Multimodal Interactive Pattern Recognition and Applications

Alejandro Héctor Toselli · Enrique Vidal ·
Francisco Casacuberta

Multimodal Interactive Pattern Recognition and Applications

Springer

Dr. Alejandro Héctor Toselli
Instituto Tecnológico de Informática
Universidad Politécnica de Valencia
Camino de Vera, s/n
46022 Valencia
Spain
ahector@iti.upv.es

Prof. Francisco Casacuberta
Instituto Tecnológico de Informática
Universidad Politécnica de Valencia
Camino de Vera, s/n
46022 Valencia
Spain
fcn@iti.upv.es

Dr. Enrique Vidal
Instituto Tecnológico de Informática
Universidad Politécnica de Valencia
Camino de Vera, s/n
46022 Valencia
Spain
evidal@iti.upv.es

ISBN 978-0-85729-478-4 e-ISBN 978-0-85729-479-1
DOI 10.1007/978-0-85729-479-1
Springer London Dordrecht Heidelberg New York

British Library Cataloguing in Publication Data
A catalogue record for this book is available from the British Library

Library of Congress Control Number: 2011929220

Cover design: VTeX UAB, Lithuania

Printed on acid-free paper

Springer is part of Springer Science+Business Media (www.springer.com)

Foreword

Traditionally, the aim of pattern recognition is to *automatically* solve complex recognition problems. However, it has been realized that in many real world applications a correct recognition rate is needed that is higher than the one reachable with completely automatic systems. Therefore, some sort of post-processing is applied where humans correct the errors committed by machine. It turns out, however, that very often this post-processing phase is the bottleneck of a recognition system, causing most of its operational costs.

The current book possesses two unique features that distinguish it from other books on Pattern Recognition. First, it proposes a radically different approach to correcting the errors committed by a system. This approach is characterized by human and machine being tied up in a much closer loop than usually. That is, the human gets involved not only after the machine has completed producing its recognition result, in order to correct errors, but during the recognition process. In this way, many errors can be avoided beforehand and correction costs can be reduced. The second unique feature of the book is that it proposes multimodal interaction between man and machine in order to correct and prevent recognition errors. Such multimodal interactions possibly include input via handwriting, speech, or gestures, in addition to the conventional input modalities of keyboard and mouse.

The material of the book is presented on the basis of well founded mathematical principles, mostly Bayes theory. It includes various fundamental results that are highly original and relevant for the emerging field of interactive and multimodal pattern recognition. In addition, the book discusses in detail a number of concrete applications where interactive multimodal systems have the potential of being superior over traditional systems that consists of a recognition phase, conducted autonomously by machine, followed by a human post-processing step. Examples of such applications include unconstrained handwriting recognition, speech recognition, machine translation, text prediction, image retrieval, and parsing.

To summarize, this book provides a very fresh and novel look at the whole discipline of pattern recognition. It is the first book, to my knowledge, that addresses the emerging field of interactive and multimodal systems in a unified and integrated way. This book may in fact become a standard reference for this emerging and fascinating new area. I highly recommend it to graduate students, academic and industrial researchers, lecturers, and practitioners working in the field of pattern recognition.

Bern, Switzerland Horst Bunke

Preface

Our interest in human–computer interaction started with our participation in the TT2 project ("Trans–Type-2", 2002–2005—http://www.tt2.atosorigin.es), funded by the European Union (EU) and coordinated by Atos Origin, which dealt with the development of statistical-based technologies for computer assisted translation.

Several years earlier, we had coordinated one of the first EU-funded projects on spoken machine translation (EuTrans, 1996–2000—http://prhlt.iti.es/w/eutrans) and, by the time TT2 started, we had already been working for years in machine translation (MT) in general. So we knew very well which was one of the major bottlenecks for the adoption of the MT technology available at that time by professional translation agencies: Many professional translators preferred to type by themselves all the text from scratch, rather than trying to take advantage of the (few) correct words of a MT-produced text, while fixing the (many) translation errors and sloppy sentences. Clearly, by post-editing the error-prone text produced by a MT system, these professionals felt they were not in command of the translation process; instead, they saw themselves just as dumb assistants of a foolish system which was producing flaky results that they had to figure out how to amend (the state of affairs about post-editing has improved over the years but the feeling of lack of control persists).

In TT2 we learnt quite a few facts about the central role of human feedback in the development of assistive technologies and how this feedback can lead to great human/machine performance improvements if it is adequately taken into account in the mathematical formulation under which systems are developed. We also understood very well that, in these technologies, the traditional, accuracy-based performance criteria is not sufficiently adequate and performance has to be mainly assessed in terms of estimated human–machine interaction effort. In one word, assistive technology has to be developed in such a way that the human user feels in command of the system, rather than the other way around, and human-interaction effort reduction must be the fundamental driving force behind system design. In TT2 we also started to realize that multimodal processing is somehow implicitly present in all interactive systems and that this can be advantageously exploited to improve overall system performance and usability.

After the success of TT2, our research group (PRHLT—http://prhlt.iti.upv.es), started to look at how these ideas could be applied in many other Pattern Recognition (PR) fields, where assistive technologies are in increasing demand. As a result, we soon found ourselves coordinating a large and ambitious Spanish research program, called Multimodal Interaction in Pattern Recognition and Computer Vision (MIPRCV, 2007–2012—http://miprcv.iti.upv.es). This program, which involves more that 100 highly qualified Ph.D. researchers from ten research institutions, aims at developing core assistive technologies for interactive application fields as diverse as language and music processing, medical image recognition, biometrics and surveillance, advanced driving assistance systems and robotics, to name but a few.

To a large extent, this book is the result of works carried out by the PRHLT research group within the MIPRCV consortium. Therefore it owes credit to many MIPRCV researchers that have directly or indirectly contributed with ideas, discussions and technical collaborations in general, as well as to all the members of PRHLT who, in one manner or another, have made it possible.

These works are presented in this book in a unified way, under the PR framework of Statistical Decision Theory. First, fundamental concepts and general PR approaches for Multimodal Interaction modelling and search (or inference) are presented. Then, systems developed on the base of these concepts and approaches are described for several application fields. These include interactive transcription of handwritten and spoken documents, computer assisted language translation, interactive text generation and parsing, and relevance-based image retrieval. Finally, several prototypes developed for these applications are overviewed in the last chapter. Most of these prototypes consist in live demonstrators which can be publicly accessed through the Internet. So, readers of this book can easily try them by themselves in order to get a first-hand idea of the interesting possibilities of placing Pattern Recognition technologies within the Multimodal Interaction framework.

Chapter 1 provides an introduction to Interactive Pattern Recognition, examining the challenges and research opportunities entailed by placing PR within the human-interaction framework. Moreover, it provides an introduction to general approaches available to solve the underlying *interactive search* problems on the basis of existing methods to solve the corresponding non-interactive counterparts and, an overview of modern machine learning approaches which can be useful in the interactive framework.

Chapter 2 establishes the common basics and framework on which are grounded the computer assisted transcription approaches described in the three subsequent *Chaps.*: *3*, *4* and *5*. On the one hand, *Chaps. 3* and *5* are devoted to handwritten documents transcription providing different approaches, which cover different aspects as multimodality, user interaction ways and ergonomics, active learning, etc. On the other hand, *Chap. 4* focuses directly on transcription of speech signals employing a similar approach described in *Chap. 3*.

Likewise, *Chap. 6* addresses the general topic of Interactive Machine Translation, providing an adequate human–machine-interactive framework to produce high-quality translation between any pair of languages. It will be shown how this also allows one to take advantage of some available multimodal interfaces to increase the productivity. Multimodal interfaces and adaptive learning in *Interactive Machine Translation* will be covered in *Chaps. 7* and *8*, respectively.

With significant differences in relation to previous chapters, *Chaps. 9–11* introduce other three Interactive Pattern Recognition topics: *Interactive Parsing*, *Interactive Text Generation* and *Interactive Image Retrieval*. The second one, for example, is characterized by not using input signal, whereas the first and third by not following the *left-to-right* protocol in the analysis of their corresponding inputs.

Finally, *Chap. 12* presents several full working prototypes and demonstrators of multimodal interactive pattern recognition applications. As previously commented, all of these systems serve as validating examples for the approaches that have been proposed and described throughout this book. Among other interesting things, they are designed to enable a true human–computer interaction on selected tasks.

Valencia, Spain

E. Vidal
A.H. Toselli
F. Casacuberta

Contents

Chapter 1
General Framework

With Contribution Of: Jesús Andrés, Verónica Romero and Alberto Sanchís.

Contents

Lately, the paradigm for Pattern Recognition (PR) systems design is shifting from the concept of full-automation to systems where the decision process is conditioned by human feedback. This shift is motivated by the fact that full automation often proves elusive, or unnatural in many applications where technology is expected to assist rather than replace the human agents.

This chapter examines the challenges and research opportunities entailed by placing PR within the human-interaction framework; namely: (a) taking direct advantage of the *feedback* information provided by the user in each interaction step to improve raw performance; (b) acknowledging the inherent *multimodality* of interaction to improve overall system behavior and usability and (c) using the feedback-derived data to tune the system to the user behavior and the specific task considered, by means of *adaptive learning* techniques.

One of the most influential factors for the rapid development of PR technology in the last few decades is the nowadays commonly adopted assessment paradigm based on labeled training and testing corpora. This chapter includes a discussion about simple but realistic "*user models*" or *interaction protocols* and *assessment criteria* which allow the successful labeled corpus-based assessment paradigm to be applied also in the interactive scenario.

This chapter also provides an introduction to general approaches available to solve the underlying *interactive search* problems on the basis of existing methods

A.H. Toselli et al., *Multimodal Interactive Pattern Recognition and Applications*,
DOI 10.1007/978-0-85729-479-1_1, © Springer-Verlag London Limited 2011

to solve the corresponding non-interactive counterparts and an overview of modern machine learning approaches which can be useful in the interactive framework.

1.1 Introduction

Classical *Pattern Recognition* (PR) has generally focused on "full automation". Traditional PR technologies have been mainly developed with the ultimate aim of fully replacing human beings in tasks that require complex perceptive and/or cognitive skills. However, full automation often proves elusive or unnatural in many applications where technology is expected to assist rather than replace the human agents. One should bear in mind that no PR system is error-free and, even in those applications where the full automation paradigm might make sense, PR developments often end up in "semiautomatic systems" or systems for "computer-assisted" operation.

On the other hand, one of the most popular and time-honored concepts in classical PR is that of relying system development on the availability of (large amounts of) *labeled data*. These data are then adequately split into *training* and *testing* sets. While this concept has proven very successful and has indeed led to very useful practical systems and devices, it is becoming increasingly clear nowadays that many practical applications do not fit well in the traditional *training* and *testing* corpora development paradigm.

An example of this kind of applications is the task (described in Chaps. 3 and 5) of transcribing a single large collection of handwritten documents. Of course one can ask the users to produce a "training set" by transcribing an adequate part of the collection manually and then consider the remaining batch of documents as a "test set". If the training set is too small, this will typically result in an undertrained system that performs poorly on the "test" part of the collection. Therefore, the users will have to devote large amounts of effort to correct system mistakes in that part. Conversely, by increasing the amount of "training" pages or documents, the system will perform better on the "test" part, but at the expense of a larger user effort required to manually transcribe the larger "training" batch. Since the task is to transcribe *this* whole collection, in the end it is the *total* user effort what matters and, the classical idea of trying to achieve a "good" *training/testing* partition of the data (and the user effort) does not seem like the best idea to follow.

Once we realize that, for one reason or another, human effort is needed not only to produce training data, but also to supervise and/or correct system outputs in the test phase, it becomes very clear that our traditional *batch-processing* paradigm needs to be changed into an explicit *person-machine interaction* framework.

These facts are seldom acknowledged in the PR mainstream. Initial problem statement typically pretends full automation and the "eventual" need for human intervention is overlooked in the mathematical formulations. By ignoring the essential need for human feedback, the resulting technologies and systems generally fail to take advantage of the opportunities underlying the interactive framework. Perhaps the most obvious of these opportunities is to *directly profit from human feedback* in order to increase raw system performance. But, as will be discussed later, the interactive framework also entails other important research challenges and opportunities such as *multi-modal* processing and *adaptive learning*.

The idea of interaction between humans and machines is by no means new. In fact, historically, tools and machines have mostly been developed with the aim of assisting human beings in their work. With the introduction of computer machinery, however, the appetence for fully automatic complex devices that would completely substitute the humans in certain types of tasks, has been gaining increasing popularity in the last few decades. This largely speculative goal notwithstanding, the interest in interactive technologies has indeed gone on over the years. An early vision of promises and challenges of the human-machine interaction framework appeared in 1974 in the Computer magazine [29]:

> "An interactive computer environment is one which attempts to facilitate the interplay between man and machine in pursuit of a goal defined by man. Presumably, to be effective, this environment should allow the calculating speed, precision, and structured logical/iterative skill of the machine to serve the conceptual, intuitive, highly associative, and contextually sensitive attributes of human mental function in the solution of problems [...] The areas of graphics, image processing, and pattern recognition are particularly appropriate candidates for this interactive approach."

This vision has actually taken on in areas such as Computer Graphics, leading nowadays to impressive graphical user interfaces and other systems such as virtual reality devices. However, only a very small fraction of the huge potential of the human interaction framework has actually been exploited so far in Image Processing, Computer Vision and Pattern Recognition [4].

Tapping this potential entails several research challenges and opportunities in order to adapt PR approaches to the dynamic and changing environments of interactive systems. Here we explore some of these opportunities and challenges. We also show how existing PR technologies can naturally evolve to help developing advanced multi-modal interactive systems that will hopefully realize the long standing promises of a seamless synergy between persons and machines.

1.2 Classical Pattern Recognition Paradigm

Let x be an input stimulus, observation or signal and h a hypothesis or output, which the system has to derive from x. Let $\mathcal{M}$ be a *model* or set of models used by the system to derive its hypotheses. In general, $\mathcal{M}$ is obtained through a "batch" training process from a given *training sequence* of pairs $(x, h)_i$ from the task being considered. Figure 1.1 shows a diagram of this kind of systems.

In traditional PR [17] decision theory is adopted to develop techniques that aim at minimizing the cost of wrong hypotheses. In the simplest case, a $0/1$ cost function is used which corresponds to minimizing the *number* of wrong hypotheses. Under this *minimal error criterion*, a best hypothesis is shown to be one which maximizes

Fig. 1.1 Diagram of a traditional PR system

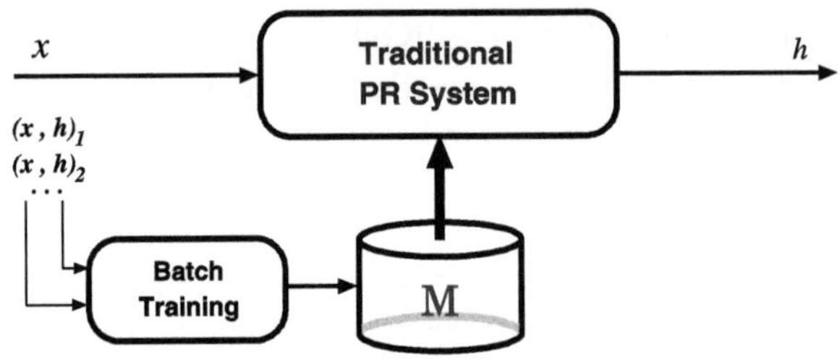

the posterior probability $\Pr(h \mid x)$. Using a model $\mathcal{M}$, this is approximated as:[1]

$$\hat{h} = \mathop{\arg\max}_{h \in \mathcal{H}} \Pr(h \mid x) \approx \mathop{\arg\max}_{h \in \mathcal{H}} P_{\mathcal{M}}(h \mid x) \tag{1.1}$$

where $\mathcal{H}$ is the (possibly infinite) set of valid hypotheses.

Minimal error is also the main criterion adopted to guide the development of *statistical learning* approaches to train (the parameters of) $\mathcal{M}$ from the training data. *Maximum likelihood* is among the most successful and popular of these approaches. However, in many cases it is difficult to directly estimate $P_{\mathcal{M}}(h \mid x)$ and it is better to apply the Bayes rule in Eq. (1.1) to achieve the following decomposition:

$$\hat{h} \approx \mathop{\arg\max}_{h \in \mathcal{H}} \frac{P(x \mid h) \cdot P(h)}{P(x)} = \mathop{\arg\max}_{h \in \mathcal{H}} P(x \mid h) \cdot P(h) \tag{1.2}$$

where the term $P(x)$ has been dropped since it does not depend on the maximization variable, h.

With this decomposition, two models have to be estimated. First the *likelihood* model $P(x \mid h)$, which can often be easily and independently estimated from the available training pairs $(x, h)_i$, following the maximum likelihood approach. And second the *prior* $P(h)$, which can be estimated by using only the output data, $(h)_i$, of the available training pairs [17].

Classification is one of the most traditional PR frameworks. Here, the set of possible hypotheses, $\mathcal{H}$ is just a finite (and typically small) set of class-labels—or just integers; i.e., $\mathcal{H} = \{1, \dots, C\}$, where C is the number of classes. In this case, the *search* needed to solve the optimization problem (1.2) (or Eq. (1.1)) amounts to a straightforward exhaustive exploration of the corresponding C probability values.

While classification is in fact a useful framework within which many applications can be naturally placed, there are many other practical problems of increasing interest which need a less restrictive framework where hypotheses are not just labels, but some kind of *structured* information. This is the case, for example, of Automatic Speech or Handwritten Text Recognition (ASR, HTR), Machine Translation (MT), etc. In these cases, the inputs, x, are structured into *sequences* of feature vectors (ASR, HTR) or words (MT) and the outputs, h, are *sequences* of words or other

[1] True probabilities will be denoted as $\Pr(\cdot)$, while modeled probabilities will be written as $P_{\mathcal{M}}(\cdot)$, where the model $\mathcal{M}$ can be omitted if it is understood from the context.

adequate linguistic units. Many applications admit this kind of input and output sequential structuring, but there are also other practical problems, many of them in the field of Image Processing and Computer Vision, which require more complex structures such as input and output *arrays* or *graphs* of vectors and labels, respectively.

When $\mathcal{H}$ is a structured space, the *search* (or *inference*) required to solve Eq. (1.2) or Eq. (1.1) can become quite complex, but several adequate algorithmic solutions or approximations, such as *Viterbi search* [30, 50], $A^\star$ [15, 39], *Probabilistic Relaxation* [8, 32, 44], *Belief Propagation* [40], etc., have been developed over the last few decades. In addition, training with structured input–output data also becomes more complex, because in many cases (such as ASR, HTR, MT, etc.) the mapping from individual input elements (vector subsequences in ASR/HTR or words in MT) to output tokens (linguistic units in these examples) is generally not explicitly available and it has to me modeled as a *hidden or latent variable*. Expectation–Maximization (EM) techniques such as the *backward–forward* algorithm [30] are available to deal with the difficult training problem in the case of sequential data and other (Bayesian) approaches such as [20, 21, 26], etc., have been developed for more complex structures.

In order to illustrate the concepts introduced so far, as well as those to be introduced later in this chapter, we will discuss in some detail a simplification of a classical PR problem: the recognition of human karyotypes. While (individual) chromosome recognition is a typical PR example of *classification*, the recognition of a whole karyotype properly corresponds to the case of *structured input/output*, as will be discussed below.

Example: Recognition of Human Karyotypes

For the sake of simplicity, we ignore here the initial image segmentation task and assume that each of the 46 chromosomes in a normal unsorted karyotype is already represented as an individual image.[2] Thus, the problem is stated as follows [43]:

> Given a set of 46 unsorted images of stained ("banded") human chromosomes, associate each image with a label from a set of 24 labels, {"1", "2", ..., "22", "X", "Y"}, in such a way that each label is assigned exactly to *two* images, except labels "X, Y", for which only the following assignment pairs are possible: ("X","X"), ("X","Y").

For the sake of illustration clarity, we will not consider the real, full karyotype recognition problem, but a simpler setting in which only single chromosome images, rather than pairs, are considered and sex chromosomes, "X", "Y", are ignored (see Fig. 1.2):

> *Simplification:* Given a set of *22 unsorted images* of banded human chromosomes, associate each image with a label from a set of *22 labels*, {"1", "2", ..., "22"}, in such a way that each label is assigned exactly to *one* image.

---

[2]Moreover, we are completely ignoring here recent advances in karyotype analysis, such as fluorescent dye-based spectral karyotyping [45], which allow obtaining colored chromosome images and may significantly simplify the real problem of human karyotyping.

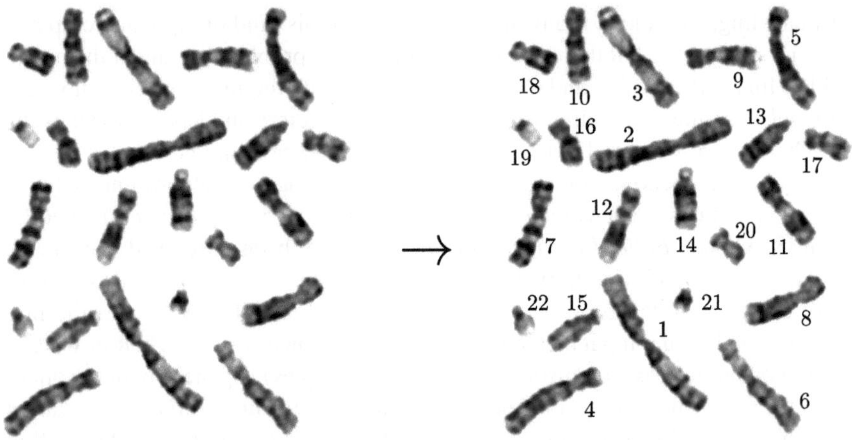

Fig. 1.2 Illustration of simplified human karyotyping. A different label from "1" to "22" has to be assigned to each chromosome. The labeling shown is the correct one in this case

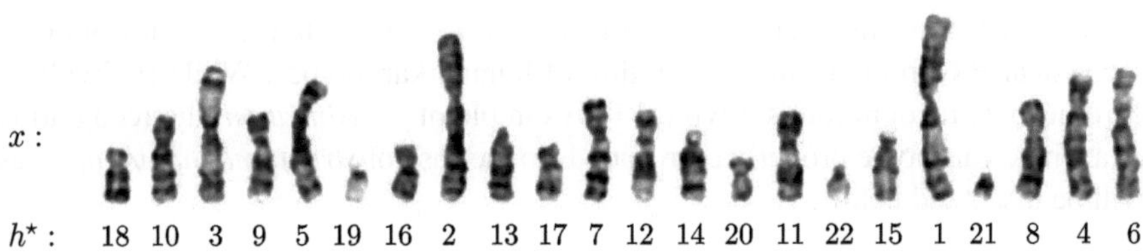

Fig. 1.3 Simplified human karyotyping: representation and notation. The correct labeling, $h^\star$, is shown

In the simplified problem statement, $x = x_1, \ldots, x_{22} \in \mathcal{X}$ is an unsorted sequence of 22 chromosome images, arranged from left to right in some arbitrary order. This sequence will be denoted as x_1^{22}. Correspondingly, $h = h_1^{22} \in \mathcal{H}$ is a sequence of 22 labels, $h_i \in \{\text{"1"}, \text{"2"}, \ldots, \text{"22"}\}$, $1 \le i \le 22$. Note that $\mathcal{H}$ is finite but huge ($|\mathcal{H}| = 22^{22}$). Figure 1.3 shows graphically this kind of representation and notation. In what follows, we assume that each individual chromosome image is parametrically represented by means of features extracted from this image; for example, each x_i can be represented as a grey-level projection profile of the chromosome image on its median axis [23, 34, 35].

Following this notation, a solution to the simplified karyotype recognition problem is given by Eq. (1.2); i.e.,

$$\hat{h} \approx \arg\max_{h \in \mathcal{H}} P(x \mid h) P(h) \tag{1.3}$$

where $P(x \mid h)$ is the probability of an image sequence x, given the sequence of labels h and $P(h)$ is the prior probability of a labeling h.

The *prior* $P(h)$ in this problem is well known, but not trivial. Ideally, it should be *null* for those h which contain repeated symbols and *flat* otherwise; that is:

$$P(h) = \begin{cases} 0, & \text{if } \exists i \neq j : h_i = h_j,\ 1 \leq i, j \leq 22, \\ \frac{1}{22!}, & \text{otherwise.} \end{cases} \tag{1.4}$$

The *likelihood*, on the other hand, $P(x \mid h)$, can be approached through a simple, naive Bayes decomposition; that is:

$$P(x \mid h) = \prod_{i=1}^{22} P(x_i \mid h_i) \tag{1.5}$$

where each $P(x_i \mid h_i)$ can be modeled, for instance, by a hidden Markov Model [34, 42].

An exact solution to the search problem (1.3) is difficult because of the huge size of $\mathcal{H}$ and the tangled restrictions entailed by $P(h)$ (no repeated labels); but simple greedy approximations can provide acceptable results [34, 35].

One of the simpler and most effective greedy approaches is as follows. First, for each individual chromosome image, x_j, compute its max-likelihood, $\max_{k\in\{1,\dots,22\}} P(x_j \mid k)$. This is exactly the computation that would be carried out for individual chromosome image classification. Now sort the images according to these scores and, from now on, assume that the images are considered in this order. Then, following this max-likelihood order, for each chromosome image, x_i, assign it the label $\hat{h}_i = \arg\max_{k\in\mathcal{K}} P(x_i \mid k)$, taking care that labels assigned to previous images can no longer be assigned; that is $\mathcal{K} = \{\text{“1”}, \dots, \text{“22”}\} - \{\hat{h}_1, \dots, \hat{h}_{i-1}\}$.

Obviously, this and other greedy solutions to Eq. (1.3) can only achieve local optimization, since other complete labelings $h \neq \hat{h}$ may exist for which $P(x \mid h)P(h) > P(x \mid \hat{h})P(\hat{h})$.

1.2.1 Decision Theory and Pattern Recognition

As briefly discussed in Sect. 1.2, the *decision theory* (*DT*) provides support to statistical PR. Traditional PR often assumes a $0/1$ *cost function*, or “*loss*”, in order to obtain the optimal decision rule of Eq. (1.1). This assumption leads to systems that aim at minimizing the number of incorrectly proposed hypotheses. However, in many problems and tasks, the $0/1$ loss cannot adequately reflect the complexity of the performance measures used in these tasks. This happens, for example, when the hypotheses are sequences, as in the MT, ASR or HTR tasks mentioned previously.

For the sake of illustration, consider the human karyotypes recognition example, which was introduced above. In this example, the $0/1$ loss has severe implications. A hypothesis h_1^{22}, would be counted as one single error independently of how many chromosomes are misclassified; i.e., independently of whether there are only two misclassified chromosomes or all the 22. In this example, one might rather prefer a system which produces a high percentage, say 50%, of wrong full hypothesis (karyotypes) with one misclassified chromosome per hypothesis, than a system that achieves a low percentage, say 5%, of wrong full hypotheses but each having all the chromosomes misclassified. Note that the first case yields a total of 2.28% misclassified chromosomes, while the latter case results in a chromosome misclassification rate of 5.00%.

This problem becomes even more important in IPR, where performance has to be gauged mainly in terms of interaction effort. As will be discussed in Sect. 1.4, human interaction effort can often be *estimated* on the base of adequately labeled test corpora. Therefore DT opens the possibility of defining cost functions whose minimization would lead to systems that, at least in theory, would perform optimally for the given task.

Two *intrinsically* related decision problems arise in PR. The first one is *hypotheses decision*; i.e., the problem of deciding which the best hypothesis is among a set of possible hypotheses. For instance, the decision rule (1.1) is the solution to a hypotheses decision problem with a $0/1$ loss. The second is *model decision* which consists in deciding which the best model $\mathcal{M}$ is, in order to approximate the probabilities used for hypotheses decision. For instance, maximum likelihood estimation is the solution to this problem under a $0/1$ loss, among other assumptions. Both decision problems become closely related under the DT framework, but here we focus only on the first one.

Formally, a *loss function* is defined as $\ell : \mathcal{X} \times \mathcal{H} \times \mathcal{H} \rightarrow \mathbb{R}$. The function $\ell(x, h, h^\star)$ defines the cost in which a system incurs if, for an input x, it *proposes* a hypothesis h, while the *correct* hypothesis is $h^\star$. For a given (PR) decision problem (characterized by ℓ), a solution is characterized by a *decision function*, $\delta : \mathcal{X} \rightarrow \mathcal{H}$, which decides an output h for each possible input, x. Given ℓ and δ, the total expected loss for unseen inputs, of "*global risk*", is defined as

$$R_\ell(\delta) = \int_{\mathcal{X}} \Pr(x) \cdot R_\ell\big(\delta(x) \mid x\big)\, dx, \tag{1.6}$$

where $R_\ell(h \mid x)$ (with $h = \delta(x)$) is the "*conditional risk*", or expected loss in which a hypothesis h is likely to incur for a given input x. The *conditional risk* is defined as:

$$R_\ell(h \mid x) = \sum_{h^\star \in \mathcal{H}} \ell(x, h, h^\star) \cdot \Pr(h^\star \mid x). \tag{1.7}$$

Note that each pair of decision and loss functions, has its own global risk.

A PR problem amounts to finding a decision function with the minimum global risk. It is well known [17] that the global risk is minimized by minimizing the conditional risk for each input. This is often known as the *optimal Bayes' decision rule*, or simply *Bayes' decision rule:*[3]

$$\hat{h} = \hat{\delta}_\ell(x) = \arg\min_{h \in \mathcal{H}} R_\ell(h \mid x). \tag{1.8}$$

If the *actual* probabilities needed to compute $R_\ell(h \mid x)$ in (1.8) were exactly known, then $R_\ell(\hat{\delta}_\ell(x) \mid x)$ is the minimum risk that can be achieved, and the corresponding global risk (1.6) is called the *Bayes' risk*.

The classical PR *minimum-error* criterion corresponds to a $0/1$ *loss function*, $\ell(x, h, h^\star)$, defined to be 0 if $h = h^\star$ and 1 otherwise. In this case [17], the conditional risk (1.7) and the corresponding Bayes' decision rule (1.8) simplify to

$$R_{\ell_{0/1}}(h \mid x) = 1 - \Pr(h \mid x), \tag{1.9}$$

$$\hat{\delta}_{\ell_{0/1}}(x) = \arg\max_{h \in \mathcal{H}} \Pr(h \mid x). \tag{1.10}$$

Note that Eq. (1.10) is the rule used in Eq. (1.1).

The previous discourse still applies to structured hypothesis spaces and, in particular, when hypotheses are sequences. However, it is very common that although the decision may have to be taken for the whole hypothesis, the loss has to be evaluated at sequence-element level. For instance, in the karyotypes example, instead of counting how many karyotypes the system has incorrectly classified, the quality is assessed by counting how many chromosomes are incorrectly tagged. In such cases, the loss is given by

$$\ell(x, h, h^\star) = \sum_{k=1}^{22} \ell(x, h_k, h_k^\star), \tag{1.11}$$

where $\ell(x, h_k, h_k^\star)$ is a single-label $0/1$ loss function. The difference between this loss function and the conventional one lies in the preferred types of hypothesis in an error-prone system. The Bayes' decision rule induced by the latter would prefer to minimize the number of wrongly proposed karyotypes, while that induced by the former would prefer to minimize the number of wrongly tagged chromosomes, even if that entails producing a larger number of wrong karyotypes.

1.3 Interactive Pattern Recognition and Multimodal Interaction

Placing PR within the human-interaction framework requires changes in the way we look at problems in these areas. Classical PR minimum-error performance criteria [17] should be complemented with more direct estimates of the amount of effort that the interactive process will demand from the user. But, to estimate this

[3]Note that each loss function has its own optimal Bayes' decision rule, although the most widespread notation, $\hat{h}$, does not explicitly highlight it.

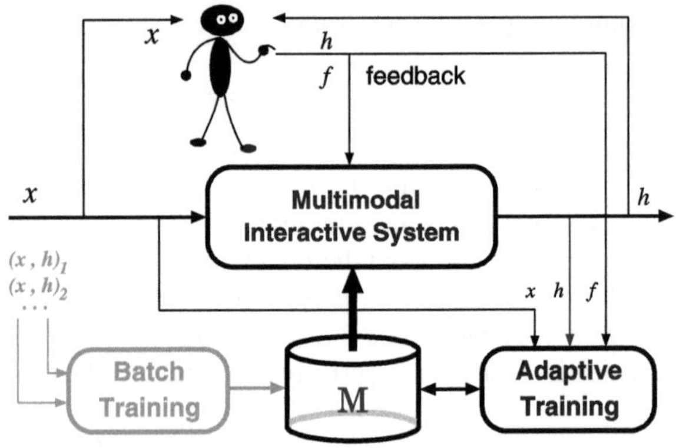

Fig. 1.4 Diagram of an Interactive Pattern Recognition (IPR) system

effort, we should stick with the traditional testing-corpus-based approach which has proved so successful in PR. Furthermore, since all the existing PR techniques are intrinsically grounded on error-minimization algorithms, they need to be revised and adapted to the new, minimum human-effort performance criterion. Interestingly, such a paradigm shift entails important research opportunities which hold promise for a new generation of truly human-friendly PR devices. Three main types of opportunities can be identified:

Feedback: Take direct advantage of the *feedback information* provided by the user in each interaction step to improve raw performance.

Multimodality: It arises as a *natural property of interaction*. By properly acknowledging this fact, improved overall system performance and usability can be achieved.

Adaptation: Use feedback-derived data to *adaptively* (re-)train the system and tune it to the user behavior and the specific task considered.

The framework for the development of these ideas will be referred to as "*Interactive Pattern Recognition*" (IPR). Figure 1.4 shows a schematic view of these ideas. As in classical PR, x is an input stimulus, observation or signal and h is a hypothesis or output, which the system derives from x. By observing x and h, an operator or user provides some (perhaps null) feedback signal, f, which may iteratively help the system refine or improve its hypothesis until it is finally accepted. $\mathcal{M}$ is a *model* or set of models which is used by the system to derive its hypotheses. In general, $\mathcal{M}$ is initially obtained in "batch mode", as in traditional PR, from training pairs $(x, h)_i$ (in grey color in the figure). Now, during the interactive operation, the valuable user feedback signals produced in each interaction step are advantageously used in an *adaptive training* process which progressively *tunes* $\mathcal{M}$ to the specific task and/or to the way the user makes use of the system in this task.

It should be noted that *Multimodal Interaction* may entail two types of multimodality. One corresponds to the input signal, which can be a complex blend of different types of data, ranging from conventional keyboard data to complex images, audio and video streams. The other, a more subtle but no less important type, is due to the generally different nature of *input* and *feedback* signals. It is this second type that makes multimodality an inherent feature of human interaction.

Consider for instance a IPR application in the context of *tele-care* for elderly people. Here, x is itself a multimodal signal which comes from human monitoring sensors such as microphones, cameras and perhaps other non-invasive medical sensors. Now x is processed by a IPR system, which tracks the human activities in order to detect possibly abnormal or risky situations. Clearly, such type of systems will never be fully automatic. Instead, the system should set adequate alarms (h) for *another* human to consider and act accordingly. It is this other human, or *operator*, the one which is depicted in Fig. 1.4. For a specific system hypothesis h, the operator may doubt about its correctness and, after examining x, may try to improve h by providing some feedback f to the system. Feedback complexity may range from simple directions for the system to improve "perceptive" parameters such as camera focus or microphone gain, to much more subtle information directly aimed at improving the system's "cognitive" or decision-making performance (cf. Sect. 1.3.1). In any case, the operator's feedback signals will rarely be of the same nature as those in x. Typically, they will probably involve keyboard-and-pointer signals and/or perhaps hand gestures or voice commands; hence the claimed inherent multimodality of interaction.

General approaches to deal with the opportunities and challenges of the IPR framework are examined in the following subsections. It is important to point out that most of the issues discussed below only make sense if the hypothesis space, $\mathcal{H}$ is "structured"; for example, spaces of sets, sequences, arrays, etc.

1.3.1 Using the Human Feedback Directly

Without varying the model $\mathcal{M}$, *human interaction* offers a unique opportunity to improve the quality of system hypotheses h, using information directly derived from the interaction process. As discussed in Sect. 1.2, for fixed $\mathcal{M}$ and x, a best hypothesis, $\hat{h}$, is one which maximizes the posterior probability $P_{\mathcal{M}}(h \mid x)$. Now interaction allows adding more *conditions*, that is:

$$\hat{h} = \arg\max_{h \in \mathcal{H}} P_{\mathcal{M}}(h \mid x, f) \tag{1.12}$$

where $f \in \mathcal{F}$ stands for the feedback, interaction-derived information; e.g., in the form of *partial hypothesis* or *constraints* on $\mathcal{H}$. The new system hypothesis, $\hat{h}$, may prompt the user to provide further feedback information, thereby starting a new interaction step. And the process continues in this way until the system output is acceptable by the user.

Clearly, the richer the feedback information, f, the greater the opportunity to obtain better $\hat{h}$. But modeling the probability distribution in Eq. (1.12) and solving the associated maximization, may be (much) more difficult than the corresponding problems with our familiar $P_{\mathcal{M}}(h \mid x)$.

Equation (1.12) corresponds to a zero-order approach, where $\hat{h}$ is derived using only the feedback obtained in the previous iteration step. However, as discussed below, feedback and prediction history can be jointly taken into account or "merged" and used in Eq. (1.12) instead of f.

1.3.2 Explicitly Taking Interaction History into Account

In general, interactive processing makes history from previous interaction steps readily available and, in many cases, taking it into account explicitly may significantly improve the prediction accuracy. Moreover, as we will see later, this does not necessarily increase the complexity of the prediction problem.

Let h' be the history. It can be represented by the optimal hypothesis, $\hat{h}$, obtained by the system in its previous interaction step[4] for the given x. Since previous hypotheses have been supervised/corrected by the user, a part of h' will be correct for the given x. In the current interaction step, the feedback f aims at further correcting element(s) of h'. Algorithm *IPR–History*, below, illustrates this interactive process. Taking history into account, Eq. (1.12) becomes:

$$\hat{h} = \arg\max_{h \in \mathcal{H}} P_{\mathcal{M}}(h \mid x, h', f). \tag{1.13}$$

It is worth noting that, by jointly considering the pair (h', f) as a kind of "consolidated history", this equation becomes formally identical to Eq. (1.12).

Algorithm IPR–History // Let x be the input and $\hat{h}$ the output hypothesis
  $\hat{h} = \arg\max_{h \in \mathcal{H}} P_{\mathcal{M}}(h \mid x)$ // Initialization
do forever { // Interaction loop
  $f =$ *user_feedback*$(\hat{h})$; **if** $(f =$ "OK"$)$ **return** $\hat{h}$
  $h' = \hat{h}$; $\hat{h} = \arg\max_{h \in \mathcal{H}} P_{\mathcal{M}}(h \mid x, h', f)$
}

1.3.3 Interaction with Deterministic Feedback

Using only traditional keyboard & mouse, and/or any other *deterministic* feedback modality, greatly simplify matters. Let $\mathcal{D}$ be the space of decoded feedback signals. Deterministic feedback decoding can then be specified as a function, $d : \mathcal{F} \rightarrow \mathcal{D}$, which maps each raw feedback signal, f, into its corresponding unique decoding $d = d(f)$. For instance, if f is the signal of a keystroke on the key "A", $d(f)$ is the symbol "A" itself (keyboards are not expected to produce erroneous output symbols!). Such determinism means that feedback signals do not need to be actually

[4] This would be a first-order approach but, more generally, h' can represent an adequate combination of the optimal hypotheses obtained in all previous interaction steps for the given x.

"decoded" and we can interchangeably use a feedback signal f and its (trivial and unique) decoding $d = d(f)$.

Using d rather than f in Eq. (1.13), applying the Bayes rule, and dropping $\mathcal{M}$ to simplify notation, we can now write the prediction of $\hat{h}$ in more detail:

$$\hat{h} = \arg\max_{h \in \mathcal{H}} P(h \mid x, h', d) = \arg\max_{h \in \mathcal{H}} P(x \mid h', d, h) P(h \mid h', d). \tag{1.14}$$

Note that $\mathcal{H}$ and $\mathcal{D}$ are typically closely related domains, in that d often embodies information aimed to modify an element or a part of h'. Therefore, the likelihood model, $P(x \mid h', d, h)$, can often be similar or identical to $P(x \mid h)$, the model used in the non-interactive version of the problem considered. On the other hand, the hypothesis prior becomes now history and feedback conditioned. The pair (h', d) can often be seen as a partially amended version of h', where one or more errors from the last step have been corrected. Therefore the conditioned prior, $P(h \mid h', d)$, will typically be (proportional to) the classical $P(h)$, except for those h *not* compatible with (h', d), for which it should be *null* (or low).

In many cases, these model changes can be interpreted just as a part of the search problem by substituting $\mathcal{H}$ with a smaller space, $\mathcal{H}' \subset \mathcal{H}$, in which the feedback-derived restrictions apply. This way, an IPR problem can often be seen as a variation of the corresponding non-interactive PR problem where identical models are used but the search strategy has to be changed.

In any case, it is worth noting that history and feedback derived constraints may significantly increase the difficulty of solving Eq. (1.14), with respect to solving the classical Eq. (1.2). Nevertheless, as we will see throughout this book, classical solutions can often be easily extended to provide at least approximate solutions to Eq. (1.14).

Example: Interactive Human Karyotyping

In the non-interactive version of human karyotype recognition introduced in Sect. 1.2, *all* the individual chromosome labeling errors made by the recognition system had to be amended, one by one, by the human operator (the karyotyping result must be completely correct before the operator can sign and supply it to the medical doctor who has ordered the karyotype analysis!).

Obviously, such a "*post-editing*" procedure does not allow the operator to take advantage of the system prediction capabilities to help her in the amending process. Conversely, under the interactive framework, the system may take advantage of each individual correction made by the operator in order to improve its hypotheses for the remaining chromosome images. Clearly, this may significantly reduce the amount of human effort needed to produce a correct karyotype.

The interactive human karyotyping problem becomes an instance of Eq. (1.14) as follows. To begin with, the system provides an initial karyotype $\hat{h}$ using Eqs. (1.3)–(1.5) (and the greedy search outlined in Sect. 1.2). In the next interaction step, $\hat{h}$ becomes the history, h', and a new $\hat{h}$ is obtained using Eq. (1.14). The same process will go on through all the successive interaction steps.

The user feedback produced in each step of this interactive process, $f \in \mathcal{F}$, consists of keystrokes to specify a position c in h' where the last correct label appears, and a label $l \in \{$"1", "2", ..., "22"$\}$ to fix the first labeling error. Since f is *deterministic*, it is trivially "decoded" as $d = d(f) \equiv (c, l) \in \mathcal{D}$. The first wrong label in h' is h'_{c+1} and its correct value should be l. Such an interaction-derived information conditions the possible values of h as follows:

$$\begin{aligned} h_1^c &= h'^c_1, \\ h_{c+1} &= l, \\ h_i &\notin \{h'_1, \ldots, h'_c, l\}, \quad c+2 \le i \le 22. \end{aligned} \tag{1.15}$$

That is, the first c elements of h must be the same as those of h', the $(c+1)$th element must be the feedback-given label and the remaining elements should be different from the first $c+1$ already validated.

If $\mathcal{H}'(h', c, l)$ is the subset of hypotheses, h, that comply with Eq. (1.15) the *conditioned prior* model can be written as

$$\begin{aligned} P(h \mid h', d) &= P(h \mid h', c, l) \\ &= \begin{cases} \alpha P(h), & \text{(as in Eq. (1.4)) if } h \in \mathcal{H}'(h', c, l), \\ 0, & \text{otherwise,} \end{cases} \end{aligned} \tag{1.16}$$

where α is an adequate normalization factor.

On the other hand, for the *likelihood* model, interaction dependencies do not make sense given the simple naive Bayes decomposition Eq. (1.5) adopted in Eq. (1.4). Therefore we use here the same model as in the non-interactive case; that is: $P(x \mid h', c, l, h) = P(x \mid h)$.

History and feedback constraints can also be interpreted in terms of *search* by constraining the optimization in Eq. (1.14) to search only for hypotheses $h \in \mathcal{H}'(h', c, l) \subset \mathcal{H}$. In addition, it is not actually necessary to search for a complete labeling, h, but just for the last $22 - c - 1$ labels of h that follow the already fixed subsequence h_1^{c+1}. In any case, exact optimization is at least as difficult as in the non-interactive case, although suboptimal non-interactive greedy approximations can be easily modified to additionally enforce the *prefix* restrictions represented by $\mathcal{H}'$.

Figure 1.5 illustrates the above discussion. Chromosome labels erroneously predicted by the system are marked in red and underlined. The first of these errors corresponds to the *fifth* image in the sequence (which is assumed to be sorted according to the greedy search carried out in the first, non-interactive step of the process). The feedback provided by the operator to fix this error is $(c, l) = (4,$ "5"$)$ and, therefore, the conditioned prior must be *null* for all h such that $h_1^5 \neq$ "18", "10", "3", "9", "5" or $\{h_6, \ldots, h_{22}\} \cap \{$"18", "10", "3", "9", "5"$\} \neq \emptyset$.

x :

h' : 18 10 3 9 $\underline{7}$ 19 $\underline{20}$ 2 13 17 $\underline{8}$ 12 14 $\underline{16}$ 11 22 15 1 21 $\underline{5}$ 4 6

$(c, l) = (4, \text{“5”})$: ↑ 5

Fig. 1.5 Example of keyboard & pointer interaction in simplified human karyotyping. Labeling errors are marked in *red* and *underlined*. User feedback consists in positioning the cursor over the last correct label ($c = 4$) and then typing the correction ($l =$ “5”) on the next position

Clearly, by fixing this error, the information gained by the system may help automatically fixing other remaining errors. For instance, now the 20th chromosome label can no longer be “$\underline{5}$” and hopefully the next-best system hypotheses for the 20th image will be the correct label, “8” (cf. Fig. 1.3); similarly, now the 11th wrong label (“$\underline{8}$”) would have to be changed, hopefully into the correct one, “7”. By actually solving Eq. (1.14), many of the remaining errors are expected to be automatically fixed without additional human intervention.

1.3.4 Interactive Pattern Recognition and Decision Theory

It is useful to recall that, in the IPR framework, performance is mainly measured in terms of *user interaction effort*, which in some cases can be roughly estimated as the *number of interactions* needed to complete a given task (cf. Sect. 1.4). Clearly, this measure is *not* necessarily optimized by minimizing the number of wrong hypotheses (i.e., the 0/1 loss).

Under the decision theory viewpoint, after I interactions, the system has received $F = f^{(1)}, \ldots, f^{(I)}$ user feedbacks and has produced $H = h^{(1)}, \ldots, h^{(I)}$ hypotheses.[5] With respect to the loss defined in Sect. 1.2.1, now the loss incurred by the system after the timespan I should take into account the new information sources, i.e., it should be defined as $\ell(x, h, h^\star, H, F)$. Typically we may wish a loss that is proportional to the number of interactions I.

As discussed in Sect. 1.2.1, for this loss function, ℓ, a best hypothesis is given by:

$$\hat{h} = \operatorname*{arg\,min}_{h \in \mathcal{H}} R_\ell(h \mid x, H, F) \tag{1.17}$$

[5]Although it might seem that under this approach the user is forced to interact after each hypothesis proposed by the IPR system; this is not the case since the set of possible feedbacks $\mathcal{F}$ can be extended with a null feedback, $\emptyset$.

where $R_\ell(h \mid x, H, F)$ is now the *interactive conditional risk*, defined as

$$R_\ell(h \mid x, H, F) = \sum_{h^\star \in \mathcal{H}} \ell(x, h, h^\star, H, F) \cdot \Pr(h^\star \mid x, H, F). \tag{1.18}$$

The way in which Eqs. (1.17) and (1.18) can be simplified mainly depends on the assumed interaction protocol (cf. Sect. 1.4). A basic simplification is to ignore the user feedback except for the last interaction and/or hypothesis; that is, define the loss as $\ell(x, h, h^\star, h^{(I)}, f^{(I)})$, or $\ell(x, h, h^\star, h', f)$, according to the notation of Sect. 1.3.2. Under this assumption, if we consider a 0/1 loss function at whole hypothesis level,

$$\ell(x, h, h^\star, h', f) = \begin{cases} 0, & h = h^\star, \\ 1, & \text{otherwise}, \end{cases} \tag{1.19}$$

then the interactive conditional risk is simplified to

$$R_\ell(h \mid x, h', f) = 1 - \Pr(h \mid x, h', f). \tag{1.20}$$

Taking into account this simplification in Eq. (1.17) leads to the following Bayes interactive decision rule, which is the same as Eq. (1.13):

$$\hat{h} = \arg\max_{h \in \mathcal{H}} \Pr(h \mid x, h', f). \tag{1.21}$$

Note that all the developments of this section are presented under these simplifying assumptions.

1.3.5 Multimodal Interaction

As has been already commented, in general, feedback information, $f \in \mathcal{F}$, does not naturally belong to the original domain from which the main data, x, come from; i.e., $\mathcal{F} \neq \mathcal{X}$. For instance, in a vehicle plate recognition system, it is quite unlikely that user's feedback comes in the form of images obtained by the same camera used to capture the plate images. Instead, it will arrive in form of keystrokes, mouse gestures, or perhaps spoken utterances.

This observation is particularly interesting in the case of non-deterministic feedback. In this case, human interaction naturally entails some sort of *multimodality*, which adds to the possible multimodal nature that input signals themselves may exhibit. Multimodality appears in many areas of Computer Science and Engineering. The challenge here is to achieve an adequate *modality synergy* which finally allows taking maximum advantage of all the modalities involved.

Basic Multimodal Fusion

Let u and v be two signals of some multimodal datum. In a non-interactive framework, the resulting *modality fusion* problem consists in finding a $\hat{h}$ which maximizes the posterior probability $P_{\mathcal{M}}(h \mid u, v)$. This can be straight-forwardly re-written as

$$\hat{h} = \arg\max_{h \in \mathcal{H}} P_{\mathcal{M}}(u, v \mid h) \cdot P_{\mathcal{M}}(h). \tag{1.22}$$

In many applications it is natural and/or convenient to assume independence of u and v given h. Consider for instance an image description or labeling problem where u is an image and v the acoustic signal of a spoken utterance about the image. In this case, a naive Bayes decomposition leads to

$$\hat{h} = \arg\max_{h \in \mathcal{H}} P_{\mathcal{M}_U}(u \mid h) \cdot P_{\mathcal{M}_V}(v \mid h) \cdot P_{\mathcal{M}_H}(h) \tag{1.23}$$

which allows a separate estimation of independent models, $\mathcal{M}_U$, $\mathcal{M}_V$ and $\mathcal{M}_H$, for the image and speech components, and the labeling language, respectively. The only "joint" problem here is the joint optimization in Eq. (1.23). In the multimodal processing literature, this approximation is often known as "*late fusion*" [28].

In our IPR framework, u would correspond to the input signal, x, and v to the feedback, f. Note, however, that this simplistic formulation does not care about possible explicit decoding of the (non-deterministic) feedback information which, in most cases, is one of the most important and interesting issues of multimodal processing in IPR.

Using Interaction Information to Help Decoding Non-deterministic Feedback Signals

In the previous formulation, the decoding of f, d, was a *hidden variable*. We can uncover it as follows:

$$\hat{h} = \arg\max_{h} \Pr(h \mid x, h', f) = \arg\max_{h} \sum_{d} \Pr(h, d \mid x, h', f). \tag{1.24}$$

Approximating the sum with the value of the mode, applying basic probability rules and ignoring terms which do not depend on the optimization variables (h and d):

$$\hat{h} \approx \arg\max_{h} \max_{d} \Pr(h \mid h', d, x, f) \cdot \Pr(d \mid h', x) \cdot \Pr(f \mid d, h', x). \tag{1.25}$$

Then, applying the Bayes rule and assuming independence of $\Pr(h \mid h', d, x, f)$ on f given h', d, x and of $\Pr(f \mid d, h', x)$ on h', x given d:

$$\hat{h} \approx \arg\max_{h} \max_{d} \Pr(f \mid d) \cdot \Pr(d \mid h', x) \cdot \Pr(h \mid h', d, x). \tag{1.26}$$

A final assumption is to consider that $\Pr(d \mid h', x)$ is independent[6] on x given h'. Then, decomposing the last term by means of the Bayes rule and assuming the probabilities are modeled by adequate models:

$$\hat{h} \approx \arg\max_{h} \max_{d} P(f \mid d) \cdot P(d \mid h') \cdot P(x \mid h', d, h) \cdot P(h \mid h', d). \qquad (1.27)$$

The last two terms of Eq. (1.27) are the same used in Eq. (1.14) for the basic IPR formulation with deterministic feedback. The other two terms are now needed to deal with the non-deterministic feedback:

- $P(f \mid d)$ is a *feedback likelihood* model, as in conventional PR for recognizing f.
- $P(d \mid h')$ is a history-conditioned *feedback decoding prior.*

That is, except for the history condition on the prior, these two terms are the same as those that would be needed to apply Eq. (1.1) of conventional PR for the recognition of feedback signals. But now we can condition the prior by the interaction history and, moreover, Eq. (1.27) entails a joint optimization for simultaneous recognition of main (x) and feedback (f) data. Obviously, this offers clear opportunities for more accurate feedback decoding than using just a conventional, off-the-shelf PR system for feedback signals recognition.

Unfortunately, the joint optimization Eq. (1.27) generally involves additional difficulties and it seldom admits exact and efficient search solutions. Nevertheless, simple approximations often prove useful enough in many applications. Perhaps the simplest idea for a suboptimal solution is to decompose Eq. (1.27) into a two-phase computation:

First an "optimal" feedback decoding, $\hat{d}$, is obtained by using the available history, but ignoring information directly related with the main data, (x):

$$\hat{d} = \arg\max_{d} P(f \mid d) \cdot P(d \mid h'). \qquad (1.28)$$

Second, using the fixed $\hat{d}$, the first two terms of the optimization Eq. (1.27) become independent of both d and h, which leads to the following expression, identical to Eq. (1.14).

$$\hat{h} \approx \arg\max_{h} P\big(x \mid h', \hat{d}, h\big) \cdot P\big(h \mid h', \hat{d}\big). \qquad (1.29)$$

This simple idea can be easily improved to actually take into account information from the main data to some extent. To this end, in the first phase, rather than computing just an "optimal" $\hat{d}$, we obtain a list of the n most probable decodings:

$$\begin{aligned} \{\hat{d}_1, \ldots, \hat{d}_n\} &= n\text{-}\underset{d}{\text{best}}\, P(f \mid d) \cdot P(d \mid h'), \\ \hat{h} &\approx \arg\max_{h} \max_{1 \le i \le n} P\big(f \mid \hat{d}_i\big) \cdot P\big(\hat{d}_i \mid h'\big) \cdot P\big(x \mid h', \hat{d}_i, h\big) \cdot P\big(h \mid h', \hat{d}_i\big). \end{aligned} \qquad (1.30)$$

[6] A less drastic assumption would keep the cross dependencies of f and x, leading to more interesting, *intermediate fusion* schemes [28].

Note that the optimization (1.30) can be easily solved by applying n times the same techniques used to solve Eq. (1.29) or Eq. (1.14) and, as a byproduct, an optimal $\hat{d}$, possibly better than the one given by Eq. (1.28), is obtained.

It is important to understand that non-deterministic feedback decoding will never be error-free. Consequently, with respect to using deterministic feedback, non-deterministic multimodal interfaces will always lead to an increase in the number of interaction steps needed to accomplish a given task. In other words, some degree of performance has to be sacrificed for a potentially improved ergonomy and/or user friendliness. Therefore, the design of a good non-deterministic multimodal feedback interface ultimately amounts to achieving a maximum feedback decoding accuracy by taking the maximum possible advantage of contextual information provided by the interactive framework. The concepts and formulation introduced in this section may prove helpful for the development of this kind of feedback interfaces.

Example: Non-deterministic Feedback in Human Karyotyping

For the sake of illustration, we assume now that feedback is provided by an *e-pen* interface. Thus f is a sequence of points or "*trajectory*" of the pen tip, which has to be decoded using *on-line* Handwritten Text Recognition (HTR) technology [38, 41].

This sequence of points encompasses two different parts. The first one, denoted by τ, is essentially deterministic: it is the first point of f, which is assumed to unambiguously determine the position, $c+1$, of the first wrong label in h'. The second one, denoted by t, is *non-deterministic* and corresponds to the remaining points of f which define the actual trajectory of amending pen-strokes. This trajectory has to be actually *decoded* into an optimal label, $\hat{l}$. That is, for a feedback signal $f \equiv (\tau, t)$, its decoding will be $d \equiv (c, \hat{l})$.

This is illustrated in Fig. 1.6, where the first error (*fifth* label: "7") is amended by handwriting with an e-pen the correct label (in blue) over the wrong one. The (horizontal coordinate of the) first point in the resulting trajectory unambiguously determines which is the first wrong label (the *fifth* in this case), thereby determining the last correct label $c = 4$. The whole trajectory is now submitted to the HTR subsystem, which may provide several label decoding hypotheses, such as "3", "5", "6", etc., (hopefully) including the correct decoding, "5".

In order to apply Eq. (1.27) here, the following modeling choices can be made:

- *Feedback decoding likelihood models*: $P(f \mid d) \equiv P(\tau, t \mid c, l) = P(t \mid l)$, because τ is deterministic and $P(t \mid l, \tau, c)$ can be assumed to be independent on the place (τ or c) were the correction is written. $P(t \mid l)$ can be modeled as in conventional *on-line* HTR; e.g., using Hidden Markov Models [41, 48].
- *History-conditioned chromosome label prior*: $P(d \mid h') \equiv P(c, l \mid h') = P(l \mid h', c)$, because c is deterministic. This conditioned prior should be null for already validated labels in ${h'}_1^c$ and for the wrong ${h'}_{c+1}$; flat for the other labels. It is interesting to note that if no interaction-derived information were taken into account, the best prior would be just a uniform distribution over {"1", "2", ..., "22"}.

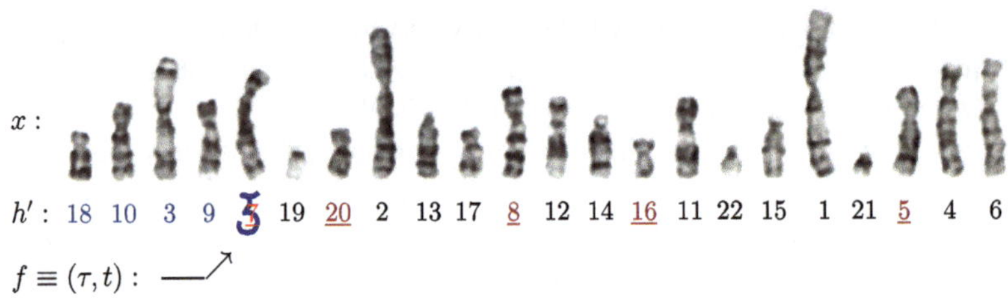

Fig. 1.6 Example of e-pen multimodal interaction in simplified human karyotyping. Labeling errors are marked in *red* and *underlined*. The correction made by the e-pen is shown in *blue*: a digit "5", handwritten over the first wrong (printed) label, "7". The possible decodings of this feedback, f, would be pairs (c, l) such as (4, "3"), (4, "5"), (4, "6"), ..., hopefully including the correct decoding, "5"

- The other two models are as in the deterministic feedback case. In particular, $P(h \mid h', c, l)$ must be null for all h with repeated symbols and for those h such that $h_1^{c+1} \neq h'_1, \ldots, h'_c, l$ or $h_i \in \{h_1, \ldots, h_c, l\}$, $c + 2 \leq i \leq 22$; flat otherwise.

To solve Eq. (1.27), on the other hand, both search solutions Eqs. (1.28)–(1.29) and (1.30) can be used, along with the greedy search of the conventional, non-interactive case.

Of course, despite using all the available interaction-derived information to increase feedback decoding accuracy, decoding errors will eventually occur. In these situations, the operator may want to just try again the failed correction, or perhaps simply resort to a fail-proof, deterministic device such as the keyboard.

1.3.6 Feedback Decoding and Adaptive Learning

As outlined at the beginning of Sect. 1.3, one of the main opportunities of the IPR framework is that it very naturally allows using feedback-derived data to adaptively tune the system to the user behavior and the specific task considered.

Now it is interesting to add that this concept applies not only for *Adaptive Learning* of the main system models (i.e., models needed to obtain hypotheses $\hat{h}$ for given input data x). Models needed for feedback decoding can also be adapted by just using training data effortless derived from the very interaction process. More specifically, the data needed for such a model adaptation are directly available from the explicit feedback decoding, as given by the solution of Eq. (1.27), or its approximations Eq. (1.28) or Eq. (1.30).

Figure 1.7 shows an IPR diagram where this kind of learning is considered. In this figure, $\mathcal{M}$ is assumed to include models for both *main* and *feedback* data. Both types of models can be initially trained in batch mode and then successively *adapted* to the task and/or the user by using training pairs derived from the user feedback information.

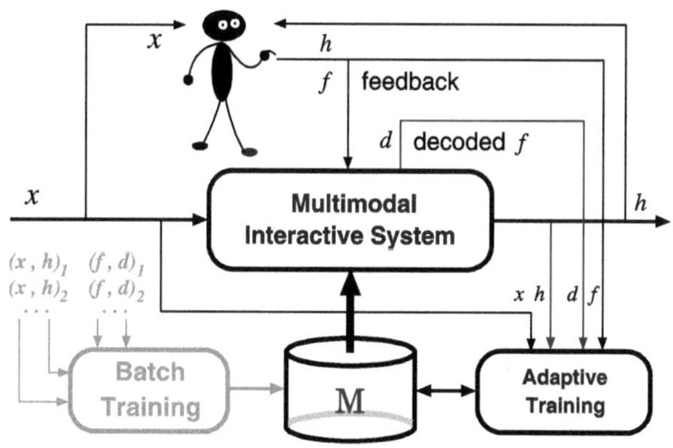

Fig. 1.7 Feedback decoding is useful for Adaptive Learning

Example: Adapting HTR Feedback Models in Human Karyotyping

In the case of interactive karyotyping with e-pen feedback, the HTR likelihood (HMM) models, $P(t \mid l)$, needed for feedback decoding, can be easily adapted to the specific handwriting style of the operator who is using the system. The training data needed in this case are pairs (t, l), where t is an *e-pen* trajectory and l is the correct text associated with t (a one- or two-digits label from "1" to "22"). Clearly, these pairs become readily available after every successful corrective interaction step.

Similarly, rather than using a flat feedback decoding prior model, as suggested in Sect. 1.3.5, $P(l)$ can be adapted to the typical errors made by the chromosome recognizer by increasing the prior probability of those handwriting labels that are frequently needed in the interactive corrections. The data required for this adaptation are just counts of the number of times the different labels have been used for corrections, information which is also readily available after each successful interaction step.

1.4 Interaction Protocols and Assessment

In multimodal interactive systems, the human operator may interact with the system in an unimaginable number of ways. Not only because many (combinations of) feedback modalities are possible, but also because there may generally be many ways or "*actions*" the operator can choose to provide the interaction feedback. Obviously, in order to allow for proper implementations of (the models needed in) an IPR system, human creativity has to be limited or predicted in some way so that the system can take maximum advantage of the allowed or expected interactive actions.

In the HCI literature, this kind of limitation or prediction of operator actions is often referred to as *User Model* [14, 18, 52]. Here only very simple, mathematically tractable user models will be considered and we will prefer to use the more modest term "*Interaction Protocol*" to refer to the set of allowed interactive actions and the ways the user is allowed or expected to make use of these actions.

Depending on the application and on the feedback modalities used, very different types of protocols can be assumed for the operator to interact with the system in a comfortable and productive manner. But the chosen protocols must also allow efficient implementations because, to be effective, interactive processing is generally highly demanding in terms of response times. In the end, the design of a good, friendly, effective and efficient interaction protocol is perhaps the most sensible design task for a given IPR application. Unfortunately, no adequate mathematical tools are typically available for such a design task and only intuition and trial-and-error can be used generally.

Once a specific interaction protocol has been defined it should be possible to apply decision theory in order to model the expected interaction effort of this protocol in terms of an adequate loss function. This would allow one to search for a corresponding decision function that minimizes the loss; i.e., the expected effort. While this is certainly an exciting research direction, for the time being we will only assume the simplifications of Sect. 1.3 that lead to the basic IPR Eq. (1.12), as discussed in Sect. 1.3.4.

The definition of an interaction protocol has also implications in system testing, as will be discussed latter.

1.4.1 General Types of Interaction Protocols

Perhaps the most basic taxonomy of interaction protocols attends to the way it is decided which hypothesis elements (are likely to) require human supervision.

In the examples discussed so far, the operator was assumed to systematically supervise each successive system hypothesis and find the point where the next labeling error appears. From the system's point of view this protocol is considered "*passive*", in that the system just waits for the human feedback, without concern about how she makes her supervision decisions. In contrast, in "*active*" protocols it is the system, rather than the human, which is in charge of making the relevant decisions about the need of operator supervision. Typically, the system makes the required computations on its own predictions to estimate for which hypothesis elements it may pay off to ask for operator supervision in order to optimize the overall system–human performance.

Clearly, with a *passive* protocol, "perfect" results from the human point of view can be guaranteed, since it is the operator herself who is fully responsible of the accurateness of these results. With the *active* protocol, on the other hand, the quality of the results may depend on the system ability to select appropriate hypothesis elements for supervision. But *active* interaction may provide for better compromises between overall human interaction effort and final accuracy.

In the case of *passive* protocols, the order in which hypothesis elements are presented to the user may be relevant; both in terms of efficiency and usability. For instance, in a handwritten text transcription task (cf. Sect. 3), the hypothesis elements are natural language words and it would be a bad idea to present these words in any order other than the right sentence order. But in a task such as the one considered in the interactive karyotyping examples, no natural ordering of the input images exists and hypothesis elements could in principle be presented in any arbitrary order.

For the sake of specifying an interaction protocol, output hypotheses can generally be represented in terms of *sequences* of hypothesis elements. This is often possible even if the outputs are naturally structured into more complex objects such as sets, arrays, trees, etc. (see an example in Chap. 9). In this case, a secondary dichotomy of *passive* protocols can be established.

The simplest of these protocol types corresponds to a "*left-to-right order*". In this case hypothesis elements are presented in a pre-specified or input-data-dependent order and the operator supervises the sequence from left to right (or right to left). In the other type of protocol a "*desultory order*" is assumed. At each interaction step, the operator chooses which hypothesis element(s) might be more convenient to be supervised, without following any systematic or precomputed order.

Obviously, with respect to the simple passive, left-to-right interaction, the greater flexibility entailed by others forms of interaction may allow reducing the number of required interaction steps, thereby reducing the overall human effort. But some type of *middle-out* optimization may be required which, in general, may become more complex than the simple *left-to-right* search required in the simplest case. On the other hand, a common variant of all the protocols discussed above consist on allowing the operator to supervise and/or fix herself more than one error in a single interaction step, rather than amending just one and waiting for the system reaction before carrying out further amendments. Clearly this may also lead to increased search difficulty, but the greater flexibility achieved might pay off in terms of overall user effort and usability.

The following hierarchy summarizes the interaction protocol types discussed so far:

Passive: The operator decides which hypothesis elements need supervision

- *Left-to-right order*: Hypothesis elements are supervised in fixed order
- *Desultory order*: Hypothesis elements are supervised in unspecified order

Active: The system decides which hypothesis elements undergo operator supervision and in which order they are considered.

Example: Human Karyotyping Interaction Protocols

Passive, left-to-right. Is the protocol that has been assumed in all the examples so far. First, chromosome images are sorted according to their max-posterior probability in order to use the greedy search outlined in Sect. 1.2. In the successive interaction steps, the operator is assumed to follow this order for supervision.

Passive, desultory. The operator might well prefer not to check the partial karyotype correctness in a strict left-to-right order, but perhaps by choosing herself which is "the worst" or most notorious labeling error at each interaction step.

Active. At each interaction step, the system computes some *confidence measure* for each chromosome label provided in that step. The one with lowest confidence is proposed for operator supervision. Then the operator validates or corrects *this* label and the system uses the corresponding feedback (and history) to compute its next prediction.

1.4.2 Left-to-Right Interactive–Predictive Processing

The passive, left-to-right protocol discussed above is perhaps the simplest and most natural protocol when *output hypotheses* can naturally be structured in terms of *sequences*. This protocol will be often referred to as "*left-to-right interactive–predictive processing*".

Let h in Eq. (1.14) be a sequence of elementary output hypotheses, $h_1, h_2, \ldots$. In this case, the history h' and the (deterministic) corrective feedback d can be jointly considered as a correct *prefix*, p, of h and Eq. (1.14) becomes

$$\hat{h} = \arg\max_{h \in \mathcal{H}} P(h \mid x, p). \tag{1.31}$$

Here $P(h \mid x, p)$ should be null for those h that do not have p as a prefix, which implies that $\hat{h}$ must be the concatenation of the given p and some optimal *suffix* $\hat{s}$. Correspondingly, Eq. (1.14) can be simplified to

$$\hat{s} = \arg\max_{s \in \mathcal{H}'} P(s \mid x, p) = \arg\max_{s \in \mathcal{H}'} P(x \mid p, s)\, P(s \mid p) \tag{1.32}$$

where $\mathcal{H}'$ is the set of possible suffixes.

Most of the applications to be described throughout this book correspond to left-to-right interactive–predictive processing, or quite natural variants thereof.

1.4.3 Active Interaction

As previously discussed, in this case it is the system, rather than the human, which proposes the next element of h to be supervised by the operator.

Let $\mathcal{S}(h)$ be a system-computed "*supervision*" function, which determines which element of a given hypothesis h has to be supervised, and $\mathcal{C}(h, k)$ a "*correction*" function, which represents a (may be void) corrective action made by the operator on the hypothesis element h_k. This way, the (deterministic) feedback, d, in Eq. (1.14) is $\mathcal{C}(h', \mathcal{S}(h'))$, and we can write:

$$\hat{h} = \arg\max_{h \in \mathcal{H}} P\bigl(h \mid x, h', \mathcal{C}\bigl(h', \mathcal{S}(h')\bigr)\bigr). \tag{1.33}$$

An interesting feature of this way of interaction is that it can be easily formulated to achieve adequate tradeoffs between human supervision effort and errors remaining at the end of the process. This is in contrast with other protocols, which aim to achieve perfect output with minimum supervision effort.

This way of interaction will be discussed in Chap. 5.

1.4.4 Interaction with Weaker Feedback

In the interactive karyotyping example, the operator may like to just point the place where an error exists and wait for the system to change its hypothesis, in an attempt to anticipate the correction which she has in mind. Interestingly, this simple but quite effective and user friendly interactive action can often be implemented easily and with a low search complexity.

Departing again from Eq. (1.14), let now d be just the *index* of the wrong hypothesis element. Then

$$\hat{h} = \arg\max_{h \in \mathcal{H}} P(x \mid h', d, h) P_d(h \mid h') \tag{1.34}$$

where

$$P_d(h \mid h') = \begin{cases} 0, & \text{if } h_d = h'_d, \\ \alpha P(h \mid h'), & \text{otherwise}, \end{cases} \tag{1.35}$$

were α is an adequate normalization factor and $P(h \mid h')$ accounts for the prior probability of a hypothesis, conditioned only by the (uncorrected) history, h'.

Alternatively, this can be formulated as a change in the underlying search problem. Again departing from Eq. (1.14):

$$\hat{h} = \arg\max_{h \in \mathcal{H}_d} P(x \mid h', h) P(h \mid h') \tag{1.36}$$

where $\mathcal{H}_d = \{h \in \mathcal{H}, h_d \neq h'_d\}$. That is, the wrong hypothesis element is excluded from the search space.

In any case, since this simple interactive action is often used repeatedly, the successive values of h'_d must be cached and $P_d(h \mid h')$ (or $\mathcal{H}_d$) must be computed taking into account all the previously discarded values of h'_d (not just the one from the previous step).

1.4.5 Interaction Without Input Data

There are interactive applications in which no input data, x, are given. An example of this kind of applications is the interactive generation of text, which will be discussed in detail in Chap. 10. In this application, the IPR system assists the user in writing text by predicting what are the most probable continuations of the text produced so far. Other applications, such as Relevance-based Image Retrieval (see Chap. 9), can also be considered to fall in this category. In these cases the formulation is essentially a trivial simplification of Eq. (1.14):

$$\hat{h} = \arg\max_{h \in \mathcal{H}} P(h \mid h', d). \tag{1.37}$$

This simplification, however, allows taking further considerations into account which will be discussed in detail in Chaps. 9 and 10.

1.4.6 Assessing IPR Systems

The definition of an interaction protocol has strong implications in system testing. Real testing, with a real operator working with the system, is much too expensive to be used in the day-to-day system development work. In all the cases, we should try our best to devise "objective" testing procedures which can be based on *labeled testing corpora*, as in the time-honored tradition of classical PR. Obviously, for this to be possible, an unambiguously defined interaction protocol is needed. However, not every interaction protocol lends itself to corpus-based testing and this adds to the set of tradeoffs that have to be considered when specifying a good interaction protocol.

As previously commented, decision theory does provide an adequate framework to rigorously define assessment criteria in terms of loss functions. Nevertheless, again, not every loss function leads to mathematically tractable decision functions and, for the moment, only the most basic simplifications are considered.

1.4.7 User Effort Estimation

Perhaps one of the most important factors of the rapid development of PR technology in the last few decades, is the nowadays commonly adopted *assessment paradigm* based on *labeled training and testing corpora*. In this paradigm, different approaches or algorithms can be easily, objectively and automatically tested and compared, without having to implement complete prototypes or requiring human intervention in the assessment procedures.

In the IPR framework, a human being is embedded "in the loop", and system performance has to be gauged mainly in terms of how much human effort is required to achieve the goals of the considered task. Apparently, evaluating system performance in this scenario should require human work and judgment. However, by carefully specifying precise goals and ground-truth, the corpus-based assessment paradigm is still applicable in most IPR tasks.

A corpus designed for testing a *traditional, non-interactive* PR system typically consists of a collection of objects, each one accompanied by its corresponding correct (structured) labeling. Performance is typically assessed in terms of elementary hypothesis errors; i.e., by counting the number of times the a system hypothesis element differs from the corresponding correct label.

As we will see throughout this book, natural interaction protocols can often be assumed for which the very same corpus and labeling can be directly used for assessing *interactive performance*. In this case, we no longer focus only on errors (the operator will ensure the required level of accuracy) but the correct, reference labeling for each object can be used to determine how many interaction steps are needed to produce a fully correct hypothesis. This will allow us to obtain adequate *estimates* of the amount of user interaction effort that would be needed to perform the considered task, under the assumed interaction protocol.

For example, if the interaction protocol is *left-to-right*, we can properly estimate user interaction effort in terms of the number of user corrective interactions needed to produce a given test-set labeling. At each interaction step, user behavior is simulated by computing the *longest common prefix*, p' between the current system hypothesis and the corresponding reference labeling. Then the first system wrong hypothesis element after this common prefix is replaced with the correct reference label, r, and the number of corrective interactions is increased by one. Finally, the resulting correct prefix, $p = p'r$, is used by the IPR system to compute a new suffix prediction, $\hat{s}$, as in Eq. (1.32).

In many applications discussed throughout this book, system hypotheses (and test-set labelings) are (natural–language) *sequences of words* and the *left-to-right* protocol applies very naturally. In these applications IPR performance is mainly assessed by means of the so-called "*Word Stroke Ratio*" (WSR) which is just the average number of (simulated) user corrective interactions needed to produce the reference word labelings of the test-set data.

It should be noted that assessment measures such as the WSR ignore user *supervision* effort; that is, only *corrective* interaction steps are considered relevant in order to measure (or estimate) system/user performance. This can be an adequate assumption in some practical applications. In particular, this is the case with passive interaction, which is often used when perfect results have to be guaranteed (by the user). Clearly, this entails a complete supervision of all the system hypotheses and only corrective effort may make a difference in system performance. Nevertheless, in general, performance measures should take into account (perhaps with different weights) the cost of both *corrective* and *supervision* interaction steps.

Of course, when an IPR system is considered sufficiently mature, final testing should be based on performance evaluations with human operators actually working with the real tasks the system is designed for. As previously mentioned, this kind of evaluation is generally extremely expensive and time consuming and cannot be carried out frequently. Moreover, the results of this kind of test are typically affected by many factors which are far away from the fundamental principles upon which system design is based. How the final *User Interface* (UI) is designed is one of these important factors. A good design should take into account the IPR design principles used in system development and, in particular, it should be finely tuned to the *interaction protocol* assumed in that development.

While the design of good IPR UIs and human subjective testing are clearly beyond the scope of this book, in the last chapter we present a series of prototypes developed for the different applications considered. Most of these prototypes are publicly available through the Internet, thereby allowing the readers to judge by themselves the practical potential of the ideas presented in this book for the different applications considered.

1.5 IPR Search and Confidence Estimation

In many of the applications to be presented in this book, multimodal interaction will lead to difficult search problems for which adequate approximations are needed. For all the problems in which (input and) output data and can be arranged sequentially, a useful tool for these approximations is the so-called *word graph*. In this section general word-graph concepts are introduced. Among other things, word graphs are useful tools to efficiently estimate *confidence measures* for hypothesis elements. This is also briefly outlined at the end of this section.

1.5.1 "Word" Graphs

The term "*word*" is used here to denote an *element* of a structured hypothesis, h. This use obeys historical reasons. Word graphs were first proposed by several authors some decades ago during the development of Automatic Speech Recognition technology. They were introduced as a data structure to very efficiently represent a large amount of sequences of words whose posterior probability is large enough, according to the acoustic (likelihood) and language (prior) models used to decode a spoken utterance, represented as a sequence of acoustic vectors.

Formally, a word graph (WG) is a weighted directed acyclic graph (weighted DAG) defined by the eight-tuple $(Q, n_I, F, A, t, V, \omega, p)$, where:

- Q is a *finite set of nodes*. Since a WG is a DAG a topological order on the nodes is assumed. Each node n is labeled with its corresponding index in this order: $Q = \{0, 1, 2, \dots, |Q| - 1\}$.
- $n_I \in Q$ is a special *initial node*: $n_I = 0$.
- $F \subseteq Q$ is the set of *final nodes*.
- $A \subset Q \times Q$ is a *finite set of edges*. Each edge e is denoted by its departing and ending nodes: $e = (i, j)$, where $i, j \in Q$ and $i < j$.
- $t : Q \to \{0, 1, \dots, T\}$ is a *position function* that associates each node (except n_I) with a position of the input sequence $x = x_1^T$. It must comply: $t(n_I) = 0$ and $\forall_{n \in F}\, t(n) = T$.
- V is a *vocabulary*; i.e., is a non-empty set of all the possible hypothesis elements or "words".
- $\omega : A \to V$ is a *word function* that assigns a word, $\omega(e)$, to each edge, $e = (i, j)$. This word corresponds to an element hypothesized between input sequence positions $t(i) + 1$ and $t(j)$.
- $p : A \to [0, 1]$ is an *edge probability function*. For a given edge, $e = (i, j)$, $p(e)$ is the probability of the hypothesis that $\omega(e)$ appears between $t(i) + 1$ and $t(j)$.

The word sequence hypotheses represented by a WG are the concatenations of words on paths in the WG from the initial node to a final node. Formally, a path in a WG is a sequence of consecutive edges $\phi = e_1, e_2, \dots, e_{|\phi|} = (0, q_1), (q_1, q_2), \dots, (q_{|\phi|-1}, q_{|\phi|})$, where $q_k \in Q - \{n_I\}$, $1 \le k \le |\phi|$ and $q_{|\phi|} \in F$. The probability of this path is computed as the product of the probabilities of the edges along the path:

$$P(\phi) = \prod_{k=1}^{|\phi|} p(e_k). \tag{1.38}$$

The word sequence hypothesis associated with the path ϕ is $h = \omega(e_1), \omega(e_2), \ldots, \omega(e_{|\phi|})$. Given that WGs are generally ambiguous (for each node and word several next nodes are possible), there may be more than one path associated with the sequence h. Let $\gamma(h)$ be the set of all the paths associated with h and let ϕ_h be one of these paths, the probability of the word sequence h is computed as:

$$P(h) = \sum_{\phi_h \in \gamma(h)} P(\phi_h). \tag{1.39}$$

Given a WG, the most probable word sequence can be written as:

$$\hat{h} = \arg\max_h \sum_{\phi_h \in \gamma(h)} P(\phi_h). \tag{1.40}$$

In general, this maximization problem is NP-hard [6]. Nevertheless, adequate approximations can be obtained by approximating the sum in Eq. (1.39) by the dominant addend. The resulting approximate probability, denoted by $\tilde{P}(\cdot)$, and the corresponding approximately optimal word sequence, $\tilde{h}$, are defined as:

$$P(h) \approx \tilde{P}(h) = \max_{\phi_h \in \gamma(h)} P(\phi_h), \tag{1.41}$$

$$\hat{h} \approx \tilde{h} = \arg\max_h \max_{\phi_h \in \gamma(h)} P(\phi_h). \tag{1.42}$$

These optimization equations can be efficiently solved by means of dynamic programming search algorithms, similar to Viterbi [50].

It is worth noting that the maximization Eq. (1.40) becomes quite simple in the case of an unambiguous WG. In this case, since $|\gamma(h)| = 1\ \forall h$, there is only one addend in the sum of Eq. (1.39) and Eq. (1.40) simplifies to:

$$\hat{h} = \arg\max_h P(\phi_h) \tag{1.43}$$

where ϕ_h is now the unique path associated with h. This optimization amounts to finding the best path in a DAG, a problem for which very well know simple exact solutions are available.

Sometimes it may be necessary not only to compute the best word sequence, but also the n-best word sequences in the word graph. To this end, the algorithm known as "Recursive Enumeration Algorithm" (REA) [31] is particularly useful here, because of its ability to efficiently provide next-best paths on demand.

In (sequential) IPR problems, WGs may help solving optimization equations such as Eq. (1.14). First, for a given input, x, a WG is computed, generally as a byproduct of the non-interactive search used to solve Eq. (1.2). Therefore, according to Eqs. (1.40), (1.42), or Eq. (1.43), the most probable word sequence in this WG is the optimal (non-interactive) solution to Eq. (1.2). Then, in a given interaction step, some elements of the history, h', have been validated and are therefore fixed. These elements can be searched for in the WG. With this information, we can search for complete hypotheses, h, compatible with the fixed parts of h' and select the one for which the probability $P(h \mid x, h', d)$ is maximum. Also, the edges associated with the fixed elements and their neighbor edges hold all the context information needed for the improved decoding Eq. (1.27) of non-deterministic feedback signals required for multimodal IPR.

Given that the WG is a DAG, these computations can generally be made efficiently using Dynamic Programming methods. The computations become even simpler in the case of *left-to-right* interaction protocols. Details of these procedures will be given for specific applications presented in the following chapters of this book.

Example: Word Graph of Human Karyotypes

In this case, a word graph represents the sequences of 22 labels with highest posterior probability $\Pr(h \mid x)$ for a given sequence of 22 chromosome images, x. Since, for the sake of simplicity, we have ignored here the initial image segmentation task and we assume that each chromosome is already represented as an individual image, the word graphs for this problem are unambiguous.[7]

An example of a word graph for this application is shown in Fig. 1.8. This kind of graph can typically be obtained as a byproduct of solving Eq. (1.3), using the prior and likelihood models given by Eqs. (1.4) and (1.5) and the greedy search procedure outlined in the example of Sect. 1.2.

The function t associates each node (except the initial one) with a chromosome image. On the other hand, the function $\omega(e)$ assigns a chromosome label to the edge $e = (i, j)$. This label is the hypothesis for the chromosome image associated with the node j. The function $p(e)$ is the probability of this hypothesis.

In this example, the two paths in black correspond to the correct labeling shown in Fig. 1.3 and the erroneous hypothesis predicted by the system as in Fig. 1.5. The probability of an arbitrary path such as:

$$\begin{aligned}\phi_1 = {} & (0,1),(1,4),(4,6),(6,8),(8,10),(10,13),(13,16),(16,19),(19,22),\\ & (22,25),(25,28),(28,31),(31,36),(36,41),(41,46),(46,49),(49,52),\\ & (52,55),(55,58),(58,61),(61,64),(64,66)\end{aligned}$$

is computed as:

$$\begin{aligned}P(\phi_1) = {} & p(0,1)p(1,4)p(4,6)p(6,8)p(8,10)p(10,13)p(13,16)p(16,19)\\ & p(19,22)p(22,25)p(25,28)p(28,31)p(31,36)p(36,41)p(41,46)\\ & p(46,49)p(49,52)p(52,55)p(55,58)p(58,61)p(61,64)p(64,66)\end{aligned}$$

[7] A more general example is given in Chap. 2.

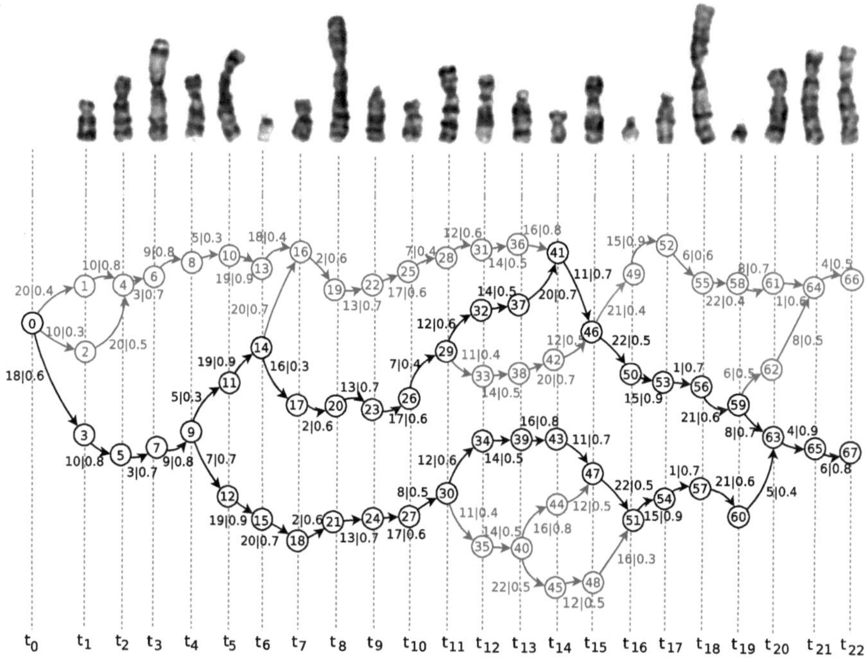

Fig. 1.8 Example of word graph used in Recognition of Human Karyotypes. Positions t_i are associated with the nodes as: $t(0) = t_0 = 0$, $t(1) = t(2) = t(3) = t_1$, $t(4) = t(5) = t_2$, $t(6) = t(7) = t_3, \ldots$

$$= 0.4 \cdot 0.8 \cdot 0.7 \cdot 0.8 \cdot 0.3 \cdot 0.9 \cdot 0.4 \cdot 0.6 \cdot 0.7 \cdot 0.6 \cdot 0.4 \cdot 0.6 \cdot 0.5 \cdot 0.8$$
$$\cdot 0.7 \cdot 0.4 \cdot 0.9 \cdot 0.6 \cdot 0.4 \cdot 0.7 \cdot 0.6 \cdot 0.5 = 5.94 \cdot 10^{-6}.$$

The label sequence associated with this path is $h^{(1)} =$ "20, 10, 3, 9, 5, 19, 18, 2, 13, 17, 7, 12, 14, 16, 11, 21, 15, 6, 22, 8, 1, 4". Given that this WG is not ambiguous, each sequence h has a unique path associated with it. So, according to Eq. (1.39) (or Eq. (1.43)), the exact probability of $h^{(1)}$ is

$$P\left(h^{(1)}\right) = P(\phi_1) = 5.94 \cdot 10^{-6}.$$

To obtain the most probable label sequence, all the word sequences on the WG must be taken into account. Some of the label sequences on the WG in Fig. 1.8 and their corresponding paths and probabilities are:

- $h^{(1)} =$ "20, 10, 3, 9, 5, 19, 18, 2, 13, 17, 7, 12, 14, 16, 11, 21, 15, 6, 22, 8, 1, 4", $\phi_1 = (0,1), (1,4), (4,6), (6,8), (8,10), (10,13), (13,16), (16,19), (19,22), (22,25), (25,28), (28,31), (31,36), (36,41), (41,46), (46,49), (49,52), (52,55), (55,58), (58,61), (61,64), (64,66)$,
  $P(h^{(1)}) = P(\phi_1) = 5.94 \cdot 10^{-6}$

  ...

- $h^{(9)}$ = "18, 10, 3, 9, 5, 19, 20, 2, 13, 17, 7, 12, 14, 16, 11, 22, 15, 1, 21, 8, 4, 6",
  ϕ_9 = (0, 3), (3, 5), (5, 7), (7, 9), (9, 11), (11, 14), (14, 16), (16, 19), (19, 22), (22, 25), (25, 28), (28, 31), (31, 36), (36, 41), (41, 46), (46, 50), (50, 53), (53, 56), (56, 59), (59, 63), (63, 65), (65, 67),
  $P(h^{(9)}) = P(\phi_9) = 8.19 \cdot 10^{-5}$
  ...
- $h^{(12)}$ = "18, 10, 3, 9, 5, 19, 16, 2, 13, 17, 7, 12, 14, 20, 11, 22, 15, 1, 21, 8, 4, 6",
  ϕ_{12} = (0, 3), (3, 5), (5, 7), (7, 9), (9, 11), (11, 14), (14, 17), (17, 20), (20, 23), (23, 26), (26, 29), (29, 32), (32, 37), (37, 41), (41, 46), (46, 50), (50, 53), (53, 56), (56, 59), (59, 63), (63, 65), (65, 67),
  $P(h^{(12)}) = P(\phi_{12}) = 3.07 \cdot 10^{-5}$
  ...
- $h^{(16)}$ = "18, 10, 3, 9, 7, 19, 20, 2, 13, 17, 8, 12, 14, 16, 11, 22, 15, 1, 21, 5, 4, 6",
  ϕ_{16} = (0, 3), (3, 5), (5, 7), (7, 9), (9, 12), (12, 15), (15, 18), (18, 21), (21, 24), (24, 27), (27, 30), (30, 34), (34, 39), (39, 43), (43, 47), (47, 51), (51, 54), (54, 57), (57, 60), (60, 63), (63, 65), (65, 67),
  $P(h^{(16)}) = P(\phi_{16}) = 1.4 \cdot 10^{-4}$
  ...

The most probable word sequence is $\hat{h} = h^{(16)}$ = "18, 10, 3, 9, 7, 19, 20, 2, 13, 17, 8, 12, 14, 16, 11, 22, 15, 1, 21, 5, 4, 6", with $P(\hat{h}) = 0.00014$. This is the optimal solution to Eq. (1.3) (and Eq. (1.43)), and corresponds to the label sequence predicted by the system in Fig. 1.5.

Since the interaction protocol assumed in this example is *left-to-right*, this sequence is supervised by the operator in this direction until the first wrong label is detected, which corresponds to the fifth image in the sequence. After correcting this error, the prefix "18, 10, 3, 9, 5" becomes fixed. The search for this prefix ends in node 11. Departing from this node, the system searches for an optimal suffix in the WG and proposes the next-best hypotheses compatible with the prefix, $h^{(9)}$. This is in fact the result of solving Eq. (1.14) or, more specifically, Eq. (1.32), given that the protocol is *left-to-right*. In this new system hypotheses, the 20th and the 11th wrong labels are corrected automatically. Then, in a new interaction step, the user corrects the next error, in this case the 7th label in the sequence. Finally, the system uses this new validated prefix to search for the next-best prefix-compatible hypothesis in the WG. This yields $h^{(12)}$, which is already the correct chromosome label sequence.

As previously mentioned, all the required computations can be efficiently carried out by simple and well-known graph-processing algorithms.

In the case of *multimodal* feedback, the WG can also be used to (approximately) deal with the optimization Eq. (1.27), needed for improved decoding of non-deterministic e-pen feedback signals (some details of this procedure will be given in Chap. 3).

1.5.2 Confidence Estimation

Given that PR systems are in general error-prone, a desirable feature of these systems is the capability of predicting the reliability of the system hypotheses. A large research effort has been devoted to this topic in the last two decades for many classical PR problems, e.g.: speech recognition [51], machine translation [49], handwritten text recognition [3]; and nowadays is being applied for different purposes in IPR [22, 46].

Confidence Estimation (CE) deals with the problem of assessing the correctness of PR system outputs. CE is performed by computing a score $C(h,x)$ (usually between 0 and 1), called *confidence measure*, which reflects the reliability of any PR system output. Confidence measures can be useful in many IPR scenarios, such as *active* interaction protocols (see Sect. 1.4.1) and different learning paradigms (see Sect. 1.6). In this book, active learning techniques within an active interaction protocol based on CE is applied for computer-assisted transcription of handwritten text (see Chap. 5). Also, an active interaction protocol based on CE is applied for interactive machine translation (see Chap. 6).

Perhaps the simplest approach for CE is to measure the confidence of a hypothesis h by its (properly normalized) posterior probability, $\Pr(h \mid x)$. From Eq. (1.2), this is computed as

$$C(h,x) = \Pr(h \mid x) = \frac{\Pr(x \mid h) \cdot \Pr(h)}{\Pr(x)} = \frac{\Pr(x \mid h) \cdot \Pr(h)}{\sum_{h' \in \mathcal{H}} \Pr(x \mid h') \cdot \Pr(h')}. \tag{1.44}$$

Equation (1.44) measures the reliability of a whole hypothesis h (e.g., a sequence of 22 labels in the case of human karyotypes). However, for many IPR applications it is more useful to predict the reliability of each one of the specific hypothesis elements (e.g., individual chromosome labels in the case of human karyotypes). Given a hypothesis h, the confidence measure (or posterior probability) for a specific hypothesis element h_i, $1 \leq i \leq |h|$, is computed by summing up the posterior probabilities of all decoding hypotheses which contain h_i at position i:

$$C(h_i,x) = \Pr(h_i \mid x) = \sum_{h' \in \mathcal{H}(i)} \Pr(h' \mid x), \qquad \mathcal{H}(i) = \{h' \in \mathcal{H} \mid h'_i = h_i\}. \tag{1.45}$$

In general, the hypothesis space, $\mathcal{H}$, may be infinite or exponentially large and it can be hard to compute the posterior probabilities in Eq. (1.44) or Eq. (1.45) using all possible hypotheses. Therefore, some approximations are needed for the sake of efficiency.[8] A simple approximation consists in using not all but a (large) number of most probable whole hypotheses, represented as a WG or an n-best list. Given that a WG can represent a huge number of best hypotheses in a very compact way, comparatively better performance is generally achieved using posterior probabilities computed over WGs. The computation of these probabilities can be efficiently

[8]Note that we have been able to avoid the use of the unconditional probability $\Pr(x)$ in all the all the PR and IPR optimization (search) equations discussed in the previous sections.

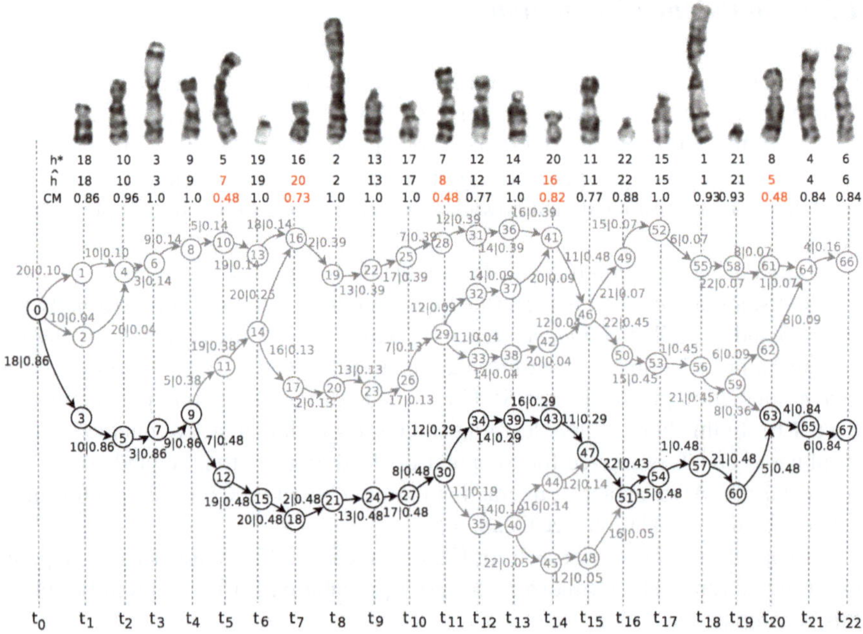

Fig. 1.9 Example of the computation of the confidence measures (CM) for the most probable decoded hypothesis, $\hat{h}$, over the word graph used in Recognition of Human Karyotypes. Each edges is tagged with the chromosome label and its posterior probability. The CM for each chromosome label at position t_i is computed by summing up the posterior probabilities of all edges which contain this chromosome label and end at position t_i. The correct labeling is h^* and CM is the confidence measure of each hypothesis element of $\hat{h}$. The recognition errors are shown in *red*. Using a threshold $\tau = 0.75$, four out of the five recognition errors would be rightly considered wrong while the rest of the hypothesis elements would be considered correct

carried out using *Dynamic Programming* techniques, such as (a WG version of) the well-known *forward–backward algorithm* [30].

Once the element-level (or hypothesis-level) confidence measure has been computed, an adequate decision threshold τ can be used to consider the element (or the hypothesis) either *correct* or *incorrect* depending on whether its confidence exceeds τ or not.

Example: Estimating Confidence Measures of Human Karyograms

Figure 1.9 shows an example of confidence estimation over the same WG shown in Fig. 1.8. Here posterior probabilities computed as explained above are assigned to the edges. For example, the posterior probability of a given edge such as $e = (15, 18)$, with chromosome label "20", is computed by summing up the posterior probabilities of the *three* paths containing this edge; i.e.:

- $\phi_{16} = (0,3),(3,5),(5,7),(7,9),(9,12),(12,15),(15,18),(18,21),(21,24),$ $(24,27),(27,30),(30,34),(34,39),(39,43),(43,47),(47,51),(51,54),$ $(54,57),(57,60),(60,63),(63,65),(65,67),$
  $P(\phi_{16}) = 1.4 \cdot 10^{-4}$,
- $\phi_{17} = (0,3),(3,5),(5,7),(7,9),(9,12),(12,15),(15,18),(18,21),(21,24),$ $(24,27),(27,30),(30,35),(35,40),(40,44),(44,47),(47,51),(51,54),$ $(54,57),(57,60),(60,63),(63,65),(65,67),$
  $P(\phi_{17}) = 6.50 \cdot 10^{-5}$,
- $\phi_{18} = (0,3),(3,5),(5,7),(7,9),(9,12),(12,15),(15,18),(18,21),(21,24),$ $(24,27),(27,30),(30,35),(35,40),(40,45),(45,48),(48,51),(51,54),$ $(54,57),(57,60),(60,63),(63,65),(65,67),$
  $P(\phi_{18}) = 2.43 \cdot 10^{-5}$,

$$P\big(e = (15, 18) \mid x\big) = \frac{(1.4 \cdot 10^{-4} + 6.50 \cdot 10^{-5} + 2.43 \cdot 10^{-5})}{4.75 \cdot 10^{-4}} = 0.48$$

where $P(x) = 4.75 \cdot 10^{-4}$ is the sum of the probabilities $P(\phi)$ of all WG paths ϕ.

Note that the posterior probability of an edge $e = (i, j)$ is not necessarily the confidence measure of the chromosome label $w(e)$ at position $t(j)$, since different edges $e' = (i', j')$ can end at same position $t(j')$ with the same chromosome label $w(e') = w(e)$. For this reason, the confidence measure for a specific hypothesis element which finish at position t_k is computed by summing up the posterior probabilities of all edges which contain this hypothesis element and finish at position t_k. For example, in Fig. 1.9, the confidence measure for the most probable hypothesis element at position t_7 (chromosome label 20) is computed by summing up the posterior probabilities of the *two* edges which contain the chromosome label 20 and finish at position t_7, i.e.: $P(e_1 = (15, 18)|x) + P(e_2 = (14, 16)|x) = 0.48 + 0.25 = 0.73$.

1.6 Machine Learning Paradigms for IPR

So far all models, $\mathcal{M}$, needed for IPR have been assumed to be fixed. But now *human interaction* offers another unique opportunity to improve system's behavior by tuning the models, $\mathcal{M}$. The feedback produced at each step of the interaction process can generally be converted into new, fresh training information, useful for *adapting* the system to changing environment.

For many years, *adaptive learning* and other related learning paradigms such as *on-line*, *semi-supervised*, *reinforcement*, *active*, etc.) have been the focus of thorough studies. However, most of these studies are mainly theoretically oriented. Practical applications of the theoretical results are generally scarce. Now the *interactive* paradigm offers a natural framework where these learning paradigms can be used advantageously.

The application of these ideas in our IPR framework require establishing adequate training criteria. These criteria should allow the development of adaptive training algorithms that take the maximum advantage of the interaction-derived data to ultimately minimize the overall human effort in the long term. Although a deep review of these topics is clearly beyond the scope of this book, the main ideas will be presented in some detail in this section.

1.6.1 Online Learning

During the interactions with the user, an IPR system obtains correct hypotheses for unseen inputs. This feedback gives a great opportunity to learn from the new data. As stated in Sect. 1.2, in IPR, the models $\mathcal{M}$ that approximate the probabilities of the optimal decision rules, are initially estimated by a model trained with a batch corpus $T = \{(x, h)_i\}$, as is done in traditional PR. After I interaction rounds, the system has gathered a new corpus $T' = \{(x', h')_j\}$ of correct hypotheses and input stimulus. *Online learning* aims at learning in scenarios like this, where the samples can be considered as a stream of data.

It is worth highlighting that the initial or seed corpus and the online gathered corpus have different properties. The former is intended to be a large corpus that comprises several use cases. The latter corpus, is domain specific which comprises an initially small number of training pairs that slowly grow with the user interactions. Then, the on-line corpus summarizes information from two sources: the specific domain of the current task and the user preferences. For instance consider an example of handwritten recognition in which a corpus of text sentences is needed to estimate *language models*. In this case, the more sentences are used to train the seed corpus, the more general the language model would be and the less likely it is to find *out of vocabulary words*.[9] However, as the system interacts with the user, the system is fed with language constructions and vocabulary that are specific to the document that is being supervised.

There are two approaches for a IPR system to make profit from the new hypotheses supervised by the user. On the one hand, IPR systems can learn from them. On the other hand, while performing online learning, IPR systems need to adapt to different domains. These two objectives are often opposed to each other. For instance, in order to properly adapt, the system should be able to forget what it learnt from old samples. However, by forgetting what old samples taught, the system performance can decrease.

A simple online learning approach is to train the model by merging both corpora: the seed corpus, T, and the online gathered corpus, T'. This approach is equivalent to assume that initially, both corpora were part of the seed corpus. This technique is usually called *incremental learning*, since we only increment the seed corpus. In practice, this incremental learning can be efficiently implemented for many cases. Specially, if maximum likelihood is taken as the modeling technique, then incremental learning boils down to update the sufficient statistics. These sufficient statistics

[9] Words for which the system has no previous example.

mostly are the counts needed to estimate the model parameters if the model has no latent variable.

In the case of latent variable models, the maximum likelihood estimates cannot be computed in a closed form solution. A typical approach is to iteratively ascend the gradient by means of the Expectation and Maximization (EM) algorithm [16]. Given an initial parameter estimate, the EM algorithm computes, in the E(xpectation) step, a set of sufficient statistics that are afterwards used in the M(aximization) step to compute a new parameter estimate. This process is held until convergence. There is an incremental version of the EM algorithm [36] that keeps track of the sufficient statistics computed in the E-step. When a new training pair is observed, the sufficient statistics computed in the incremental E-step are updated and a new M-step is computed yielding new adapted parameters.

Incremental learning assumes that both corpora have the same bias in the system modeling. Obviously, the online corpus resembles the probabilities of the task, which the system is dealing with, better than the seed corpus does. However, the initial corpus is larger and, consequently, better estimated models can be built with it. Therefore, a trade-off should be found between the two corpora; or in other words, a trade-off between reliability and domain adaptation must be found. There are several extensions to the incremental learning techniques that aim at finding this tradeoff. For instance, for the case of latent variable models there are some online versions of the EM algorithm [5, 36].

A simple approach that aims at finding a trade-off between both corpora is to use a linear interpolation of two models: one trained with the seed corpus and another trained with the online corpus. For instance, consider the modeling of the hypothesis prior probability distribution. In this case the initial model $P_{\mathcal{M}}(h)$, and the on-line model $P_{\mathcal{M}'}(h)$ can be combined to obtain an on-line model $P_\alpha(h)$ as follows

$$P_\alpha(h) = \alpha \cdot P_{\mathcal{M}}(h) + (1-\alpha) \cdot P_{\mathcal{M}'}(h) \tag{1.46}$$

with α being an adaptation ration that if close to 1 generates a fixed system that slowly learns from new inputs; and if it is close to 0, quickly takes into account the new inputs. Ideally, at the beginning, when the on-line corpus is small, the adaptation ratio should be almost 1; and as the on-line corpus is fed with new data the ratio will drop to values closer to 0. The interpolation parameter α can be estimated by a Bayesian approach [17].

A recurrent idea of adaptive learning methods is to find a trade-off between the on-line corpus and the seed corpus. This problem is extended to the online corpus itself since it is common that the on-line corpus varies from one domain to another. For instance, in an interactive handwritten text recognition system, the user may use the system to transcribe different books; or different users can use the same system for transcribing parts of the same book.

A simple approach to adapt in changing environments, such as the one discussed, is to consider a set of models $\{\mathcal{M}_1, \dots, \mathcal{M}_K\}$ to be estimated instead of a simple one, $\mathcal{M}'$. Each model would gather a proportion of the online corpus to train its parameters. For instance, each model can sample at exponentially decreasing time intervals [25]. Finally, the adapted model would be a combination of the initial model and the online models. In this scenario a log-linear adaptation model is specially appealing

$$P_{\boldsymbol{\lambda}}(h) = \frac{1}{\mathcal{Z}_{\boldsymbol{\lambda}}(h)} \exp\left(\sum_{k=1}^{K} \lambda_k \log\left(P_{\mathcal{M}_k}(h)\right)\right) \tag{1.47}$$

where $\boldsymbol{\lambda}$ stands for the adaptation weights, and $\mathcal{Z}_{\boldsymbol{\lambda}}(h)$ is a normalization constant to ensure the probability to sum up to one. The previous idea can be extended to any score as follows:

$$P_{\boldsymbol{\lambda}}(h) = \frac{1}{\mathcal{Z}_{\boldsymbol{\lambda}}(h)} \exp\left(\sum_{k=1}^{K} \lambda_k f_k(h)\right) \tag{1.48}$$

where $f_k(h)$ can be any suitable score such as the logarithm of a probability distribution model. This modeling technique is know as *maximum entropy models* [2] or *log-linear models* [37]. Maximum entropy models are not exclusive for model adaptation, and as a matter of fact, they have been applied for modeling probability distributions in many traditional PR tasks such as statistical machine translation [37], or language modeling [33].

An alternative approach is to start with an initial model and adapt it to each newly acquired sample pair as long as the model does not have to modify its parameter significantly. For instance, the *online passive aggressive* technique [10], is an adaptive training algorithm for linear classifiers that adapts to the new samples as long as they do not require to modify the decision boundary more than a given threshold (aggressive case). In such case, the classifier is modified so that the decision boundary is modified just as much as the threshold (passive case). This technique, however, is difficult to extend to many PR classifiers.

Bayesian Statistics

In the context of adaptative learning, Bayesian statistics is a very appealing framework, which applies decision theory to the parameter selection phase. In conventional statistics, each model is parametrized with a set of parameters, say $\boldsymbol{\theta}$. The inferring problem is, then, stated as the problem of finding those parameters that optimize a given criterion such as maximum likelihood. In this case, there is no uncertainty assumed over the parameters. In other words, during the training phase, it is assumed that there is enough information to obtain a reliable estimation of the actual parameters.

In the Bayesian framework, parameters are considered random variables and, hence, they are treated as such. Therefore, there are no optimal parameters to select, but a probability distribution over those parameters to model. A model in this framework, is given by two probability distributions: a *likelihood distribution* and a *parameter-prior distribution*. The likelihood distribution is the probability of the random variable given the parameters; in other words, it corresponds to traditional models. The parameter-prior distribution is a probability distribution over the value of the parameters that codifies our previous knowledge regarding to the parameters. Note that the question of deciding one or another prior probability distribution is a modeling issue.

Consider the example of modeling the input probability $\Pr(x \mid h)$ in Eq. (1.2). This probability is traditionally modeled with a set of parameters $\boldsymbol{\theta}$. Given a training sample, T, the optimal parameters, $\hat{\boldsymbol{\theta}}$, are selected so that they maximize the likelihood of the training sample. Therefore, we can say that the model $\mathcal{M}$ is given by this set of parameters and a known probability distribution, i.e., $\mathcal{M} = \{P_{\boldsymbol{\theta}}(x \mid h), \hat{\boldsymbol{\theta}}\} = P_{\hat{\boldsymbol{\theta}}}(x \mid h)$. A Bayesian model is defined by two probability distributions, i.e. $\mathcal{M} = \{P(x \mid h, \boldsymbol{\theta}), \pi(\theta)\}$, where $P(x \mid h, \boldsymbol{\theta})$ is equivalent to $P_{\boldsymbol{\theta}}(x \mid h)$, i.e., the likelihood of x given the parameters $\boldsymbol{\theta}$; and where $\pi(\boldsymbol{\theta})$ is a prior probability distribution over the parameters. Finally, in order to predict the probability of a new input x given the model $\mathcal{M}$ and the training data T, the parameters have to be marginalized in order to compute the *predictive probability distribution*

$$P_{\mathcal{M}}(x \mid h, T) = \int_{\boldsymbol{\Theta}} P(x \mid h, \boldsymbol{\theta}) \cdot P(\boldsymbol{\theta} \mid T)\, d\boldsymbol{\theta} \tag{1.49}$$

where $P(x \mid h, \boldsymbol{\theta})$ is the likelihood probability distribution and where $P(\boldsymbol{\theta} \mid T)$ is the *parameter-posterior probability distribution.*

The posterior probability distribution is a distribution over the parameters that adjust the prior knowledge encoded into the parameter-prior distribution, π, to the events observed in the "training" sample T. The parameter-posterior probability is usually decomposed as

$$P(\boldsymbol{\theta} \mid T) = \frac{P(T \mid \boldsymbol{\theta})\pi(\boldsymbol{\theta})}{P(T)} \tag{1.50}$$

where $P(T)$ is a normalization constant that can be computed integrating out the parameters of the numerator; and $P(T \mid \boldsymbol{\theta})$ is the traditional maximum likelihood probability of the training sample.

As stated above, the "training" sample is not used for training a model but for refining the system knowledge about the parameters. Although there is no training stage in Bayesian framework, the integrations needed to compute the parameter-posterior and the predictive probability distributions, have to be approximated, which is typically done by means of sampling techniques such as Markov chain Monte Carlo [1].

Theoretically, the Bayesian framework is very appealing in adaptive learning since the effect that a new observation has over the model is simply to modify the parameter-posterior probability distribution. Therefore, in theory, a Bayesian model is easily adaptable to new evidence by simply updating the parameter-prior distribution with the parameter-posterior. In this way, the parameter-posterior becomes the parameter-prior of the model for the following outcome, and so on.

More specifically, in IPR, an initial Bayesian model can be defined with the parameter-prior initialized to the parameter-posterior distribution computed over the initial batch training sample. Afterwards, this parameter-prior probability distribution would be adapted to the online corpus while it grows as given by Eq. (1.50).

This approach, however, has a great practical disadvantage, since most of the traditional PR models are not easily extended to the Bayesian framework, due to computational requirements.

1.6.2 Active Learning

In Sect. 1.4.1 we differentiated between two kinds of interactive protocols: passive and active. In the former case, the user is monotonically inquired to fully correct the proposed hypothesis for each input x in the same order they occur. In the latter case, the system decides the order in which the hypotheses and inputs would be supervised. In active interaction protocols, the system might decide to stop inquiring the user if the assessment quality is beyond a given threshold, finishing in this way the interaction with the user.

The active interaction protocols are closely related with the active learning. In active learning [12], there is a pool of input samples for which correct hypotheses are not known. There is also an oracle that is able to give the correct hypothesis to each input stimulus. The objective is to minimize the number of queries to the oracle while maximizing the performance. In order to do that, an active selection criterion is applied to all the samples and then the best one is selected. The selected sample is, then, queried to the oracle in order to obtain its correct hypothesis. This process is repeated until no more samples are needed.

There are several active learning strategies [24] such as selecting the sample that is closer to the bounds or the sample with the smaller confidence intervals, among many others. Many active learning techniques are aimed to work in an online learning scenario. In general, we can classify active strategies into two categories depending on the degree of modification an online model would suffer: aggressive and mellow. Examples of aggressive techniques are for instance query by committee [19] or splitting index [11]. Most of the mellow techniques are based on the generic mellow learner [9, 13].

One core idea in active learning that is important to keep in mind is the *sampling bias* [12]. The sampling bias, can be stated as the distortion in the sample probability distribution generated by the active sampling strategy. If no active learning strategy is applied then all the training examples occur with the actual probability distribution of the data. However, when an active learning strategy is applied, the sample probability is distorted provided that there are inputs that are not corrected. For instance, consider the case of selecting the sentence with more out-of-vocabulary words in an interactive machine translation system. In this scenario, the user is asked to correct a translation that has more out of vocabulary words than the other source sentences. In doing so, the system quickly extends its vocabulary. However, the actual data probability is being distorted, since out-of-vocabulary words are rare and by actively selecting those sentences, unlikely events become likely. This could eventually lead to a drop in the system performance.

A very interesting scenario in IPR is the active interaction protocol in which a given threshold of error is required. In this scenario, the system selects inputs to query to the user until the system estimates that the error of the task is lower than a given threshold. If we use an active learning in order to reduce the user effort, we can produce quite the opposite if the active strategy is too aggressive. Therefore, the sampling bias should be kept in mind while designing an active learning strategy.

1.6.3 Semi-Supervised Learning

In some IPR interactive active protocols, the system has two kinds of hypotheses:

- *Validated hypotheses*: the hypotheses that the user has supervised so far,
- *Automatic hypotheses*: the hypotheses produced by the system without user supervision.

The validated hypotheses can be used to make the system better by online training or adaptation techniques. However, the automatic hypotheses that may contain errors can also be used in order to improve the system performance. There are several techniques fitted to this sort of problems, the so called semi-supervised learning [7]. Semi-Supervised learning is stated as the problem of designing the best system using two kind of corpus: one that is tagged with the correct hypotheses for each input; and another that is composed only of input stimuli.

Although the semi-supervised learning does not totally fit the IPR learning problem, it is very common in semi-supervised learning to complete the sample with the hypotheses given by an automatic system. Afterwards, many semi-supervised techniques are built on this completed sample. For instance, a simple technique is to use confidence intervals to select those samples that are reliable enough accordingly to a confidence measure. Then, those reliable samples are used as if they where user validated hypotheses. This process can be generalized giving at each sample a reliability weight.

Another very common technique is to use the inputs without their corresponding hypotheses to infer the input probability distribution. One way of accomplishing it consists in building clusters with all the data (supervised and unsupervised). Afterwards, the supervised data are used to infer the best hypothesis for each cluster [12]. This technique is usually combined with active learning techniques so that new corrected hypotheses can be queried whenever a cluster is confusing with regards to which the best hypothesis is.

1.6.4 Reinforcement Learning

In some interaction protocols, the feedback given by the user is not always totally informative. This is the case of *weak feedback* discussed in Sect. 1.4.1, where an interactive system may receive the feedback that the hypothesis is not correct without the actual correction. In those cases, the system can use this information to propose a new hypothesis. However, it could also inquire to the user additional information regarding the previous hypothesis. Obviously, the aim of such question is to improve the models so that the next time the system observes similar inputs it would correctly classify them. This process may, in principle, increase the number of interactions with the user. This problem is known in the machine learning literature as *learning with limited-feedback* [47].

Limited-feedback can be understood as a branch of reinforcement learning [27]. In these problems, the system has a benefit function that rewards and reinforces the system actions over time. Therefore, the system wishes to maximize the benefit (or minimize the loss) that it can obtain from the environment while working. For doing this, the system has to optimize two confronted objectives:

- *Exploration*: the system has to explore many possibilities in order to know its surrounding "environment", and
- *Exploitation*: the system uses its knowledge about the environment to make profit from it.

A system that only explores would give a low benefit because it would use resources to explore hypothesis that give low benefit in an attempt of obtaining a very accurate probability distribution model. Oppositely, a system that only exploits would obtain a pour benefit, because it would have a weak environment model. This duality is usually formalized in terms of "*regret*". The *regret* is the difference between the reinforcement or benefit that the system has obtained from the environment with respect to the maximum benefit it could have obtained during a past period of time T, for which the system has already taken its hypotheses. In this context, the best system is the one that minimizes the regret.

Formally, if $h^{(1)}, \ldots, h^{(T)}$ are the T proposed hypotheses during a period of time; and the function $B(h^{(1)}, \ldots, h^{(T)})$ quantifies the benefit obtained from these hypotheses, then the regret is

$$R\big(h^{(1)}, \ldots, h^{(T)}\big) = B\big(h^{(1)}, \ldots, h^{(T)}\big) - \underset{m^{(1)}, \ldots, m^{(T)}}{\arg\max}\; B\big(m^{(1)}, \ldots, m^{(T)}\big). \quad (1.51)$$

A very simple IPR example is to model the user preferences. In an IPR task, we can have two different IPR systems, each minimizing different loss functions. Assuming that none of those loss functions minimizes the interactions with the user directly, there is no way to know which is better in practice. Then, we can use reinforcement learning strategies on the fly in order to infer which the best system is while the system is interacting with the user. A possible approach, would be to use the system A for a while and then change to the system B for another period of time. After that sampling, we could have recorded some statistics, such as number of corrections by the user, or number of proposed hypotheses. It is important to highlight that this is an exploration phase. Once we have a proper model of the environment, the best system can be used for a while in an exploitation phase. Note that none of both strategies can be held forever if we want to minimize the regret.

References

1. Andrieu, C., de Freitas, N., Doucet, A., & Jordan, M. I. (2003). An introduction to mcmc for machine learning. *Machine Learning*, *50*(1–2), 5–43.
2. Berger, A. L., Pietra, S. A. D., & Pietra, V. J. D. (1996). A maximum entropy approach to natural language processing. *Computational Linguistics*, *22*, 39–71.
3. Bertolami, R., Zimmermann, M., & Bunke, H. (2006). Rejection strategies for offline handwritten text recognition. *Pattern Recognition Letters*, *27*, 2005–2012.
4. Canny, J. (2006). The future of human-computer interaction. *ACM Queue*, *4*(6), 24–32.
5. Cappé, O., & Moulines, E. (2009). Online EM algorithm for latent data models. *Journal of the Royal Statistical Society Series B*, *71*(3), 593–613.
6. Casacuberta, F., & Higuera, C. D. L. (2000). Computational complexity of problems on probabilistic grammars and transducers. In *ICGI'00: Proceedings of the 5th international colloquium on grammatical inference* (pp. 15–24), London, UK. Berlin: Springer.
7. Chapelle, O., Schölkopf, B., & Zien, A. (2006). *Semi-supervised learning*. Cambridge: MIT Press.
8. Christmas, W. J., Kittler, J., & Petrou, M. (1995). Structural matching in computer vision using probabilistic relaxation. *IEEE Transactions on Pattern Analysis and Machine Intelligence*, *17*, 749–764.
9. Cohn, D., Atlas, L., & Ladner, R. (1994). Improving generalization with active learning. *Machine Learning*, *15*(2), 201–221.
10. Crammer, K., Dekel, O., Keshet, J., Shalev-Shwartz, S., & Singer, Y. (2006). Online passive–aggressive algorithms. *Journal of Machine Learning Research*, *7*, 551–585.
11. Dasgupta, S. (2005). Coarse sample complexity bounds for active learning. In *Neural information processing systems*.
12. Dasgupta, S. (2009). The two faces of active learning. In *Discovery science* (p. 35).
13. Dasgupta, S., Hsu, D., & Monteleoni, C. (2008). A general agnostic active learning algorithm. In J. C. Platt, D. Koller, Y. Singer & S. Roweis (Eds.), *Advances in neural information processing systems* (Vol. 20, pp. 353–360). Cambridge: MIT Press.
14. De Bra, P., Kobsa, A., & Chin, D. E. (2010). *Lecture notes in computer science: Vol. 6075. User modeling, adaptation, and personalization. Proceedings of the 18th international conference UMAP 2010.*
15. Dechter, R., & Pearl, J. (1985). Generalized best-first search strategies and the optimality of *A**. *Journal of the ACM*, *32*, 505–536.
16. Dempster, A. P., Laird, N. M., & Rubin, D. B. (1977). Maximum likelihood from incomplete data via the EM algorithm (with discussion). *Journal of the Royal Statistical Society, Series B*, *39*, 1–38.
17. Duda, R. O., & Hart, P. E. (1973). *Pattern classification and scene analysis*. New York: Wiley.
18. Fischer, G. (2001). User modeling in human–computer interaction. *User Modeling and User-Adapted Interaction*, *11*, 65–86.
19. Freund, Y., Seung, H. S., Shamir, E., & Tishby, N. (1995). Selective sampling using the query by committee algorithm. In *Machine learning* (pp. 133–168).
20. Frey, B. J., & Hinton, G. E. (1999). Variational learning in nonlinear Gaussian belief networks. *Neural Computation*, *11*, 193–213.
21. Geman, S., & Geman, D. (1987). Stochastic relaxation, Gibbs distributions, and the Bayesian restoration of images. In *Readings in computer vision: issues, problems, principles, and paradigms* (pp. 564–584). San Mateo: Morgan Kaufmann.
22. González-Rubio, J., Ortiz-Martínez, D., & Casacuberta, F. (2010). Balancing user effort and translation error in interactive machine translation via confidence measures. In *Proceedings of the 48th annual meeting of the association for computational linguistics (ACL10)* (pp. 173–177).
23. Groena, F. C. A., tenKateb, T. K., Smeuldersc, A. W. M., & Youngd, I. T. (1989). Human chromosome classification based on local band descriptors. *Pattern Recognition Letters*, *9*(3), 211–222.

24. Hanneke, S. (2009). *Theoretical foundations of active learning*. Machine Learning Department, School of Computer Science, Carnegie Mellon University, Pittsburgh, USA. Advisors: Blum, A., Dasgupta, S., Wasserman, L., & Xing, E. P.
25. Hazan, E., & Seshadhri, C. (2009). Efficient learning algorithms for changing environments. In *Proceedings of the 26th annual international conference on machine learning*.
26. Hinton, G. E. (2002). Training products of experts by minimizing contrastive divergence. *Neural Computation*, *14*, 1771–1800.
27. Jaksch, T., Ortner, R., & Auer, P. (2010). Near-optimal regret bounds for reinforcement learning. *Journal of Machine Learning Research*, *99*, 1563–1600.
28. Jaimes, A., & Sebe, N. (2006). Multimodal human–computer interaction: A survey. *Computer Vision and Image Understanding*, *108*(1–2), 116–134. Special Issue on Vision for Human-Computer Interaction.
29. Jarvis, R. A. (1974). An interactive minicomputer laboratory for graphics, image processing, and pattern recognition. *Computer*, *7*(10), 49–60.
30. Jelinek, F. (1998). *Statistical methods for speech recognition*. Cambridge: MIT Press.
31. Jiménez, V. M., & Marzal, A. (1999). Computing the k shortest paths: a new algorithm and an experimental comparison. In J. S. Viter & C. D. Zaraliagis (Eds.), *Lecture notes in computer science: Vol. 1668. Algorithm engineering* (pp. 15–29). Berlin: Springer.
32. Kittler, J., & Illingworth, J. (1986). Relaxation labelling algorithms-a review. *Image and Vision Computing*, *3*, 206–216.
33. Martin, S. C., Ney, H., & Hamacher, C. (2000). Maximum entropy language modeling and the smoothing problem. *IEEE Transactions on Speech and Audio Processing*, *8*(5), 626–632.
34. Martínez, C., García, H., & Juan, A. (2003). Chromosome classification using continuous hidden Markov models. In *LNCS*. *Pattern recognition and image analysis* (pp. 494–501). Berlin: Springer.
35. Martínez, C., Juan, A., & Casacuberta, F. (2007). Iterative contextual recurrent classification of chromosomes. *Neural Processing Letters*, *26*(3), 159–175.
36. Neal, R. M., & Hinton, G. E. (1998). A view of the em algorithm that justifies incremental, sparse, and other variants. In *Learning in graphical models* (pp. 355–368). Dordrecht: Kluwer Academic.
37. Och, F. J., & Ney, H. (2002). Discriminative training and maximum entropy models for statistical machine translation. In *Proc. of ACL* (pp. 295–302).
38. Pastor, M., Toselli, A. H., & Vidal, E. (2005). Writing speed normalization for on-line handwritten text recognition. In *Proc. of the eighth international conference on document analysis and recognition (ICDAR '05)* (pp. 1131–1135), Seoul, Korea.
39. Pearl, J. (1984). *Heuristics: intelligent search strategies for computer problem solving*. Reading: Addison-Wesley.
40. Pearl, J. (1988). *Probabilistic reasoning in intelligent systems: networks of plausible inference*. San Mateo: Morgan Kaufmann.
41. Plamondon, R., & Srihari, S. N. (2000). On-line and off-line handwriting recognition: a comprehensive survey. *IEEE Transactions on Pattern Analysis and Machine Intelligence*, *22*(1), 63–84.
42. Rabiner, L. (1989). A tutorial of hidden Markov models and selected application in speech recognition. *Proceedings of the IEEE*, *77*, 257–286.
43. Ritter, G., Gallegos, M. T., & Gaggermeier, K. (1995). Automatic context-sensitive karyotyping of human chromosomes based on elliptically symmetric statistical distributions. *Pattern Recognition*, *28*(6), 823–831.
44. Rosenfeld, A., Hummel, R. A., & Zucker, S. W. (1976). Scene labeling by relaxation operations. *IEEE Transactions on Systems, Man, and Cybernetics*, *6*(6), 420–433.
45. Schröck, E., du Manoir, S., Veldman, T., Schoell, B., Wienberg, J. W., Ferguson-Smith, M. A., Ning, Y., Ledbetter, D. H., Bar-Am, I., Soenksen, D., Garini, Y., & Ried, T. (1996). Multicolor spectral karyotyping of human chromosomes. *Science*, *273*(5274), 494–497.
46. Serrano, N., Sanchis, A., & Juan, A. (2010). Balancing error and supervision effort in interactive-predictive handwriting recognition. In *Proceedings of the international conference on intelligent user interfaces (IUI 2010)* (pp. 373–376).

47. Shalev-shwartz, S., & Tewari, A. (2008). Efficient bandit algorithms for online multiclass prediction sham m. kakade. In *Proc. of the 25th international conference on machine learning*.
48. Toselli, A. H., Pastor, M., & Vidal, E. (2007). On-line handwriting recognition system for Tamil handwritten characters. In *Lecture notes in computer science: Vol. 4477. 3rd Iberian conference on pattern recognition and image analysis* (pp. 370–377), Girona (Spain). Berlin: Springer.
49. Ueffing, N., & Ney, H. (2007). Word-level confidence estimation for machine translation. *Computational Linguistics*, *33*(1), 9–40.
50. Viterbi, A. (1967). Error bounds for convolutional codes and an asymptotically optimal decoding algorithm. *IEEE Transactions on Information Theory*, *13*, 260–269.
51. Wessel, F., Schlüter, R., Macherey, K., & Ney, H. (2001). Confidence measures for large vocabulary continuous speech recognition. *IEEE Transactions on Speech and Audio Processing*, *9*(3), 288–298.
52. Zaphiris, P., & Ang, C. S. (2008). *Cross-disciplinary advances in human computer interaction: user modeling, social computing, and adaptive interfaces. Advances in technology and human interaction book series*. Information Science Reference.

Chapter 2
Computer Assisted Transcription: General Framework

With Contribution Of: Verónica Romero and Luis Rodriguez.

Contents

This chapter described the common basics on which are grounded the computer assisted transcription approaches described in the three subsequent chapters: Chaps. 3, 4 and 5. Besides, a general overview is provided of the common features characterizing the up-to-date systems we have employed for handwritten text and speech recognition.

Specific mathematical formulation and modeling adequate for interactive transcription of handwritten text images and speech signals are derived from a particular instantiation of the interactive–predictive general framework already introduced in Sect. 1.3.3. Moreover, on this ground and by adopting the *passive left-to-right interaction protocol* described in Sect. 1.4.2, the two basic computer assisted handwriting and speech transcription approaches were developed (detailed in Chaps. 3 and 4, respectively), along with the evaluation measures used to assess their performance.

2.1 Introduction

The tasks of transcribing handwritten documents and speech signals are becoming an important research topic, specially because of the increasing number of online digital libraries publishing large quantities of digitized legacy manuscripts and

A.H. Toselli et al., *Multimodal Interactive Pattern Recognition and Applications*,
DOI 10.1007/978-0-85729-479-1_2, © Springer-Verlag London Limited 2011

audio-(visual) documents. The vast majority of this material, hundreds of terabytes worth of digital text-image and speech-signal data, remain waiting to be transcribed into a textual electronic format (such as ASCII or PDF) that would provide new ways of indexing, consulting and querying these documents.

Up-to-date systems for both handwritten text recognition (HTR) and automatic speech recognition (ASR) share the same consolidated technology based on Hidden Markov Models (HMMs), whose fundamentals will be given in the succeeding Sect. 2.2. Unfortunately, these systems are not accurate enough to substitute the users in these tasks. The open vocabulary issue added to the existing variety of handwriting styles and the intrinsic complexity of the acoustic signal, explain most of the difficulties encountered by these recognition systems. In order to produce adequately good transcriptions using such systems, once the full automatic recognition process of one document has finished, heavy human expert revision is required. But usually, given the high error rates involved, such a post-editing solution is quite inefficient and uncomfortable for the human correctors.

Depending on the specific requirements of the different transcription tasks, two kind of produced transcription qualities are distinguished: transcriptions containing some controlled amount of errors and totally correct transcriptions. Transcriptions of the first type can be used as metadata for indexing, consulting and querying (handwriting/audio) documents, while the second type corresponds to the conventional literal transcriptions, such as, for example, the so-called *paleographic transcription* in the case of old manuscript documents.

Transcription systems of the first type look for reducing error location effort, by marking (if needed) recognized words for the user to supervise and correct, for which the recognition system is not confident enough. While this partial supervision does not guarantee perfect transcriptions, it does help the system to adaptively train its statistical models for greater accuracy. Moreover, if (hopefully minor) recognition errors can be tolerated in non-supervised parts, it might result in considerable supervision effort reduction. This *semisupervised, active learning* approach has been developed within the GIDOC system [6] for handwriting transcription, which is extensively described in Chap. 5.

In the case of totally correct transcriptions are needed, the approaches of the so-called *Computer Assisted Transcription of Text Images* (CATTI) and *Computer Assisted Speech Transcription* (CATS) can be used as an effective alternative to post-editing. In these *interactive–predictive approaches*, the recognition system and the human transcriber tightly cooperate to generate the final transcription, thereby combining human accuracy with recognition system efficiency. The two implemented systems (CATTI and CATS) are presented in detail in Chaps. 3 and 4, while the remaining sections of this chapter are devoted to the common general framework on which these two approaches are based.

2.2 Common Statistical Framework for HTR and ASR

Following the classical pattern recognition paradigm exposed in Sect. 1.2, both handwriting and speech recognition tasks seek to decode their respective symbolic and phonetic representation in terms of characters and/or words. In the already consolidated approach for both systems, the input pattern x is a sequence of feature vectors describing a *text image or speech signal* along its corresponding horizontal or time axis. On the other hand, system hypotheses are sequences of transcribed words, w, from a certain language. In this context, following a similar procedure as for Eqs. (1.1) and (1.2) (see Sect. 1.2):

$$\hat{w} = \arg\max_{w} \Pr(w \mid x) = \arg\max_{w} \Pr(x \mid w) \cdot \Pr(w)$$
$$\approx \arg\max_{w} P(x \mid w) \cdot P(w), \tag{2.1}$$

where $P(x \mid w)$ is given by morphological word models and $P(w)$ by a language model.

Morphological word models are built from respective *lexical entries (words)*, each of them modeled by a stochastic finite-state automaton which represents all possible concatenations of individual characters/phonemes that may compose the word. In turn, each character/phoneme is modeled by continuous density left-to-right HMM, with a Gaussian mixture per state. This mixture serves as a probabilistic law to the emission of feature vectors on each model state. By embedding the character/phoneme HMMs into the edges of the word automaton, a *lexical HMM* is obtained. These HMMs (morphological word models) estimate the word-conditional probabilities $P(x \mid w)$ of Eq. (2.1). The number of states as well as Gaussians of the HMMs define the total amount of parameters to be estimated. Therefore, these numbers need to be empirically tuned to optimize the overall performance for the given amount of training vectors available.

In general, the true probability $\Pr(w)$ of a specific concatenation of words w into text lines or sentences is given by

$$\Pr(w) = \Pr(w_1) \cdot \prod_{i=2}^{l} \Pr\left(w_i \mid w_1^{i-1}\right), \tag{2.2}$$

where $\Pr(w_i \mid w_1^{i-1})$ is the probability of the word w_i when we have already seen the sequence of words $w_1 \cdots w_{i-1}$. The sequence of words prior to w_i is the so-called history. In practice, estimating the probability $\Pr(w)$ for each possible w sequence can become difficult since sentences can be arbitrarily long and, in fact, many of them may be missing in the training set used for estimation process. Noting that for a vocabulary of $|V|$ different words, the number of distinct histories of length i is $|V|^{i-1}$. Therefore, the correct estimation of $\Pr(w)$ can be really unworkable, and for which reason this is often approximated using smoothed n-gram models, which use the previous $n-1$ words to predict the next one:

$$\Pr(w) \approx P(w) = P(w_1) \cdot \prod_{i=2}^{n-1} P\left(w_i \mid w_1^{i-1}\right) \cdot \prod_{i=n}^{l} P\left(w_i \mid w_{i-n+1}^{i-1}\right). \tag{2.3}$$

In this chapter, as well as in Chaps. 3, 4 and 5, we are going to use n-grams *language model* (bi-grams in most of the cases), with Kneser–Ney back-off smoothing [3, 4], estimated from the given transcriptions of the trained set. Bi-gram models estimate the probability $P(w)$ in Eq. (2.1), and are the basis for the "dynamic", prefix-conditioned language model $P(s \mid p)$ of Eq. (2.8), as will be explained in Sect. 2.4.

To train HMMs and n-gram language model, a corpus is required in which each training sample (handwritten text image or speech utterance) is accompanied by its correct transcription. These transcriptions must accurately describe all the elements appearing in each sample, such as phonemes in the case of speech or letters (lower-case and upper-case), symbols, abbreviations, etc., in the case of handwriting images. On one hand, HMMs are trained using a well-known instance of the expectation-maximization (EM) algorithm called forward–backward or Baum–Welch re-estimation [2]. And on the other hand, n-gram language model probabilities can be estimated from the raw text of the training transcriptions (or from external text corpora) based on the relative frequency of word sequences.

Once all the *character/phoneme*, *word* and *language* models are available, recognition of new test sentences can be performed. Thanks to the homogeneous finite-state (FS) nature of all these models, they can be easily *integrated* into a single *global* (huge) FS model, on which Eq. (2.1) is easily solved. Given an input sequence of feature vectors, the output word sequence hypothesis corresponds to a path in the integrated network that, with highest probability, produces the input sequence. This optimal path search is very efficiently carried out by the well-known (*beam-search*-accelerated) Viterbi algorithm [2]. This technique allows integration to be performed "on the fly" during the decoding process. In this way, only the memory strictly required for the search is actually allocated. The Viterbi algorithm can also be easily adapted to solve Eq. (2.6) required in the CATTI and CATS interactive framework, as will be seen in Sect. 2.3.

It should be mentioned that, in practice, HMM and bi-grams (log-)probabilities are generally "balanced" before being used in Eqs. (2.1) or (2.6). This is carried out by using a "*Grammar Scale Factor*" (GSF), the value of which is tuned empirically.

2.3 Common Statistical Framework for CATTI and CATS

The IPR paradigm framework using human feedback outlined in Sect. 1.3.3 (for *interaction with deterministic feedback*) can be directly applied to the transcription of handwritten documents and speech signals. According to this IPR paradigm, in the interactive transcription framework the system should take into account the current state to improve the following predictions. To start the process, the system makes an initial prediction consisting in a whole transcription of the input image/speech signal. Then, the user reads this prediction until an error is found. At this point, the user corrects this error, generating a new, extended prefix (the previous validated prefix plus the amendments introduced by the user). This new prefix is used by the recognition system to attempt a new prediction, thereby starting a new cycle that is repeated until a final correct transcription is achieved. This interactive process follows the so-called "*left-to-right interactive–predictive processing protocol*" stated in Sect. 1.4.2.

Ergonomics and user preferences dictate exactly when the system should start a new cycle. Typically, it can start after each new user keystroke or after each user-entered whole word. A timed system reaction scheme is also possible, where new predictions are computed only upon detecting a short period of user inactivity. Even though keystroke-level interaction is most preferable in practice, for the sake of clarity and unless stated otherwise, only whole-word interactions will be considered in the present study. This will allow us to properly estimate the user-effort reduction achieved by the interactive transcription with respect to conventional post-editing of automatic transcriptions (see Sect. 2.6).

Formally, the interactive transcription approach can be seen as an instantiation of the problem formulated in Eq. (1.14) where, in addition to the given sequence of feature vectors x, a user-validated *prefix* p of the transcription is available. This prefix, which corresponds to the pair (h', d) in Eq. (1.14), contains information from the previous system's prediction (h') plus user's actions, in the form of amendment keystrokes (d). In this way, the HTR system should try to complete this prefix by searching for the most likely *suffix* according to the already-given Eq. (1.32) (see Sect. 1.4), which, for convenience, is shown again below:

$$\begin{aligned} \hat{s} = \arg\max_{s} \Pr(s \mid x, p) &\approx \arg\max_{s} P(s \mid x, p) \\ &= \arg\max_{s} P(x \mid p, s) \cdot P(s \mid p). \end{aligned} \tag{2.4}$$

Equation (2.4) is very similar to Eq. (2.1), where w is the concatenation of p and s. The main difference is that here p is given. Therefore, the search must be performed over all possible suffixes s of p and the language model probability $P(s \mid p)$ must account for the words that can be written after the fixed prefix p.

In order to solve Eq. (2.4), the image x can be considered split into two fragments, x_1^b and x_{b+1}^M, where M is the length of x. By further considering the boundary point b as a hidden variable, we can write:

$$\hat{s} \approx \arg\max_{s} \sum_{0 \leq b \leq M} P(x, b \mid p, s) \cdot P(s \mid p). \tag{2.5}$$

We can now make the *naïve* (but realistic) assumption that the probability of x_1^b given p does not depend on the suffix and the probability of x_{b+1}^M given s does not depend on the prefix and, approximating the sum over all the possible segmentations by the dominating term, Eq. (2.5) can be rewritten as

$$\hat{s} \approx \arg\max_{s} \max_{0 \leq b \leq M} P\bigl(x_1^b \mid p\bigr) \cdot P\bigl(x_{b+1}^M \mid s\bigr) \cdot P(s \mid p). \tag{2.6}$$

This optimization problem entails finding an optimal boundary point, $\hat{b}$, associated with the optimal suffix decoding, $\hat{s}$. That is, the signal x is actually split into two segments, $x_p = x_1^{\hat{b}}$ and $x_s = x_{\hat{b}+1}^{M}$, the first one corresponding to the *prefix* and the second to the *suffix*. Therefore, the search can be performed just over segments of the signal corresponding to the possible suffixes and, on the other hand, we can take advantage of the information coming from the prefix to implement the language model constraints modeled by $P(s \mid p)$.

2.4 Adapting the Language Model

Perhaps the simplest way to deal with $P(s \mid p)$ is to adapt an n-gram language model to cope with the consolidated prefix. Given that a conventional n-gram models the probability $P(w)$ (where w is the concatenation of p and s, i.e the whole sentence), it is necessary to modify this model to take into account the conditional probability $P(s \mid p)$.

Let $p = w_1^k$ be a consolidated prefix and $s = w_{k+1}^l$ be a possible suffix. We can compute $P(s \mid p)$, as is shown in Eq. (2.7):

$$\begin{aligned} P(s \mid p) &= P(p, s)/P(p) \\ &= \frac{\prod_{i=1}^{l} P(w_i \mid w_{i-n+1}^{i-1})}{\prod_{i=1}^{k} P(w_i \mid w_{i-n+1}^{i-1})} = \prod_{i=k+1}^{l} P\big(w_i \mid w_{i-n+1}^{i-1}\big). \end{aligned} \tag{2.7}$$

Moreover, for the terms from $k+1$ to $k+n-1$ of this factorization, we have additional information coming from the already known words w_{k-n+2}^{k}, leading to:

$$\begin{aligned} P(s \mid p) &= \prod_{i=k+1}^{k+n-1} P\big(w_i \mid w_{i-n+1}^{i-1}\big) \cdot \prod_{i=k+n}^{l} P\big(w_i \mid w_{i-n+1}^{i-1}\big) \\ &= \prod_{j=1}^{n-1} P\big(s_j \mid p_{k-n+1+j}^{k}, s_1^{j-1}\big) \cdot \prod_{j=n}^{l-k} P\big(s_j \mid s_{j-n+1}^{j-1}\big), \end{aligned} \tag{2.8}$$

where $p_1^k = w_1^k = p$ and $s_1^{l-k} = w_{k+1}^l = s$. The first term of Eq. (2.8) accounts for the probability of the $n-1$ words of the suffix, whose probability is conditioned by words from the validated prefix, and the second one is the usual n-gram probability for the rest of the words in the suffix.

2.5 Search and Decoding Methods

In this section, we are going to proceed to discuss briefly some possible implementations of interactive transcription decoders based on Eq. (2.6). To begin with, a simple possibility would be to perform the decoding in two steps: first, the validated prefix p could be used to segment the signal x into x_p and x_s and, then, x_s

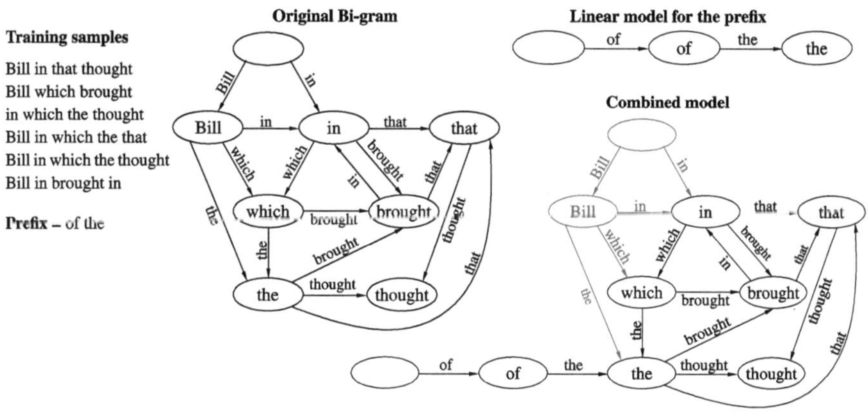

Fig. 2.1 Example of interactive transcription dynamic language model building. First, a bi-gram for the training set of the figure is obtained. Then, a linear model which accounts for the prefix "*of the*" is constructed. Finally, these two models are combined into a single *prefix-constrained model*

could be decoded by using a "suffix language model" (SLM) as in Eq. (2.8). The problem here is that the signal cannot be optimally segmented into x_p and x_s if only the information of the prefix p is considered.

A better approach is to explicitly rely on Eq. (2.6) to implement a decoding process in one step, as in classical handwriting/speech recognition. The decoder should be forced to match the previously validated prefix p and then continue searching for a suffix $\hat{s}$ according to the constraints in Eq. (2.8). Two different possible implementations for this last approach have been considered. The first one is based on the well-known Viterbi algorithm [2], while the second one is based on word-graph techniques similar to those described in [1, 5] for Computer Assisted Translation and for multimodal speech post-editing. Both implementations are described in the following sections.

2.5.1 Viterbi-Based Implementation

In this case, the search problem corresponding to Eqs. (2.6) and (2.8) can be straightforwardly solved by building a special language model which can be seen as the "concatenation" of a *linear* model which strictly accounts for the successive words in p and a "suffix language model" of Eq. (2.8). First, an n-gram with the available training set is built. Then, a linear model which accounts for the validated prefix is constructed. Finally, these two models are combined into a single model as shown in Fig. 2.1. Owing to the finite-state nature of this special language model, the search involved in Eq. (2.6) can be efficiently carried out using the Viterbi algorithm [2]. Apart from the optimal suffix decoding, $\hat{s}$, a correspondingly optimal segmentation of the x is then obtained as a by-product.

It should be noted that a direct adaptation of the Viterbi algorithm to implement these techniques leads to a computational cost that grows quadratically with the number of words of each sentence. As for each user interaction a new derived language model is dynamically built for performing the decoding search, this can be problematic (very high time-consuming process) for large sentences and/or for fine-grained (character-level) interaction schemes. Nevertheless, using word-graph techniques similar to those described in [1, 5], very efficient, linear cost search can be easily achieved.

2.5.2 Word-Graph Based Implementation

As previously explained in Sect. 1.5.1, a word graph (WG) is a data structure that represents a set of strings in a very efficient way. In handwritten text as well as speech recognition, a WG represents the transcriptions with the highest $P(w \mid x)$ (see Eq. (2.1)) of the given text image or speech utterance. In this case, the word graph is just (a pruned version of) the Viterbi search trellis obtained when transcribing the given input x.

According to Eqs. (1.38) and (1.39) (Sect. 1.5.1), the probability of a word sequence, w, in a word-graph is computed as the sum of the probabilities of all the paths that generate w, $\gamma(w)$:

$$P(w) = \sum_{\phi_w \in \gamma(w)} \prod_{i=1}^{l} p(e_i), \tag{2.9}$$

where ϕ_w is a sequence of edges $e_1, e_2, \ldots, e_l$ such that $w = \omega(e_1), \omega(e_2), \ldots, \omega(e_l)$. Given a WG, a word sequence with the greatest probability can be written as

$$\hat{w} = \arg\max_{w} \sum_{\phi_w \in \gamma(w)} \prod_{i=1}^{l} p(e_i). \tag{2.10}$$

However, as this maximization problem is NP-hard, we approximate it by means of the efficient Viterbi search algorithm:

$$P(w) \approx \max_{\phi_w \in \gamma(w)} \prod_{i=1}^{l} p(e_i), \tag{2.11}$$

$$\hat{w} \approx \arg\max_{w} \max_{\phi_w \in \gamma(w)} \prod_{i=1}^{l} p(e_i). \tag{2.12}$$

The edge probability function, $p(e)$, where $e = (i, j)$, is equal to the product of the morphological/acoustic word probability $P(x_{t(i)+1}^{t(j)} \mid \omega(e))$ of the feature vector subsequence $x_{t(i)+1}^{t(j)}$ between i and j WG nodes, and the language model probability $P(\omega(e))$ of the given word at the edge e. That is,

$$p(e) = P\left(x_{t(i)+1}^{t(j)} \mid \omega(e)\right) \cdot P\left(\omega(e)\right). \tag{2.13}$$

During the interactive transcription process the system has to make use of this word graph in order to complete the prefixes accepted by the human transcriptor. In other words, the search problem consists in finding the target suffix s that maximizes the posterior probability $P(s \mid x, p)$ given a prefix p as described in Eq. (2.4).

The search on the WG involves two phases. The first one deals with the parsing of the previously validated prefix p over the WG, looking for a set of end nodes Q_p of the paths, whose associated word sequence is p. In the second phase, the decoder continues searching for the suffix s, from any of the nodes in Q_p, that maximizes the posterior probability given by Eq. (2.4). In terms of WG, an analogous expression of Eq. (2.6) can be obtained:

$$\hat{s} = \arg\max_{s} \max_{q \in Q_p} P\left(x_1^{t(q)} \mid p\right) \cdot P\left(x_{t(q)+1}^{m} \mid s\right) \cdot P(s \mid p). \tag{2.14}$$

The boundary point b in Eq. (2.6) is now restricted to values $t(q)\ \forall q \in Q_p$.

This search problem can be efficiently carried out using dynamic programming. In order to make the process faster, first, we apply a dynamic-programming Viterbi-like algorithm backwards from the final node to the initial one. In this way, we compute the best path and its probability from any node to the final node. Then, we look for the set of boundary nodes Q_p. Then we should only have to multiply the probability computed from the initial node to any node $q \in Q_p$ by the probability from q to the final node (previously computed), and finally, choose the node with the maximum probability score.

As the WG is a representation of a *subset* of the possible transcriptions for a source handwritten text image or the speech signal, it may happen that some prefixes given by the user cannot be exactly found in the WG. To circumvent this problem some error-correcting parsing algorithms have been implemented as we will see throughout this book for the different systems studied.

Example: Word Graph of Handwritten Text

Although the following example focuses on a specific WG obtained from the recognition of a handwritten text image, this is completely analogous to one obtained from the recognition of a speech signal. In Fig. 2.2 an example of a WG that represents a set of the possible transcriptions of the handwritten sentence “antiguos ciudadanos que en Castilla se llamaban” is shown. In this case, the function t associates each node with a horizontal position of the handwritten image. Following the WG notation given in Sect. 1.5.1, the function $\omega(e)$ relates each edge with a word hypothesis between horizontal image positions $t(i)+1$ and $t(j)$, and the function $p(e)$ returns the probability of the hypothesis that $\omega(e)$ appears between $t(i)+1$ and $t(j)$.

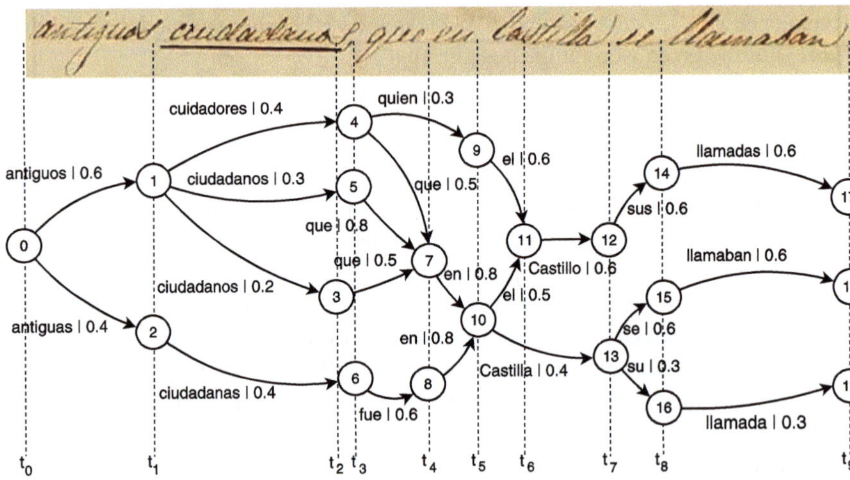

Fig. 2.2 Image positions t_i are associates with the nodes $t(0) = t_0 = 0$, $t(1) = t(2) = t_1$, $t(3) = t_2$, $t(4) = t(5) = t(6) = t_3$, $t(7) = t(8) = t_4$, $t(9) = t(10) = t_5$, $t(11) = t_6$, $t(12) = t(13) = t_7$, $t(14) = t(15) = t(16) = t_8$, $t(17) = t(18) = t(19) = t_9$

Given a path on the WG represented on Fig. 2.2, for example the path ϕ_1:

$$\phi_1 = \{(0,1),(1,5),(5,7),(7,10),(10,11),(11,12),(12,14),(14,17)\} \tag{2.15}$$

whose probability is computed as

$$\begin{aligned} P(\phi_1) &= p(0,1)p(1,5)p(5,7)p(7,10)p(10,11)p(11,12)p(12,14)p(14,17) \\ &= 0.6 \cdot 0.3 \cdot 0.8 \cdot 0.8 \cdot 0.5 \cdot 0.6 \cdot 0.6 \cdot 0.6 = 0.012. \end{aligned}$$

And the word sequence associated with it is $w^{(1)} =$ "*antiguos ciudadanos que en el Castillo sus llamadas*". However, ϕ_1 is not the unique path that generates $w^{(1)}$. We also have

$$\phi_2 = \{(0,1),(1,3),(3,7),(7,10),(10,11),(11,12),(12,14),(14,17)\}.$$

Therefore, the exact probability of $w^{(1)}$ is

$$P(w^{(1)}) = P(\phi_1) + P(\phi_2) = 0.012 + 0.005 = 0.017$$

and approximating that by the Viterbi algorithm, $P(w^{(1)})$ will be the probability of the path with the maximum probability, i.e:

$$P(w^{(1)}) \approx P(\tilde{w}^{(1)}) = P(\phi_1) = 0.012.$$

Now, to obtain the word sequence with the greatest probability, all the word sequences on the WG must be taken into account. Figure 2.2 shows all the word sequences on the WG and their corresponding paths:

- $w^{(1)} =$ "*antiguos ciudadanos que en el Castillo sus llamadas*",
  $\phi_1 = \{(0,1),(1,5),(5,7),(7,10),(10,11),(11,12),(12,14),(14,17)\}$,
  $\phi_2 = \{(0,1),(1,3),(3,7),(7,10),(10,11),(11,12),(12,14),(14,17)\}$,
- $w^{(2)} =$ "*antiguos ciudadanos que en Castilla se llamaban*",
  $\phi_3 = \{(0,1),(1,5),(5,7),(7,10),(10,13),(13,15),(15,18)\}$,
  $\phi_4 = \{(0,1),(1,3),(3,7),(7,10),(10,13),(13,15),(15,18)\}$,
- $w^{(3)} =$ "*antiguos ciudadanos que en Castilla su llamada*",
  $\phi_5 = \{(0,1),(1,5),(5,7),(7,10),(10,13),(13,16),(16,19)\}$,
  $\phi_6 = \{(0,1),(1,3),(3,7),(7,10),(10,13),(13,16),(16,19)\}$,
- $w^{(4)} =$ "*antiguos cuidadores quien el Castillo sus llamadas*",
  $\phi_7 = \{(0,1),(1,4),(4,9),(9,11),(11,12),(12,14),(14,17)\}$,
- $w^{(5)} =$ "*antiguos cuidadores que en el Castillo sus llamadas*",
  $\phi_8 = \{(0,1),(1,4),(4,7),(7,10),(10,11),(11,12),(12,14),(14,17)\}$,
- $w^{(6)} =$ "*antiguos cuidadores que en Castilla se llamaban*",
  $\phi_9 = \{(0,1),(1,4),(4,7),(7,10),(10,13),(13,15),(15,18)\}$,
- $w^{(7)} =$ "*antiguos cuidadores que en Castilla su llamada*",
  $\phi_{10} = \{(0,1),(1,4),(4,7),(7,10),(10,13),(13,16),(16,19)\}$,
- $w^{(8)} =$ "*antiguas ciudadanas fue en el Castillo sus llamadas*",
  $\phi_{11} = \{(0,2),(2,6),(6,8),(8,10),(10,11),(11,12),(12,14),(14,17)\}$,
- $w^{(9)} =$ "*antiguas ciudadanas fue en Castilla se llamaban*",
  $\phi_{12} = \{(0,2),(2,6),(6,8),(8,10),(10,13),(13,15),(15,18)\}$,
- $w^{(10)} =$ "*antiguas ciudadanas fue en Castilla su llamada*",
  $\phi_{13} = \{(0,2),(2,6),(6,8),(8,10),(10,13),(13,16),(16,19)\}$,

and their probabilities are

$$P\big(w^{(1)}\big) = P(\phi_1) + P(\phi_2) = 0.012 + 0.005 = 0.017, \quad P\big(w^{(6)}\big) = P(\phi_9) = 0.014,$$
$$P\big(w^{(2)}\big) = P(\phi_3) + P(\phi_4) = 0.016 + 0.007 = 0.023, \quad P\big(w^{(7)}\big) = P(\phi_{10}) = 0.003,$$
$$P\big(w^{(3)}\big) = P(\phi_5) + P(\phi_6) = 0.004 + 0.002 = 0.006, \quad P\big(w^{(8)}\big) = P(\phi_{11}) = 0.008,$$
$$P\big(w^{(4)}\big) = P(\phi_7) = 0.009, \quad P\big(w^{(9)}\big) = P(\phi_{12}) = 0.011,$$
$$P\big(w^{(5)}\big) = P(\phi_8) = 0.010, \quad P\big(w^{(10)}\big) = P(\phi_{13}) = 0.003.$$

Finally, the word sequence with the greatest probability is $w^{(2)}$ for both the exact approach ($P(w^{(2)}) = 0.023$) and the approximated by the Viterbi algorithm ($P(\tilde{w}^{(2)}) = 0.016$).

Throughout the interactive transcription process, when the user validates a prefix, the system uses this WG in order to complete this validated prefix following the already above-explained WG search phases. For example, given the prefix "*antiguos ciudadanos*", on the first phase, the decoder parses this prefix over the WG finding the set of nodes $Q_p = \{3, 5\}$, which correspond to paths from the initial node whose associated word sequence is "*antiguos ciudadanos*". Then, the decoder continues searching for the suffix s that maximizes the posterior probability from any of the nodes in Q_p. In this example, the suffix that maximizes the posterior probability is $\hat{s} =$"*que en Castilla se llamaban*".

2.6 Assessment Measures

As was commented in Sect. 1.4.6, the corpus-based assessment paradigm could be still applicable to IPR tasks. Although recognition errors are meaningless in IPR (as the user will ensure that no errors will be produced), the correct labeling for each object can be used to determine how many interaction steps are needed to produce a correct hypothesis. In the case of interactive transcription systems, the effort needed by a human transcriber to produce correct transcriptions is estimated by the *Word Stroke Ratio* (WSR), which can be computed using the reference transcriptions. After each recognized hypothesis, the longest common prefix between the hypothesis and the reference is obtained and the first unmatching word from the hypothesis is replaced by the corresponding reference word. This process is iterated until a full match with the reference is achieved. Therefore, the WSR can be defined as the number of (word level) user interactions that are necessary to achieve the reference transcription of the text image considered, divided by the total number of reference words.

On the other hand, the quality of non-interactive transcriptions can be properly assessed with the well-known *Word Error Rate* (WER). It is defined as the minimum number of words that need to be substituted, deleted or inserted to convert a sentence recognized by the system into the corresponding reference transcription, divided by the total number of reference words. The WER is a good estimate of post-editing user effort.

These definitions make WER and WSR comparable. Moreover, the relative difference between them gives us a good estimate of the reduction in human effort that can be achieved by using an interactive transcription system with respect to using a conventional transcription system followed by human post-editing. This *estimated effort reduction* will be denoted hereafter as "EFR".

Another measure for assessing non-interactive transcriptions is the well-known *Sentence Error Rate* (SER), also called string error, defined as the number of sentences that have at least one misrecognized word. Because of SER is really stricter than WER, it is not used at all in transcription evaluation, mainly because it does not reflect the effort needed to correct all the misrecognized words within sentences. However, it is rather widely used in speech recognition (Chap. 4), machine translation (Chaps. 4 and 7) and interactive text generation (Chap. 10).

References

1. Barrachina, S., Bender, O., Casacuberta, F., Civera, J., Cubel, E., Khadivi, S., Ney, A. L. H., Tomás, J., & Vidal, E. (2009). Statistical approaches to computer-assisted translation. *Computational Linguistics*, *35*(1), 3–28.
2. Jelinek, F. (1998). *Statistical methods for speech recognition*. Cambridge: MIT Press.
3. Katz, S. M. (1987). Estimation of probabilities from sparse data for the language model component of a speech recognizer. *I.E.E.E. Transactions on Acoustics, Speech, and Signal Processing*, *ASSP-35*, 400–401.

4. Kneser, R., & Ney, H. (1995). Improved backing-off for n-gram language modeling. In *Proceedings of the international conference on acoustics, speech and signal processing (ICASSP)* (Vol. 1, pp. 181–184).
5. Liu, P., & Soong, F. K. (2006). Word graph based speech recognition error correction by handwriting input. In *Proceedings of the international conference on multimodal interfaces (ICMI'06)* (pp. 339–346), New York, NY, USA. New York: ACM.
6. Serrano, N., Sanchis, A., & Juan, A. (2010). Balancing error and supervision effort in interactive–predictive handwritten text recognition. In *Proceedings of the international conference on intelligent user interfaces (IUI'10)* (pp. 373–376), Hong Kong, China.

References

Chapter 3
Computer Assisted Transcription of Text Images

With Contribution Of: Verónica Romero and Moisés Pastor.

Contents

Grounded in the interactive–predictive transcription framework drawn in the previous chapter, an interactive approach for efficient transcription of handwritten text images, along with its more ergonomic and multimodal variants are presented. All these approaches, rather than full automation, aim at assisting the expert in the proper transcription process in an efficient way. In this sense, an interactive scenario is stated, where both automatic handwriting recognition system and human transcriber (user) cooperate to produce the final transcription of text-images.

Additionally, an explanation of both basic off- and on-line HTR systems used embedded in the CATTI approaches is given in some detail. This focusing mainly on the preprocessing, feature extraction and on specific aspects of the modeling and decoding-searching process, which complement the ones already introduced in Sect. 2.2.

Moreover, in this chapter, it will be shown how user-interaction feedback directly allows us to improve system accuracy, while multimodality increases system ergonomics and user acceptability. Multimodal interaction is approached in such a way that both the main and the feedback data streams help each-other to optimize overall performance and usability. All these are supported by experimental results obtained on three cursive handwritten tasks suggesting that, using these approaches,

DOI 10.1007/978-0-85729-479-1_3,

considerable amounts of user effort can be saved with respect to both pure manual work and non-interactive, post-editing processing.

3.1 Computer Assisted Transcription of Text Images: CATTI

So far, the interactive transcription framework, search approaches and assessment measures presented in Sects. 2.3, 2.5 and 2.6, respectively, can be straightforwardly applied to the transcription task of handwritten documents. The application performing this kind of task, resulting from applying all the before-mentioned concepts, shall be called from now on *Computer Assisted Transcription of Text Images* (CATTI) [28, 30].

The CATTI application involves an interactive scenario, where both automatic *handwritten text recognition* system (HTR) and human transcriber (which henceforth will be referred to as the user) cooperate together to produce the final transcription of text-images. During the CATTI process, the user is directly involved in the transcription process since he/she is responsible of validating and/or correcting the HTR output. As illustrated in Fig. 3.1, and following the *left-to-right* protocol for interactive transcription laid down in Sect. 2.3, the process starts when the HTR system proposes a full transcription $\hat{s}$ (or a set of n-best transcriptions) of a given feature vector sequence x, representing a handwritten text line image.[1] Then, the user reads this transcription until he or she finds a mistake; i.e, he or she validates a prefix p' of the transcription which is error-free. Now, the user can enter some keystrokes (letters or whole-words), κ, to correct the erroneous text that follows the validated prefix. This action produces a new prefix p (the previously validated prefix, p' followed by κ). Taking into account this new prefix p, the HTR system suggests a suitable continuation (or a set of the best possible continuations) to this prefix (i.e., a new $\hat{s}$), thereby starting a new cycle. This process is repeated until a correct, full transcription T of x is accepted by the user. A key point of this interactive process is that, at each user-system iteration, the system can take advantage of the prefix validated so far to attempt to improve prediction.

The example shown in Fig. 3.1 illustrates how a 67% *estimated effort reduction* (EFR) is achieved (cf. Sect. 2.6). It is worth nothing that in this example the non-interactive post-editing operation would have required the user to correct *six* errors from the original recognized hypothesis whereas with the interaction feedback, only *two* user-corrections (the red color text in the final transcription T) are necessary to get the final error-free transcription. In spite of Fig. 3.1, which shows an example of interaction-correction at character level, only whole-word correction interactions will be considered in this chapter for the reasons already commented in Sect. 2.3,

Next section is mostly devoted to explain the implementation details of the search techniques based on word-graphs, employed to solve the optimization problem set

[1] For simplicity henceforward, we will refer x directly as the input handwritten text image.

	x						
STEP-0	p						
STEP-1	$\hat{s} \equiv \hat{w}$	opposite	this	Comment	Bill	in that	thought
	p'	oppos					
	κ	ed					
	p	opposed					
STEP-2	$\hat{s}$		the	Government	Bill	in that	thought
	p'	opposed	the	Government	Bill		
	κ					which	
	p	opposed	the	Government	Bill	which	
FINAL	$\hat{s}$						brought
	p'	opposed	the	Government	Bill	which	brought
	κ						
	$p \equiv T$	opposed	the	Government	Bill	which	brought

Fig. 3.1 Example of CATTI interaction to transcribe an image sentence "*opposed the Government Bill which brought*". Initially the prefix p is empty, and the system proposes a complete transcription $\hat{s} \equiv \hat{w}$ (as happens in the normal non-interactive HTR) of the input x. In each interaction step the user reads this transcription, accepting a prefix p' of it. Then, he or she types in some keystrokes, κ, to correct some words of the transcription provided by the system, thereby generating a new prefix p (the accepted one p' plus the text κ added by the user). At this point, the system suggests a suitable continuation $\hat{s}$ of this prefix p and this process is repeated until a complete and correct transcription of the input image is reached. In the final transcription, T, the user-typed text is typeset in different font and *red* color. In this example the correct transcription has six words and the initial hypothesis, $\hat{w}$, has six errors. Therefore, the estimated post-editing effort (WER) is 100%, while in the corresponding interactive estimate (WSR) is 33%, since only two (word) corrections are needed. This results in an estimated effort reduction (EFR) of $100 - 33/100 = 67\%$ (see Sect. 2.6 for definitions of WER, WSR and EFR)

up by Eq. (2.6). Section 3.3 depicts an additional interaction issue, along with the involved theoretical background, which increases the performance of CATTI, mainly, in terms of ergonomics and usability. Section 3.4 introduces and describes the multimodal version of CATTI. Complementing the information already given in Sect. 2.2, a general description of the *off-* and *on line* text processing systems is given in Sect. 3.5. Application tasks, experimental data and reported results are finally shown in Sect. 3.6.

3.2 CATTI Search Problem

As explained in Sect. 2.5.1, the optimal solution for the search problem set up by Eq. (2.6) is solved by using the Viterbi algorithm on the corresponding finite-state network restricted by a special language model built by the concatenation of a *linear* model (which accounts for the words of the prefix p) and a conventional n-gram model (which models all the possible words of the suffix s). However, given that the direct adaptation of the Viterbi algorithm leads to a computational cost that grows quadratically with the number of words of each sentence, more efficient techniques based on word-graphs (WG) can be used to obtain a linear cost search.

3.2.1 Word-Graph-Based Search Approach

As was stated in Sect. 2.5.2, a WG derived from a handwriting recognition process can be seen as a compact representation of the highest $P(w \mid x)$ transcriptions of a given text image x. Moreover, the probability of a given WG edge $p(e)$ is defined by Eq. (2.13). Here, in order to avoid the numeric underflow problem, mainly occurring during repeated multiplication of probabilities, we are going to use instead log-probabilities. With this in mind, Eq. (2.13) can be rewritten in these terms as follows:

$$\log p(e) = \log P\bigl(x_{t(i)+1}^{t(j)} \mid \omega(e)\bigr) + \log P\bigl(\omega(e)\bigr). \tag{3.1}$$

Similarly, as was pointed out at the end of Sect. 2.2, in order to balance the absolute values of these both (log-) probability terms, they are weighted by the so-called *grammar scale factor* (GSF) α, and the *word insertion penalty* (WIP) β (see [16]). Hence, the final resulting score of each edge is then computed as

$$\varphi(e) = \log P\bigl(x_{t(i)+1}^{t(j)} \mid \omega(e)\bigr) + \alpha \log P\bigl(\omega(e)\bigr) + \beta. \tag{3.2}$$

Note that Eqs. (3.1) and (3.2) become identical far $\alpha = 1$ and $\beta = 0$.

During the CATTI process, the two step search approach previously explained in Sect. 2.5.2 is performed on the above-defined WG in order to complete the prefixes accepted by the user. That is, the decoder first parses the validated prefix p, defining in this way a set of path end nodes Q_p (cf. Sect. 2.5.2), and then, the most likely transcription suffix departing from any of the nodes in Q_p is obtained.

3.2.2 Word Graph Error-Correcting Parsing

As already commented, a WG is a compact representation of a large *subset* of the highest possible likely transcriptions for a given input handwritten text image, whose number depends mainly of the WG density. Hence, it may happen that some prefixes given by the user cannot be exactly found in the WG. The solution is not to use p, but using the prefix $\tilde{p}$ from all the possible prefixes on the WG that best matches p. This prefix $\tilde{p}$ (that best matches the validated prefix p) can be considered as a hidden variable, so departing from Eq. (2.4), the problem of searching the most likely suffix $\hat{s}$ given p can be formulated as

$$\begin{aligned}
\hat{s} &= \arg\max_s \Pr(s \mid x, p) \\
&\approx \arg\max_s P(s \mid x, p) \\
&= \arg\max_s \sum_{\tilde{p}} P(s, \tilde{p} \mid x, p)
\end{aligned}$$

$$= \arg\max_{s} \sum_{\tilde{p}} P(x \mid p, \tilde{p}, s) \cdot P(\tilde{p}, s \mid p)$$

$$= \arg\max_{s} \sum_{\tilde{p}} P(x \mid p, \tilde{p}, s) \cdot P(s \mid p, \tilde{p}) \cdot P(\tilde{p} \mid p)$$

$$= \arg\max_{\tilde{p},s} \sum_{\tilde{p}} \sum_{q \in Q_{\tilde{p}}} P(x, q \mid p, \tilde{p}, s) \cdot P(s \mid p, \tilde{p}) \cdot P(\tilde{p} \mid p). \qquad (3.3)$$

We can make the naïve assumption that $P(x, q \mid p, \tilde{p}, s)$ and $P(s \mid p, \tilde{p})$ do not depend of p given $\tilde{p}$, to rewrite Eq. (3.3) as

$$\hat{s} \approx \arg\max_{s} \sum_{\tilde{p}} \sum_{q \in Q_{\tilde{p}}} P(x, q \mid \tilde{p}, s) \cdot P(s \mid \tilde{p}) \cdot P(\tilde{p} \mid p) \qquad (3.4)$$

and following similar assumptions made on Eq. (2.6), previous equation can be rewritten as

$$\hat{s} \approx \arg\max_{s} \max_{\tilde{p}} \max_{q \in Q_{\tilde{p}}} P\big(x_1^{t(q)} \mid \tilde{p}\big) \cdot P\big(x_{t(q)+1}^{M} \mid s\big) \cdot P(s \mid \tilde{p}) \cdot P(\tilde{p} \mid p) \qquad (3.5)$$

where $P(\tilde{p} \mid p)$ models the similarity distribution probability between $\tilde{p}$ and p. Moreover, $P(\tilde{p} \mid p)$ can be modeled in terms of probabilistic error correcting parsing. To do so, firstly we add to each original WG edge e, a set of extra edges representing different editing operations [1]. In Fig. 3.2, it is shown an example of all the added new edges between two adjacent nodes i and j. The probabilities of the added edges are considered to be proportional to $\exp^{-d(\omega(e),v)}$, where V is a task vocabulary (cf. Sect. 1.5.1), $v \in V \cup \{\lambda\}$ and $d(\cdot,\cdot)$ is the Levenshtein distance between $\omega(e)$ and v. As was seen in Sect. 1.5.1, an edge has been defined by its start and end nodes. However, this is not longer possible due to the fact that now there is more than one edge between two adjacent nodes. For this reason, each edge must now be defined by its start and end nodes, and a word label related with this edge: $e' = (i, j, v)$. Using log-probabilities, the score of the different edges can be

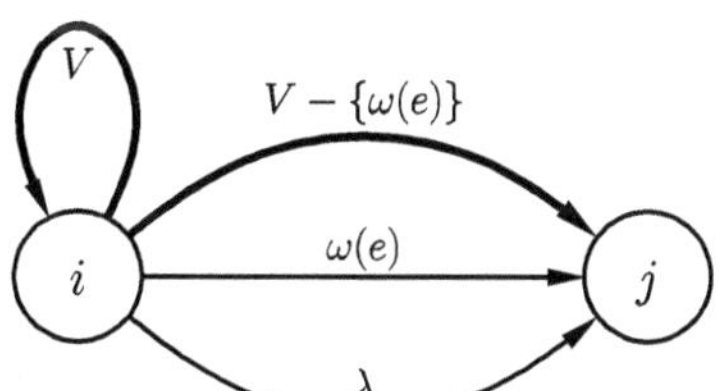

Fig. 3.2 Example of edges added between two adjacent nodes i and j of a WG for probabilistic error correcting parsing. The edge labeled with the word $\omega(e)$ is the original edge and corresponds to the operation of substitution of word $\omega(e)$ with itself. The group of edges labeled with $V - \{\omega(e)\}$ represents the substitution of $\omega(e)$ with any other word in the vocabulary excepting $\omega(e)$. The edge labeled with λ (empty symbol) models a deletion operation, whereas the last group V models insertion operations, involving an edge for each word in the vocabulary from the state i to itself

reformulated as

$$\varphi(i, j, v) = \begin{cases} \log P(x_{t(i)+1}^{t(j)} \mid \omega(e)) + \alpha \log P(\omega(e)) + \beta - \gamma d(\omega(e), v), & i \neq j, \\ \beta - \gamma d(\lambda, v), & i = j, \end{cases} \tag{3.6}$$

where e is the original edge between the nodes i and j, and γ is a penalization factor applied to control the number of different characters between $\omega(e)$ and v. The γ value should be greater than 0 because, otherwise, we would be encouraging WG paths, whose corresponding associated word-label sequences are more different from the given prefix's one. Note further that, if $\omega(e) = v$, then the number of different characters will be 0 and therefore Eqs. (3.6) and (3.2) become identical.

This heuristic can be implemented using dynamic programming and it can be further improved by visiting the WG nodes in topological order [1], and by incorporating beam search techniques [12] to discard those nodes whose scores are worse than the best score at the current stage of the parsing. Moreover, given the incremental nature of p, the error-correcting algorithm takes advantage of this peculiarity to parse only the new appended words of p provided by the user in the last interaction.

3.3 Increasing Interaction Ergonomics in CATTI: PA-CATTI

In CATTI application, user is repeatedly interacting with transcription process, thus trying to make this interaction process easier is really crucial for the success of such application.

Section 3.1 describes the CATTI process in which the user, before typing a new word in order to correct progressively a given hypothesis, needs first to position the cursor in the place where he or she wants to type such word. This is done by performing what, from now on, we will call *Pointer Action* (PA), which involves any kind of pointer-device like a typical mouse for example. By doing so, the user is already providing some very useful information to the system: he/she is validating a prefix up to the position where he placed the cursor, and, additionally, is signaling that the following word located after the cursor is incorrect. Hence, the system can already capture this fact and directly propose a new suitable suffix in which its first word is different from the first one in the previous suffix. This way, many explicit user corrections are avoided.

In Fig. 3.3 we can see an example of the CATTI process with the new interaction mode, which will be referred henceforth as PA-CATTI. As in the conventional CATTI, the process starts when the HTR system proposes a full transcription $\hat{s} \equiv \hat{w}$ of the input image x. Then, the user reads this prediction until a transcription error is found (denoted in this case by v) and makes a PA to position the cursor at this point. This way, the user validates an error-free transcription prefix p'. Now, before the user introduces a word to correct the erroneous one (as happens with the conventional CATTI), the HTR system, taking into account this validated prefix and the

	x	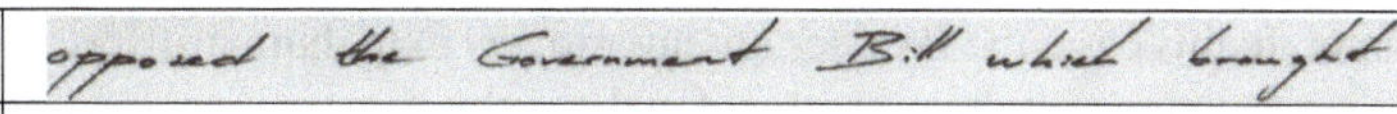					
STEP-0	p						
STEP-1	$\hat{s} \equiv \hat{w}$	**opposite**	**this**	**Comment**	**Bill**	**in that**	**thought**
	PA	↑					
	p'						
	----	----					
	$\hat{s}$	**opposition**	**this**	**Comment**	**Bill**	**in that**	**thought**
	κ	opposed					
	p	**opposed**					
STEP-2	$\hat{s}$		**the**	**Government**	**Bill**	**in that**	**thought**
	PA					↑	
	p'	**opposed**	**the**	**Government**	**Bill**		
FINAL	$\hat{s}$					**which**	**brought**
	PA						
	$p' \equiv T$	**opposed**	**the**	**Government**	**Bill**	**which**	**brought**

Fig. 3.3 Example of CATTI operation with pointer actions (PA). Starting with an initial recognized hypothesis $\hat{s} \equiv \hat{w}$, the user validates through a PA its longest well-recognized prefix p', which is used then by the system to suggest a new recognized hypothesis $\hat{s}$. In case the first word of $\hat{s}$ is also incorrect (see interaction 1), the user types the correct word κ (as in conventional CATTI process), generating a new consolidated prefix p (p' concatenated to κ), used later by the system to suggest a new hypothesis $\hat{s}$ starting again a new cycle. On the other hand, in case the word following to p' has been corrected in the new suggested hypothesis $\hat{s}$ (see interaction 2), no further corrective actions are required and the system start a new cycle. This whole process is repeated until the final error-free transcription T is obtained. In this final transcription, words in *red* color represent those which were corrected by user. Note that in the iteration 1, an unsuccessful PA was performed followed by the necessary typing of the correct word "`opposite`", whereas in the iteration 2, the performed PA was successful in predicting the correct word "`which`" and also the final full correct transcription is obtained

wrong word (v) that follows it, suggests a suitable continuation (i.e., a new $\hat{s}$). If the wrong word v appears corrected in this new $\hat{s}$, then a new cycle starts. Otherwise, as in the conventional CATTI, the user proceeds to correct it by directly typing the correct word, κ, producing a new consolidated prefix p (the previously validated prefix p' followed by κ) which is used by the HTR system to suggest a new suffix and a new cycle starts again. This process is repeated until a correct transcription of x is accepted by the user.

In the example shown in Fig. 3.3, without interaction, a user should have to correct about *six* errors from the original recognized hypothesis $\hat{w}$. If the conventional CATTI were used, *two* word corrections would have had to be performed. However in this new PA-based interaction, which somehow tries to anticipate the possible corrections that should be carried out by the user in the conventional CATTI context, just one user-correction is required to get the final error-free transcription. Note that in the iteration 1, the performed single PA is unsuccessful and the correct word is finally typed.

This new kind of interaction needs not be restricted to a single PA. Several scenarios arise, depending on the number of times the user performs a PA. In the simplest one, the user only makes one PA (i.e. single PA) when it is necessary to displace the cursor. In this case, the PA does not involve any extra human effort, because it is also the same action that the user should make in the conventional CATTI to position the cursor before typing the correct word. Another interesting scenario to be considered consists in performing systematically a PA before writing, although the cursor is already in the correct position. In this case, however, there is a cost associated to this kind of PAs, since the user does need to perform additional actions, which may or may not be beneficial. Finally, this last scenario can be easily extended, allowing the user to make several PAs before deciding to write the correct word.

Since we have already dealt with the problem of finding a suitable suffix $\hat{s}$ for a given consolidated prefix p (p' plus κ), we focus now on the problem in which the user only performs a single PA. In this case, in order to search for the best transcription suffix $\hat{s}$, the decoder has to cope with the input image x, the validated prefix p' and its following wrong word v:

$$\hat{s} = \arg\max_{s} \Pr(s \mid x, p', v) \approx \arg\max_{s} P(x \mid p', s, v) \cdot P(s \mid p', v). \tag{3.7}$$

PA-CATTI interaction falls within what was described in Sect. 1.4.4: *Interaction with Weaker Feedback* where Eq. (1.34) is close related with Eq. (3.7), with h', d and h instantiated, respectively, by p', v and s. Concerning the first term of Eq. (3.7), $P(x \mid p', s, v)$, can be modeled following similar assumptions and developments made for Eq. (2.6) (cf. Sect. 2.3). On the other hand, $P(s \mid p', v)$ can be provided by a language model constrained by the validated prefix p' and by the erroneous word v that follows it.

With respect to the scenario which allows the user to perform several PAs before deciding to write the correct word, the successive corresponding values of v must be cached and $P(s \mid p', v)$ must be computed taking into account all the previously discarded values of v (not just the one from the previous step).

3.3.1 Language Model and Search

$P(s \mid p', v)$ can be approached by adapting an n-gram language model so as to cope with the validated prefix p' and with the erroneous word v that follows it. The language model described in Sect. 2.4 would provide a direct way to model the probability $P(s \mid p')$, but as in addition we have to take into account that the first word of s is conditioned by v, some extra considerations are needed to model adequately $P(s \mid p', v)$.

Let $p' = w_1^k$ be a validated prefix and $s = w_{k+1}^l$ be a possible suffix, considering that the wrong-recognized word v only affects the first word of the suffix w_{k+1}. Then, after following similar procedure to obtain Eq. (2.8), $P(s \mid p', v)$ can be computed as

$$P(s \mid p', v) \simeq P\big(w_{k+1} \mid w_{k+2-n}^{k}, v\big) \cdot \prod_{i=k+2}^{k+n-1} P\big(w_i \mid w_{i-n+1}^{i-1}\big) \cdot \prod_{i=k+n}^{l} P\big(w_i \mid w_{i-n+1}^{i-1}\big)$$

$$= P\big(s_1 \mid p'^k_{k-n+2}, v\big) \cdot \prod_{j=2}^{n-1} P\big(s_j \mid p'^k_{k-n+1+j}, s_1^{j-1}\big) \cdot \prod_{j=n}^{l-k} P\big(s_j \mid s_{j-n+1}^{j-1}\big) \tag{3.8}$$

where $p'^k_1 = w_1^k = p'$ and $s_1^{l-k} = w_{k+1}^l = s$. Now, taking into account that the first word s_1 of the possible suffix has to be different from the erroneous word v, $P(s_1 \mid p'^k_{k-n+2}, v)$ can be formulated as follows:

$$P\big(s_1 \mid p'^k_{k-n+2}, v\big) = \begin{cases} 0, & s_1 = v, \\ \frac{P(s_1 \mid p'^k_{k-n+2})}{1 - P(v \mid p'^k_{k-n+2})}, & s_1 \neq v. \end{cases} \tag{3.9}$$

As in the conventional CATTI, the search problem involved by Eq. (3.7) can be solved by building a special language model, where the "suffix language model" of the Eq. (3.8) is modified in accordance with Eq. (3.9). Thanks to the finite-nature of this special language model, the search involved in Eq. (3.7) can be carried out using the Viterbi algorithm.

Due to the nature of PA-CATTI approach, where the system must react immediately by emitting a new suggested suffix after each pointer action performed by the user, the response speed becomes a very crucial factor to be taking into account. For this reason, search implementation based on WG technique results the more convenient solution. The restriction entailed by Eq. (3.9) can be easily implemented by directly deleting the WG edge labeled with v after the prefix has been matched. An example of this is shown in Fig. 3.4, where we have assumed that the user validated the prefix "`antiguos ciudadanos que en`" and the wrong-recognized word was "`el`". Hence, the WG has the edge labeled with "`el`" disabled.

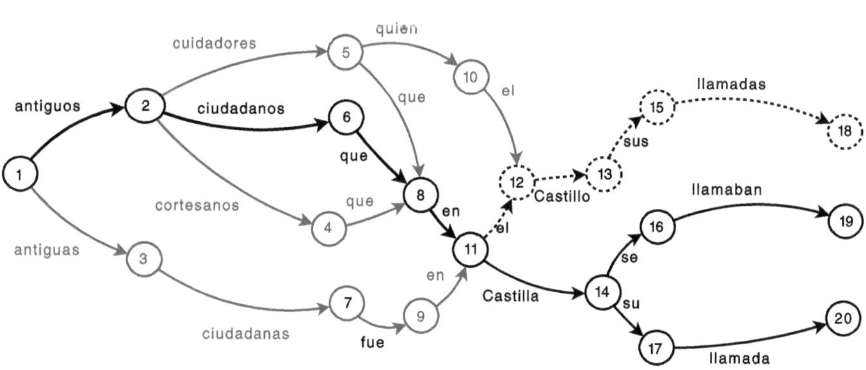

Fig. 3.4 Example of the WG generated after the user validates the prefix "`antiguos ciudadanos que en`" (represented by thicker-edges path). The edge corresponding to the wrong-recognized word "`el`" was disabled (*dashed-line path*)

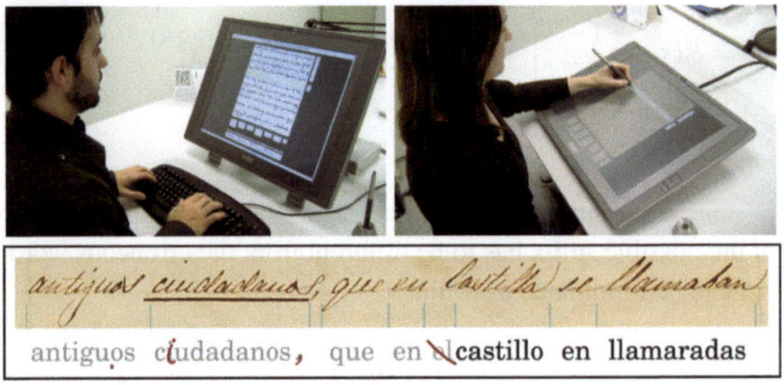

Fig. 3.5 *Top*: illustrations of CATTI multimodal user-interaction using keyboard and electronic-pen, respectively, on a touch-screen device. *Bottom*: page fragment showing a line image being processed, with a partially corrected system suggestion (in *grey* and *black* roman font) and the (previous) corrections made by the user through pen strokes and handwriting input marked in *bold red*

3.4 Multimodal Computer Assisted Transcription of Text Images: MM-CATTI

As was described in the CATTI approach (see Sect. 3.1), the user is recurrently interacting with the system in order to produce the final required transcription. Hence, the quality and ergonomics of the interaction process is crucial for the success of the system. Traditional peripherals like keyboard and mouse can be used to unambiguously provide the feedback associated with the validations and/or corrections of the successive system predictions. In this sense, in the previous Sect. 3.3, it has been shown, based on the concept of what we have called PA, how the use of pointer-devices like (for example) a mouse can foster the CATTI interaction process to easily provide such a corrective feedback.

Nevertheless, using more ergonomic multimodal interfaces should result in an easier and more comfortable human-machine interaction, at the expense of the feedback being less deterministic to the system. Different possibilities can be explored: gaze and gesture tracking, spoken commands, etc. Here we will focus on *touch-screen* communication, which is perhaps the most natural modality to provide the required feedback in CATTI systems. Figure 3.5 (top) shows a user interacting with a CATTI system using the keyboard and another one interacting by means of a touch-screen. Both the original image and the successive *off-line* HTR system's transcription hypotheses can be easily aligned and jointly displayed on the touchscreen, as shown in Fig. 3.5 (bottom).

More formally speaking, let x be the input image and s' a suffix suggested by the system as continuation of a consolidated prefix p in the previous interaction step (see Fig. 3.6). Hence, ps' constitutes a whole recognized hypothesis. Let t be the on-line *touchscreen pen strokes* provided by the user, which are sequences of real-valued vectors as described in Sect. 3.5.2. Let also p' be the longest error-free prefix validated by the user on the recognized hypothesis ps', thereby resulting that $ps' \equiv p'\sigma$, where σ corresponds to the remaining word sequence whose first word(s) was/were incorrectly recognized. Actually, the validated prefix p' is implicitly stated when the user performs some pen strokes t aiming at correcting the first wrong word in ps' or, what is the same, the first word of σ. Moreover, the user may additionally type some keystrokes (κ) on the keyboard in order to correct (other) parts of this σ and/or to add more text. Using this information, the system has to suggest a new suffix s for the next interaction, as a continuation of the user-validated prefix p', conditioned by the on-line touchscreen pen-strokes t and the typed text κ. That is, the problem is to find s given x and a feedback information composed of $p'\sigma$, t and κ, considering all possible *decodings*, d, of the on-line data t (i.e., letting d be a hidden variable). After some mathematical formulation development, this general set-up scenario can be seen as an instantiation of the problem already formulated in Eq. (1.27), where the (p', σ) and (t, κ) correspond with h' and f, respectively:

$$\hat{s} \approx \arg\max_s \max_d P(t \mid d) \cdot P(d \mid p', \sigma) \cdot P(x \mid p', \sigma, d, \kappa, s) \cdot P(s \mid p', \sigma, d, \kappa). \tag{3.10}$$

According to this very general discussion, it might be assumed that the user can type with independence of the result of the on-line handwritten decoding process. However, it can be argued that this generality is not realistically useful in practical situations. Alternatively, it is much more natural that the user waits for a specific system outcome ($\hat{d}$) from the on-line touchscreen feedback data (t), prior to start typing amendments (κ) to the (remaining part of the previous) system hypothesis. Furthermore, this allows the user to fix possible on-line handwritten recognition errors in $\hat{d}$.

For this more pragmatic and simpler scenario, following a similar approach presented in Sect. 1.3.5, each interaction step can be formulated in two phases. In the first one, the user produces some (may be null) on-line touchscreen data t (to correct part of σ) and the system has to decode t into a word (or word sequence) $\hat{d}$ using the previous hypothesis $p'\sigma$:

$$\hat{d} = \arg\max_d P(t \mid d) \cdot P(d \mid p', \sigma). \tag{3.11}$$

Once $\hat{d}$ is available, the user can enter adequate amendment keystrokes κ, if necessary, and produce a new consolidated prefix p (based on the validated prefix p', the first incorrectly recognized words of σ, $\hat{d}$ and κ), which leads to the following expression, identical to Eq. (2.4):

$$\begin{aligned} \hat{s} &\approx \arg\max_s P(x \mid p', \sigma, \hat{d}, \kappa, s) \cdot P(s \mid p', \sigma, \hat{d}, \kappa) \\ &= \arg\max_s P(x \mid p, s) \cdot P(s \mid p). \end{aligned} \tag{3.12}$$

The process continues in this way until p is accepted by the user as a full correct transcription of x.

	x						
STEP-0	p						
STEP-1	$\hat{s} \equiv \hat{w}$	**opposite**	**this**	**Comment**	**Bill**	**in that**	**thought**
	p', t, σ	*opposed*	this	Comment	Bill	in that	thought
	$\hat{d}$	opponent					
	κ	`sed`					
	p	**opposed**					
STEP-2	$\hat{s} \equiv s'$		**the**	**Government**	**Bill**	**in that**	**thought**
	p', t, σ	**opposed**	**the**	**Government**	**Bill**	*which*	thought
	$\hat{d}$					which	
	κ						
	p	**opposed**	**the**	**Government**	**Bill**	**which**	
FINAL	$\hat{s} \equiv s'$						**brought**
	p', t, σ	**opposed**	**the**	**Government**	**Bill**	**which**	**brought**
	κ						
	$p \equiv T$	oppo<u>sed</u>	**the**	**Government**	**Bill**	which	**brought**

Fig. 3.6 Example of MM-CATTI interaction with a CATTI system, to transcribe an image sentence "*opposed the Government Bill which brought*". Each interaction step starts with a transcription prefix p that has been consolidated in the previous step. First, the system suggests a suffix $\hat{s}$ and the user handwrites some touchscreen text, t, to amend $\hat{s}$. This action also validates a correct prefix p' (and a remaining word sequence σ starting with the first wrong recognized word of $\hat{s}$), which can be used by the on-line HTR subsystem to obtain a decoding of t. After observing this decoding, $\hat{d}$, the user may type additional keystrokes, κ, to correct possible errors in $\hat{d}$ (and perhaps to amend other parts of $\hat{s}$). A new consolidated prefix, p, is built from the previous correct prefix p', the decoded on-line handwritten text, $\hat{d}$, and the typed text κ. System suggestions are printed in **boldface** and typed text in typewriter font. User corrections are shown in *different font* and *red* color. In the final transcription, T, typed text is additionally *underlined*. Assuming all interactions as whole-word corrections, the post-editing WER would be 100% (5 substitutions plus one insertion out of 6 correct words), while the MM-CATTI WSR is 50%; i.e., 2 touch-screen + 1 keyboard word corrections (see definitions of WER and WSR in Sect. 2.6)

An example of this kind of inter-leaved off-line image recognition and on-line touchscreen interaction is shown in Fig. 3.6. In this example, we are assuming that on-line handwriting is the modality preferred by the user to make corrections, relaying on the keyboard mainly (or only) to correct eventual on-line text decoding errors. Note that the potential increase in comfort of this setting comes at expense of a hopefully small number of additional interaction steps using the keyboard. In this example the user would need *three* interactions using MM-CATTI, compared with the *two* interactive corrections needed by CATTI (in Fig. 3.1) and *six* post-editing corrections required by the original, off-line recognized hypothesis.

Although Fig. 3.6 may suggest otherwise, we should remind that, as mentioned in Sect. 3.1, only whole-word interactions are considered in the present chapter. Furthering this assumption, but without loose of generality, we consider here that, in each interaction, the user only attempts to correct the single word σ_1 (first word of the word sequence σ); that is, $\hat{d}$ consists in a single, whole word.

Since we have already dealt with Eq. (3.12) in Sect. 2.3 (Eqs. (2.4)–(2.6)), we focus now on Eq. (3.11). As in Sect. 3.1, $P(t \mid d)$ is provided by (HMM) morphological models of the word(s) in d (see Sect. 3.5.2). On the other hand, here, $P(d \mid p', \sigma)$ can be provided by a language model constrained by information derived from the validated error-free prefix p' and by the remaining words sequence σ produced at the previous iteration. Equation (3.11) may lead to several scenarios depending on the assumptions and constraints adopted for $P(d \mid p', \sigma)$. We examine some of them hereafter.

The simplest one corresponds to a conventional, non-interactive on-line HTR setting, where all the available conditions are ignored; i.e., $P(d \mid p', \sigma) \equiv P(d)$. This scenario is considered here as a *baseline*.

A more informative setting arises by taking into account part of the information derived from the previous off-line HTR prediction σ. The user introduces the touchscreen data t in order to correct the first m wrong words σ_1^m that follows the validated prefix p'. Therefore, we can assume an *error-conditioned* model such as $P(d \mid p', \sigma) \equiv P(d \mid \sigma_1^m)$; clearly, knowing the word(s) that the user has already deemed incorrect should prevent the on-line decoder making the same error(s).

If, in addition to σ_1^m, the information derived by the accepted prefix p' is also taken into account, a particularly useful scenario arises. In this case the decodings of t are further constrained to be suitable continuations of the prefix accepted; that is: $P(d \mid p', \sigma) \equiv P(d \mid p', \sigma_1^m)$ and Eq. (3.11) becomes

$$\hat{d} \approx \arg\max_d P(t \mid d) \cdot P\big(d \mid p', \sigma_1^m\big). \tag{3.13}$$

This *multimodal* model, referred to as MM-CATTI [29, 30], is the one studied in more detail in this chapter.

3.4.1 Language Model and Search for MM-CATTI

Language modeling and search techniques needed for the on-line HTR feedback subsystem in MM-CATTI are essentially similar to those described in Sect. 2.4 for the main, off-line HTR system. Language model constraints are implemented on the base of n-grams, depending on each multimodal scenario considered.

The simplest *baseline* scenario does not take into account any interaction-derived information and $P(d)$ could be provided by the same n-gram used for the off-line decoder. However, if only single whole-word touchscreen corrections are assumed, as discussed in the previous subsection, only *uni*-grams actually make sense.

The whole-word assumption also simplifies the *error-conditioned* model, $P(d \mid \sigma_1^m)$, because only the first (wrong) word of σ is to be taken into account. Let $v = \sigma_1$ be this wrong word. Therefore the *error-conditioned* language model probability can be written as

$$P(d \mid v) = \begin{cases} 0, & d = v, \\ \frac{P(d)}{1-P(v)}, & d \neq v. \end{cases} \tag{3.14}$$

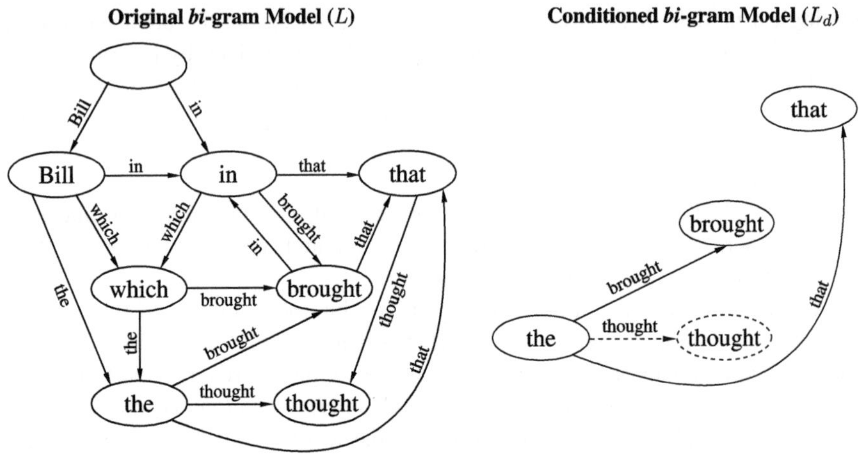

Fig. 3.7 Example of MM-CATTI dynamic *bi*-gram language model generation. L is the original *bi*-gram model used by off-line HTR system, whereas L_d is the *bi*-gram sub-model, derived from L, which takes as initial state that corresponding to the prefix "`the`". This simplified language model is used by the on-line HTR subsystem to recognize the touchscreen handwritten word "`brought`", intended to replace the wrong off-line recognized word "`thought`", which was disabled in L_d (displayed in *dashed line*)

Finally, in MM-CATTI the language model probability is approximated by $P(d \mid p', v)$. That is, the on-line HTR subsystem should produce a hypothesis $\hat{d}$ for the touchscreen strokes t, taking into account a user-validated prefix, p', and the first wrong word, $v = \sigma_1$, in the off-line HTR suggestion. In this case, arguments similar to those in Sect. 3.3.1 apply and, under the same single whole-word assumption, we can use Eq. (3.9) changing s_1 with d, leading to

$$P(d \mid p', v) = \begin{cases} 0, & d = v, \\ \frac{P(d \mid p'^{k}_{k-n+2})}{1 - P(v \mid p'^{k}_{k-n+2})}, & d \neq v \end{cases} \tag{3.15}$$

where k is the length of p'.

A simple implementation of Eq. (3.15) is shown in Fig. 3.7, based on the same language model example of Fig. 2.1. In this case, p' ="`of the`" and the user wants to correct the wrong off-line recognized word "`thought`", by handwriting the word "`brought`" (for example) on the touchscreen. The on-line HTR subsystem uses a *bi*-gram model, conditioned by the context word "`the`" (which is now the initial state) and the word transition edge "`thought`" is disabled.

As shown in the example, and unlike it happened in CATTI (cf. Fig 2.1), the linear language model of the prefix p' is no longer required, because the corresponding on-line touchscreen data of the prefix p' do no exist in this case. Moreover, as we are assuming only single whole-word corrections, only the direct transitions from the starting node (the "`the`" node in the example) need be considered.

As in CATTI searching (Sect. 3.2), owing to the finite-state nature of the n-gram language model, the search involved in Eqs. (3.13) and (3.15) can be efficiently carried out using the Viterbi algorithm [10]. Note that under the assumption of just one whole-word correction per interaction, Viterbi search implementation is the only choice that makes sense for the on-line HTR feedback decoding. Moreover, and as in CATTI, decoding search in MM-CATTI (specially decoding related to Eq. (3.12)) can be implemented using one of the two different approximations presented in Sect. 2.5. The on-line decoding phase (Eq. (3.13)) may also be implemented using WGs, particularly for the case we decide that it is possible to write/correct more than one word with the e-pen touchscreen.

3.5 Non-interactive HTR Systems

This section is devoted to describe in more detail the HTR systems employed for both the off-line and the on-line versions. In particular, it will be shed more light on the preprocessing and feature extraction phases carried out for each HTR version, along with additional specific information related to the modelling topic itself used in each case.

3.5.1 Main Off-Line HTR System Overview

The off-line HTR system used here follows a classical architecture composed of three modules: (a) *preprocessing*, aimed at correcting image degradations and geometry distortions, and dedicated to decompose page images into their constituent line images; (b) *feature extraction*, where a real-value vector sequence representation of each line image is obtained; and (c) *recognition*, which obtains a most likely word sequence for the given input sequence of feature vectors. The following subsections describe the three modules in some detail.

Off-Line HTR Preprocessing

Image degradation is a quite common problem in many text images and more so in ancient documents [6]. Typical degradations include the presence of smear and skew, backgrounds with big variations and uneven illumination, spots due to the humidity or marks resulting from the ink that goes through the paper (commonly called bleed-through). In addition, other kinds of difficulties appear in these images, such as different character styles and sizes, underlined and/or crossed-out words, etc. The combination of these problems contributes to make the recognition process difficult. Therefore, preprocessing becomes essential to reduce the impact of these problems, as well as to extract the actual (line) images of the text to be recognized. A survey of preprocessing techniques proposed for text images can be seen in [17, 21]. In this

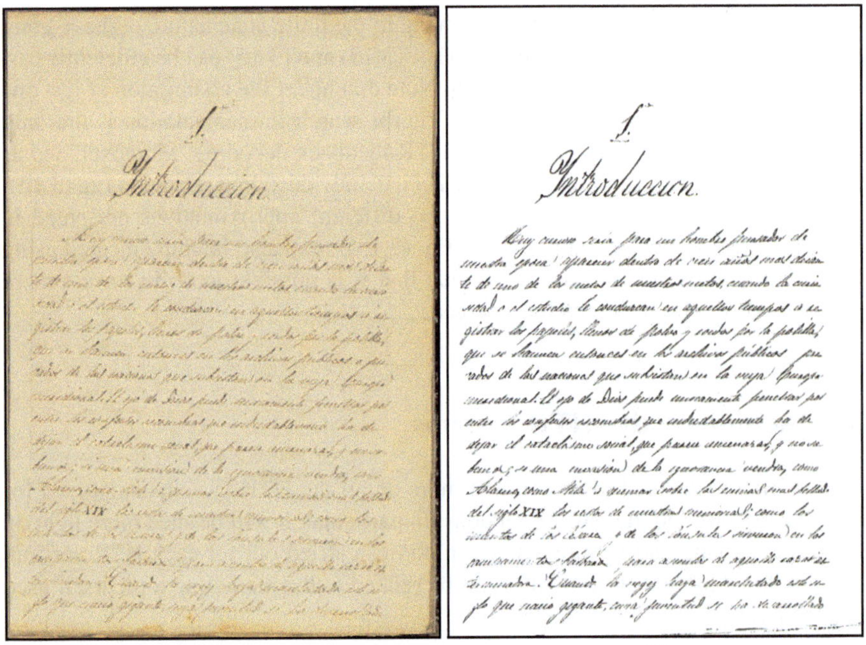

(a) (b)

Fig. 3.8 Preprocessing example: (**a**) original page image; (**b**) result after page skew correction, background removal, noise reduction and increase of contrast

work, the following preprocessing steps take place in order: background removal and noise reduction, skew correction, line extraction, slope-slant correction and size normalization.

Background removal and noise reduction are performed by applying a 2-dimensional median filter [5, p. 540] on the whole page image and subtracting the result from the original image. This is often followed by a grey-level normalization to increase the foreground/background image contrast (see Figs. 3.8a and 3.8b).

Skew is one of the distortions introduced during document scanning process. It is understood as the angle of the document paper image with respect to the horizontal x-axis. *Skew correction* is carried out globally on each page image by searching for the angle which maximizes the variance of the horizontal projection profile. It is assumed here that this maximal variance value should correspond with the horizontal projection profile of the de-skewed text lines [19, 26] (see again Figs. 3.8a and 3.8b).

Line detection is based again on the horizontal projection profile of the optimally de-skewed input image. Local minima in this curve are potential cut-points between consecutive text lines (see Fig. 3.9a). Obviously, clear separation is not always possible and cut-points detection needs to be adequately combined with connected components techniques [14]. Figure 3.9b shows some line images obtained with this method.

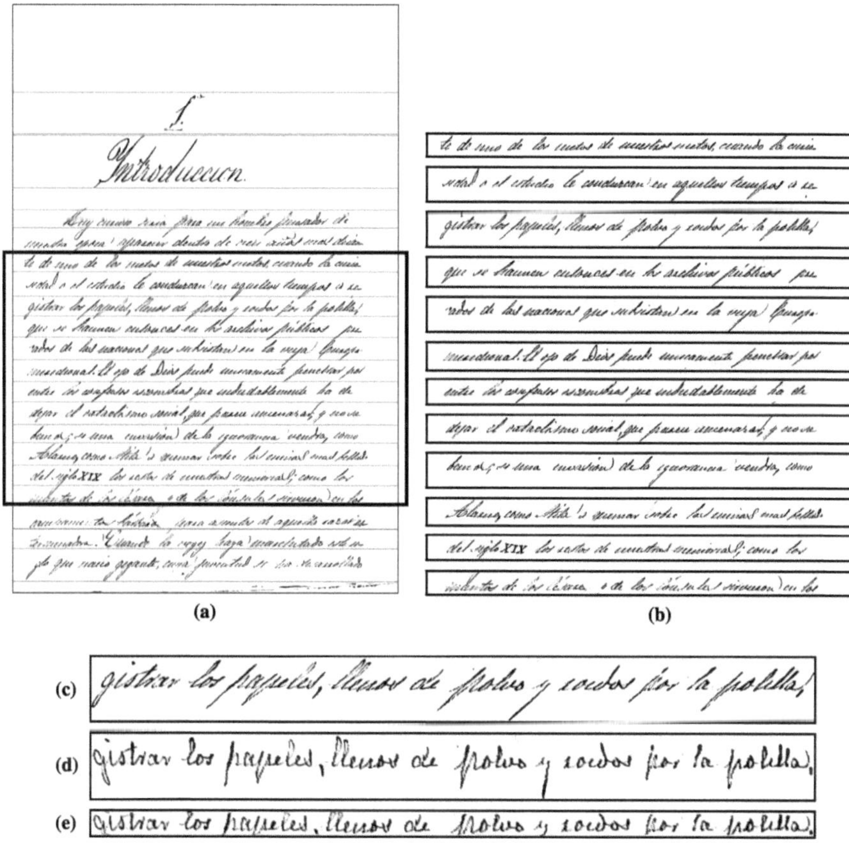

Fig. 3.9 Preprocessing example: (a) image with cutting lines computed from the horizontal projection profile; (b) separated line images from the highlighted region; (c) a separated line image; (d) slant correction; (e) size normalization

The slant is the angle between the vertical and the dominant direction of the written vertical strokes. *Slant correction* is applied to each previously separated line image. Much in the same way as in the case of line detection, the slant is computed by searching for the angle which maximizes the variance of the vertical projection profile of the de-slanted text [19]. This tends to render the written text strokes in an upright position (see Fig. 3.9d) and significantly improves the accuracy of the HMM recognition techniques.

The slope is the angle between the direction of the line on which the writer aligned the words on a text line and the horizontal direction. The *slope correction* processes an original image to put the text line into horizontal position by applying a rotation operation with the same slope angle, but in the opposite direction. To obtain the angle we use a method based on horizontal projections, very similar to the method used on the skew correction operation.

Finally, (non-linear) *size normalization* aims at making the optimally de-slanted line images invariant to character size and attempts to reduce large areas of background pixels which remain on the image because of the presence of long ascenders and descenders of some letters [23] (see Fig. 3.9e).

Off-Line HTR Feature Extraction

As our HTR system is based on HMMs, each preprocessed text line image has to be represented as a sequence of feature vectors. Several approaches have been proposed to obtain this kind of sequences [2, 3, 14]. The approach used in this chapter follows the ideas described in [2].

First, a grid is applied to divide the text line image into $N \times M$ rectangular cells. N is chosen empirically, whereas M is such that M/N is proportional to the original text line image aspect ratio, with a proportionality coefficient tuned empirically. Each cell of the grid is characterized by three features: *average gray level, horizontal gray level derivative* and *vertical gray level derivative* [26], which are computed from a $n \times m$ pixels analysis window, S, centered in that cell. The size of the analysis window (centered in a cell) is also empirically adjusted and its area typically overlaps partially (or completely) the neighbor cell areas.

The *average gray level*, $\overline{g}$, is computed through convolution with two 1-d Gaussian filters, w_i and w_j:

$$\overline{g} = \frac{1}{nm} \sum_{i=0}^{n-1} \sum_{j=0}^{m-1} S(i,j) \cdot w_i \cdot w_j,$$

$$w_i = \exp\left(-\frac{1}{2} \frac{(i - n/2)^2}{(n/4)^2}\right), \quad w_j = \exp\left(-\frac{1}{2} \frac{(j - m/2)^2}{(m/4)^2}\right). \tag{3.16}$$

The *horizontal gray level derivative*, d_h, is calculated as the slope of the line which best fits the horizontal function of column-average gray level in the analysis window. The fitting criterion is the sum of squared errors weighted by a 1-d Gaussian filter:

$$d_h = \frac{(\sum_{j=0}^{m-1} w_j g_j)(\sum_{j=0}^{m-1} w_j j) - (\sum_{j=0}^{m-1} w_j)(\sum_{j=0}^{m-1} w_j g_j j)}{(\sum_{j=0}^{m-1} w_j j)^2 - (\sum_{j=0}^{m-1} w_j)(\sum_{j=0}^{m-1} w_j j^2)} \tag{3.17}$$

where g_j is, in this case, the column-average gray level at column j, defined by

$$g_j = \frac{\sum_{i=0}^{n-1} S(i,j)}{n}.$$

The *vertical gray level derivative*, d_v, is computed in a similar way.

Columns of cells (also called *frames*) are processed from left to right and a feature vector is constructed for each *frame* by stacking the three features computed in their constituent cells. Hence, at the end of this process, a sequence of M $(3N)$-dimensional feature vectors is obtained. Figure 3.10 shows a graphical representation of the feature vectors sequence extracted for the word image *sometimes*.

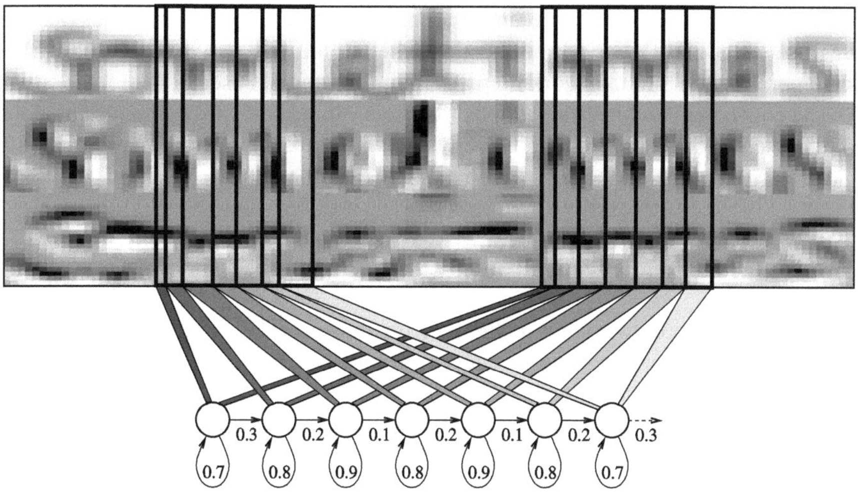

Fig. 3.10 Example of feature-vector sequence and HMM modeling of instances of the character "`m`" within the word "`sometimes`". The model is shared among all instances of characters of the same class. The zones modeled by each state show graphically subsequences of feature vectors compounded by stacking the normalized grey level and its both derivatives features

Modeling and Search

As already explained in Sect. 2.2, *characters* (considered in this case as the basic recognition units) are modeled by continuous density left-to-right HMMs, with state emission probabilities given by mixtures of Gaussian densities. The number of Gaussian densities of the mixtures as well as the number of states were empirically chosen after tuning the system. It is also important to mention here that all the experimental results reported in Sect. 3.6.2 have been obtained using HMM topologies with the same number of states for all the character classes. Figure 3.10 shows an example of how a HMM models two feature vector subsequences corresponding to the character "`m`".

Concerning to the modeling of lexical entries (words) and syntactic constraints derived from each specific task, as well as the way they are used to perform the search decoding, have been already described in Sect. 2.2.

3.5.2 On-Line HTR Subsystem Overview

The on-line HTR subsystem is intended to decode the feedback touchscreen data for multimodal text correction; i.e. to recognize the pen strokes (words) written by the user in successive CATTI interactions in order to correct or replace the errors produced by the main, off-line HTR decoder. In general, touchscreen data consist of a series of pen-positions (x_t, y_t), sampled at regular time instants $t = 1, 2, \ldots$.

Each sample of this *trajectory* can be accompanied by information about the pen pressure, or at least by one bit indicating whether the pen is actually touching the screen or it is "up". In this work no pressure information is used.

The conceptual architecture adopted for the on-line HTR subsystem is analogous to that used in the main off-line HTR system, with exception of the preprocessing and feature extraction modules, which are explained hereafter.

On-Line HTR Preprocessing

An overview of preprocessing techniques for on-line HTR can be seen in [8]. In this chapter, the preprocessing of each trajectory involves only two simple steps: repeated points elimination and noise reduction. *Repeated points* appear in a trajectory when the pen remains down and motionless for some time. These uninformative data are trivially removed, along with the points marked as "*pen-up*". *Noise* in pen strokes is due to erratic hand motion and inaccuracy of the digitalization process. To reduce this kind of noise, a simple smoothing technique is used which replaces every point (x_t, y_t) in the trajectory by the mean value of its neighbors [9]. Note that the temporal order of the data points is preserved throughout these preprocessing steps.

On-Line HTR Feature Extraction

Each preprocessed trajectory is transformed into a new temporal sequence of 6-dimensional real-valued feature vectors [27]. These time-domain features are point locations (although in this case only y coordinate is considered), first and second time derivatives and curvature.

Normalized Vertical Position: first, the coordinate pairs of each trajectory point are linearly scaled and translated to obtain new pairs of values (x_t, y_t), so that y_t is in the range $[0, 100]$ and the original aspect-ratio of the trajectory is preserved.

Normalized First Derivatives: x'_t and y'_t are calculated using the method given in [32]:

$$x'_t = \frac{\Delta x_t}{\|\nabla\|}, \qquad y'_t = \frac{\Delta y_t}{\|\nabla\|}, \tag{3.18}$$

where

$$\Delta x_t = \sum_{i=1}^{r} i \cdot (x_{t+i} - x_{t-i}), \qquad \Delta y_t = \sum_{i=1}^{r} i \cdot (y_{t+i} - y_{t-i}),$$

$$\|\nabla\| = \sqrt{\Delta {x_t}^2 + \Delta {y_t}^2},$$

and r defines a window of size $2r + 1$ which determines the neighbor points involved in the computation. Setting $r = 2$ has provided satisfactory results in this case.

It is worth noting that the normalization of derivatives by $\|\nabla\|$ implicitly entails an effective *writing speed normalization*. In our experiments, this has proved to lead to better results than using explicit speed normalization preprocessing techniques such as *trace segmentation*, based on re-sampling the trajectory at equal-length (rather than equal time) intervals [20, 31].

Second derivatives: x''_t and y''_t, are computed in the same way as the first derivatives, but using x'_t and y'_t instead of x_t and y_t.

Curvature: k_t, is the inverse of the local radius of the trajectory in each point. It is calculated as

$$k_t = \frac{x'_t \cdot y''_t - x''_t \cdot y'_t}{(x'^2_t + y'^2_t)^{3/2}}. \tag{3.19}$$

Although this feature is an explicit combination of the previous features, it has lead to slightly but consistently improved results in our experiments.

Character, Word and Language Modeling and Search

Modeling and search for on-line recognition follow almost the same schemes used in off-line recognition, described in Sect. 3.5.1.

As in the off-line case, we use continuous density left-to-right character HMMs with Gaussian densities assigned to each state mixture. However, instead of using a fixed number of states for all HMMs, it is variable for each character class. The number of states s_c chosen for each HMM character class M_c was computed as $s_c = l_c/f$, where l_c is the average length of the sequences of feature vectors used to train M_c, and f is a design parameter measuring the average number of feature vectors modeled per state (*state load factor*). This rule of setting up s_c tries to balance modeling effort across states and, for our task, has significantly improved the recognition accuracy. On the other hand, lexical modeling is carried out in exactly the same way as in the off-line HTR case.

Language modeling and search are simpler in this case because, as discussed in Sect. 3.4.1, we have restricted our present MM-CATTI study to single whole-word touchscreen corrections. That is, the language models used in the MM-CATTI search only allow one word per user-interaction. As mentioned at the end of Sect. 2.2, a GSF is also used here in practice to balance the HMM and language model probabilities of Eq. (3.11).

3.6 Tasks, Experiments and Results

The experimental framework adopted to assess the effectiveness of the basic HTR systems (off-line and on-line) and for the three approaches proposed in this chapter: CATTI, PA-CATTI and MM-CATTI, is described in the following subsections. This includes information about the different corpora and performance measures employed in the experiments as well as the obtained results.

3.6.1 HTR Corpora

Three off-line corpora were employed in the experiments. Two of them, ODEC-M3 [25] and IAMDB [13, 15], contain handwritten text in modern Spanish and English, respectively. IAMDB is publicly available, thereby serving as a reference to compare the obtained results. The third corpus, CS [24], consists of cursive handwritten page images in old Spanish, which allow us to report results on the kind of legacy documents.

Sentence-segmented images are used both in ODEC-M3 and IAMDB, while only *line-segmented* images are available in CS. Each sentence or line image is accompanied by its ground truth transcription as the corresponding sequence of words. To better focus on the essential issues of the considered problems, no punctuation marks, diacritics, or different word capitalizations are included in the transcriptions. These transcriptions are used to train the *bi*-gram language models for ODEC-M3 and CS. IAMDB, on the other hand, consists of hand-copied sentences from the much larger electronic text LOB corpus [11] which contains about 1 000 000 running words. Therefore, in this case, the whole LOB corpus (after removing all the test sentences) was used for *bi*-gram training. Finally, the lexicon of each task is defined as the set of words found in training or in test transcriptions. Such a "closed vocabulary" scheme is commonly used in Automatic Speech Recognition [4, 10] to ease results reproducibility.

On the other hand, to train the on-line HTR feedback subsystem and test the MM-CATTI approach, the on-line handwriting UNIPEN corpus, which also is publicly available, was chosen.

In the next subsections, detailed descriptions of all off-line corpora as well the on-line corpus are given.

ODEC-M3

This corpus consists of images of casual handwritten Spanish paragraphs. It was compiled from spontaneous answers extracted from survey forms made for a telecommunication company.[2] These answers were written by a heterogeneous group of people, without any explicit or formal restriction. In addition, since no guidelines were given as to the kind of pen or the writing style to be used, paragraphs are very variable and noisy. Many of them were written using different case and font types, variable sizes and include words which are underlined, crossed-out or contain orthographic mistakes, unusual abbreviations, symbols, etc. Examples of these difficulties are shown in Fig. 3.11.

Because of some of these difficulties, line extraction was carried out in a semi-automatic way, based on a conventional line-extraction method mentioned in Sect. 3.5.1. Most of the phrases were processed automatically, but manual supervision was applied to difficult line-overlapping cases such as that shown in Fig. 3.11

[2]Data kindly provided by ODEC, S.A. (www.odec.es).

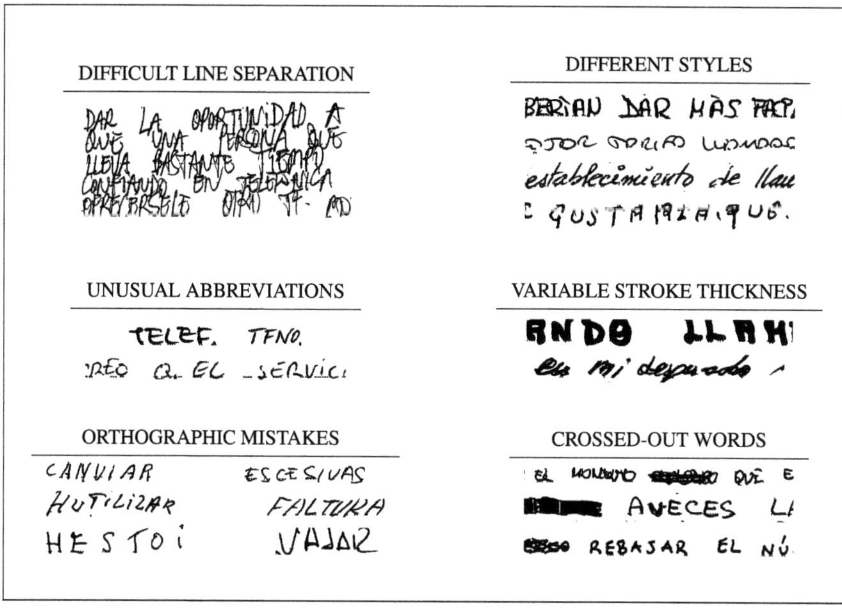

Fig. 3.11 Examples of difficulties found in several paragraphs of the ODEC-M3 Corpus

Table 3.1 Basic statistics of the database ODEC, where OOV stands for *out-of-vocabulary* words

Number of	Training	Test	Total	Lexicon	OOV	Tr. Ratio
Writers/phrases	676	237	913	–	–	–
Words	12 287	4 084	16 371	2 790	518	4.4
Characters	64 666	21 533	86 199	80	0	808

(top-left). By adequately pasting the lines extracted from each paragraph, a single-line (long) image which encompasses the whole paragraph was obtained. This resulted in 913 binary images, which were partitioned into a training set of 676 images and a test set of 237 images. The transcriptions of all the images are also available, containing 16 371 words with a vocabulary of 2 790 different words. It is important to remark that we do not distinguish between words written in lowercase characters or uppercase. Therefore, to train the n-gram models, the transcription of the 676 training images were converted to uppercase and the punctuation signs $\{-/;:+*()|,\ !?\}$ were eliminated. The average ratio for n-gram training is 4.4 running word instances per vocabulary word. Nevertheless, to train the character HMMs we use the transcription that describes with detail and accuracy all the elements appearing in each handwritten text images, such as lowercase or uppercase letters, symbols, abbreviations, spacing between words and characters, crossed-words, etc. All this information is summarized in Table 3.1. More information on this corpus can be found in [25].

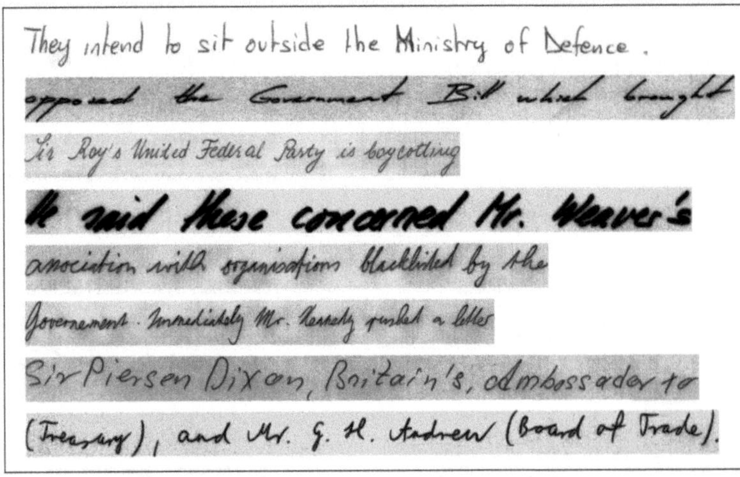

Fig. 3.12 Examples of handwritten lines from the IAMDB corpus

IAMDB

This corpus was compiled by the Research Group on Computer Vision and Artificial Intelligence (FKI) at Institute of Computer Science an Applied Mathematics (IAM) in Bern (Switzerland). The IAM Handwriting Database [13, 15] (IAMDB) consists of grey-level images of unconstrained handwritten English text forms. It is publicly accessible and freely available upon request for non-commercial research purposes.[3] The IAMDB images correspond to handwritten texts copied from the Lancaster-Oslo/Bergen Corpus [11] (LOB), which encompasses around 500 printed English texts of about 2 000 words each and about 1 000 000 total running words.

The IAMDB version 3.0 (the latest at this moment) is composed of 1 539 scanned text pages, handwritten by 657 different writers. No restriction was imposed on the writing style or the type of pen to be used. This dataset is also provided at sentence level. Line detection and extraction, as well as (manually) detecting sentence boundaries, was carried out by the IAM institute [14]. Using this information, lines could be easily merged into whole sentence line-images. Figure 3.12 shows examples of handwritten lines images from this corpus. This corpus was partitioned into a training set composed of 2 124 sentences, handwritten by 448 different writers, and a writer independent test set composed of 200 sentences written by 100 writers. Table 3.2 summarizes all this information.

Note that the amount of data available for training the (n-gram) language models for this task (the whole LOB corpus) is very much larger than the amount of data contained in the transcriptions of the available text images. Following [33], we take advantage of this opportunity by using the whole LOB corpus (except the

[3] http://iamwww.unibe.ch/~fki/iamDB

Table 3.2 Basic statistics of the database IAM, where OOV stands for *out-of-vocabulary* words

Number of	Training	Test	Total	Lexicon	OOV	Tr. Ratio
Writers	448	100	548	–	–	–
Sentences	2 124	200	2 324	–	–	–
Words	42 832	3 957	46 789	8 017	921	81
Characters	216 774	20 726	237 500	78	0	2 779

Fig. 3.13 Examples of pages images from CS corpus

200 sentences of the image test set) for n-gram training, while setting a reduced vocabulary which encompasses only the 8 017 different words found in the IAMDB text images. Only 651 462 running words of the LOB corpus belong to the IAMDB vocabulary proper. Therefore, for n-gram training we have a quite good effective average ratio of 81 word instances per IAMDB vocabulary word. As in the ODEC-M3 corpus, here we do not distinguish between words written in lowercase characters or uppercase.

CS MANUSCRIPT

This corpus was compiled from a XIX century Spanish manuscript identified as "Cristo-Salvador" (CS), which was kindly provided by the *Biblioteca Valenciana Digital* (BiVaLDi).[4] This is a rather small document composed of 50 color images of text pages, written by a single writer. Some examples are shown in Fig. 3.13.

The page images were preprocessed and divided into lines, as described in Sect. 3.5.1. The results were visually inspected and the few detection errors

[4]http://bv2.gva.es

Table 3.3 Basic statistics of the partition *page* of the database Cristo-Salvador. OOV stands for *out-of-vocabulary* words

Number of	Training	Test	Total	Lexicon	OOV	Tr. Ratio
Pages	53	53	53	–	–	–
Text lines	681	491	1 172	–	–	–
Words	6 435	4 483	10 918	2 277	1 010	2.8
Characters	36 729	25 487	62 216	78	0	470

(around 4%) were manually corrected, resulting in a dataset of 1 172 text line images. It is worth mentioning that, unlike the two previous corpora, in this case the extracted lines are not merged into sentence or paragraph images. The transcriptions of these line images are also available, containing 10 918 running words with a vocabulary of 2 277 different words. Note that as in the other two corpora, we do not distinguish between words written in lowercase characters or uppercase.

Two different partitions, *page* (or "*soft*") and *book* (or "*hard*") are defined for this dataset [24]. Here we only consider the (easier) *page* partition. Its test set contains 491 samples corresponding to the last ten lines of each document page, whereas the training set is composed of the 681 remaining lines. Table 3.3 summarizes this information.

For n-gram training, the average ratio of running word instances per vocabulary word is 2.8. It is important to remark that such a small ratio will certainly result in under-trained language models, which clearly increase the difficulty of the recognition task and prevent CATTI, PA-CATTI or MM-CATTI to take much advantage of prefix-derived constraints.

UNIPEN Corpus

The UNIPEN `Train-R01/V07` dataset[5] comes organized into several categories [7] such as lower- and uppercase letters, digits, symbols, isolated words and full sentences. Unfortunately, the UNIPEN isolated words category does not contain all (or almost none of) the required word instances to be handwritten by the user in the MM-CATTI interaction process with the ODEC, IAMDB, or CS text images. Therefore, they were generated by concatenating random character instances from three UNIPEN categories: `1a` (digits), `1c` (lowercase letters) and `1d` (symbols). Table 3.4 shows the basic statistics of these words, needed to test the HTR feedback subsystem for each off-line HTR task. We have just taken into account here, for each task (corpus), all the words that the user must introduce in a standard CATTI iteration process when the Viterbi-search implementation is used (cf. Sect. 2.5.1). Note that in the case of WG-search implementation had been used, probably slightly different words and/or number of their instances would have been obtained. Anyway,

[5] For a detailed description of this dataset, see http://www.unipen.org.

Table 3.4 For each off-line HTR task: number of *on-line* unique words and word instances needed as feedback to correct the word errors made by the plain off-line HTR system

Task	Unique words	Word instances
ODEC-M3	378	753
IAMDB	510	755
CS	648	1 196

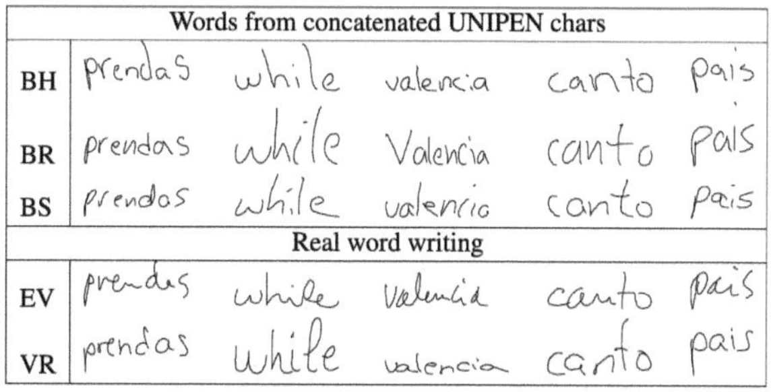

Fig. 3.14 Examples of words generated using characters from the three selected UNIPEN test writers (BH, BR, BS), along with samples of the same words written by two other writers in our labs

since we are interested in evaluating the feedback decoding subsystem (i.e. the on-line HTR subsystem), only Viterbi-search implementation is going to be considered. Even so, as we will see in Sect. 12.2, the demonstrator of MM-CATTI (MM-IHT) is implemented using an hybrid search-decoding scheme; that is, the off-line decoding phase is based on WG, whereas the feedback decoding phase relies directly on Viterbi.

To increase realism, the generation of each of these test words was carried out employing characters belonging to a same writer. Three different writers were randomly chosen, taking care that sufficient samples of all the characters needed for the generation of the required word instances were available from each writer. Each character needed to generate a given word was plainly aligned along a common word baseline, except if it had a descender, in which case the character baseline was raised 1/3 of its height. The horizontal separation between characters was randomly selected from *one* to *three* trajectory points. The selected writers are identified by their name initials as BS, BH and BR. Figure 3.14 shows some examples of words generated in this way, along with real samples of the same words written by two writers (EV and VR).

Training data were produced in a similar way using 17 different UNIPEN writers. For each of these writers, a sample of each of the 42 symbols and digits needed was randomly selected and one sample of each of the 1 000 most frequent Spanish and English words was generated, resulting in 34 714 training tokens (714 isolated characters plus 34 000 generated words). To generate these tokens, 186 881 UNIPEN character instances were used, using as many repetitions as required out of the 17 177 *unique* character samples available. Table 3.5 summarizes the amount of UNIPEN training and test data used in the experiments.

Table 3.5 Basic statistics of the UNIPEN training and test data used in the experiments

Number of different	Train	Test	Lexicon
Writers	17	3	–
Digits (1a)	1 301	234	10
Letters (1c)	12 298	2 771	26
Symbols (1d)	3 578	3 317	32
Total characters	17 177	6 322	68

3.6.2 Results

The three measures (WER, WSR and EFR) adopted to assess interactive transcription systems in Sect. 2.6 have been used to evaluate CATTI performance. In addition, to assess the new interaction mode of PA-CATTI approach, it has been introduced the so-called *Pointer Action Rate* (PAR). This can be defined as the number of additional PAs per word that the user has to do using the new user interaction mode. Note that the human effort needed for the verification of the transcription and positioning the cursor in the appropriate place in the conventional CATTI is the same as in the new CATTI system using single-PA interactions. In both cases the user should read the transcription proposed by the system until he or she finds an error and then positions the cursor in the place where the new word has to be typed. Moreover, since only single-word corrections have been considered, the *feedback decoding error rate* (FER) (that is, the conventional classification error rate) will be used to assess the accuracy of the on-line HTR feedback subsystem under the different constraints entailed by the MM-CATTI interaction process.

Different experiments have been carried out to assess the feasibility and potential of CATTI, PA-CATTI and MM-CATTI. In addition, non-interactive (off- and on-line) handwritten text recognition experiments have been performed to establish baseline performance figures.

Baseline Off-Line HTR Results

Conventional, non-interactive off-line HTR experiments were performed on the three off-line corpora described in Sect. 3.6.1, ODEC-M3, IAMDB and CS, using the basic system explained in Sect. 3.5.1. All the morphological (HMMs) and language (*bi*-gram) models were trained from the respective training images and transcriptions of each corpus. Although, as was noted earlier, in the training of IAMDB *bi*-gram language model not only the own IAMDB transcription corpus, but also the whole LOB corpus was used to. The HTR WER percentages obtained for the test images of each corpus were 22.9, 25.3 and 28.5, for ODEC-M3, IAMBD and CS, respectively. All these results have been obtained after optimizing the parameters values corresponding to the preprocessing and the feature extraction processes explained in Sect. 3.5.1 for each of the tasks. The WER obtained for IAMDB (25.3%) is comparable with non-interactive, state-of-the-art results published for this dataset [33].

Baseline On-Line HTR Results

These experiments were carried out using the basic on-line HTR subsystem explained in Sect. 3.5.2. As discussed in Sect. 3.6.1, UNIPEN data were used to assess the performance of the on-line HTR feedback subsystem.

All the samples were preprocessed using the preprocessing and feature extraction methods outlined in Sect. 3.5.2. In order to tune the parameters of the 68 on-line character HMMs needed, isolated character recognition experiments were carried out on each of the `1a`, `1c` and `1d` UNIPEN categories. The *classification error rates* (ER) obtained for test digits, letters and symbols were 1.7%, 5.9% and 21.8%, respectively. These results are comparable with state-of-the-art results obtained for this dataset [18, 22].

In order to establish a word decoding baseline accuracy for the on-line HTR feedback subsystem, a simple word recognition experiment was carried out. The words needed to train and test the feedback subsystem for each task were generated by concatenating adequate UNIPEN characters. Therefore, new character HMMs were trained from these training words, using the parameters previously tuned through the isolated character recognition experiments. On the other hand, since only single words are to be recognized, a *uni*-gram language model was trained (from the training transcriptions of each off-line task) to estimate the corresponding prior word probabilities. The following word recognition error percentages (FER) were observed for ODEC-M3, IAMDB and CS, respectively: 5.1, 4.6 and 6.4.

Note that these FER values are obtained without taking advantage of any interaction-derived contextual information (i.e., just using plain *uni*-grams). Therefore these figures represent the highest accuracies that could be expected if, e.g., an off-the-shelf on-line HTR system were adopted to implement the MM-CATTI feedback decoder.

CATTI Results

The CATTI approach presented in Sect. 3.1 was applied to the three off-line HTR tasks before-described, using the same parameter values used for the baseline, non-interactive off-line HTR results presented earlier. Table 3.6 shows the estimated interactive human effort (WSR) required for each task using the Viterbi-based implementation presented in Sect. 2.5.1, in comparison with the corresponding estimated post-editing effort (WER) before reported in the subsection of baseline off-line HTR results. Besides, it shows the *estimated effort reduction* (EFR), computed as the relative difference between WER and WSR (see Sect. 2.6).

Table 3.6 Performance of non-interactive off-line HTR (baseline WER) and CATTI (WSR), along with their relative difference (Estimated Effort Reduction—EFR) using the Viterbi-based search. All results are percentages

Corpus	WER	WSR	EFR
ODEC-M3	22.9	18.9	17.5
IAMDB	25.3	21.1	16.6
CS	28.5	26.9	5.7

According to these results, to produce 100 words of a correct transcription in the ODEC-M3 task, for example, a CATTI user should have to type only less than 20 words; the remaining 80 are automatically predicted by CATTI. That is to say, the CATTI user would save about 80% of the (typing and, in part thinking) effort needed to produce all the text manually. On the other hand, when interactive transcription is compared with post-editing, from every 100 (non-interactive) word errors, the CATTI user should have to interactively correct only less than 78. The remaining 17 errors would be automatically corrected by CATTI, thanks to the feedback information derived from other interactive corrections.

The different performance figures achieved in the different tasks can be explained by quality differences in the original images and also by the relative lexicon sizes and *bi*-gram estimation robustness. The later is particularly problematic in the case of CS which, in addition, suffers from a segmentation into relatively short, syntactically meaningless lines, which further hinders the ability of the *bi*-gram language model to capture relevant contextual information.

It is interesting to realize that CATTI is more effective for lines or sentences that have several errors; clearly, if a sentence has just one (word) error, it *must* be interactively corrected by the user and the best CATTI can do is to keep the remaining text unchanged. Obviously, this is not guaranteed by Eq. (2.4) and, in the worst case, a single word change made by the user may lead to more errors; that is, WSR might be greater than WER. To analyze this behavior, Fig. 3.15 presents WER, WSR and EFR values for increasing initial numbers of errors per sentence, for ODEC-M3 and IAMDB (similar tendencies are observed for CS).

As expected, the estimated effort reduction increases with the number of errors per sentence, which clearly assess the ability of CATTI to correct more than one error per interaction step in sentences with several wrong-recognized words. Also, for sentences with a single error, CATTI does not help at all or is even worse than post-editing. Therefore, in practice, a good implementation of a CATTI user interface should allow the user to disable CATTI predictions when doing some (single-word) corrections. Taking this into account, the results of Table 3.6 can be recomputed after excluding all the sentences with zero or one errors, leading to better EFR. Namely, the EFR becomes 17.9%, 18.4% and 6.9% for ODEC-M3, IAMDB and CS, respectively.

On Table 3.7 we can see the WSR and the EFR obtained for each task using WG search (see Sect. 3.2.1) in comparison with the corresponding WER. The WGs used in the experiments were generated with the same GSF and WIP values used

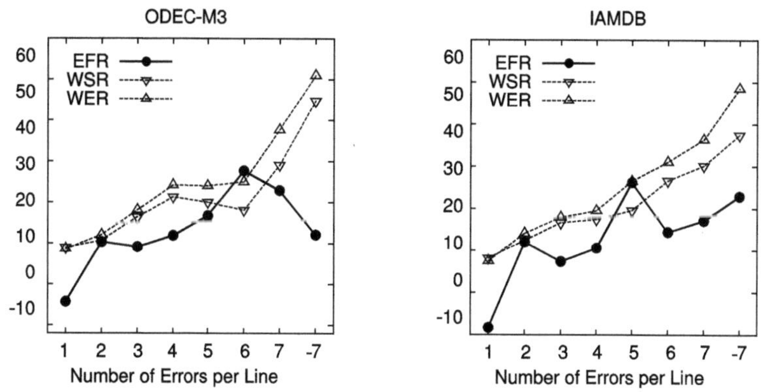

Fig. 3.15 WER, WSR and EFR (all in %) for varying number of errors per sentence, for ODEC-M3 (*left*) and IAMDB (*right*) corpora

Table 3.7 Performance of non-interactive off-line HTR (WER) and CATTI (WSR), along with the relative difference between them (Estimated Effort-Reduction—EFR) using the WG-based search approach. All results are percentages

Corpus	WER	WSR	EFR
ODEC-M3	22.9	21.5	6.1
IAMDB	25.3	22.5	11.1
CS	28.5	27.7	2.8

for the baseline results. As we have expected, the results obtained using the Viterbi-based search are better than those obtained with WGs. This is owing to the fact that the WG is just a pruned version of the Viterbi search trellis. Therefore, not all the possible transcriptions for the input handwritten text image are available, leading to some loss of system accuracy. However, the computational cost of using WGs is much lower than that using Viterbi adaptation, allowing in the former case, the user to interact in real-time with the system.

Nevertheless, from the reported results of Tables 3.6 and 3.7, it is clear that the estimated saved human effort (EFR) to produce error-free transcriptions with this CATTI approach is reduced in all the tasks. Furthermore, as previously explained, CATTI has the change to be more effective for lines/sentences with several errors. The EFR recomputed after excluding all the sentences with zero or one errors using the WG search approach are 6.8%, 12.9% and 3.8% for ODEC-M3, IAMDB and CS, respectively.

PA-CATTI Results

As commented at the end of Sect. 3.3.1, in order to be effective and fully useful, PA-CATTI approach requires short response times to emit a new suffix each time a

Table 3.8 Performance of the PA-CATTI with the single-PA interaction mode scenario (WSR single PA), along with the Estimated Effort-Reduction computed for WSR single PA with respect to conventional CATTI WSR (EFR_{CATTI}) and WSR single PA with respect to the non-interactive HTR WER (EFR_{PEDIT}). All results are percentages

Corpus	WSR single PA	EFR_{CATTI}	EFR_{PEDIT}
ODEC-M3	18.2	15.3	20.5
IAMDB	18.6	17.3	26.5
CS	23.7	14.4	16.8

PA is performed. A search implementation based on WG techniques is the solution which best fits this requirement. Table 3.8 reports the results obtained with the new single-PA interaction mode, which is the simplest one of the PA-related scenarios explained in Sect. 3.3. The first column shows the WSR obtained using the single-PA interaction mode, whereas the second and third columns show respectively the relative differences between the WSR single PA with respect to the conventional CATTI WSR (see second column of Table 3.7), and with respect to the WER of a conventional HTR system followed by human post-editing (see first column of Table 3.7).

According to Table 3.8, the estimated human effort to produce error-free transcription using PA-CATTI is significantly reduced with respect to using the conventional CATTI approach, and of course, with respect to the non-interactive HTR followed by manual post-editing. For example, in the IAMDB task, the new interaction mode can save about 26% of the overall effort, whereas the conventional CATTI would only save 11.1% using the WG-based search approach, or 16.6% using the Viterbi-based search approach (reported in Table 3.6).

Figure 3.16 plots the WSR, the EFR and the *Pointer-Action Rate* (PAR) as a function of the maximum number of allowed PAs before the user decides to write the correct word. These results are reported for both ODEC-M3 and IAMDB corpora (similar tendency has been observed for CS corpus as well). The EFR values have been computed between corresponding WSR and WER. From the both plots, it is revealed that a good trade-off between EFR and PAR can be obtained, for example, by setting the maximum number of PAs to 3, for which a significant amount of expected user effort is saved with a fairly low number of extra PAs per word.

MM-CATTI Results

The aim of these experiments is to assess the effectiveness of MM-CATTI in the scenarios described in Sect. 3.4.1. Multimodal operation offers ergonomics and increased usability at the expense of the system having to deal with non-deterministic feedback signals. Therefore, the main concern here is the accuracy of the on-line HTR feedback decoding and the experiments aim to determine how much this accuracy can be boosted by taking into account information derived from the proper

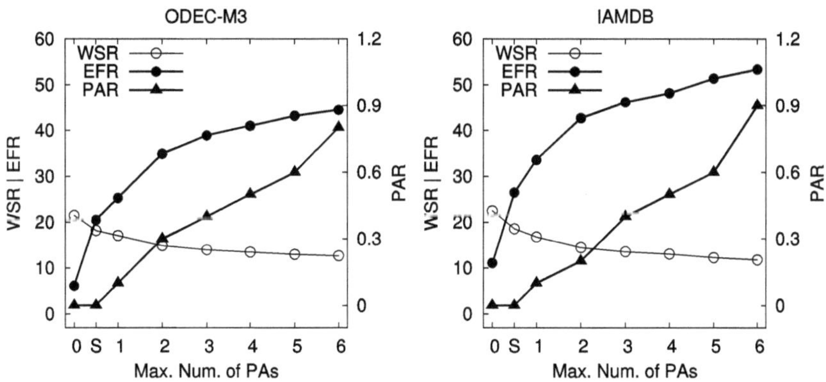

Fig. 3.16 *Word stroke ratio* (WSR), *estimated effort reduction* (EFR) and *pointer-action rate* (PAR) as a function of the maximum number of PAs allowed before the user decides to write the correct word. The first point "0" corresponds (without performing any PA) to the conventional CATTI, whereas the point "S" corresponds to the single-PA interaction scenario already discussed in Sect. 3.3

Table 3.9 Writer average MM-CATTI *feedback decoding error rates* (FER) for the different corpora and three language models: plain *uni*-gram (U, *baseline*), error-conditioned *uni*-gram (U_v) and prefix-and-error-conditioned *bi*-gram (B_v). The relative accuracy improvements for U_v and B_v with respect to U are shown in the last two columns

Corpus	FER (%)			Relative Improv. (%)	
	U	U_v	B_v	U_v	B_v
ODEC-M3	5.1	5.0	3.1	1.9	39.2
IAMDB	4.6	4.3	3.5	6.5	23.9
CS	6.4	6.2	5.8	3.1	9.3

interaction process. Ultimately, experiments aim at assessing which degree of synergy can actually be expected by taking into account *both* interactivity and multimodality.

Table 3.9 presents the writer average *feedback decoding error rates* (FER) for the different corpora considered and three language models which embody increasingly strong interaction-derived constraints (see Sect. 3.4.1). The first one corresponds to a plain *uni*-gram estimate of $P(d)$, already reported in "Baseline On-line HTR Results" in Sect. 3.6.2 as a *baseline*. The second corresponds to an error-conditioned *uni*-gram estimate of $P(d \mid v)$ (Eq. (3.14)). The third model is a prefix-and-error-conditioned *bi*-gram estimate of $P(d \mid p', v)$ (Eq. (3.15)). These models are derived from the original language models employed for the main, off-line HTR system, as explained in Sect. 3.4.1. As observed in Table 3.9, feedback decoding accuracy increases significantly as more interaction-derived constraints are taken into account.

As a final overview, Table 3.10 summarizes all the CATTI and MM-CATTI results obtained in this chapter. The forth and fifth columns show respectively the

Table 3.10 From left-to-right: post-editing corrections (WER), interactive corrections needed (WSR), e-pen *feedback decoding error rate* for baseline case (FER_{BL}) and multimodal decoding (FER_{MM}), overall multimodal interactive corrections (WSR_{MM}), and overall estimated effort reduction (EFR) achieved by the proposed approaches. All results are percentages

Corpus	Post-edit	CATTI	MM-CATTI			Overall EFR	
	WER	WSR	FER_{BL}	FER_{MM}	WSR_{MM}	CATTI	MM-CATTI
ODEC-M3	22.9	18.9	5.1	3.1	19.5	17.5	14.8
IAMDB	25.3	21.1	4.6	3.5	21.8	16.6	13.8
CS	28.5	26.9	6.4	5.8	28.4	5.6	0.4

e-pen FER baseline (BL) and FER multimodal decoding (MM), while the sixth column reports the total MM-CATTI WSR achieved. These figures correspond to the three-writers averaged decoding errors reported in Table 3.9. The last two columns show the overall estimated effort reductions (EFR) in both the conventional CATTI and MM-CATTI approaches.

The MM-CATTI EFR is calculated under the simplifying (but reasonable) assumption that the cost of keyboard-correcting a feedback on-line decoding error is similar to that of another on-line touchscreen interaction step.[6] That is, each correction using keyboard is counted twice: one for the failed touch-screen attempt and another for the keyboard correction itself. According to these results, the expected user effort for the more ergonomic and user-preferred touch-screen-based MM-CATTI is only moderately higher than that of CATTI in the ODEC-M3 and on the IAMDB corpora. On the CS corpora the results shown that the expected user effort is very similar to the expected effort on a post-editing system. However, this extra human effort entails an human-machine interaction more easier and comfortable.

3.7 Conclusions

In this chapter, the approaches CATTI, PA-CATTI and MM-CATTI presented in Sects. 3.1, 3.3 and 3.4 have been tested in three different tasks: ODEC, IAMDB and CS. These tasks involve the transcription of handwritten answers from survey forms, handwritten full English sentences of different categories (editorial, religion, fiction, love, humor, ...) and an ancient handwritten document from 1853, respectively.

At deeper depths it has been proposed a new interactive, on-line framework, which combines the efficiency of automatic HTR system with the accuracy of the user in the transcription of handwritten documents. We have called this approach

[6]This is most probably a pessimistic assumption since, in this application, interaction through touch-screen is clearly more ergonomic than through keyboard. Moreover, in practice, it seems often preferable to try again a failed touch-screen correction, rather than typing a definitive fix on the keyboard.

"Computer Assisted Transcription of Text Images" (CATTI). Here, the words corrected by user become part of increasingly longer prefixes of the final target transcription. These prefixes are used by the CATTI system to suggest new suffixes that user can iteratively accept or modify until a satisfactory, correct target transcription is finally produced. The experimental results obtained in the three above-mentioned tasks are encouraging and show that the CATTI approach speed up the human error-correction process.

Moreover, two different search-decoding implementations have been tested. The first one is based directly on the Viterbi algorithm, whereas the second one on word-graph techniques. From the obtained results, it can be concluded that, although the results obtained using the Viterbi-based approach are better than those using word-graph, the last one is preferable because the accuracy loss is not too high and the computational cost is much lower. In fact, this last issue allows the human transcriber to interact with the system in real time.

In order to foster the usability and ergonomics of CATTI, a new interaction way was proposed by considering what we called "Pointer Action" (PA-CATTI). This consists in that the system takes advantage of the positioning made by the user prior to correct the following word error, by proposing quickly (from that position) a new, hopefully more correct prediction. Therefore, PA-based user-feedback goes some way to anticipating upcoming user corrections. Implementation of PA-CATTI was carried out also on the base of word-graphs, which are the best solution to the fast-reaction-time required by PA-CATTI to have an acceptable usability. From experimental results it can be seen that this new kind of user-feedback can produce significant benefits, in terms of word stroke reductions, and this is specially noticeable for single-PA interaction scenario where the new prediction is obtained practically without extra human effort.

We have also studied the use of on-line touch-screen handwritten pen strokes as a complementary means to input the required CATTI correction feedback. We have called this multimodal approach "MM-CATTI". From the results, we observe that the use of this more ergonomic feedback modality comes at the cost of only a reasonably small number of additional interaction steps needed to correct the few feedback decoding errors. The number of these extra steps is kept very small thanks to the MM-CATTI ability to use interaction-derived constraints to considerably improve the on-line HTR feedback decoding accuracy. Clearly, this would have not been possible if just a conventional, off-the-shelf on-line HTR decoder were trivially used for the correction steps.

The advantage of CATTI, PA-CATTI and MM-CATTI over traditional HTR followed by post-editing goes beyond the good estimates of human effort reductions achieved. When difficult transcription tasks with high WER are considered, expert users generally refuse to post-edit conventional HTR output. In contrast, the proposed interactive approaches constitute a much more natural way of producing correct text. With an adequate user interface, CATTI, PA-CATTI or MM-CATTI let the users be dynamically in command: if predictions are not good enough, then the user simply keeps typing at his/her own pace; otherwise, he/she can accept (partial) predictions and thereby save both thinking and typing effort.

It should be mentioned here that, in addition to the laboratory experiments reported in previous section, a complete CATTI prototype (which includes PA and multimodality) has been implemented (see Sect. 12.2) and already submitted to preliminary, informal tests with real users. According to these tests, the system does meet the expectations derived from the laboratory experiments; both in terms of usability and performance. This is particularly true for the on-line HTR feedback decoding accuracy: even though the on-line HTR HMMs were trained from artificially built words using UNIPEN character samples, the accuracy in real operation with real users is observed to be similar to that shown in the laboratory results here reported. Of course even higher accuracy can be easily achieved by retraining the models with the text handwritten by the actual users.

References

1. Amengual, J. C., & Vidal, E. (1998). Efficient error-correcting Viterbi parsing. *IEEE Transactions on Pattern Analysis and Machine Intelligence*, *20*(10), 1109–1116.
2. Bazzi, I., Schwartz, R., & Makhoul, J. (1999). An omnifont open-vocabulary OCR system for English and Arabic. *IEEE Transactions on Pattern Analysis and Machine Intelligence*, *21*(6), 495–504.
3. Brakensiek, A., Rottland, J., Kosmala, A., & Rigoll, G. (2000). Off-line handwriting recognition using various hybrid modeling techniques and character n-grams. In *Proceedings of the international workshop on frontiers in handwriting recognition (IWFHR'00)* (pp. 343–352), Amsterdam, The Netherlands.
4. Chelba, C., & Jelinek, F. (1999). Recognition performance of a structured language model. In *Proceedings of European conference on speech communication and technology (Eurospeech)* (Vol. 4, pp. 1567–1570).
5. Chen, C. H. (Ed.) (2003). *Frontiers of remote sensing information processing*. Singapore: World Scientific.
6. Drira, F. (2006). Towards restoring historic documents degraded over time. In *Proceedings of the international conference on document image analysis for libraries (DIAL'06)* (pp. 350–357), Washington, DC, USA. Los Alamitos: IEEE Computer Society.
7. Guyon, I., Schomaker, L., Plamondon, R., Liberman, M., & Janet, S. (1994). UNIPEN project of on-line data exchange and recognizer benchmarks. In *Proceedings of the international conference on pattern recognition (ICPR'94)* (pp. 29–33), Jerusalem, Israel.
8. Huang, B. Q., Zhang, Y. B., & Kechadi, M. T. (2007). Preprocessing techniques for online handwriting recognition. In *Proceedings of the international conference on intelligent systems design and applications (ISDA'07)* (pp. 793–800), Washington, DC, USA. Los Alamitos: IEEE Computer Society.
9. Jaeger, S., Manke, S., Reichert, J., & Waibel, A. (2001). On-line handwriting recognition: the NPen++ recognizer. *International Journal on Document Analysis and Recognition*, *3*(3), 169–181.
10. Jelinek, F. (1998). *Statistical methods for speech recognition*. Cambridge: MIT Press.
11. Johansson, S., Atwell, E., Garside, R., & Leech, G. (1996). *The tagged LOB corpus, user's manual*. Norwegian Computing Center for the Humanities, Bergen, Norway.
12. Lowerre, B. T. (1976). *The harpy speech recognition system*. Ph.D. thesis, Carnegie Mellon University, Pittsburgh, PA, USA.
13. Marti, U.-V., & Bunke, H. (1999). A full English sentence database for off-line handwriting recognition. In *Proceedings of the international conference on document analysis and recognition (ICDAR'99)* (pp. 705–708), Washington, DC, USA. Los Alamitos: IEEE Computer Society.

14. Marti, U.-V., & Bunke, H. (2001). Using a statistical language model to improve the preformance of an HMM-based cursive handwriting recognition system. *International Journal of Pattern Recognition and Artificial Intelligence*, *15*(1), 65–90.
15. Marti, U.-V., & Bunke, H. (2002). The IAM-database: an English sentence database for off-line handwriting recognition. *International Journal on Document Analysis and Recognition*, *5*(1), 39–46.
16. Ogawa, A., Takeda, K., & Itakura, F. (1998). Balancing acoustic and linguistic probabilities. In *Proceedings of the IEEE conference acoustics, speech and signal processing (ICASSP'98)* (Vol. 1, pp. 181–184), Seattle, WA, USA.
17. O'Gorman, L., & Kasturi, R. (Eds.) (1995). *Document image analysis*. Los Alamitos: IEEE Computer Society.
18. Parizeau, M., Lemieux, A., & Gagné, C. (2001). Character recognition experiments using UNIPEN data. In *Proceedings of the international conference on document analysis and recognition (ICDAR'01)* (pp. 481–485).
19. Pastor, M., Toselli, A. H., & Vidal, E. (2004). Projection profile based algorithm for slant removal. In *Lecture notes in computer science: Vol. 3212. Proceedings of the international conference on image analysis and recognition (ICIAR'04)* (pp. 183–190), Porto, Portugal. Berlin: Springer.
20. Pastor, M., Toselli, A. H., & Vidal, E. (2005). Writing speed normalization for on-line handwritten text recognition. In *Proceedings of the international conference on document analysis and recognition (ICDAR'05)* (pp. 1131–1135), Seoul, Korea.
21. Plamondon, R., & Srihari, S. N. (2000). On-line and off-line handwriting recognition: a comprehensive survey. *IEEE Transactions on Pattern Analysis and Machine Intelligence*, *22*(1), 63–84.
22. Ratzlaff, E. H. (2003). Methods, report and survey for the comparison of diverse isolated character recognition results on the UNIPEN database. In *Proceedings of the international conference on document analysis and recognition (ICDAR'03)* (Vol. 1, pp. 623–628), Edinburgh, Scotland.
23. Romero, V., Pastor, M., Toselli, A. H., & Vidal, E. (2006). Criteria for handwritten off-line text size normalization. In *Proceedings of the IASTED international conference on visualization, imaging, and image processing (VIIP'06)*, Palma de Mallorca, Spain.
24. Romero, V., Toselli, A. H., Rodríguez, L., & Vidal, E. (2007). Computer assisted transcription for ancient text images. In *Lecture notes in computer science: Vol. 4633. Proceedings of the international conference on image analysis and recognition (ICIAR'07)* (pp. 1182–1193). Berlin: Springer.
25. Toselli, A., Juan, A., & Vidal, E. (2004). Spontaneous handwriting recognition and classification. In *Proceedings of the international conference on pattern recognition (ICPR'04)* (pp. 433–436), Cambridge, UK.
26. Toselli, A. H., Juan, A., Keysers, D., González, J., Salvador, I., Ney, H., Vidal, E. & Casacuberta, F. (2004). Integrated handwriting recognition and interpretation using finite-state models. *International Journal of Pattern Recognition and Artificial Intelligence*, *18*(4), 519–539.
27. Toselli, A. H., Pastor, M., & Vidal, E. (2007). On-line handwriting recognition system for Tamil handwritten characters. In *Lecture notes in computer science: Vol. 4477. Proceedings of the Iberian conference on pattern recognition and image analysis (IbPRIA'07)* (pp. 370–377), Girona, Spain. Berlin: Springer.
28. Toselli, A. H., Romero, V., Rodríguez, L., & Vidal, E. (2007). Computer assisted transcription of handwritten text. In *Proceedings of the international conference on document analysis and recognition (ICDAR'07)* (pp. 944–948), Curitiba, Paraná, Brazil. Los Alamitos: IEEE Computer Society.
29. Toselli, A. H., Romero, V., & Vidal, E. (2008). Computer assisted transcription of text images and multimodal interaction. In *Lecture notes in computer science: Vol. 5237. Proceedings of the joint workshop on multimodal interaction and related machine learning algorithms* (pp. 296–308), Utrecht, The Netherlands.
30. Toselli, A. H., Romero, V., Pastor, M., & Vidal, E. (2009). Multimodal interactive transcription of text images. *Pattern Recognition*, *43*(5), 1814–1825.

31. Vuori, V., Laaksonen, J., Oja, E., & Kangas, J. (2001). Speeding up on-line recognition of handwritten characters by pruning the prototype set. In *Proceedings of the international conference on document analysis and recognition (ICDAR'01)* (pp. 0501–0507), Seattle, Washington.
32. Young, S., Odell, J., Ollason, D., Valtchev, V., & Woodland, P. (1997). *The HTK book: hidden Markov models toolkit V2.1*. Cambridge Research Laboratory Ltd.
33. Zimmermann, M., Chappelier, J.-C., & Bunke, H. (2006). Off-line grammar-based recognition of handwritten sentences. *IEEE Transactions on Pattern Analysis and Machine Intelligence*, *28*(5), 818–821.

Chapter 4
Computer Assisted Transcription of Speech Signals

With Contribution Of: Luis Rodríguez.

Contents

Automatic Speech Recognition has been widely employed in the last years. However, when a perfect transcription of the input is required, it is still necessary to rely on a human operator that supervises and corrects the mistakes that recognition systems usually make. Although the use of automatic systems can speed up the transcription process significantly, the intervention of these human supervisors can slow down this job considerably. Owing to this fact, the application of the *Interactive Pattern Recognition* approach to this task turns out to be a good opportunity to improve the cooperation between the computer and the human when an error-free transcribed document is needed.

In this chapter, an interactive multimodal approach for efficient transcriptions of speech signal is presented. This approach, rather than full automation, aims at assisting the expert in the proper transcription process. In this sense, an interactive scenario is proposed and it is based on a cooperative process between an automatic recognition system and a human transcriber to generate the final transcription of the speech signal. It will be shown how user's feedback directly allows one to improve

A.H. Toselli et al., *Multimodal Interactive Pattern Recognition and Applications*,
DOI 10.1007/978-0-85729-479-1_4,

the system accuracy, while multimodality increases system ergonomics and user acceptability.

4.1 Computer Assisted Transcription of Audio Streams

Speech recognition is a good candidate to apply the approach described in Chap. 2 since *Automatic Speech Recognition* (ASR) systems are far from being perfect. Complex tasks with large vocabularies, noisy environments, spontaneous speech, etc. result in a significant number of errors in transcriptions. When high quality transcriptions are needed, a human transcriber is required to verify and correct the (imperfect) system's transcriptions.

This process is usually performed *off-line*. First, the system returns a full transcription of the input audio signal. Next, the human transcriber reads it sequentially (while listening to the original audio signal) and corrects the possible mistakes made. This solution is rather uncomfortable and inefficient for the human corrector.

As in the case of the CATTI application described in Chap. 3, an interactive *on-line* scenario can allow for a more efficient approach. Again, the ASR and the human transcriber cooperate to generate the final transcription of the input signal. The rationale behind this approximation is to combine the accuracy provided by the human transcriber with the efficiency of the ASR. This approach is called "Computer Assisted Transcription of Speech" (CATS).

4.2 Foundations of CATS

This section overviews our approach to CATS. The process is quite similar to what was described for CATTI. As illustrated in Fig. 4.1, the process starts when the ASR system proposes a full *transcription* $\hat{s}$ (or a set with N-best transcriptions) of a suitable segment of the *input signal* x. Then, the human transcriber (named *user* from now on) reads this transcription until he or she finds a mistake; i.e., he or she validates a prefix p' of the transcription which is error-free. Now, the user can enter a word (or words), κ, to *correct* the erroneous text that follows the validated prefix. This action produces a new *prefix* p (the previously validated prefix, p', followed by κ). Then, the ASR system takes into account the new prefix to suggest a suitable continuation (or a set of best possible continuations) to this prefix (i.e., a new $\hat{s}$), thereby starting a new cycle. This process is repeated until a correct, full transcription T of x is accepted by the user. A key point on this interactive process is that, at each user-system iteration, the system can take advantage of the prefix validated so far to attempt an improved prediction.

	(x)	
ITER-0	(p)	( )
ITER-1	$(\hat{s})$	*(Nine extra soul are planned half beam discovered these years)*
	$(\hat{s_p})$	**(Nine)**
	(c)	(extrasolar)
	(p)	(Nine extrasolar)
ITER-2	$(\hat{s})$	*(planets have been discovered these years)*
	$(\hat{s_p})$	**(planets have been discovered)**
	(c)	(this)
	(p)	(Nine extrasolar planets have been discovered this)
FINAL	$(\hat{s})$	*(year)*
	(c)	(#)
	$(p \equiv \mathbf{t})$	**(Nine extrasolar planets have been discovered this year)**

Fig. 4.1 Example of CATS. See the text for details

4.3 Introduction to Automatic Speech Recognition

An automatic speech recognition (ASR) system takes an input audio signal and decodes this signal producing a text transcription of the words uttered. We will start by describing all the stages needed to achieve this goal.

4.3.1 Speech Acquisition

The human voice generates a series of variations in the air pressure that are transmitted through the air. These pressure changes can be captured by using a special type of transducer (microphone). As a result, this transducer produces an analog electric signal suitable to be stored and processed. However, analog processing presents important drawbacks (noise, need of specific hardware, etc.). Computers, on the other hand, are digital systems unable to directly deal with analog inputs. Hence, this signal is converted into the digital domain. In this process, the analog input is periodically sampled and a set of discrete samples is produced as a result. The sampling frequency (that is, the number of samples taken per second) is crucial to ensure an accurate codification of the original signal. According to the Nyquist–Shannon theorem [8] the sampling frequency must be, at least, two times the maximum frequency in the signal. Otherwise, it is not possible to obtain a perfect representation. The maximum frequencies present in a speech signal are around 8 KHz and, therefore, a sampling frequency of 16 KHz is typically used.

4.3.2 Pre-process and Feature Extraction

Once the signal is in the digital domain, the relevant information for speech recognition has to be extracted. Different representations have been proposed for speech signals. One of the most widely employed in ASR is based on the use of the so-called *Mel Frequency Cepstrum Coefficients* (MFCCs). These coefficients are obtained as follows. Initially, the signal is split into a sequence of overlapped fragments ("windows" or "frames") where each fragment of signal can be considered a stationary process (each window typically has a size between 10 and 20 milliseconds). The spectrum of every window is then computed and frequencies are grouped into a (non-linear) series of bands (collectively known as filter bank) according to the Mel scale, which is, approximately, linear below 1 KHz and logarithmic above. This way, each speech window (frame) is represented as a vector storing the average of the energy of the frame after passing through the corresponding filter (usually from 20 to 40 filters are employed). Finally, the Discrete Cosine Transform (DCT) is applied to each output vector and the first DCT components (usually from 10 to 15) are chosen. The first and second time-derivative of each DCT vector are usually computed as well.

As a result of this process, the signal is represented as a sequence of feature vectors of dimension between 30 and 40. This signal representation will be used in a latter stage to produce the transcription of the original input signal.

4.3.3 Statistical Speech Recognition

Now that we have the input signal properly pre-processed and represented as a sequence x of feature vectors, we can discuss the recognition process itself. In statistical ASR, given an input signal x, we have to obtain the optimal sequence of uttered words w as was stated in Eq. (2.1):

$$\hat{w} = \arg\max_{w} P(x \mid w) \cdot P(w). \tag{4.1}$$

As was explained in Sect. 2.2, the first term $P(x \mid w)$ corresponds to an *acoustic word model*, which accounts for the distribution of word sounds present in the signal. Acoustic word models are seen as being composed of valid concatenations of phonetic sounds, which are modeled by Hidden Markov Models (HMMs), so far the most successful paradigm for stochastic modeling of phonetic units.

The second term $P(w)$ is called *language model* and deals with the distribution of the sentences in the language so that correct sentences in the language are (hopefully) scored with high probability and, consequently, incorrect sentences are scored with low probability. This can be estimated by a n-gram model (see Eq. (2.3)), where each word is conditioned by just the $n - 1$ previous words.

Once all the models are available, the transcription is obtained by constructing an integrated network, where each word in the language model is expanded as a set of HMMs. This network produces words according to the acoustic and language model probabilities. The *Viterbi* algorithm is applied to obtain the most likely path in the network, thereby solving the maximization stated in Eq. (2.1).

4.4 Search in CATS

As explained in Sect. 2.5.1, the optimal solution for the searching problem given by Eq. (2.6) can be approached by using the *Viterbi* algorithm over the corresponding finite-state network restricted by an special language model (Eq. (2.6)) built by the concatenation of a *linear* model (which accounts for the words of the prefix p) and a conventional n-gram model (which models all the possible words of the suffix s).

Nevertheless, this *direct* approach can lead to a slow system response, since the computational cost entailed by a complete speech recognition search is usually high.

4.5 Word-Graph-Based CATS

CATS is an interactive application and, as such, some specific requirements have to be fulfilled. For instance, no matter how precise the ASR can be if the time needed to obtain a hypothesis is too high. In the most extreme case, if the prediction system is as slow as the user performing the task manually, CATS does not make any sense. To summarize, we can claim that, in order for the user to feel comfortable with the system, we have to ensure an appropriate time response. Although some experiments in this sense will be described later, we can say, for the time being, that the *direct* implementation presents a response time higher than 3 *seconds* in some tasks. In consequence, we need to explore an alternative CATS implementation.

In speech decoding, there are many computations to be performed for each frame of the input signal. The acoustic score, for instance, requires to calculate the probability of a Gaussian mixture for each state in all the actives HMMs. We could save a lot computation effort if we were able to obtain, for each input to be transcribed, a representation that stores a sufficient number of decoding hypotheses along with their scores. This way, all the interactive CATS search would be performed on this model, achieving a better time response.

The previous discussion suggests the use of a well known ASR data structure, a word graph (WG). Formally defined in Sect. 1.5.1, a WG is, indeed, a compact way to represent a very large set of n-best hypotheses along with additional information about how they were produced.

WGs can be constructed as a byproduct of the speech decoding process by storing the best acoustic and language model probabilities for each partial hypothesis. Then all the paths starting from initial states and reaching final states are added to the graph [7, 9].

Once the WG is available for a specific input, it can be used to perform the search described in Eq. (2.6). Now, we will study how to address this search. Basically, the idea consists in, when a new user prefix is available, parsing this prefix over the word graph. This is aimed at obtaining a set of nodes that approximates the best signal segmentation (the first two terms in Eq. (2.6)). Moreover, the prefix-based language model probability in Eq. (2.6) can be easily computed from the arcs leaving these nodes. Once this set of nodes is available, we can produce a CATS hypothesis (suffix) by searching for the best (or the n-best) path starting from these nodes. In the upcoming sections, different details of this process are discussed.

4.5.1 Error Correcting Prefix Parsing

In our case, we have a directed acyclic graph and have to find the best path *compatible* with the prefix. Ideally, this graph would contain all the possible recognition outcomes for the input signal but, unfortunately, this is not actually true in practice.

Firstly, the stochastic model that conducts the WG generation has been trained from a finite set of samples (although smoothed models can be used, there is still the problem of out-of-vocabulary words). Secondly, a pruning search is usually applied because of computer memory constraints. As a result of this, we cannot expect the WG to account for every possible user prefix. For that reason, a more sophisticated approach has to be adopted. This is the case of the *Error Correcting Parsing* (ECP) described as follows. To start with, we can define an error model to address the problem of generating a string $y = y_1, \dots, y_n$ from another string $z = z_1, \dots, z_m$. This generation is based on a well defined set of operations:

- Substitution: Consists in replacing a symbol y_i in the source string with a symbol z_j in the target string (denoted as $y_i \to z_j$).
- Deletion: Consists in removing a symbol y_i in the source string (denoted as $y_i \to \lambda$).
- Insertion: Consists in inserting a symbol z_j in the target string (denoted as $\lambda \to z_j$).

Each operation has an associated cost. This cost is usually chosen according to the specific task to be solved. The overall cost of generating one string from another is computed by summing up all the editing costs involved in transforming the source string into the target one. For a given sequence of editing operations $\epsilon = \epsilon_1, \dots, \epsilon_L$ the total cost of ϵ is then defined as

$$\mathcal{C}(\epsilon) = \sum_{l=1}^{L} c(\epsilon_l), \tag{4.2}$$

where $c(\epsilon_l)$ denotes the cost of the editing operation ϵ_l. It is easy to see that a specific target string can be generated from a given source in very different ways. Generally, we are only interested in the sequence of minimum cost. This *optimal* sequence is known as the (weighted) *Levenshtein* distance [11]:

$$d(y, z) = \min_{\epsilon}\{\mathcal{C}(\epsilon) \mid y \xrightarrow{\epsilon} z\}, \tag{4.3}$$

where $y \stackrel{\epsilon}{\rightarrow} z$ denotes a sequence of edition operations to reach z from y. To compute the *Levenshtein* distance in a polynomial time, the following dynamic programming algorithm can be followed (notice that i and j denote positions in the source and the target sentence respectively). Given two strings y and z, $d(y, z)$ is computed as

- Recursive general term:

$$\begin{aligned} d(i, j) = \min\{&d(i-1, j-1) + c(y_i \rightarrow z_j), \\ &d(i-1, j) + c(y_i \rightarrow \lambda),\ d(i, j-1) + c(\lambda \rightarrow z_j)\}. \end{aligned}$$

- Base case:

$$\begin{aligned} & d(0,0) = 0, \\ \forall i \quad & d(i,0) = d(i-1,0) + c(y_i \rightarrow \lambda), \\ \forall j \quad & d(0,j) = d(0,j-1) + c(\lambda \rightarrow z_j). \end{aligned}$$

In CATS we have a string (prefix) and a representation of many strings along with their probabilities (word graph) and we have to parse the prefix over this graph. This problem is similar to the problem of finding the minimum distance between a regular language and a given string [1].

This algorithm returns the *Levenshtein* distance along with the graph nodes ("non-terminals") reached after parsing the input string. The search for the best suffix can then be performed by applying a *Viterbi*-like search from these nodes.

4.5.2 A General Model for Probabilistic Prefix Parsing

So far, we have a tool (Error Correcting Parsing) that allows us to perform a CATS search within WGs. However, there are some issues to be discussed before going on with this approach. On the one hand, it is not clear how to relate the ECP procedure to Eq. (2.4). On the other, as a result of the ECP, we have a set of states with an associated cost (the ECP cost) and probability (the probability given by the path(s) in the word graph that reaches the state). The question is how to combine these two terms to carry out the search for the suffix as Eq. (2.4) shows.

To overcome this problem, a new formulation can be attempted in order to properly include ECP into WG CATS approximation. Starting from Eq. (2.4), we can introduce a hidden variable q_b to represent a possible boundary node between the prefix and the suffix in the WG:

$$\begin{aligned} \hat{s} &= \arg\max_s P(s \mid p) \cdot P(x \mid p, s) \\ &= \arg\max_s P(s \mid p) \cdot \sum_{q_b \in Q} P(x, q_b \mid p, s) \end{aligned}$$

$$= \arg\max_{s} P(s \mid p) \cdot \sum_{q_b \in Q} P(x \mid q_b, p, s) \cdot P(q_b \mid p, s). \tag{4.4}$$

Notice that in Eq. (2.5) the boundary point b was defined on the input signal. Here that point has to be approximated according to the nodes in the word graphs (which are tied to a specific frame in the input signal). We can make the assumption that $P(x \mid q_b, p, s)$ does not depend of p given q_b to rewrite Eq. (2.4) as

$$\hat{s} = \arg\max_{s} P(s \mid p) \cdot \sum_{q_b \in Q} P(x \mid q_b, s) \cdot P(q_b \mid p, s).$$

Additionally, we can assume that q_b only depends on the prefix (this issue will be discussed later), leading to

$$\hat{s} = \arg\max_{s} P(s \mid p) \cdot \sum_{q_b \in Q} P(x \mid q_b, s) \cdot P(q_b \mid p).$$

Finally, the usual approximation of the sum by the dominating term can be adopted to obtain

$$\hat{s} \approx \arg\max_{s} P(s \mid p) \cdot \max_{q_b \in Q} P(x \mid q_b, s) \cdot P(q_b \mid p),$$

where the first term corresponds the already known prefix-conditioned language model, the second one to the probability given by the acoustic word HMMs, and the last one, $P(q_b \mid p)$, to the computed probability-like ECP cost. In other words, $P(q_b \mid p)$ is the probability with which p can be distorted to produce the best prefix reaching the WG node q_b; that is:

$$P(q_b \mid p) = \max_{\tilde{p} \in \mathcal{P}(q_b)} P(\tilde{p} \mid p),$$

where $\mathcal{P}(q_b)$ is the set of prefixes reaching q_b and $P(\tilde{p} \mid p)$ is the maximum probability of edition p into $\tilde{p}$. Assuming editing operations independently applied, the edition probability is computed as the product of the probability of elementary insertion, deletion and substitution probabilities. Therefore, we need to define the editing operations in a probabilistic way. This can easily be done by constructing an stochastic automaton representing the string to be parsed (in our case, the prefix) so that the different editing operations can be modeled as in Sect. 3.2.2, as groups of arcs in the automaton (see Fig. 3.2).

In the ECP cost-based approach, all the operations are usually defined to have a similar cost except the substitution of a symbol by itself which is usually a no-cost operation. Directly translating these costs into probabilities is not trivial at all. Intuitively, the case of the no-cost could be mapped to a probability of one, since the substitution of a symbol by itself does not entail a real transformation of the string. However, this would imply to use a *null* score for the remaining set of operations. Alternatively, some uncertainty can be assigned to this *special* operation and, this way, some probability mass is available to be distributed among the other ones.

To start with, we can consider any editing operation equivalent. To this end, we can group the probability so that any insertion, deletion and real substitution are equally likely. This actually means that all the arcs in the ECP automaton should be labeled with the same probability. Those arcs not involving a real transformation of the string, however, will have a different treatment in which much higher probability should be considered for them. By assigning, for instance, half of the overall probability mass to these arcs and equally distributing the other half among the other operations, we can reach the following expressions:

$$P(\epsilon_{p_i \tilde{p}_j}) = P(p_i \to \tilde{p}_j) = \begin{cases} \frac{1}{2}, & p_i = \tilde{p}_j, \\ \frac{1}{4|V|}, & p_i \neq \tilde{p}_j, \\ \frac{1}{4|V|}, & p_i = \lambda, \\ \frac{1}{4|V|}, & \tilde{p}_j = \lambda, \end{cases} \tag{4.5}$$

where V represents the vocabulary. Here, the score of each editing operation is set so that each arc in the ECP automaton has the same probability (except those arcs that do not transform the input string). Notice that in the case of substitutions and insertions, the probability mass is grouped for all the symbols in the vocabulary (the amount of probability assigned to these groups of arcs would be $\frac{|V|-1}{4|V|}$ and $\frac{|V|}{4|V|}$ for substitutions and insertions respectively). For that reason, a specific insertion of substitution will be scored with the same probability as a deletion.

Now, we can define $\epsilon_{pq} = \epsilon_{pq_1}, \ldots, \epsilon_{pq_L}, q_L = q$, as a sequence of L editing operations that allows to reach the node q given the current prefix p. Assuming independence among these operations, we can compute this sequence probability as

$$P(\epsilon_{pq}) = \max_{\tilde{p} \in \mathcal{P}(q)} \prod_{l=1}^{L} P(\epsilon_{p\tilde{p}}), \tag{4.6}$$

where $P(\epsilon_{pq})$ is the maximum probability of transforming p into $\tilde{p}$, according to the elementary edition probabilities of Eq. (4.5).

From this, we can easily define the optimal sequence $\hat{\epsilon}_{pq}$ as

$$\hat{\epsilon}_{pq} = \arg\max_{\epsilon_{pq}} P(\epsilon_{pq}) \tag{4.7}$$

to finally compute the probability $P(q_b \mid p)$ as

$$P(q_b \mid p) = \frac{P(\hat{\epsilon}_{pq_b})}{\sum_{q \in Q} P(\hat{\epsilon}_{pq})}, \tag{4.8}$$

where Q is the set of all nodes in the WG.

4.6 Experimental Results

In the following sections, our CATS experimental framework is described in detail.

Table 4.1 Features of the EuTrans, Xerox and WSJ test corpora

	EuTrans	Xerox	WSJ 5k	WSJ 20k
Test sentences	336	875	330	333
Running words	3 340	8 569	5 683	5 974
Test-set perplexity (3-grams)	7	41	60	155

Table 4.2 Features of the Spanish Albayzin and English WSJ acoustic training corpus (K = ×1 000)

	Spanish Albayzin	English WSJ
Speakers	164	45
Running words	42K	136K

Table 4.3 Features of the EuTrans, Xerox and WSJ LM-training corpora

	EuTrans	Xerox	WSJ 5k	WSJ 20k
Training sentences	10k	55k	1 612k	1 612k
Running words	97k	627 581	38 500k	38 500k
Vocabulary size	684	10 835	4 989	19 982

4.6.1 Corpora

Two different tasks have been mainly used. The first one corresponds to the EuTrans corpus [2], composed of sentences used in conversations between a tourist and a hotel receptionist. The second one is the Xerox corpus [5], consisting of spoken utterances from printer manuals. The initial version of this corpus consisted of fragment sentence utterances aimed at testing a speech interface proposal for Computer Assisted Translation (CAT) systems. It was later extended to be employed in CATS. The main features of both corpora are presented in Table 4.1. In addition, the well known *Wall Street Journal* (WSJ) corpus [10] was used in the word graph CATS experiments.

Regarding the training corpora, the acoustic models, on the one hand, were estimated from the Albazyin and WSJ corpora, as shown in Table 4.2. In the EuTrans and Xerox experiments, monophone HMMs (obtained with the HTK toolkit [14]) were employed. For WSJ, triphones were used. Speech pre-processing and feature extraction consisted in speech boundary detection, followed by the computation of the first ten MEL cepstral coefficients plus the energy, along with the corresponding first and second derivatives [6].

On the other hand, the language models for both tasks were estimated from the corpora described in Table 4.3. The SRILM toolkit [12] was used to estimate Kneser–Ney smoothed 3-grams [3].

4.6.2 Error Measures

The metrics used in the experiments tries to gives an estimation of the user effort required to transcribe a set of sentences through a CATS approach. As already introduced in Sect. 2.6, the well known *word error rate* (WER) and the *word stroke ratio* (WSR [4, 5]) measures have been adopted.

As explained, the WSR is computed by using reference transcriptions of the speech segments considered. After a first CATS hypothesis, the longest common prefix between this hypothesis and the reference sentence is obtained, and the first unmatching word from the hypothesis is replaced by the corresponding reference word. This process is iterated until a full match with the reference sentence is achieved. The WSR is, therefore, the number of required corrections divided by the overall number of reference words.

The comparison between WER and WSR would give us an idea about the amount of effort required by a CATS user with respect to the effort needed by using a classical speech recognition system followed by a manual post-editing process (see Sect. 2.6 for more details). Henceforth, we will refer to this as *Estimated effort reduction* (EFR).

4.6.3 Experiments

The experiments consisted in a series of block validation on the test corpora. Training is always carried out on the whole set of acoustic and text training data summarized in Tables 4.2 and 4.3. This way of proceeding slightly resembles the approach called K-fold cross validation but, in this case, one block (development) was chosen for optimizing some parameters of the search. Once these parameters have been set on the development block, the remaining blocks (test) were used as the proper test set. This framework is aimed at trying to draw more general conclusions on the sparse test data available. In the usually employed holdout method, one single partition of the original test data into development and test sets is considered. In our experiments, the original test was split into several blocks so that different development and test sets could be derived from these blocks. Specifically, five blocks, with sizes of 67 and 175 sentences, have been considered for EuTrans and Xerox, respectively. The experiments were actually carried out in five trials. In trial number i the block number i was used as development set and the four remaining blocks were used as test. Here we are trying to follow a realistic approach, where only a small development set is available during the system design. The real test for the system is bigger since it consists of all the transcriptions obtained during its normal operation mode. Notice that in K-fold cross validation only one block is used as test and the remaining ones are used for training.

On the other hand, WSJ 5k and WSJ 20k corpora have also been used to test the WG-based approximation, which constitutes the most feasible technique to actually use CATS in real environments.

Table 4.4 Results obtained on the EuTrans, Xerox and WSJ corpora. The mean and the standard deviation for the test sets in the five block validation series are shown. The first row corresponds to the post-editing approach. The second and the third rows show the results for the interactive baseline approach and the ECP word-graph-based approach described in Sect. 4.5.1 respectively. In the fourth row, the results correspond to the Probabilistic Word ECP (PWECP) discussed in Sect. 4.5.2. All results are percentages

		EuTrans		Xerox		WSJ 5k		WSJ 20k	
		mean	sd	mean	sd	mean	sd	mean	sd
Direct	WER	7.7	1.3	22.9	2.4	6.2	1.5	10.6	1.7
	WSR	4.7	1.4	18.6	2.1	–	–	–	–
Word graph	ECP WSR	4.8	1.4	19.5	2.1	5.9	1.3	9.9	1.6
	PWECP WSR	4.7	1.3	19.3	2.1	5.6	1.4	9.5	2.0

The development sets were specifically used to tune the *Language Model Scale Factor* which, as was mentioned, is basically a scaling factor for the second term in Eq. (4.1).

4.6.4 Results

In Table 4.4 the mean and the standard deviation of the results on the five test sets obtained as described in Sect. 4.6.3 are reported. In the first two rows, a comparison between two estimations of the off-line (WER) and interactive (WSR) user effort is shown. As can be observed, significant improvements are obtained when using the CATS approach with respect to the classical ASR followed by a human post-processing approach. In addition, the WSR results for the WG-based techniques are also presented (third and four rows).

As can be noticed, the use of the WGs does not affect the performance significantly, while improving the WER baseline. The results obtained by the initial ECP presented in Sect. 4.5.1 and the *probabilistic word* ECP (PWECP) described in Sect. 4.5.2 are quite similar. However, we have to take into consideration that the margin of improvement is actually constrained by the WSR results on the original CATS implementation. On the other hand, a significant number of sentences in both corpora require no interactions (see Fig. 4.2), which causes some improvements to have a small impact on the overall results. In order to clarify this a little more, the Xerox corpus has been split into different sets based on the cumulative distribution, shown in Fig. 4.2; that is, the first set contains all the sentences that require at least one interaction, the second one contains the sentences that require at least two interactions and so on.

Table 4.5 shows the WSR results for the baseline CATS approach, the initial ECP and the new PWECP based on this sentence distribution. Notice that for sentences with exactly one error, the post-editing approach should be similar to CATS in effort terms, since a properly designed user interface should permit to disable the

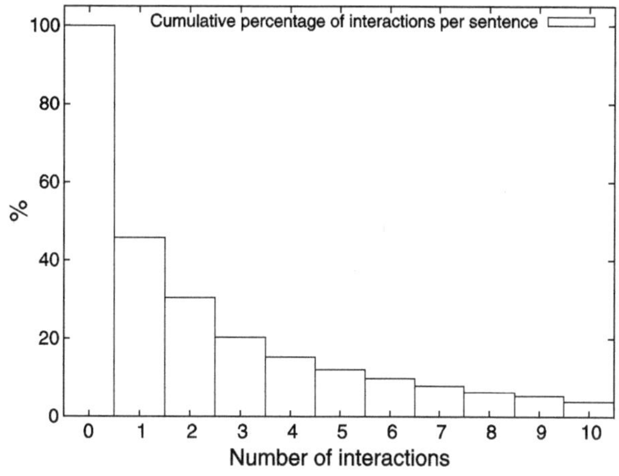

Fig. 4.2 Cumulative sentence distribution of the XEROX corpus, based on the number of user interactions needed to obtain a perfect transcription. The *first bar* shows the percentage of sentences that are perfectly transcribed with zero or more interactions (the whole corpus in this case), the *second bar* the percentage for one or more interactions and so on

Table 4.5 Results (WER and WSR) on the XEROX corpus for different CATS techniques based on the distribution of the sentences shown in Fig. 4.2. The baseline column shows the results obtained by the original CATS approach without using word graphs. All results are percentages

	WER	WSR		
		Baseline	ECP	PWECP
1 interaction or more	39.6	33.1	35.1	34.3
2 interactions or more	50.9	40.1	44.3	43.2
3 interactions or more	54.6	45.6	51.0	49.8

Table 4.6 Average interaction time response. The first row shows the time response of the baseline approach to CATS. The second row reports the interactive time response of the word-graph approximation. Finally, in the third row the average time needed to generate the WGs is shown. All the times are in seconds

Approach	EUTRANS	XEROX
Baseline CATS	0.9	3.3
Word-graph CATS	0.4	0.5
Including word-graph generation time	1.7	1.9

prediction engine when only one mistake is found (for sentences with more than one interaction an EFR of 22.4% is achieved, as is shown in Table 4.5).

The previous results show that the use of WGs is competitive in terms of WSR. However, it is still necessary to check whether this new approximation can actually improve or not the system time response. To this end, the CATS system latency was measured in the following way. First, experiments corresponding to the *direct* approach (in the first two rows of Table 4.4) were carried out, where, for each user interaction, a complete speech recognition process is conducted. Since an exhaustive search in speech recognition is usually prohibitive, a pruned search approach was

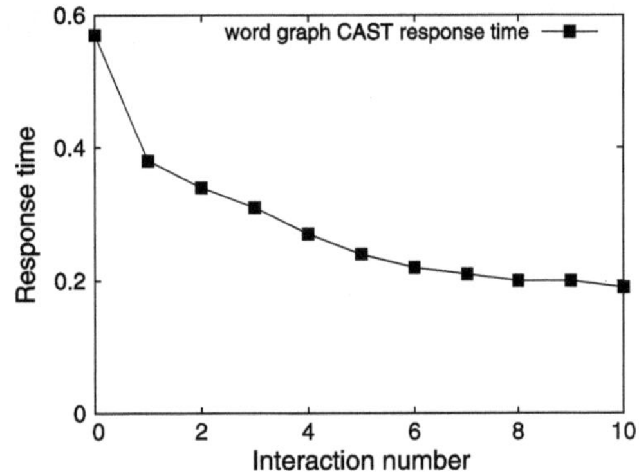

Fig. 4.3 Average word-graph CATS time response based on specific interaction number within a sentence

adopted in these experiments to achieve an appropriate tradeoff between accuracy and time response as shown in Tables 4.4 and 4.6.

In the case of the WG approaches, we have to take into account two different kinds of computations. Firstly, we have to generate the WG from the input signal. This process entails a standard speech decoding plus some additional work necessary to obtain the word graph. Nevertheless, it is reasonable to assume that we can generate the WGs "in advance" before starting a CATS session (or as a look-ahead background computation). This assumption is based on the fact that, in our case, speech transcription is carried out from recorded signals. Therefore, we can consider the construction of the WGs as a batch and separate process from the interactive transcription task itself. In any case, this WG generation time is included in the third row in Table 4.6 for informative purposes. In the case of the direct approach, it is not possible to perform any off-line work apart from the usual signal pre-processing and feature extraction. To summarize, the interactive WG time response is exclusively given by the cost of the search for the suffix on the WGs.

As expected, the WG approach notably outperforms the baseline. Especially, in the case of XEROX, where the baseline technique seems to be too slow to be even considered and the WG approach proves to be the best solution to implement CATS in a real environment. In addition, we can expect a diminishing time response when using WGs as the number of interactions grows for a sentence. Whereas the initial system hypothesis is actually a whole sentence prediction, the following predictions tend to be shorter as the prefix length increases. Since the computational cost of the prefix parsing is significantly lower than the search for the suffix, the time response goes down. To quantify this fact, Fig. 4.3 shows the average response (XEROX corpus) time based on the specific number of interaction performed; that is, the first point in the graph is for the initial system prediction, the second one for the prediction after one user interaction and so on. The cumulative distribution histogram shown in Fig. 4.2 for the XEROX may help to better understand the previous results.

In order to give a reference point for the different time results, we can mention that all the experiments were performed on a 3.2 GHz Intel Xeon CPU.

4.7 Multimodality in CATS

As was mentioned in Chap. 1, multimodality is a natural part of IPR systems. In the case of CATS, we have two different inputs: a speech signal to be transcribed and the user feedback. This user feedback is mainly aimed at selecting parts of the system suggestions as well as at introducing some corrections to these suggestions. This interaction can be performed by means of typical input interfaces (i.e., mouse and/or keyboard) but we can naturally introduce in CATS alternative interaction modalities, hopefully leading to a more friendly multimodal interface.

Speech is a very natural way for humans to communicate. In the case of human-computer interaction speech recognition-based feedback is really appreciated by the users if the decoding accuracy is high enough.

Speech feedback can be introduced into CATS as a completely "decoupled" process. This way, we can approach the problem of decoding the user feedback as a classical speech recognition problem, where we have the user feedback in the form of a speech signal x_f and we are interested in obtaining the sequence of words w_f in x as (notice that this is basically Eq. (4.1)):

$$\hat{w}_f = \arg\max_{w_f} P(w_f \mid x_f). \tag{4.9}$$

Clearly, it can be argued that this approach can be followed with any kind of application (the only difference is that in CATS a speech recognizer is already included as part of the application itself). On account of this, we could regard this problem as a mere implementation issue. However, in IPR, the user feedback is clearly embedded into the very interaction process. In our CATS application, the user feedback utterances are intended to correct part of the system suggestion to the input signal x to be transcribed. We can take advantage to this fact to rewrite Eq. (4.9) as

$$\hat{w}_f = \arg\max_{w_f} P(w_f \mid x_f, x). \tag{4.10}$$

Notice that we can consider this problem as a familiar "re-speaking" problem, where the user is actually re-speaking part of the input utterance. Nevertheless, in a CATS environment we can benefit from additional information as follows. Let w be the concatenation of p and s in the previous CATS iteration, which represents the whole transcription of the input signal currently returned by the CATS system; the user amendments will be based on this transcription. After decoding the user feedback, a new CATS iteration will be performed obtaining in a new transcription for the input speech signal x, according to

$$\hat{s} = \arg\max_{s} P(s \mid x, w, x_f). \tag{4.11}$$

The transcription of the user feedback speech w_f can be seen as a hidden variable, leading to

$$\hat{s} = \arg\max_{s} \sum_{w_f} P(s, w_f \mid x, w, x_f)$$

$$= \arg\max_{s} \sum_{w_f} P(x \mid s, w_f, w, x_f) \cdot P(x_f \mid s, w_f, w)$$
$$\cdot P(s \mid w_f, w) \cdot P(w_f \mid w). \tag{4.12}$$

By assuming that $P(x \mid s, w_f, w, x_f)$ does not depend on x_f given w_f, and that $P(x_f \mid s, w_f, w)$ does not depend on s and w given w_f, we reach the following expression:

$$\hat{s} = \arg\max_{s} \sum_{w_f} P(x \mid s, w_f, w) \cdot P(x_f \mid w_f) \cdot P(s \mid w_f, w) \cdot P(w_f \mid w). \tag{4.13}$$

Finally, adopting the usual approximation of the sum by the dominating term and rearranging the terms, we achieve the following expression:

$$(\hat{s}, \hat{w}_f) = \arg\max_{s, w_f} P(x_f \mid w_f) \cdot P(w_f \mid w) \cdot P(x \mid s, w_f, w) \cdot P(s \mid w_f, w) \tag{4.14}$$

which can be seen essentially as an instantiation of the problem already formulated in Eq. (1.27), where the w, x_f, s and w_f correspond with h', h, f and d, respectively.

At this point we can discuss what the terms in Eq. (4.14) represent. On the one hand, the first two terms are a classical speech recognition model for the user feedback utterance. The only difference is that the words decoded are somehow related to the CATS current hypothesis w. The other two terms are, basically, a CATS search, that is: the search for a suffix after the user amends the previous CATS hypothesis.

Now we are going to adopt a specific interaction scenario aimed at both clarifying how Eq. (4.14) can be implemented and allowing for an appropriate experimental framework. Let us suppose that, given the current CAT hypothesis, the user is going to select an error-free prefix in this utterance and, at the same time, to introduce a correction after this prefix by uttering exactly two words. The first uttered word will correspond to the last word in this error-free prefix and the second one is the word that should be after this prefix. As a result, we will have a new prefix p to start a new CATS iteration as is shown in Eq. (2.6). Now that a scenario for the user feedback has been defined, we can approach the implementation of Eq. (4.14). The first two terms can be seen, as was commented, as a classical speech recognition problem. The only difference is that the language model probability is conditioned by the current system suggestion w. Since this constraint comes from the fact that the first word in w_f has to be a word in w, we can simply consider a model where all the w_f hypotheses having a first word not appearing in w are scored with null probability.

Regarding the last two models, they correspond to a CATS search in which the prefix is constructed according to w and $\hat{w}_f$. This prefix can be instantiated by concatenating all the words in w that come before the first word in $\hat{w}_f$ with the second word in $\hat{w}_f$ (remember that, in this scenario, the first word in the user utterance is

Table 4.7 Features of the Xerox corpora

	Full	Fragments
Test utterances	875	775
Speakers	5	10
Running words	3 340	1 550

used to set the prefix and the second one is used to dictate a new word after this prefix).

The implementation of the whole model in Eq. (4.14) can be approached as follows. Firstly a list of n-best hypotheses is obtained according to first two terms in the formula. Then, each element in the n-best list is re-scored according to the last two terms. In order to perform this re-scoring, a prefix from each n-best hypothesis, obtained as explained in the previous paragraph, is completed according to the CATS search implementation.

Finally, it is worth mentioning that this speech interface is introduced into the system not to replace the classical interaction modalities (keyboard, mouse) but as a multimodal alternative.

4.8 Experimental Results

To assess the CATS multimodal approximation, different experiments were carried out. These experiments are intended, in the one hand, to test the accuracy of the CATS approach and, on the other, to assess the multimodal interface here proposed.

4.8.1 Corpora

In the experiments, the *Xerox* corpus [5], consisting of spoken utterances from printer manuals, was used. This corpus was originally designed to be used in interactive pattern recognition experiments. Specifically, the initial version of this corpus consisted of fragments of whole sentence utterances aimed at testing a speech interface proposal for Computer Assisted Translation (CAT) systems [13] and will be used here to test the CATS speech interface. This corpus was posteriorly extended by adding whole sentence utterances to be employed in CATS. The main features of both corpora are presented in Table 4.7.

Regarding the corpora used to train the CATS models, the acoustic models, on the one hand, were estimated from the corpus shown in Table 4.8. In all the experiments, monophone HMMs (obtained with the HTK toolkit [14]) were employed. Speech pre-processing and feature extraction consisted in speech boundary detection, followed by the computation the first ten MEL cepstral coefficients plus the energy, along with the corresponding first and second derivatives [6].

Table 4.8 Features of the acoustic training corpus (K= ×1 000)

Speakers	164
Running words (4 hours)	42K

Table 4.9 WER and SER results for the user speech interface. The numbers in the first column have been obtained by performing a completely separated ASR process. In the second column, the recognition is based on the constraints included in Eq. (4.14). All results are percentages

	Baseline	CATS ASR	Improvement
WER	7.3	5.0	31.0
SER	12.0	9.8	19.4

4.8.2 Experiments

For the speech feedback experiments, a real CATS session was simulated according to the corpus shown in the first column of Table 4.7 so that each user feedback speech utterance in the corpus shown in the second column of Table 4.7 corresponds to a user interacting in a real CATS session.

In Table 4.9, the WER and SER for the user feedback speech interface are reported. The first column corresponds to the baseline described in Eq. (4.9) while the second column shows the results for the coupled speech interface shown in Eq. (4.14). The average size of the n-best list employed is 496. We can see how the performance of the speech feedback interface can be significantly improved by taking advantage of the constraints provided by the CATS environment.

4.9 Conclusions

The CAST approach described in this chapter constitutes an alternative approximation to the subject of obtaining perfect speech transcriptions. In this new paradigm, an automatic speech recognition system is used within an interactive system that allows a human user to take advantage of the efficiency of this kind of automation. The key point here is that the user takes active part of the process, correcting the different transcription suggestions that the recognition system makes and allowing, on the other hand, the automatic system to take advantage of these user interactions.

The results reported show that the adoption of CAST can reduce the amount of effort that a human transcriber has to make in the case of correcting the outputs of an automatic speech recognition system. This is even more noticeable when comparing to a completely manual transcription process. However, real transcription sessions involving a CAST application and a real human transcriber should be conducted in order to draw more reliable conclusions about the real gain that could be reached by adopting this sort of interactive paradigm.

References

1. Amengual, J. C., & Vidal, E. (1998). Efficient error-correcting Viterbi parsing. *IEEE Transactions on Pattern Analysis and Machine Intelligence, PAMI-20*(10), 1109–1116.
2. Amengual, J. C., Benedí, J. M., Casacuberta, F., Castaño, A., Castellanos, A., Jiménez, V., Llorens, D., Marzal, A., Pastor, M., Prat, F., Vidal, E., & Vilar, J. M. (2000). The EuTrans-I speech translation system. *Machine Translation, 15*, 75–103.
3. Chen, S. F., & Goodman, J. (1996). *An empirical study of smoothing techniques for language* (Technical Report).
4. Civera, J., Vilar, J. M., Cubel, E., Lagarda, A. L., Casacuberta, F., Vidal, E., Picó, D., & González, J. (2004). A syntactic pattern recognition approach to computer assisted translation. In A. Fred, T. Caelli, A. Campilho, R. P. Duin & D. de Ridder (Eds.), *Lecture notes in computer science. Advances in statistical, structural and syntactical pattern recognition—joint IAPR international workshops on syntactical and structural pattern recognition (SSPR 2004) and statistical pattern recognition (SPR 2004)*. Berlin: Springer.
5. Cubel, E., Civera, J., Vilar, J. M., Lagarda, A. L., Barrachina, S., Vidal, E., Casacuberta, F., Picó, D., González, J., & Rodríguez, L. (2004). Finite-state models for computer assisted translation. In *Proceedings of the 16th European conference on artificial intelligence (ECAI04)* (pp. 586–590), Valencia, Spain.
6. Llorens, D., Casacuberta, F., Segarra, E., Sánchez, J. A., & Aibar, P. (1999). Acoustical and syntactical modeling in ATROS system. In *Proceedings of international conference on acoustic, speech and signal processing (ICASSP99)* (pp. 641–644), Phoenix, Arizona, USA.
7. Ney, H., & Ortmanns, S. (1997). Extensions to the word graph method for large vocabulary continuous speech recognition. In *IEEE international conference on acoustics, speech, and signal processing* (Vol. 3, pp. 1791–1794), Munich, Germany.
8. Nyquist, H. (2002). Certain topics in telegraph transmission theory. *Proceedings of the IEEE, 90*(2), 280–305.
9. Ortmanns, S., Ney, H., & Aubert, X. (1997). A word graph algorithm for large vocabulary continuous speech recognition. *Computer Speech and Language, 11*(1), 43–72.
10. Paul, D. B., & Baker, J. M. (1992). The design for the wall street journal-based csr corpus. In *HLT'91: Proceedings of the workshop on speech and natural language* (pp. 357–362), Morristown, NJ, USA. Menlo Park: Association for Computational Linguistics.
11. Sankoff, D., & Kruskal, J. B. (1983). *Time warps, string edits, and macromolecules: The theory and practice of sequence comparison*. Reading: Addison-Wesley.
12. Stolcke, A. (2002). SRILM—an extensible language modeling toolkit. In *Proceedings of the international conference on spoken language processing (ICSLP02)* (pp. 901–904), Denver, Colorado, USA.
13. Vidal, E., Casacuberta, F., Rodríguez, L., Civera, J., & Martínez, C. (2006). Computer-assisted translation using speech recognition. *IEEE Transactions on Speech and Audio Processing, 14*(3), 941–951.
14. Young, S. J. (1994). The htk hidden Markov model toolkit: Design and philosophy. *Entropic Cambridge Research Laboratory, Ltd, 2*, 2–44.

Chapter 5
Active Interaction and Learning in Handwritten Text Transcription

With Contribution Of: Nicolás Serrano, Adrià Giménez, Alberto Sanchís and Alfons Juan.

Contents

Computer-assisted systems are being increasingly used in a variety of real-world tasks, though their application to handwritten text transcription in old manuscripts remains largely unexplored. The basic idea explored in this chapter is to follow a sequential, line-by-line transcription of the whole manuscript in which a continuously retrained system interacts with the user to efficiently transcribe each new line. User interaction is expensive in terms of time and cost. Our top priority is to take advantage of these interactions, while trying to reduce them as most as possible.

To this end, we study three different frameworks: (a) improve a recognition system from newly recognized transcriptions via adaptation techniques, using semi-supervised learning techniques; (b) study how to best adapt from limited user supervisions, which is related to active learning; and (c) develop a simple error estimate, which is used to let the user adjust the error in a computer-assisted transcription task. In addition, we test these approaches in the sequential transcription of two old text documents.

5.1 Introduction

Transcription of handwritten text in (old) documents is an important, time-consuming task for digital libraries. It might be carried out by first processing all

A.H. Toselli et al., *Multimodal Interactive Pattern Recognition and Applications*,
DOI 10.1007/978-0-85729-479-1_5,

document images off-line, and then manually supervising system transcriptions to edit incorrect parts. However, state-of-the-art technologies for automatic page layout analysis, text line detection and handwritten text recognition are still far from perfect [4, 6], and thus post-editing automatically generated output is not clearly better than simply ignoring it.

A more effective approach to transcribe old text documents is to follow an interactive–predictive paradigm in which both, the system is guided by the human supervisor, and the supervisor is assisted by the system to complete the transcription task as efficiently as possible. This computer-assisted transcription approach has been successfully followed in the DEBORA [3] and iDoc [7] research projects, for old-style printed and handwritten text, respectively. In the case of iDoc, a computer-assisted transcription system prototype called GIDOC (Gimp-based Interactive transcription of old text DOCuments) has been developed to provide user-friendly, integrated support for interactive–predictive page layout analysis, text line detection and handwritten text transcription. A detailed description of the GIDOC prototype can be found in Chap. 12.

All works presented in this chapter were performed using GIDOC. As in most of the advanced handwriting recognizers today, it is based on standard speech technology adapted to handwritten text images; that is, HMM-based text image modeling and n-gram language modeling, as introduced in Chap. 2 of this book. The system is trained from manually transcribed text lines during early stages of the transcription task. Then, each new text line image is processed in turn, by first predicting its most likely transcription, and then locating and editing system errors. In order to reduce the effort in locating these errors, GIDOC again resorts to standard speech technology and, in particular, to confidence measures (at word level), which are calculated as posterior word probabilities estimated from word graphs [10]. Recognized words below a given confidence threshold are marked as possible errors, and the decision on how to proceed is left to the user. For instance, if a small number of transcription errors can be tolerated for the sake of efficiency, then the user might validate the system output after only supervising (a few) marked words.

Following previous ideas in the areas of machine translation and speech recognition, a prefix-based interactive–predictive approach is proposed in previous chapters of this book in which the user supervises each new line, in the usual reading order, and corrects the first incorrectly recognized word, if any. The prefix of the current hypothesis is thus validated up to the corrected word, and hence the system updates the current hypothesis by searching for the most probable suffix after the validated prefix. This two-step interactive–predictive process is continued until validation of the whole current hypothesis. It is worth noting that this approach is designed to produce complete, error-free transcriptions of handwritten text. According to the taxonomy outlined in Sect. 1.4.1, this corresponds to a *Passive, Left-to-right* interaction protocol in which the user has to supervise all recognized words. In contrast, the ideas presented in this chapter assume an *Active* interaction protocol which does not need complete supervison (and does not guarantee error-free results).

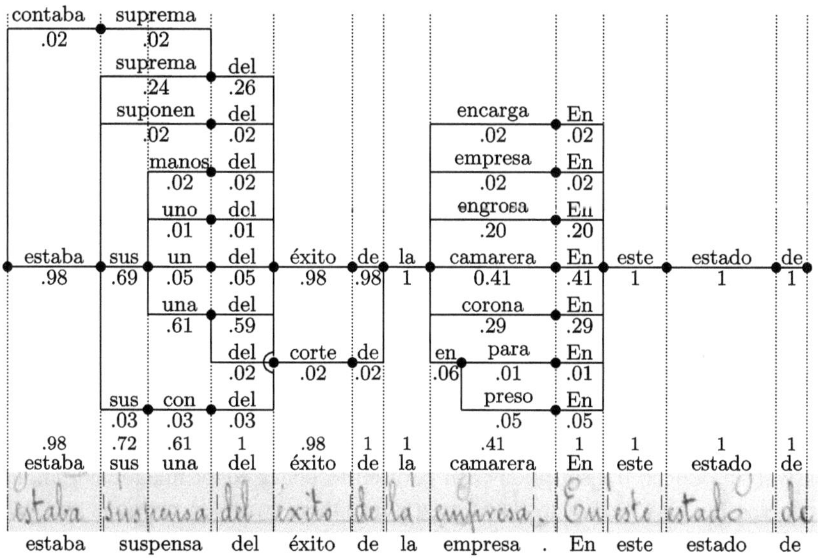

Fig. 5.1 Word-graph example aligned with its corresponding text line image and its recognized and true transcriptions. Each recognized word is labeled (*above*) with its associated confidence measure

The remainder of this chapter is organized as follows: in Sect. 5.2 the use of confidences measures for error locating is explained. Sections 5.3, 5.4 and 5.5 described in detail the main contributions under three different frameworks: adaptive learning, active interaction and learning, and development of simple good error estimate to allow user adjust the error in a computer-assisted transcription task. In the last Sect. 5.6, we test the presented approaches in two real handwriting tasks.

5.2 Confidence Measures

As indicated in the introduction, confidence measures on recognized words are calculated as posterior word probabilities estimated from word graphs. Generally speaking, word graphs are used to represent, in a compact form, large sets of transcription hypotheses with relatively high probability of being correct. See Sect. 1.5.1 for details.

Consider the example in Fig. 5.1, where a small (pruned) word graph is shown aligned with its corresponding text line image and its recognized and true transcriptions.

Each word-graph node is aligned with a discrete point in space, and each edge is labeled with a word (above) and its associated posterior probability (below). For instance, in Fig. 5.1, the word "sus" has a posterior probability of 0.69 to occur between "estaba" and "un", and 0.03 to occur between "estaba" and "con". Note that all word posteriors sum to 1 at each point in space. Therefore, the posterior probability for a word w to occur at a specific point p is given by the sum of all edges labeled with w that are found at p; e.g. "sus" has a posterior probability of 0.72 at any point in which the two edges labeled with "sus" are simultaneously found. As discussed in Sect. 1.5.2, the confidence measure of a recognized word is calculated from these point-dependent posteriors, by simply maximizing over all points where it is most likely to occur (Viterbi-aligned). As an example, each recognized word in Fig. 5.1 is labeled (above) with its associated confidence measure. Please see [10] for more details.

5.3 Adaptation from Partially Supervised Transcriptions

In this section, we introduce an interactive transcription framework, where successively produced transcriptions can be used to better adapt image and language models to the task by, for instance, re-training them from the previous and newly acquired transcribed data. However, if transcriptions are only partially supervised, then (hopefully minor) recognition errors may go unnoticed to the user and have a negative effect on model adaptation.

We study this effect as a function of the degree of supervision, i.e. the number of words supervised per line, and as a function of the adaptation strategies used to re-train the system. Concretely, we consider three adaptation strategies: from all data, only from supervised parts, and from high-confidence parts. Re-training from all data is commonly known as unsupervised learning, where a system learns from its own (unmodified) output. Given the user supervisions we can choose to train uniquely from user supervised transcription, as it is typically performed in active learning systems. In the last strategy, re-training from high-confidence parts, we use the best of the two previous approaches. It is inspired in [11], where confidence measures were successfully used to restrict unsupervised learning of acoustic models for large vocabulary continuous speech recognition. It must be noted that, high-confidence parts include both, unsupervised words above certain confidence threshold, and supervised words. Figure 5.2 shows an example of the three strategies.

5.4 Active Interaction and Active Learning

Active learning strategies are being increasingly used in a variety of real-world tasks where user supervision is difficult, time-consuming, or expensive to obtain [9]. Active learning is particularly adequate for *active interaction* protocols, as those studied in this chapter. In interactive transcription of old text documents, the simplest active interaction strategy is to supervise the least confident words of a given recognizer output. Next, active learning consists in adapting the system models by means of these corrected transcriptions, as discussed in the previous section.

0.98 0.72 0.61 1 0.98 1 1 1 1 1 1
estaba sus una del éxito de la empresa . En este estado de

From all data (Unsupervised)

estaba sus una del éxito de la empresa . En este estado de

From user supervised parts

estaba sus una del éxito de la empresa . En este estado de

From high confidence parts ($cm > 0.95$)

estaba sus una **del éxito de la empresa . En este estado de**

Fig. 5.2 Example showing words (marked in *bold*) which will be used in the next re-training, when using the different adaptation technique. The *first row* shows the recognized line along with its confidence measure (*above*), as well as the words "empresa" and "." supervised by the user

In this section, we focus on *active interaction* and explore how it can be used to further enhance system performance. That is, we take advantage of the user feedback, in form of corrected words, to further improve the transcription accuracy. The conventional, non-interactive recognition strategy is improved by letting the system recompute the most probable hypotheses with the constraints imposed by user supervisions. In particular, two strategies, called *iterative* and *delayed*, are studied which differ in the frequency of hypothesis recomputation on the current line.

An application example of the conventional, iterative and delayed strategies is shown in Fig. 5.3, with user supervision limited to three words. The conventional approach leads to the correction of the three words recognized with less confidence (`ras`, `me` and `&`), resulting in a corrected transcription which still contains two incorrectly recognized words (`vn` and `Aguas`). The iterative strategy first asks for the supervision of `ras`, which is substituted by `Pirus`, and then recomputes the most probable hypothesis, where four more recognized words of the previous hypothesis are substituted or deleted (`me`, `Aguas`, `&` and `vn`). The second iteration reduces to substituting `te` for `me`. In the third iteration, the user substitutes `Vegas` for `vengar`, which results in the correct transcription but, somewhat surprisingly, recomputation of the most probable hypothesis ends up with a recognition error (`vna`). The delayed strategy, shown at the bottom of Fig. 5.3, simply amounts to recompute the most probable hypothesis after the conventional (manual) correction of the three words recognized with less confidence. In contrast to the conventional approach, only one recognition error remains in the final transcription (`vengar`).

An important issue regarding the implementation of the iterative and delayed strategies is how to compute a most probable hypothesis compatible with user supervisions and corrections. Following Kristjansson [2], we have implemented a constrained Viterbi decoding algorithm in which the search for the most probable path is constrained to pass through subpaths that conform user supervisions and corrections. More precisely, word scores in supervised segments are set to null for all words but those supervised and possibly corrected.

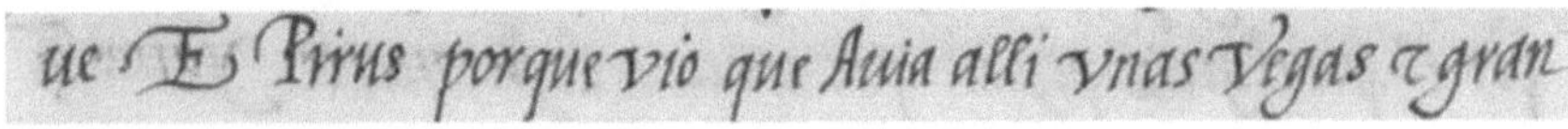

ue. E Pirus porque vio que Auia alli vnas Vegas & gran

Conventional:

.5 .7 .9 .4 1 1 1 1 1 1 .9 .9 1 1
me & E ras porque vio que Auia alli vnas vn Aguas & gran

ue. E Pirus porque vio que Auia alli vnas vn Aguas & gran

Iterative:

.5 .7 .9 .4 1 1 1 1 1 1 .9 .9 1 1
me & E ras porque vio que Auia alli vnas vn Aguas & gran

.5 1 1 1 .9 1 1 1 .8 .6 1 1
te E Pirus porque vio que Auia alli vnas vengar & gran

1 1 1 1 .9 1 1 1 .8 .6 1 1
ue. E Pirus porque vio que Auia alli vnas vengar & gran

ue. E Pirus porque vio que Auia alli vna Vegas & gran

Delayed:

.5 .7 .9 .4 1 1 1 1 1 1 .9 .9 1 1
me & E ras porque vio que Auia alli vnas vn Aguas & gran

ue. E Pirus porque vio que Auia alli vnas vengar & gran

Fig. 5.3 Application example of the conventional, iterative and delayed strategies for interactive–predictive transcription of a text line image with user supervision limited to three words. Recognized words are labeled above with their associated confidence measures. Supervised words and transcription errors are marked with *plain* and *wavy underlining*, respectively

5.5 Balancing Error and Supervision Effort

In this section, we study how to automatically balance recognition error and supervision effort. Our starting point is a system applying the best adaptation strategy from Sect. 5.3, where we have compared several model adaptation techniques from partially supervised transcriptions. Experiments showed that it is better not to adapt models from all data, but only from high-confidence parts, or just simply from supervised parts. More importantly, it has been shown that a certain degree of supervision is required for model adaptation, although it remains unclear how to adjust it properly. To this end, we propose a simple yet effective method to find an optimal balance between recognition error and supervision effort. The user decides on a maximum tolerance threshold for the recognition error (in non-supervised parts), and the system "*actively*" adjusts the required supervision effort on the basis of an estimate for this error.

Recognition error is measured in terms of Word Error Rate (WER); that is, as the average number of elementary editing operations needed to produce a reference (correctly transcribed) word from recognized words. Given a collection of reference-recognized transcription pairs, its WER may be simply expressed as

$$\mathrm{WER} = \frac{E}{N},$$

where E is the total number of editing operations required to transform recognized transcriptions into their corresponding references, and N is the total number of reference words. In this work, however, we need to decompose these three variables additively, as

$$\mathrm{WER} = \mathrm{WER}^+ + \mathrm{WER}^-,$$
$$E = E^+ + E^- \quad \text{and} \quad N = N^+ + N^-,$$

where the superscripts $^+$ and $^-$ denote supervised and unsupervised parts, respectively, and thus

$$\mathrm{WER}^+ = \frac{E^+}{N} \quad \text{and} \quad \mathrm{WER}^- = \frac{E^-}{N}.$$

In order to balance error and supervision effort, we propose the system to ask for supervision effort only when WER^- becomes greater than a given, maximum tolerance threshold, say WER^*. However, as we do not know the values of E^- and N^-, they have to be estimated from the available data. A reasonable estimate for N^- is simply

$$\hat{N}^- = \frac{N^+}{R^+} R^-,$$

where R^+ and R^- denote the number of recognized words in the supervised and unsupervised parts, respectively. Similarly, a reasonable estimate for E^- is

$$\hat{E}^- = \frac{E^+}{R^+} R^-$$

and thus the desired estimate for WER^- is

$$\widehat{\mathrm{WER}}^- = \frac{\frac{E^+}{R^+} R^-}{N^+ + \frac{N^+}{R^+} R^-}.$$

Each recognized word will be accepted without supervision if it does not lead to a WER^- estimate greater that WER^*.

Note that the above estimate for WER^- is pessimistic, since it assumes that, on average, correction of unsupervised parts requires similar editing effort to that required for supervised parts. However, the user is asked to supervise recognized words in increasing order of confidence, and hence unsupervised parts should require less correction effort. In order to better estimate WER^-, we may group recognized words by their level of confidence c, from 1 to a certain maximum level C, and compute a c-dependent estimate for E as above,

$$\hat{E}_c^- = \frac{E_c^+}{R_c^+} R_c^-$$

where E_c^+, R_c^+ and R_c^- are c-dependent versions of E^+, R^+ and R^-, respectively. The global estimate for E is obtained by simply summing these c-dependent estimates,

$$\hat{E}^- = \sum_{c=1}^{C} \hat{E}_c^-$$

and, therefore, the estimate for WER$^-$ becomes

$$\widehat{\text{WER}}^- = \frac{\sum_{c=1}^{C} \frac{E_c^+}{R_c^+} R_c^-}{N^+ + \frac{N^+}{R^+} R^-}$$

which reduces to the previous, pessimistic estimate when only a single confidence level is considered ($C = 1$).

5.6 Experiments

In the following sections, the active learning and interactive transcription strategies described are applied in two real handwritten tasks: GERMANA and RODRIGO.

5.6.1 User Interaction Model

In order to validate our interactive transcription techniques, we need to perform a high number of experiments. As our experiments require from user supervision, dealing with real users would be impossible because of time and cost. In this section, we propose a simple yet realistic user interaction model to simulate user actions at different degrees of supervision. The degree of supervision is modeled as the (maximum) number of recognized words (per line) that are supervised: 0 (unsupervised), $1, \ldots, \infty$ (fully supervised). It is assumed that recognized words are supervised in non-decreasing order of confidence.

In order to predict the user actions associated with each word supervision, we first compute a minimum edit (Levenshtein) distance path between the recognized and true transcriptions of a given text line. For instance, the example text line image in Fig. 5.1 is also used in Fig. 5.4 to show an example of minimum edit distance path between its recognized and true transcriptions. As usual, three elementary editing operations are considered: substitution (of a recognized word by a different word), deletion (of a recognized word) and insertion (of a missing word in the recognized transcription). Substitutions and deletions are directly assigned to their corresponding recognized words. In Fig. 5.4, for instance, there is a substitution assigned to "sus", a deletion assigned to "una", and a second substitution that corresponds to "camarera". Insertions, however, have not direct assignments to recognized words and, hence, it is not straightforward to predict when they are carried out by the user.

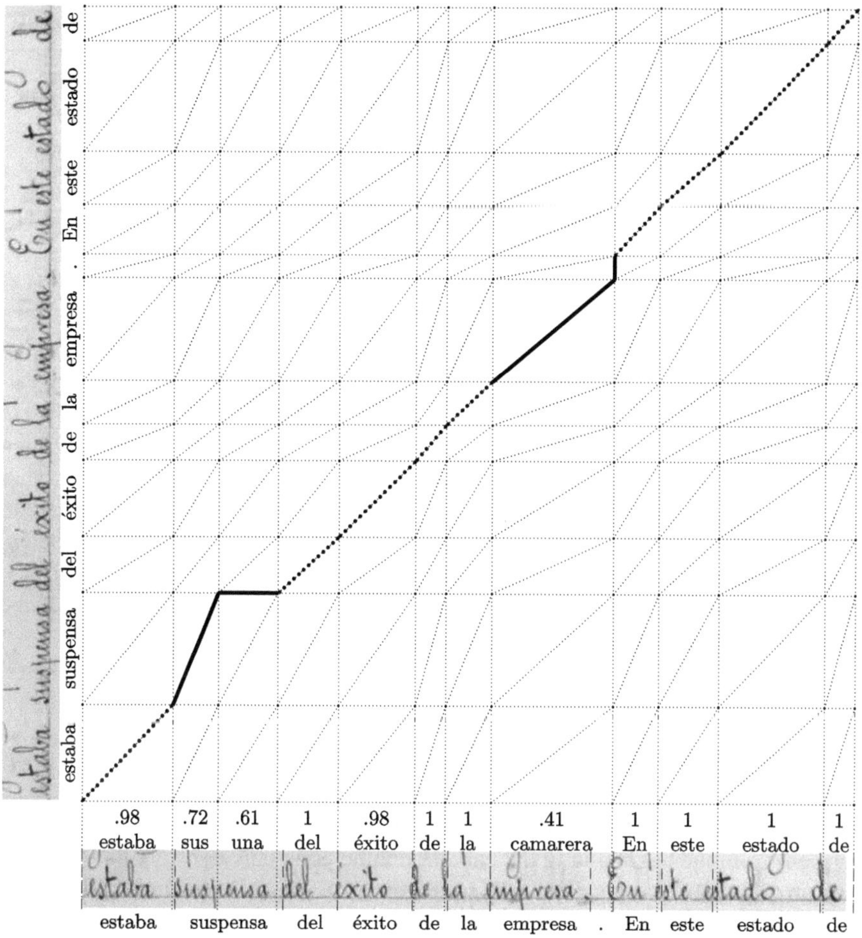

Fig. 5.4 Example of minimum edit distance path between the recognized and true transcriptions of a text line image

To this end, we first compute the Viterbi segmentations of the text line image from the true and recognized transcriptions. Given a word to be inserted, it is assigned to the recognized word whose Viterbi segment covers most part of its true Viterbi segment. For instance, in Fig. 5.4, the period is completely covered by "camarera", and thus its insertion is assumed to be done when "camarera" is supervised.

5.6.2 Sequential Transcription Tasks

Experiments were carried out on two datasets recently introduced: GERMANA [5] and RODRIGO [8]. GERMANA is the result of digitizing and annotating a 764-

Table 5.1 Statistics of GERMANA and RODRIGO. Singletons corresponds to words appearing once in the document. Perplexity drawn from a bigram language model in a ten-fold validation

	GERMANA	RODRIGO
Pages	764	853
Lines	20 529	20 357
Running words (K)	217	232
Lexicon size (K)	27.1	17.3
Singletons (%)	57.4	54.4
Character set size	115	115
Perplexity	290	166

page Spanish manuscript from 1891, in which most pages only contain nearly calligraphed text written on ruled sheets of well-separated lines. The example shown in Fig. 5.1 contains a text line image from GERMANA. GERMANA is solely written in Spanish up to p. 180, but then it includes many parts written in languages other than Spanish. RODRIGO is similar to GERMANA both, in size and page layout. However, it comes from a much older manuscript, from 1545, and it is completely written in Spanish. As can be seen in text line image shown at the top of Fig. 5.3, which was extracted from p. 65, the writing style has clear Gothic influences. Some basic statistics of GERMANA and RODRIGO are provided in Table 5.1.

5.6.3 Adaptation from Partially Supervised Transcriptions

Due to its sequential book structure, the very basic task on GERMANA is to transcribe it from the beginning to the end, though here we only consider its transcription up to p. 180. Starting from p. 3, we divided GERMANA into nine consecutive blocks of 20 pages each (18 in block 9). The first two blocks (pp. 3–42) were used to train initial image and language models from fully supervised transcriptions. Then, from block 3 to 8, each new block was recognized, partially supervised and added to the training set built from its preceding blocks.

As it has been said in Sect. 5.3, we perform the sequential transcription of GERMANA as function of: the degree of supervision and the adaptation technique used. We considered three degrees of supervision: zero (unsupervised), one and three supervised words per line; and the three adaptation (re-training) strategies: from all data, only from high-confidence parts, and only from supervised parts. The results are shown in Fig. 5.5 in terms of Word Error Rate (WER) on block 9 (pp. 163–180).

From the results in Fig. 5.5, it becomes clear that baseline models can be improved by adaptation from partially supervised transcriptions, though a certain degree of supervision is required to obtain significant improvements. In particular, supervision of three words per line leads to a reduction of more than a 10% of WER with respect to unsupervised learning (baseline models), though there is still room for improvement since full supervision achieves a further reduction of 5% (34%). The adaptation strategy, on the other hand, has a relatively minor effect on

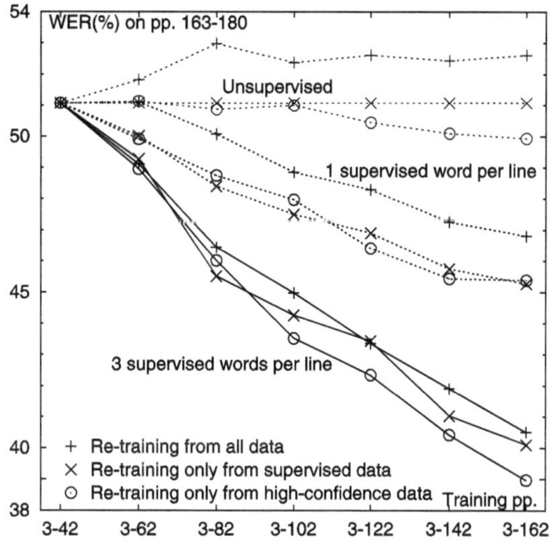

Fig. 5.5 Test-set Word Error Rate (WER) on GERMANA as a function of the training set size (in pages), for varying degrees of supervision (supervised words per line)

the results. Nevertheless, it seems better not to re-train from all data, but only from high-confidence parts, or just simply from supervised parts.

Apart from the above experiment on GERMANA, we did a similar experiment on the well-known IAM dataset, using a standard partition into a training, validation and test sets [1]. The training set was further divided into three subsets; the first one was used to train initial models, while the other two were recognized, partially supervised (four words per line) and added to the training set. The results obtained in terms of test-set WER are: 42.6%, using only the first subset; 42.8%, after adding the second subset; and 42.0%, using also the third subset. In contrast to GERMANA, there is no significant reduction in terms of WER after adding partially supervised data to the training set. We think that this result is due to the more complex nature of the IAM task.

5.6.4 Active Interaction and Learning

In this section, we describe the experiments done to test the active learning strategies referred in Sect. 5.4. In this set of experiments, we used the best system from the previous experiment. Again, the quality of the successively produced models was measured in terms of WER on block 9, and it is shown in Fig. 5.6 (left). Full supervision (∞) and the conventional strategy (C) are compared with the two strategies discussed; that is, iterative (I) and delayed (D). The C, I and D strategies were limited to three supervised words per line, which is not too much since, on average, text lines are of 11 words approximately.

Experiments similar to those previously described were also carried out on RODRIGO. The 20K lines of RODRIGO were divided into 20 consecutive blocks of 1 000 lines approximately, except for the first 1 000 lines, which were divided into

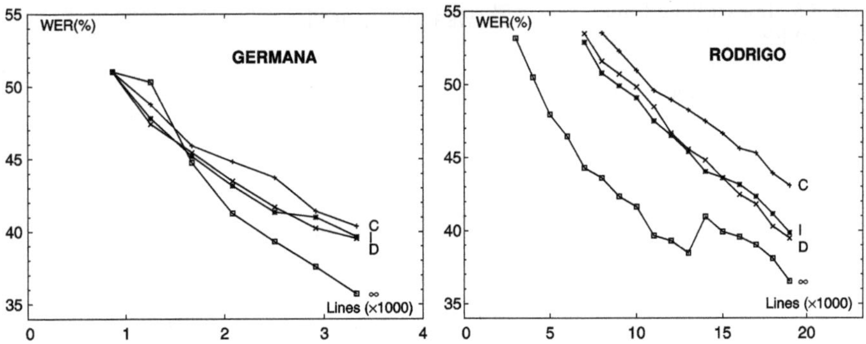

Fig. 5.6 Word Error Rate (WER) on the last block of lines, as a function of the number of training lines, for full supervision (∞), and partial supervision (of three words per line), using three active learning strategies: conventional (C), iterative (I), and delayed(D). *Left*: GERMANA. *Right*: RODRIGO

the line blocks 1–100, 101–200, 201–500 and 501–1 000. The results are also shown in Fig. 5.6 (right).

From the results in Fig. 5.6, it becomes clear that the proposed iterative and delayed strategies are better than the basic, conventional approach. In the case of RODRIGO, conventional supervision of three words per line results in a WER of 43.1%, which is 6.6 points above full supervision (36.5%). By contrast, the iterative and delayed strategies are only 3.3 and 3.0 points above, respectively. That is, the increase of WER due to supervising only three words per line is halved by using the proposed strategies. Moreover, it is worth noting that this increase of 3 points over a WER of 36.5% is just a small degradation in terms of WER, as compared with the considerable user effort reduction achieved by only supervising three out of 11 words per line. On the other hand, it seems that the iterative and delayed strategies produce nearly identical results, though this should be further explored by also considering the effect of varying the supervision degree (number of supervised words per line).

In the case of GERMANA, the iterative and delayed strategies also provide better results than the conventional approach, though the WER improvements are more moderate. This might be due to the fact that GERMANA models are produced from training sets much smaller than those used for RODRIGO. Note that GERMANA is easier to recognize than RODRIGO, since WER results similar to those obtained on RODRIGO are achieved from much less training lines.

5.6.5 Balancing User Effort and Recognition Error

Perfect transcription of old text documents is not always mandatory. Transcriptions containing a few number of errors are perfectly readable and can be easily obtained using a computer-assisted system. In Sect. 5.5 we introduce a simple yet effective

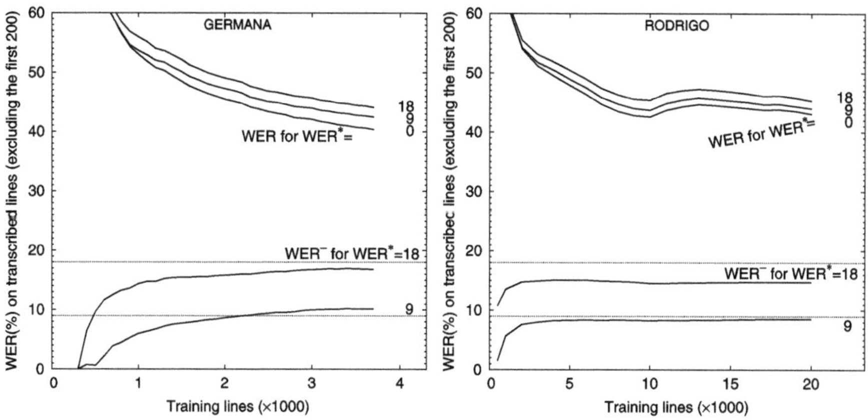

Fig. 5.7 Word Error Rate (WER) on transcribed lines (excluding the first 200), as a function of the (number of) training lines, for varying tolerance thresholds on the recognition error (in unsupervised parts). *Left*: GERMANA dataset. *Right*: RODRIGO dataset

method to balance error and user effort. Here, we consider the transcription under three tolerance thresholds on the recognition error (in unsupervised parts): 0% (fully supervised), 9% (one recognition error per line, on average) and 18%.

In this case, we divided GERMANA into consecutive blocks of 100 lines each (37 blocks). The first two blocks were used to train initial image and language models from fully supervised transcriptions. Then, from block 3 to 37, each new block was recognized, partially supervised as discussed in Sect. 5.5 for $C = 4$ confidence levels, and added to the previous training set. The first three confidence levels correspond, respectively, to the first three words in each line that were recognized with smaller confidence; the remaining recognized words were all grouped into the fourth level. Re-training of image and language models was carried out from only high-confidence parts [7]. The results are shown in Fig. 5.7 (left) in terms of WER on transcribed lines (excluding the first 200).

From the results in Fig. 5.7 (left), it becomes clear that the proposed balancing method takes full advantage of the allowed tolerance to reduce the supervision effort. Moreover, the total WER of the system trained with partial transcriptions does not deviate significantly from that of the fully supervised system. The average user effort reduction ranges from 29% (for $\text{WER}^* = 9\%$) to 49% (for $\text{WER}^* = 18\%$). That is, if one recognition error per line is allowed for on average ($\text{WER}^* = 9\%$), then the user will save 29% of the supervision actions that are required in the case of a fully supervised system. Here, supervision actions refers to elementary editing operations, and also to check that a correctly recognized word is certainly correct.

In order to better assess the proposed method, a larger experiment was also conducted on RODRIGO, which was divided into blocks of 1 000 lines each, except for the first 1 000 lines, which were divided into the line blocks 1–100, 101–200, 201–500 and 501–1 000. The experiment and results, shown in Fig. 5.7 (right), are analogous to those described above for GERMANA.

Although the results presented in Fig. 5.7 are quite satisfactory, we have observed that the proposed balancing method does not clearly favor supervision of low confidence words over those recognized with high confidence. We think that this is mainly due to the fact that it works on a word-by-word basis and, in order to decide whether a given word has to be supervised or not, its contribution to the current estimate of WER^- is not as important as the closeness of this estimate to WER^*. We think that this behavior can be alleviated by using more confidence levels or, more directly, by working on a line-by-line basis. That is, by first assuming that all balancing error recognized words in a line are not supervised, and then supervising words in increasing order of confidence while the current estimate of WER^- is above WER^*.

5.7 Conclusions

In this chapter we described three different frameworks to deal with the interactive transcription process of handwritten documents, where the recognizer output is partially supervised. The basic idea is to assist the user in the transcription process, while keeping his interactions as low as possible. It has been shown that, a system can be trained from partially (and possibly erroneous) supervised transcription, while achieving similar results to a fully supervised trained system. We showed that user interaction can be used to further improve the current transcription, constraining the current hypothesis search space. Lastly, we created a framework that allows the user to adjust the error in exchange of user effort. Experiments were performed on two real transcription tasks, GERMANA and RODRIGO, showing the effectiveness of the proposed frameworks.

References

1. Bertolami, R., & Bunke, H. (2008). Hidden Markov model-based ensemble methods for offline handwritten text line recognition. *Pattern Recognition 41*, 3452–3460.
2. Kristjannson, T., Culotta, A., Viola, P., & McCallum, A. (2004). Interactive information extraction with constrained conditional random fields. In *Proceedings of the 19th national conference on artificial intelligence (AAAI 2004)* (pp. 412–418), San Jose, CA, USA.
3. Le Bourgeois, F., & Emptoz, H. (2007). DEBORA: Digital AccEss to BOoks of the RenAissance. *International Journal on Document Analysis and Recognition*, *9*, 193–221.
4. Likforman-Sulem, L., Zahour, A., & Taconet, B. (2007). Text line segmentation of historical documents: a survey. *International Journal on Document Analysis and Recognition*, *9*, 123–138.
5. Pérez, D., Tarazón, L., Serrano, N., Castro, F., Ramos-Terrades, O., & Juan, A. (2009). The GERMANA database. In *Proceedings of the 10th international conference on document analysis and recognition (ICDAR 2009)* (pp. 301–305), Barcelona, Spain.
6. Plötz, T., & Fink, G. A. (2009). Markov models for offline handwriting recognition: a survey. *International Journal on Document Analysis and Recognition*, *12*, 269–298.

7. Serrano, N., Pérez, D., Sanchis, A., & Juan, A. (2009). Adaptation from partially supervised handwritten text transcriptions. In *Proceedings of the 11th international conference on multimodal interfaces and the 6th workshop on machine learning for multimodal interaction (ICMI-MLMI 2009)* (pp. 289–292), Cambridge, MA, USA.
8. Serrano, N., Castro, F., & Juan, A. (2010). The RODRIGO database. In *Proceedings of the 7th international conference on language resources and evaluation (LREC 2010)* (pp. 2709–2712), Valleta, Malta.
9. Settles, B. (2009). *Active learning literature survey* (Computer Sciences Technical Report No. 1648). University of Wisconsin-Madison.
10. Tarazón, L., Pérez, D., Serrano, N., Alabau, V., Ramos-Terrades, O., Sanchis, A., & Juan, A. (2009). Confidence measures for error correction in interactive transcription of handwritten text. In *Proceedings of the 15th international conference on image analysis and processing (ICIAP 2009)* (pp. 567–574), Vietri sul Mare, Italy.
11. Wessel, F., & Ney, H. (2005). Unsupervised training of acoustic models for large vocabulary continuous speech recognition. *IEEE Transactions on Speech and Audio Processing*, *13*(1), 23–31.

Chapter 6
Interactive Machine Translation

With Contribution Of: Jorge Civera, Jesús González-Rubio and Daniel Ortiz-Martínez.

Contents

Achieving high-quality translation between any pair of languages is not possible with the current *Machine-Translation* (MT) technology a human post-editing of the outputs of the MT system being necessary. Therefore, MT is a suitable area to apply the *Interactive Pattern Recognition* (IPR) framework and this application has led to what nowadays is known as *Interactive Machine Translation* (IMT). IMT can predict the translation of a given source sentence, and the human translator can accept or correct some of the errors. The text amended by the human translator can be used by the system to suggest new improved translations with the same translation models in an iterative process until the whole output is accepted by the human.

As in other areas where IPR is being applied, IMT offers a nice framework for adaptive learning. The consolidated translations obtained through the successive steps of the interaction process can easily be converted into new, fresh, training data, useful for dynamically adapting the system to the changing environment. On the other hand, IMT also allows one to take advantage of some available multimodal interfaces to increase of the productivity of high-quality translations. Multimodal interfaces and adaptive learning in IMT will be covered in Chaps. 7 and 8, respectively.

A.H. Toselli et al., *Multimodal Interactive Pattern Recognition and Applications*,
DOI 10.1007/978-0-85729-479-1_6, © Springer-Verlag London Limited 2011

6.1 Introduction

The application of statistical pattern recognition techniques to the field of *Machine Translation* (MT) has allowed the development of new MT systems with less effort than was previously required under the formerly dominant rule-based paradigm [22]. These systems (which are known as *Statistical MT* systems—SMT systems) together with the *memory-based* ones constitute the *data-driven* approach to MT. However, the quality of the translations produced by any (statistical, memory-based or rule-based) MT system remains below that of human translation. This quality could be enough for many applications, but for other applications, the output of the MT systems has to be revised in a *post-editing* phase. An alternative to the use of pure post-editing is the approach proposed in the TransType project [16, 25, 26] and its successor TransType2 (TT2) [2, 11]. In this approach, a full-fledged MT engine is embedded in an interactive editing environment and used to generate suggested completions of each target sentence being translated. These completions may be accepted or partially amended by the translator; but the validated words are exploited by the MT engine to produce further, hopefully improved suggestions. This new approach is known as *Interactive Machine Translation* (IMT). TransType allowed only for single-token completions, where a token could be either a word or a short sequence of words from a predefined set of sequences. This idea was extended to complete full target sentences in the TT2 project. This interactive approach offers a significant advantage over traditional post-editing, where there is no way for the system to benefit from the corrections of the user.

Interactivity in translation (more precisely, in *Computer-Assisted Translation*—CAT) has been explored for a long time to solve different types of ambiguities [2]. However, there are only few research groups that have published, to our knowledge, contributions in this IMT topic. As we have mentioned, the first publications are related with the TransType project [16, 17, 25, 26, 29, 34, 37]. The second group of publications are around the TransType2 project [2, 3, 11–15, 32, 38]. More recently other research groups have started to work on this topic [23].

In this section, we present a summary of the state-of-the-art in SMT. Section 6.2 is devoted to the applications of IPR in MT. The specific search problem in IMT is presented in Sect. 6.3. The adopted tasks, the evaluation measures and experimental settings, and the results obtained are presented in Sect. 6.4. All the aspects related with adaptability and multi-modality in IMT are introduced in the next chapters.

6.1.1 Statistical Machine Translation

SMT is based on the application of the Bayes decision rule to the problem of conversion of a *source* sentence x from a source language $\mathcal{X}$ to a *target* sentence h from a target language $\mathcal{H}$. This decision rule can be stated as the search for a target sentence $\hat{h}$ that maximizes the posterior probability that a sentence h is a translation of a given x [5, 6]:

$$\hat{h} = \arg\max_{h} \Pr(h \mid x). \tag{6.1}$$

The state-of-the-art in SMT is based on *bilingual segments* or *bilingual phrases* as translation units and *log-linear* models to approach $\Pr(h \mid x)$ [22]. Bilingual phrases are pairs of word sequences $(\tilde{x}, \tilde{h})$ in which all words within the source-language phrase $\tilde{x}$ are aligned only to words of the target-language phrase $\tilde{h}$ and vice versa [22]. On the other hand, log-linear models [31] are combinations of N different feature functions $f_i(x, h)$ for $1 \le i \le N$:

$$\Pr(h \mid x) \approx P(h \mid x; \lambda) = \frac{\exp \sum_{i=1}^{N} \lambda_i f_i(x, h)}{\sum_{h'} \exp \sum_{i=1}^{N} \lambda_i f_i(x, h')}. \tag{6.2}$$

A feature function $f_i(x, h)$ [22] can be any model that represents an important feature for the translation. N is the number of models (or features) and λ_i are the weights of the log-linear combination.

Some of these feature functions are based on the segmentation of the pair (x, h) in terms of a sequence of phrases $\tilde{x}_1, \dots, \tilde{x}_K$ ($x = \tilde{x}_1 \cdots \tilde{x}_K$) and $\tilde{h}_1, \dots, \tilde{h}_K$ ($h = \tilde{h}_1 \cdots \tilde{h}_K$) for a given K. If the correspondence (*alignment*) between source and target phrases is represented as a function $a : \{1, \dots, K\} \to \{1, \dots, K\}$, Eq. (6.1) can be rewritten using a modified version of Eq. (6.2) as

$$\hat{h} = \arg\max_{h} \max_{a} \sum_{i} \lambda_i f_i(x, h, a). \tag{6.3}$$

One of these feature functions can represent the direct translation:

$$f_i(x, h, a) = \sum_{k=1}^{K} \bigl(\log p(a_k \mid a_{k-1}) + \log p(\tilde{h}_k \mid \tilde{x}_{a_k})\bigr), \tag{6.4}$$

where $p(a_k \mid a_{k-1})$ is the probability that a source phrase in position k is aligned with a target phrase in position a_k, given that a previous source phrase in position $k-1$ was aligned with a target phrase in position a_{k-1}, and $p(\tilde{h}_k \mid \tilde{x}_{k'})$ is the probability that a target phrase $\tilde{h}_k$ is the translation of a given source phrase $\tilde{x}_{k'}$. Another feature function is based on a target language model, typically a n-gram model (trigrams for example for a target sentence of length J):

$$f_i(x, h, a) = \sum_{j=1}^{J} \log p(h_j \mid h_{j-2}, h_{j-1}). \tag{6.5}$$

Other feature functions are based on the inverse version of Eq. (6.4) and on other target-language models and diverse (target and/or source) length models. There is an interesting feature function that is based on a language model (trigrams for example and with $a(j) = j$) of bilingual phrases:

$$f_i(x,h,a) = \sum_{k=1}^{K} \log p(\tilde{x}_k, \tilde{h}_k \mid \tilde{x}_{k-2}, \tilde{h}_{k-2}, \tilde{x}_{k-1}, \tilde{h}_{k-1}). \quad (6.6)$$

This model can also be efficiently implemented with *Stochastic Finite-state Transducers* (SFSTs) [9, 10] or as another feature in the log-linear modeling [28].

In the learning phase, all bilingual phrases are extracted from a bilingual training corpus and the normalized counts of how often a bilingual phrase occurred in the aligned training corpus are computed [22, 24, 33]. The parameters of the n-grams are estimated by a counting process on a target training set. On the other hand, the weights of the log-linear combination in Eq. (6.2) are computed by means of *Minimum Error Rate Training* (MERT) [30]. In the case that SFSTs are adopted, the Grammatical Inference Algorithms for Transducer Inference (GIATI) algorithm can be used [9].

The search for the best translation of a given source sentence x is carried out by producing the target sentence in left-to-right order using the log-linear model in Eq. (6.2). At each step of the generation algorithm, a set of active hypotheses are maintained and one of them is chosen for extension. A segment of the target language is then added to the chosen hypothesis and its costs get updated [22, 31]. If SFSTs are adopted, the Viterbi algorithm can used for the generation of the target sentence [10]. In both cases, the search space can be huge and pruning techniques have to be used.

6.2 Interactive Machine Translation

The systems described in Sect. 6.1.1 are still far from perfect. This implies that, in order to achieve good, or even acceptable, translations, manual post-editing is needed. An alternative to this serial approach (first MT, then manual correction) is given by the IMT paradigm. This approach is exemplified in Fig. 6.1. Let us suppose that a source English sentence $x =$ "Click OK to close the print dialog" is to be translated into a target Spanish sentence h. Initially, with no user information, the system provides a complete translation suggestion ($s =$ "Haga clic para cerrar el diálogo de impresión"). From this translation, the user marks a prefix as correct ("Haga clic") and begins to type the rest of the target sentence. Depending on the system or the user's preferences, the new input can be the next word or some letters from it (in our example, the input is the next correct word, "en"). A new target prefix p is then defined by the previously validated prefix together with the new input the user has just typed ($p =$ "Haga clic en"). The system then generates a new suffix s to complete the translation: "ACEPTAR para cerrar el diálogo de impresión". The interaction continues with a new validation, followed, if necessary, by new input from the user, and so on, until a complete and satisfactory translation is obtained.

	Input	(x)	Click OK to close the print dialog
0	System	$(\hat{s})$	Haga clic para cerrar el diálogo de impresión
1	User	(p)	Haga clic en
	System	$(\hat{s})$	ACEPTAR para cerrar el diálogo de impresión
2	User	(p)	Haga clic en ACEPTAR para cerrar el cuadro
	System	$(\hat{s})$	de diálogo de impresión
3	User	(p)	Haga clic en ACEPTAR para cerrar el cuadro de diálogo de impresión #
	Output	(h)	Haga clic en ACEPTAR para cerrar el cuadro de diálogo de impresión

Fig. 6.1 An example of IMT with keyboard interaction. The aim is to translate the English sentence "*Click OK to close the print dialog*" into Spanish. Each step starts with a previously fixed target-language prefix p, from which the system suggests a suffix $\hat{s}$ (in *blue* color). Then the user accepts a part of this suffix (in *black* color) and types some key-strokes (in *red* color), possibly in order to amend the remaining part of s. This produces a new prefix, composed by the prefix from the previous iteration and the accepted and typed text, to be used as p in the next step. The process ends when the user enters the special keystroke "#". System suggestions are printed in *italics* and user input in *boldface* typewriter font. In the final translation h, text that has been typed by the user is *underlined*

In this problem, we can apply the concepts and ideas that have been developed in Sect. 1.4.2 in the algorithm IPR-History of Sect. 1.3.2. More specifically, we can use the concepts of prefix and suffix introduced in the left-to-right interactive-predictive processing: Given a source sentence x and a target prefix p validated by the human, the optimization problem can be stated as the search for a target suffix s that completes p as a translation of the source sentence x:

$$\hat{s} = \arg\max_{s} \Pr(s \mid x, p). \tag{6.7}$$

This equation can be rewritten as

$$\hat{s} = \arg\max_{s} \Pr(p, s \mid x). \tag{6.8}$$

Since $ps = h$, this equation is very similar to Eq. (6.1). The main difference is that the maximization search now is performed over the set of suffixes s that complete p instead of complete sentences (h in Eq. (6.1)). This implies that we can use the same models if the search procedures are adequately modified [2].

The optimization problem in IMT have been reduced as a search problem constrained by the prefix; obviously, there can be other alternatives, but this one has the advantage that in this approach we used the same models as for SMT and therefore we use the same training algorithm as for SMT [2]. On the other hand, the search for IMT is similar as for SMT but constrained by a fixed prefix in each iteration. This search can be carried out by a modification of the available search algorithms [2]. However, high speed is needed because typically a new system hypothesis must be produced in real time after each user keystroke [2, 32], therefore, we use a word graph that represents all (or a selected part of) possible translations of the given source sentence.

6.2.1 Interactive Machine Translation with Confidence Estimation

Under the IMT paradigm, the user is asked to mark a correct prefix and, possibly, type some corrections for each suffix provided by the system. To interact with the system, the user makes use of his knowledge about the languages being translated, but, potentially, user effort reductions could be achieved if information about the correctness of the suffixes provided by the system is made available to the user. This information can be derived by estimating the confidence the system has on their predicted suffixes, as introduced in Sect. 1.5.2. For a given source sentence x and a validated target prefix p we compute the confidence measure $CM(\hat{s}, x, p)$ for the target suffix $\hat{s}$ generated.

Confidence estimation have been extensively studied for other *Natural Language Processing* (NLP) applications and more recently have been applied to SMT [4, 18, 35, 39, 40]. Confidence information have been previously used in IMT to improve translation prediction accuracy [17, 18, 39]. Alternatively, confidence information can be used, not only to improve the translations provided by the system, but also to reduce the user effort.

The use of confidence information within the IMT scenario results in a modification of the interaction protocol. In the IMT scenarios discussed so far, the operator was assumed to systematically supervise each system suffix and find the point where the next translation error appears. As discussed in Sect. 1.4.1, within these "passive" protocols the system just waits for the human feedback, without taking into account how the supervision is performed by the user. In contrast, in an "active" protocol, the system is in charge of taking decisions about what needs user supervision (see Sect. 1.4.3). Suffix confidence measures can be used to estimate which hypothesis may be worth asking for user supervision in order to optimize the overall human-computer performance.

According to this "active" protocol, we define an alternative IMT scenario where not all the sentences are interactively translated by the user. Specifically, only those suffixes classified as incorrect, according to a confidence measure, are interactively amended by the user [19, 20]. Therefore, the quality of the final translations may depend on the system ability to select appropriate suffixes for supervision. However, this "active" interaction may provide a better trade-off between overall human interaction effort and translation accuracy.

This "active" protocol can be seen as a generalization of the IMT scenario in which confidence estimation acts as a regulator of the effort required for the user. Depending on the confidence threshold defined, the behavior of the system can range from a fully automatic SMT system, where all suffixes are considered to be correct, to a conventional IMT system, where all suffixes are considered to be incorrect.

Confidence Measure for IMT

We estimate the reliability of the suffixes generated by the system by combining the confidence scores of their individual words. We choose a word confidence measure based on the IBM model 1 [6]. The confidence score of a word $\hat{s}_i$ of the suffix $\hat{s}$ generated from the source sentence x given the prefix p from Eq. (6.7) is computed as

$$CM(\hat{s}_i, x, p) \approx CM(\hat{s}_i, x) = \max_{0 \leq j \leq J} P(\hat{s}_i \mid x_j) \tag{6.9}$$

where $P(\hat{s}_i \mid x_j)$ is a bilingual lexicon probability [6] J is the number of words in x and x_0 is the empty source word.

We choose this confidence measure instead of using the posterior probability due to response-time constrains. The confidence score based on the simplest model proposed in [6] (Model 1) is much faster to compute than applying the forward–backward algorithm, as described in Sect. 1.5.2. Moreover, it performs similarly to the word confidence measures based on word graphs as shown in [4, 35, 40].

The confidence measure for the full suffix $\hat{s}$ is computed as the ratio of its words classified as correct by the word confidence measure. A word $\hat{s}_i$ is classified as correct if its confidence score $CM(\hat{s}_i, x)$ exceeds a word classification threshold τ_w.

$$CM(\hat{s}, x, p) \approx CM(\hat{s}, x) = \frac{|\{\hat{s}_i \mid CM(\hat{s}_i, x) > \tau_w\}|}{|\hat{s}|}. \tag{6.10}$$

Each suffix is classified as either correct or incorrect depending on whether its confidence score does or does not exceed a suffix classification threshold τ_s. It is worth of notice that with a threshold value $\tau_s = 0.0$ all the suffixes will be classified as correct whereas with a threshold value $\tau_s = 1.0$ all the suffixes will be classified as incorrect.

6.3 Search in Interactive Machine Translation

As mentioned above, the search problem in IMT can be seen as a search constrained by the prefix p validated by the user. Real-time user interaction dictates the need of efficient search techniques, such as the word-graph representation and Viterbi algorithm presented in Sect. 1.5.1.

Analogously to the search procedure in CATTI and CAST (see Sect. 2.5), the first step is to generate a word graph as a pruned version of the search space for the translation of the source sentence x [2]. Once the word graph is constructed, error-correcting parsing is used to accommodate the user-validated prefix to those prefixes available in the word graph. This step is followed by a Viterbi suffix search to provide the most probable completion.

6.3.1 *Word-Graph Generation*

For each source sentence, a word graph representing possible translations is generated. This word graph is generated once for each source sentence, so it is repeatedly

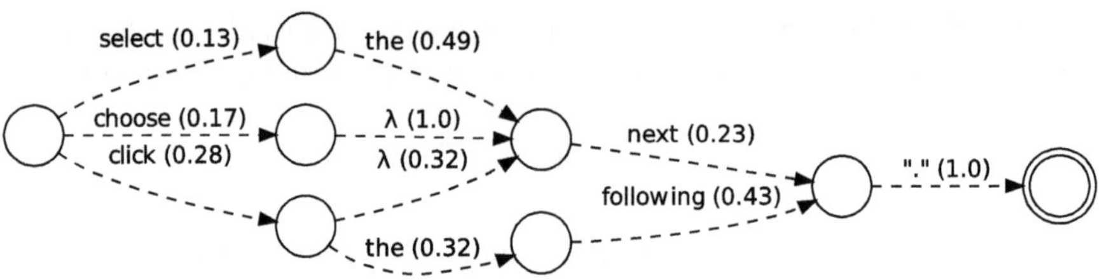

Fig. 6.2 Example of a word graph for the source Spanish sentence "seleccionar el siguiente", being the English reference translation "select the next". λ is the empty string

used to find the completions of all the different prefixes provided by the user. Using the word graph in such a way makes the system able to interact with the user under tight real-time constraints [2].

A word graph may also be understood as a weighted directed acyclic graph, in which each node represents a partial translation hypothesis, and each edge is labeled with the word or the segment of the target sentence being expanded and is weighted according to the underlying models. Indeed, if no pruning is applied in the production of the word graph, it represents all possible sequences of target words for which the posterior probability is greater than zero, according to the models used. An example of a word graph for the source Spanish sentence "seleccionar el siguiente" is shown in Fig. 6.2.

However, due to the pruning performed in the word-graph generation for efficiency and response-time constraints, the word graph only contains a subset of the possible translations. Moreover, it is also possible that the user incorporates words unknown by the system. For these reasons, it may occur that the prefix validated by the user is not present in the word graph. This problem requires the application of error-correcting parsing to allow for user prefixes that may not exist in the word graph.

6.3.2 Error-Correcting Parsing

As mentioned above, it is feasible that the user defines a prefix containing words not found in the word graph. In order to solve this problem, we take the same approximation as presented in Sect. 3.2.2, but adapted to the IMT scenario. In this scenario, the search of the most probable completion $\hat{s}$ given the source sentence x and a user-validated prefix p is formulated starting from Eq. (6.8) as follows:

$$\begin{aligned}\hat{s} &= \arg\max_s P(s, p \mid x)\\ &= \arg\max_s \sum_{p'} P(s, p, p' \mid x)\\ &= \arg\max_s \sum_{p'} P(s, p' \mid x) \cdot \Pr(p \mid x, s, p'),\end{aligned} \tag{6.11}$$

p' being a prefix in the word graph. At this point we consider the following assumption: the probability of the user-validated prefix p does not depend on the source sentence x and the suffix s given the word-graph prefix p'. By doing so and using the maximum as an approach to the sum, Eq. (6.11) becomes

$$\hat{s} \approx \arg\max_{s} \max_{p'} P(p', s \mid x) \cdot P(p \mid p'). \tag{6.12}$$

On the one hand, the first term in Eq. (6.12) is the conventional term for SMT that appears in Eq. (6.1) being $h = p's$. On the other hand, $P(p \mid p')$ is an "*error model*" which provides the probability that a word-graph prefix p' is changed into the prefix p given by the user.[1]

In practice, this last term is computed by applying a probabilistic version of the error-correcting algorithm for regular grammars [41]. As in Sect. 3.2.2, an efficient implementation is achieved by visiting the states in topological order [1], and using beam-search techniques [27]. Moreover, under the left-to-right interactive-predictive processing, we can take advantage of the incremental nature of the user prefix p, so that the error-correcting algorithm only parses the new part of this prefix.

An example of the search process is illustrated in Fig. 6.3 when translating the Spanish sentence "seleccionar el siguiente" into the English reference translation "select the next". First, the word graph is generated from the source sentence (see Fig. 6.2). Then, provided that no user prefix has been entered yet, the topmost subfigure highlights in blue the most probable path. Just underneath, we can observe how the correction of the user by typing the word "select" is reflected in the word graph defining an alternative partial path in red, compatible with this correction. Finally, considering the word-graph prefix defined by the user correction, the most probable completing path is computed according to Eq. (6.12). Obviously, the words along this path constitute the suffix suggested by the system to the user.

6.3.3 Search for n-Best Completions

A desirable feature of an IMT system is the possibility of producing a list of alternative suffixes, instead of only one. This feature can be easily added by computing the N-best suffixes.

To this purpose, an algorithm that searches for the n-best paths in a word graph is required. As mentioned in Sect. 1.5.1, among the n-best algorithms available, the *Recursive Enumeration Algorithm* (REA) described in [21] was selected. The main two features that support this decision are its simplicity to calculate best paths on demand and its smooth integration with the error-correcting parsing algorithm.

[1]Following the tradition in the error-correcting literature, it is assumed that the input data are a "distorted" version of the "correct" data represented by the model.

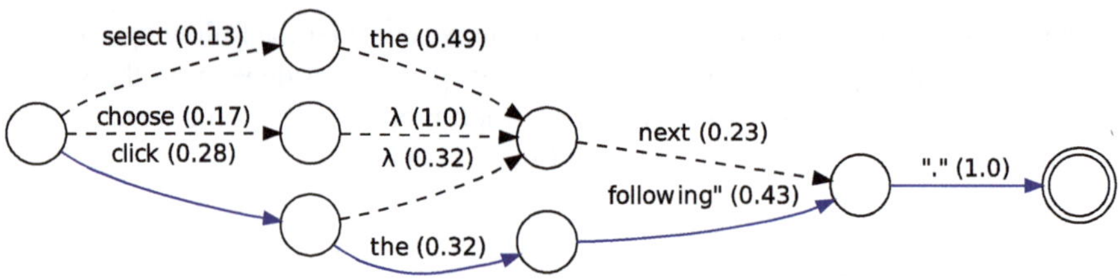

a) Most probable path in blue.

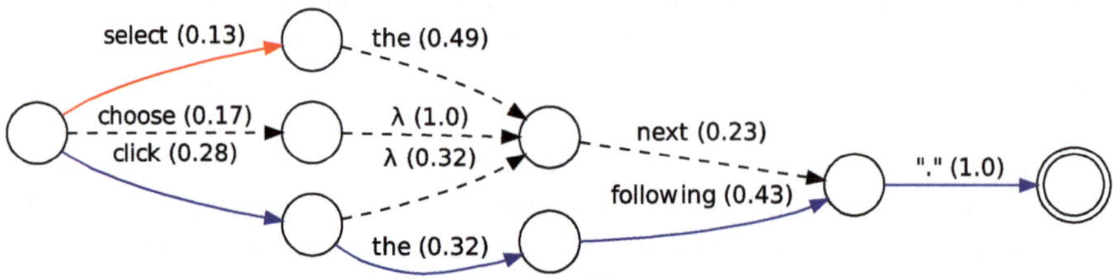

b) Alternative partial path in red after the user typing "select" as a correction.

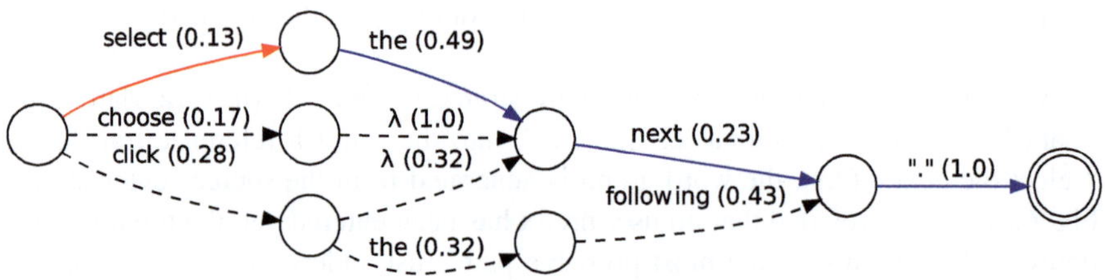

c) Most probable suffix in blue provided the user prefix "select".

Fig. 6.3 Example of the search process for the source Spanish sentence "seleccionar el siguiente", being the English reference translation "select the next". The first hypothesis generated by the system corresponds to the best path (in *blue*) in the word graph: "click the following". Then, the user types "select" to correct the first word of the first hypothesis, and the system reacts by searching the best path (in *blue*) from the node reached by the word "select"

6.4 Tasks, Experiments and Results

The IMT techniques introduced in the previous sections were assessed through a series of experiments involving different corpora. These corpora were pre-processed to obtain a simplified representation of the bilingual text which is used internally by the IMT system. This internal representation of the text is reverted by means of the application of post-processing techniques.

In the rest of this section we show a subset of the results obtained in the above mentioned experiments. The interested reader can consult the references given below for more detailed results. In addition, we briefly describe the pre- and post-processing techniques that were applied to the corpora used in the experiments.

6.4.1 Pre- and Post-processing

Pre-processing provides a simpler representation of the training corpus which makes token or word forms more homogeneous. Pre-processing involves the execution of the following steps: tokenization, removing unnecessary case information, and tagging some special tokens like numerical sequences, e-mail addresses and URLs. Post-processing takes place after the translation in order to hide the internal representation of the text from the user. In detail, post-processing involves the following steps: de-tokenization, true-casing, and replacing the tags with their corresponding words.

In an IMT scenario, the pre-/post-processing stages must run in real time and should be reversible as much as possible. In each human–machine interaction, the current prefix has to be pre-processed for the interactive-predictive engine and then the generated completion has to be post-processed for the user.

6.4.2 Tasks

Two different tasks have been selected to report IMT results: the XEROX task [36] and the European Union (EU) task [36].

The XEROX task consists in the translation of printer manuals from English to Spanish, French and German languages. Here we will only show the obtained IMT results for the English–Spanish corpus. The main figures of such corpus are shown in Table 6.1.

The EU task consists in the translation of the Bulletin of the European Union, which exists in the 23 official languages of the European Union. In this document we report results when translating from French to English. The main statistics of the French–English EU corpus are shown in Table 6.1.

It is worthy of note that the size of the vocabulary of the EU corpus is at least three times larger than that of the XEROX corpus. These figures together with the amount of running words and sentences reflect the challenging nature of this task.

6.4.3 Evaluation Measures

As mentioned in Sect. 1.4.6, the corpus-based evaluation paradigm is widely applied in MT. However, evaluation in MT is still an open problem [8], since many possible translations are acceptable for a single source sentence. This problem is further accentuated in the case of IMT, where the evaluation depends on the interaction protocol between a fictitious user that knows the reference translation and the IMT system.

In IMT systems, the effort needed by a human translator to obtain the reference translation is approximated by the measure *Word Stroke Ratio* (WSR) computed

Table 6.1 Main figures of the English–Spanish (Eng–Spa) XEROX task and the French–English (Fre–Eng) EU task (K and M denote thousands and millions, respectively). The training/test full-sentence overlap and the rate of out-of-vocabulary test-set words were less than 10% and 1%, respectively. Trigram models were used to compute the test word perplexity. A development set was used for both corpora with similar characteristics to the test set

	XEROX (Eng–Spa)	EU (Fre–Eng)
Training		
Sent. pairs (K)	56	215
Running words (M)	0.7/0.7	5.3/6.0
Vocabulary (K)	17/15	84/91
Test		
Sentences (K)	1.1	0.8
Running words (K)	10/8	20/23
Running chars. (K)	59/46	117/132
Perplexity	58/99	58/45

in a simulated user-computer scenario. The interaction protocol in this scenario is similar to that described in Sect. 2.6 for computer-assisted transcription. After each translation provided by the system, the longest common prefix is computed comparing it with a single reference translation.[2] The first unmatching word is replaced by their corresponding word in the reference translation. This process is repeated until the reference translation is produced. Thus, the WSR in IMT is redefined as the number of (word level) user interactions that are necessary to achieve the reference translation, divided by the total number of words in the reference translation.

On the other hand, the off-line measure *Word Error Rate* (WER) is also reported to gain insight into the translation quality of the underlying SMT system.[3] WER is defined in SMT as the Levenshtein (edit) distance between the system translation and the reference translation, divided by the total number of words of the reference translation. This measure is a coarse estimator of the post-editing user effort. However, WER and WSR are not directly comparable in IMT due to tight response-time constraints and a search space bounded by the limited set of translation hypotheses represented in the word graph.

6.4.4 Results

We carried out experiments to test the IMT techniques proposed here. The experiments consisted in interactively translating the test corpora of the above mentioned

[2] Although multiple reference translations would be desirable; because of the high cost of obtaining alternative reference translations only one reference translation is usually at our disposal.

[3] The interested reader is referred to [7] for a detailed comparative of SMT evaluation measures.

Table 6.2 WER results for the English–Spanish XEROX task and the French–English EU task

Task	WER
XEROX (Spa–Eng)	33.1
XEROX (Eng–Spa)	29.5
EU (Fre–Eng)	41.6
EU (Eng–Fre)	48.9

Table 6.3 WSR results for the English–Spanish XEROX task and the French–English EU task

Task	WSR
XEROX (Spa–Eng)	36.0
XEROX (Eng–Spa)	31.9
EU (Fre–Eng)	44.6
EU (Eng–Fre)	48.0

tasks using a word-graph-based IMT system. This IMT system uses phrase-based models to generate word graphs at the first interaction of the interactive translation process. After this first interaction, error-correcting techniques are applied to parse the prefixes given by the user in subsequent iterations.

As a preliminary experiment, the translation quality in terms of WER obtained by the underlying SMT system was obtained. Specifically, the WER measure is calculated from the target sentences that were generated by the IMT system at the first interaction of the IMT process. The results are shown in Table 6.2 for the English–Spanish XEROX task and the French–English EU task and for both translation directions. According to the values of the WER measure presented in the table, the XEROX English–Spanish language pair is the one for which the best translations can be produced.

As was mentioned above, the WSR measure constitutes one possible way to approximate the effort needed by IMT system users to obtain the translations of the source sentences. Table 6.3 shows the obtained WSR results when the English–Spanish XEROX corpus and the French–English EU corpus are interactively translated. The results are shown for both translation directions. According to the obtained values of the WSR measure, a human translator assisted by the IMT techniques proposed here would only need an effort equivalent to typing about 40% of the words of the translations for the French to English EU task, or only 30% for the English to Spanish XEROX task.

The obtained results are similar to those reported in [2]. That work presents IMT experiments using different translation technologies and involving all the existing language pairs and translation directions that are included in the XEROX and the EU tasks. Moreover, the IMT systems presented in [2] were evaluated by professional translators in the framework of the TT2 project. The productivity increased during the evaluation period as the participants grew accustomed to translating with this new tool. Overall, it seems fair to conclude that IMT systems can allow trans-

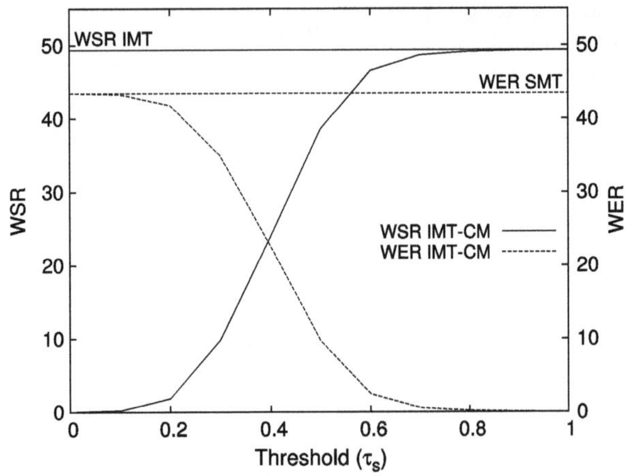

Fig. 6.4 WSR and WER obtained for different values of the suffix confidence threshold τ_s

lators to increase their productivity while maintaining a high quality; and while this increasing may not be spectacular, it is certainly substantial [11].

6.4.5 Results Using Confidence Information

A series of experiments on the English–Spanish XEROX task and the French–English EU were carried out to test the evolution of both the user effort measured in terms of WSR and the translation quality using WER, as a function of the suffix confidence classification threshold τ_s. WER allows us to gauge the quality of the translated text after supervising only those suffixes classified as incorrect. As mentioned in Sect. 6.2.1, a threshold value of $\tau_s = 0.0$ classifies all the suffixes as correct, i.e. the system behaves as a fully automatic SMT system. On the other hand, a threshold value of $\tau_s = 1.0$ implies that all the suffixes are classified as incorrect, therefore the system behavior is equal to a conventional IMT system.

Figure 6.4 shows WSR and WER for the EU task as a function of the suffix confidence threshold ranging from 0.0 to 1.0; similar curves were obtained for the XEROX task. Additionally, WER for a fully automatic SMT system is also displayed as a translation error baseline, and the WSR score of a conventional IMT system is shown as a user effort baseline. The confidence measure used in the experimentation (Sect. 6.2.1) depends on a word classification threshold τ_w. The value of τ_w modifies the smoothness of the transition between the SMT and the IMT behaviors. We present results for $\tau_w = 0.5$ because the smoothest transition is obtained for this threshold value.

This figure shows a smooth transition curve from fully automatic SMT ($\tau_s = 0.0$) through IMT scenarios enriched with confidence measures ($0.0 < \tau_s < 1.0$) to conventional IMT ($\tau_s = 1.0$). The threshold value τ_s acts as a regulator that allows one to balance the trade-off between the user effort required by the system and the final translation quality expected. Modifying the value of the threshold allows us to adapt the system to the quality requirements of the task or the limitations in human effort, and, consequently, the time needed for a professional translator to complete the task. For example, if we are allowed to provide translations with a low WER around 10, then we can reduce user effort from almost 50 (WSR IMT baseline) to less than 40 (WSR IMT-CM) setting the suffix confidence threshold (τ_s) to 0.5.

Example 6.1 shows the source sentence (src), the reference translation (ref) and the final translation (tra) for three sentences whose suffixes generated by the system were classified as correct at confidence threshold $\tau_s = 0.5$, and thus were not interactively translated by the user.

Example 6.1 Sentences in the EU task whose suffixes were classified as correct at confidence threshold $\tau_s = 0.5$.

src-1	DÉCLARATION (no 17) relative au droit d'accès à l'information
ref-1	DECLARATION (No 17) on the right of access to information
tra-1	DECLARATION (No 17) on the right of access to information
src-2	Conclusions du Conseil sur le commerce électronique et la fiscalité indirecte
ref-2	Council conclusions on electronic commerce and indirect taxation
tra-2	Council conclusions on e-commerce and indirect taxation
src-3	la participation des pays candidats aux programmes communautaires
ref-3	participation of the applicant countries in Community programmes
tra-3	the participation of applicant countries in Community programmes

6.5 Conclusions

The IMT paradigm proposed in this chapter allows for a close collaboration between a translator and an MT system. This paradigm entails an iterative process where, in each iteration, a data-driven MT system suggests a completion for the current prefix of a target sentence which a user can accept, modify, or ignore.

Behind this iterative process, there is an adaptation of the search procedure in order to take the user prefix into account for improved suffix prediction. The main components of the adapted search are error-correcting parsing and n-best completions that have been described. An additional component in these IMT systems is the integration of confidence measures to let the system play an active role in minimizing the user effort.

The evaluation procedure has simulated the behavior of a user working with an IMT system in order to assess the effort reduction with respect to a conventional post-editing system. The results reported reflect significant user effort savings in the IMT scenario, while the usage of confidence measures provides us with a powerful tool to find a trade-off between user effort and final translation quality.

However, human interaction offers a unique opportunity to improve the performance of the IMT systems by tuning the translation models. At each iteration, the translation obtained by the user in collaboration with the IMT system, together with the corresponding source sentence can generally be converted into more training data at hand to adapt the underlying models. This idea will be the central topic in Chap. 8.

Finally, one challenge in IMT is how to achieve an adequate synergy among diverse interactive feedback inputs, so that the maximum advantage of all the modalities involved is obtained. Chapter 7 is devoted to multi-modality for IMT.

References

1. Amengual, J. C., & Vidal, E. (1998). Efficient error-correcting Viterbi parsing. *IEEE Transactions on Pattern Analysis and Machine Intelligence*, *20*(10), 1109–1116.
2. Barrachina, S., Bender, O., Casacuberta, F., Civera, J., Cubel, E., Shahram, K., Lagarda, A. L., Ney, H., Tomás, J., Vidal, E., & Vilar, J. M. (2009). Statistical approaches to computer-assisted translation. *Computational Linguistics*, *35*(8), 3–28.
3. Bender, O., Hasan, S., Vilar, D., Zens, R., & Ney, H. (2005). Comparison of generation strategies for interactive machine translation. In *Proceedings of the 10th conference of the European chapter of the association for machine translation (EAMT 05)* (pp. 33–40), Budapest, Hungary.
4. Blatz, J., Fitzgerald, E., Foster, G., Gandrabur, S., Goutte, C., Kuesza, A., Sanchis, A., & Ueffing, N. (2004). Confidence estimation for machine translation. In *Proceedings of the 20th international conference on computational linguistics (COLING 04)* (p. 315), Geneva, Switzerland.
5. Brown, P. F., Cocke, J., Pietra, S. A. D., Pietra, V. J. D., Jelinek, F., Lafferty, J. D., Mercer, R. L., & Roosin, P. S. (1990). A statistical approach to machine translation. *Computational Linguistics*, *16*(2), 79–85.
6. Brown, P. F., Pietra, S. A. D., Pietra, V. J. D., & Mercer, R. L. (1993). The mathematics of statistical machine translation: Parameter estimation. *Computational Linguistics*, *19*(2), 263–310.
7. Callison-Burch, C., Fordyce, C., Koehn, P., Monz, C., & Schroeder, J. (2008). Further meta-evaluation of machine translation. In *Proceedings of the 3rd workshop on statistical machine translation (WMT 08)* (pp. 70–106), Morristown, NJ, USA.
8. Callison-Burch, C., Koehn, P., Monz, C., Peterson, K., Przybocki, M., & Zaidan, O. (2010). Findings of the 2010 joint workshop on statistical machine translation and metrics for machine translation. In *Proceedings of the joint fifth workshop on statistical machine translation and metricsMATR* (pp. 17–53), Uppsala, Sweden.
9. Casacuberta, F., & Vidal, E. (2004). Machine translation with inferred stochastic finite-state transducers. *Computational Linguistics*, *30*(2), 205–225.
10. Casacuberta, F., Ney, H., Och, F. J., Vidal, E., Vilar, J., Barrachina, S., García-Varea, I., Llorens, D., Martínez, C., Molau, S., Nevado, F., Pastor, M., Picó, D., Sanchis, A., & Tillmann, C. (2004). Some approaches to statistical and finite-state speech-to-speech translation. *Computer Speech & Language*, *18*, 25–47.
11. Casacuberta, F., Civera, J., Cubel, E., Lagarda, A. L., Lapalme, G., Macklovitch, E., & Vidal, E. (2009). Human interaction for high quality machine translation. *Communications of the ACM*, *52*(10), 135–138.
12. Civera, J., Vilar, J. M., Cubel, E., Lagarda, A. L., Barrachina, S., Vidal, E., Casacuberta, F., Picó, D., & González, J. (2004). From machine translation to computer assisted translation using finite-state models. In *Proceedings of the conference on empirical methods for natural language processing (EMNLP 04)* (pp. 349–356), Barcelona, Spain.
13. Civera, J., Vilar, J. M., Cubel, E., Lagarda, A., Barrachina, S., Casacuberta, F., Vidal, E., Picó, D., & González, J. (2004). A syntactic pattern recognition approach to computer assisted translation. In A. Fred, T. Caelli, A. Campilho, R. P. W. Duin & D. de Ridder (Eds.), *Lecture notes in computer science: Vol. 3138. Advances in statistical, structural and syntactical pattern recognition* (pp. 207–215). Berlin: Springer.

14. Cubel, E., González, J., Lagarda, A., Casacuberta, F., Juan, A., & Vidal, E. (2003). Adapting finite-state translation to the TransType2 project. In *Proceedings of the joint conference combining the 8th international workshop of the European association for machine translation and the 4th controlled language applications workshop (EAMT-CLAW 03)* (pp. 54–60), Dublin, Ireland.
15. Cubel, E., Civera, J., Vilar, J. M., Lagarda, A. L., Barrachina, S., Vidal, E., Casacuberta, F., Picó, D., González, J., & Rodríguez, L. (2004). Finite-state models for computer assisted translation. In *Proceedings of the 16th European conference on artificial intelligence (ECAI 04)* (pp. 586–590), Valencia, Spain.
16. Foster, G., Isabelle, P., & Plamondon, P. (1997). Target-text mediated interactive machine translation. *Machine Translation*, *12*(1–2), 175–194.
17. Foster, G., Langlais, P., & Lapalme, G. (2002). User-friendly text prediction for translators. In *Proceedings of the conference on empirical methods in natural language processing (EMNLP 02)* (pp. 148–155), Philadelphia, USA.
18. Gandrabur, S., & Foster, G. (2003). Confidence estimation for text prediction. In *Proceedings of the conference on natural language learning (CoNLL 03)* (pp. 315–321), Edmonton, Canada.
19. González-Rubio, J., Ortiz-Martínez, D., & Casacuberta, F. (2010). Balancing user effort and translation error in interactive machine translation via confidence measures. In *Proceedings of the 48th annual meeting of the association for computational linguistics (ACL 10)* (pp. 173–177), Uppsala, Sweden.
20. González-Rubio, J., Ortiz-Martínez, D., & Casacuberta, F. (2010). On the use of confidence measures within an interactive-predictive machine translation system. In *Proceedings of the 15th conference of the European chapter of the association for machine translation (EAMT 10)*, Saint-Raphaël, France.
21. Jiménez, V. M., & Marzal, A. (1999). Computing the k shortest paths: a new algorithm and an experimental coparison. In J. S. Viter & C. D. Zaraliagis (Eds.), *Lecture notes in computer science: Vol. 1668. Algorithm engineering* (pp. 15–29). Berlin: Springer.
22. Koehn, P. (2010). *Statistical machine translation*. Cambridge: Cambridge University Press.
23. Koehn, P., & Haddow, B. (2009). Interactive assistance to human translators using statistical machine translation methods. In *Proceedings of the 12th machine translation summit (MT Summit 09)*, Ottawa, Ontario, Canada.
24. Koehn, P., Hoang, H., Birch, A., Callison-Burch, C., Federico, M., Bertoldi, N., Cowan, B., Shen, W., Moran, C., Zens, R., Dyer, C., Bojar, O., Constantin, A., & Herbst, E. (2007). Moses: Open source toolkit for statistical machine translation. In *Proceedings of the 45th annual meeting of the association for computational linguistics (ACL 07)*, Prague, Czech Republic.
25. Langlais, P., Foster, G., & Lapalme, G. (2000). Unit completion for a computer-aided translation typing system. *Machine Translation*, *15*(4), 267–294.
26. Langlais, P., Lapalme, G., & Loranger, M. (2002). TransType: development-evaluation cycles to boost translator's productivity. *Machine Translation*, *15*(4), 77–98.
27. Lowerre, B. T. (1976). *The Harpy speech recognition system*. Ph.D. thesis, Carnegie Mellon University, Pittsburgh, PA, USA.
28. Mariño, J. B., Banchs, R. E., Crego, J. M., de Gispert, A., Lambert, P., Fonollosa, J. A. R., & Costa-jussà, M. R. (2006). N-gram-based machine translation. *Computational Linguistics*, *32*(4), 527–549.
29. Nepveu, L., Lapalme, G., Langlais, P., & Foster, G. (2004). Adaptive language and translation models for interactive machine translation. In *Proceedings of the conference on empirical methods in natural language processing (EMNLP 04)* (pp. 190–197), Barcelona, Spain.
30. Och, F. J. (2003). Minimum error rate training for statistical machine translation. In *Proceedings of the 41st annual meeting of the association for computational linguistics (ACL 03)* (pp. 160–167), Sapporo, Japan.
31. Och, F. J., & Ney, H. (2004). The alignment template approach to statistical machine translation. *Computational Linguistics*, *30*(4), 417–450.

32. Och, F. J., Zens, R., & Ney, H. (2003). Efficient search for interactive statistical machine translation. In *Proceedings of the 10th conference of the European chapter of the association for computational linguistics (EACL 03)* (pp. 387–393), Budapest, Hungary.
33. Ortiz-Martínez, D., García-Varea, I., & Casacuberta, F. (2005). Thot: a toolkit to train phrase-based statistical translation models. In *Proceedings of the 10th machine translation summit (MT Summit 05)* (pp. 141–148), Phuket, Thailand.
34. Patry, A., & Langlais, P. (2009). Prediction of words in statistical machine translation using a multilayer perceptron. In *Proceedings of the 12th machine translation summit (MT Summit 09)* (pp. 101–111), Ottawa, Ontario, Canada.
35. Sanchis, A., Juan, A., & Vidal, E. (2007). Estimation of confidence measures for machine translation. In *Proceedings of the 11th machine translation summit (MT Summit 07)* (pp. 407–412), Copenhagen, Denmark.
36. SchlumbergerSema S.A., I. T. de Informática, für Informatik VI, R. W. T. H. A. L., en Linguistique Informatique Laboratory University of Montreal, R. A., Soluciones, C., Gamma, S., and Europe, X. R. C. (2001). *TT2. TransType2—computer assisted translation.* Project Technical Annex. Information Society Technologies (IST) Programme, IST-2001-32091.
37. Simard, M., & Isabelle, P. (2009). Phrase-based machine translation in a computer-assisted translation environment. In *Proceedings of the 12th machine translation summit (MT Summit 09)* (pp. 255–261), Ottawa, Ontario, Canada.
38. Tomás, J., & Casacuberta, F. (2006). Statistical phrase-based models for interactive computer-assisted translation. In *Proceedings of the 44th annual meeting of the association for computational linguistics and 21th international conference on computational linguistics (COLING/ACL 06)* (pp. 835–841), Sydney, Australia.
39. Ueffing, N., & Ney, H. (2005). Application of word-level confidence measures in interactive statistical machine translation. In *Proceedings of the 10th conference of the European chapter of the association for machine translation (EAMT 05)* (pp. 262–270), Budapest, Hungary.
40. Ueffing, N., & Ney, H. (2007). Word-level confidence estimation for machine translation. *Computational Linguistics*, *33*(1), 9–40.
41. Wagner, R. A. (1974). Order-n correction for regular languages. *Communications of the ACM*, *17*(5), 265–268.

Chapter 7
Multi-Modality for Interactive Machine Translation

With Contribution Of: Vicent Alabau, Germán Sanchis-Trilles and Luis Rodríguez.

Contents

In the Interactive Machine Translation (IMT) framework, a human translator can interact with the IMT system to achieve a high-quality translation. This is done by basic editing operations, i.e. substitution or deletion of erroneous words or insertion of missing words. This process is usually performed with the keyboard. While keyboard is considered as the principal way of introducing text to a computer, other modalities can provide useful information to improve IMT performance or to increase system ergonomics.

Examples of modalities that can improve performance are pointer interactions, which give implicit and explicit information that can be of great use to an IMT system. Additionally, the speech and handwritten text modalities are able to increase the system's usability and ergonomics. This is specially true for the new kind of keyboard-less devices that are gaining popularity incredibly fast, as touch-screen tablets and mobile phones.

7.1 Introduction

In Chap. 6 the Interactive Machine Translation (IMT) paradigm is described. In IMT, a human translator interacts with the system to achieve a high-quality translation. This is basically done by amending iteratively the erroneous words. Unless

DOI 10.1007/978-0-85729-479-1_7,

stated to the contrary, this process is carried out using a keyboard. At best, a mouse is used to put the focus of the keyboard in the right position.

Although this paradigm has proven to be beneficial to potential users, such an interaction scheme is very restricted, and one could easily picture a scenario in which the user would desire to interact with the system in many other different ways, such as by means of spoken utterances, handwritten words, mouse gestures, or even gaze tracking. These alternative modalities could provide useful information to improve IMT performance or to increase system ergonomics in specific systems where keyboard is inadequate or even not accessible. The challenge is then to achieve an adequate modality synergy, which finally allows for taking maximum advantage of all the modalities involved, with the final purpose of allowing for a more efficient collaboration between the IMT system and the human user.

In this chapter, several ways to introduce multi-modality into the classical IMT paradigm are analyzed. Section 7.2 presents an extension of such paradigm, in which a pointer device is considered as additional interaction device between the user and the IMT system. Speech recognition is considered as an efficient modality for correcting system errors in Sect. 7.3. Alternatively, handwritten text recognition is also considered for this purpose in Sect. 7.4. Experimental results showing the performance gains achieved within these different scenarios are shown in Sect. 7.5, and the conclusions derived are presented in Sect. 7.6.

7.2 Making Use of Weaker Feedback

In the traditional IMT setting, the system only received feedback whenever the user typed in a new word. Although such a set-up has proven to provide benefits, it implies that the IMT system only relies on the information provided by the user through the keyboard. Nevertheless, a human user sitting in front of a typical desktop computer is also interacting with the machine by means of the mouse, but such an interaction is not taken into account by traditional IMT systems. In this section, we consider *Pointer Actions* (PA) as an additional information source for the system, which the user provides usually without even noticing it. In this set-up, we will consider two different PA types, i.e. *non-explicit* (or positioning) PAs and *interaction-explicit* PAs [15, 16].

7.2.1 Non-explicit Positioning Pointer Actions

The key idea behind considering PAs as an additional communication vehicle between the system and the user is that, in order to correct a hypothesis, the user first needs to position the cursor in the place where she wants to type a word, be it for correcting it, for introducing a new word, or for deleting an existing one. In this case, we will assume that this is done by performing a PA. By doing so, the user

<table>
<tr><th></th><th>Input</th><th>(x)</th><th>Click OK to close the print dialog</th></tr>
<tr><td>0</td><td>System</td><td>$(\hat{s})$</td><td>Haga clic para cerrar el diálogo de impresión</td></tr>
<tr><td>1</td><td>User</td><td>(p)</td><td>Haga clic |</td></tr>
<tr><td></td><td>System</td><td>$(\hat{s})$</td><td>en ACEPTAR para cerrar el diálogo de impresión</td></tr>
<tr><td>2</td><td>User</td><td>(p)</td><td>Haga clic en ACEPTAR para cerrar el |</td></tr>
<tr><td></td><td>System</td><td>$(\hat{s})$</td><td>de diálogo de impresión</td></tr>
<tr><td>3</td><td>User</td><td>(p)</td><td>Haga clic en ACEPTAR para cerrar el cuadro de diálogo de impresión #</td></tr>
<tr><td></td><td>Output</td><td>(h)</td><td>Haga clic en ACEPTAR para cerrar el cuadro de diálogo de impresión</td></tr>
</table>

Fig. 7.1 Example of non-explicit positioning PA which solves two errors. In this case, the system produces the correct suffix s immediately after the user validates a prefix p, implicitly indicating that she wants the suffix to be changed, without need of any further action. The character | indicates the position where a PA was performed

is already providing a very valuable information to the system. Namely, she is signaling that whatever information is located before the cursor is to be considered as correct, hence validating the current prefix p. More importantly, however, she is also signaling that she does not like whatever word comes after p, and that she is about to change it. At this point, the system can capture this fact and, knowing that such suffix is to be considered as incorrect, provide a new translation hypothesis in which the prefix remains unchanged and the suffix is replaced by a new one in which the first word is different from the first word of the previous suffix.

Obviously, having the system change the incorrect suffix does not mean that the new suffix will be correct. However, given that the system knows that the first word in the current suffix is incorrect, the worst case would only imply that the newly introduced word would still be incorrect. This entails that the user would need to type in the correct word, as she was going to do anyway. However, if the new proposed suffix happens to be correct, the system will have spared the user one interaction, which is typing in the new word, and the user will happily find that she only needs to accept such word, or perhaps even the complete suffix.

An example of such behavior can be seen in Fig. 7.1. In this example, the SMT system first provides a translation which the user does not like. Hence, she positions the cursor before word "para", with the purpose of typing in "en". By doing so, she is validating the prefix "Haga click", and signaling that she wants "para" to be replaced. Before typing in anything, the system realizes that she is going to change the word located after the cursor, and replaces the suffix by another one, which is the one the user had in mind in the first place. A similar behavior can be seen with the wrong word "diálogo". Finally, the user only has to accept the final translation.

We are naming this kind of PA *non-explicit* because the user does not need to perform an explicit action in order to inform the system that it needs to change the suffix: it is the system itself who realizes that the user is going to type in a word and anticipates the user's intentions, suggesting a new suffix hypothesis. For this reason, and given the fact that the user would need to position the cursor anyway, it is important to point out that any improvement achieved by this kind of PA is an improvement *per se*, since it requires no further effort from the user. For this reason, it is assumed to have no cost.

The positioning PAs can be formulated thus: Given a source sentence x, a consolidated prefix p and a suffix s' suggested by the system in the previous interaction, search for another suffix $\hat{s}$ such that the first word in $\hat{s}$ is different from the first word in s'

$$\hat{s} = \underset{s:s_1 \neq s'_1}{\arg\max}\, P(s \mid x, p, s'). \tag{7.1}$$

7.2.2 Interaction-Explicit Pointer Actions

In contrast to non-explicit PAs, one could easily picture a scenario where the user simply wants a given suffix to be changed, independently of the position of the cursor. Assuming that the underlying IMT system is efficient enough when attempting to provide high-quality hypotheses, the human expert would just need to click before the first word of the suffix she intends to change in order to have it replaced without any further action. This PA is named interaction-explicit [16] because, as opposed to positioning PAs, the user needs to explicitly ask the system for another hypothesis. Obviously, this could also be done by using some other different device, but in this case we assume this is done using the mouse. Note that this kind of PA does imply an added cost, since the user needs to perform an explicit action for signaling the system that she wants the suffix to be replaced. However, if the underlying MT engine providing suffixes is powerful enough, the benefit obtained may easily be worth the hassle, since performing a PA is less costly than introducing one (or several) whole new word. Of course, in this kind of PA the system is expecting a participative and collaborative attitude from the user, which was not the case in the case of non-explicit PAs. An example of such behavior is shown in Fig. 7.2.

	Input	(x)	A message appears stating that this action is processing
0	System	$(\hat{s})$	Hay un mensaje que establece que dicha acción se está realizando
1	User	(p)	|
	System	$(\hat{s})$	Aparece un mensaje que establece que dicha acción está realizándose
2	User	(p)	Aparece un mensaje que |
	System	$(\hat{s})$	afirma que dicha acción está realizándose
3	User	(p)	Aparece un mensaje que |
	System	$(\hat{s})$	indica que dicha acción está realizándose
4	User	(p)	Aparece un mensaje que indica que dicha acción está realizándose #
	Output	(h)	Aparece un mensaje que indica que dicha acción está realizándose

Fig. 7.2 Example of interaction-explicit PA which solves an error. In the case of the first error, the first word proposed by the system is considered incorrect. For this reason, the user positions the cursor before the first word, and such action already corrects the word and amends the error the user intended to correct. In the second error, the user first positions the cursor, hence performing a non-explicit PA, and then performs a second PA, an *interaction-explicit* PA, in order to ask the system for a new hypothesis. The system then returns a new suffix, which is the one the user had in mind. Finally, the user validates the complete hypothesis. As in the previous image, the character | indicates where the PA has been performed

Assuming the user has already performed n PAs until the current moment and is demanding yet another suffix $\hat{s}$ from the system, the explicit PA problem can be formalized in a very similar way to the case of non-explicit PAs:

$$\hat{s} = \operatorname*{arg\,max}_{s: s_1 \neq s_1^{(i)}, \forall i \in \{1..n\}} P\big(s | x, p, s^{(1)}, s^{(2)}, \ldots, s^{(n)}\big) \tag{7.2}$$

where $s_1^{(i)}$ is the first word of the ith suffix discarded, and $s^{(1)}, s^{(2)}, \ldots, s^{(n)}$ is the set of all n suffixes discarded.

7.3 Correcting Errors with Speech Recognition

The use of speech recognition to perform MT tasks is a topic that has received moderate attention [3–5, 11–14]. The early idea of these systems consisted on a human translator dictating aloud the translation in the target language. Then, a speech recognition system transcribed the speech signal. The recognition errors could be reduced if the source text was used by the recognition system to reduce transcription errors. These approaches, however, were focused on fully automatic systems, which needed from a human expert post-editing the system output.

Conversely, multi-modal interaction (Sect. 1.3.5) suggests a new interesting application where speech recognition can be used as an alternative modality to interact with an IMT system. Here, a human translator is allowed to make corrections to the IMT system by reading (with possible modifications) parts of the suggestions of the IMT system [17]. The IMT framework allows one to introduce a lower degree of freedom in the speech transcription process with the corresponding increasing of the recognition accuracy. On the other hand, if the recognition system is fully integrated within the IMT paradigm, the user can also make use of the conventional means (keyboard and/or mouse) to guarantee that the produced text exhibits an adequate level of quality. This idea is exemplified in Fig. 7.3.

The following is a formalization of this problem. Let x be the source text and p a "correct" prefix of the target sentence. The user is now allowed to utter some words, v, generally aimed at amending parts of the suffix s' suggested by the system in the previous iteration. Then, the most probable suffix $\hat{s}$ is searched by the system. Following Eq. (1.26), the feedback is introduced by an utterance $f = v$ and assuming a left-to-right protocol ($h = p, s$; $h' = p, s'$), the search problem can be formulated as

$$\hat{s} \approx \operatorname*{arg\,max}_{s} \max_{d} P(v \mid d) \cdot P(d \mid p, s', x) \cdot P(s \mid p, s', d, x), \tag{7.3}$$

where d is the transcription of the utterance v. Finally, the user can enter additional amendment keystrokes to produce a new consolidated prefix, p, based on the previous p, d and parts of s.

This maximization is typically carried out in two steps (Sect. 1.3.5), since the joint optimization does not usually admit an efficient solution. First, the *feedback*

	Input	(x)	Click OK to close the print dialog
0	System	$(\hat{s})$	Haga clic para cerrar el diálogo de impresión
1	Utterance	(v)	
	System	(d)	Haga clic a
	User	(p)	Haga clic en
	System	$(\hat{s})$	ACEPTAR para cerrar el diálogo de impresión
2	Utterance	(v)	
	System	(d)	cerrar el cuadro
	User	(p)	Haga clic en ACEPTAR para cerrar el cuadro↑
	System	$(\hat{s})$	de diálogo de impresión
3	User	(p)	Haga clic en ACEPTAR para cerrar el cuadro de diálogo de impresión #
	Output	(h)	Haga clic <u>en</u> ACEPTAR para cerrar el <u>cuadro</u> de diálogo de impresión

Fig. 7.3 An example of IMT with speech and keyboard interaction. The aim is to translate the English sentence "*Click OK to close the print dialog*" into Spanish. Each step starts with a previously fixed target-language prefix p, from which the system suggests a suffix $\hat{s}$. Then the user utters some words for positioning (and accepting some words) and correcting a word in the $\hat{s}$. In iteration 1, the utterance is to position and to accept "Haga clic" and to correct "para", however, the user does not agree with the decoding of the last word of the utterance and then she types another word. The system suggests a new suffix to complete the translation. In the iteration 2 the user accepts the decoding proposed by the system using some special stroke (↑). In the final translation h, text that has been typed by the user is underlined

data v are "optimally" decoded into $\hat{d}$,

$$\hat{d} = \arg\max_{d} P(v \mid d) \cdot P(d \mid p, s', x) \tag{7.4}$$

where $P(v \mid d)$ is implemented using acoustic models, typically *Hidden Markov Models* (HMM, see Sect. 4.3.3) and $P(d \mid p, s', x)$ by a language model constrained by the prefix, the previous suffix and the input.

Second, assuming that $P(s \mid p, s', d, x)$ does not depend on the previous suffix s', Eq. (7.3) can be rewritten using the fixed $\hat{d}$ into

$$\hat{s} \approx \arg\max_{s} P\big(s \mid p, \hat{d}, x\big). \tag{7.5}$$

Note that the last term of Eq. (7.5) is equivalent to the basic formulation of IMT in Eq. (6.7) since a new validated prefix can be created concatenating p and d in an appropriate manner.

There are different scenarios, depending on the assumptions of the constraints made on language modeling in Eq. (7.4). What follows is a comprehensive list of such scenarios.

7.3.1 Unconstrained Speech Decoding (DEC)

The less restrictive one (referred as DEC) is the case where the language model is approximated as $P(d)$, dropping all dependencies on the prefix, previous suffix and input. As a result, the problem can be solved by regular speech decoding:

$$\hat{d} = \arg\max_{d} P(d) \cdot P(v \mid d). \tag{7.6}$$

The language model for $P(d)$ is implemented as a (smoothed) n-gram, estimated from the same target sentences used to estimate the translation models for other scenarios. Since the n-gram is estimated from complete target sentences, but v is typically an utterance of a sentence fragment, this language model has to be adapted to properly accept any possible subsequence of words. To this end, the language model is modified adequately and the resulting search space is significantly larger than that of the original n-gram. The acoustic models for $P(v \mid d)$ are conventional HMMs of monophone units.

DEC is more difficult than the translation dictation setting discussed at the beginning of this section, not only because DEC does not take advantage of the information provided by the source-language text, but also because it deals with the decoding of fragments of the target sentence, rather than whole sentences as in [2–4].

7.3.2 Prefix-Conditioned Speech Decoding (DEC-PREF)

The second pure speech-decoding scenario is referred to as DEC-PREF. Now the available prefix p is introduced as an additional constraint; but, again, no information about the source text is used. In this case,

$$\hat{d} = \arg\max_{d} P(d \mid p) \cdot P(v \mid d). \tag{7.7}$$

The implementation of Eq. (7.7) is similar to that of Eq. (7.6), except for the search, which is now constrained to start only with the final n-grams in p.

7.3.3 Prefix-Conditioned Speech Decoding (IMT-PREF)

The least constrained IMT scenario is called IMT-PREF. It corresponds to a realization of Eq. (7.4), where the source sentence, x, the previous prefix, p, and a human-translator utterance, v, are available. The goal of the IMT system is to decode v into an optimal $\hat{d}$ and to produce a suggested suffix $\hat{s}$ as a continuation of this decoding,

$$\hat{d} = \arg\max_{d} P(d \mid x, p) \cdot P(v \mid d). \tag{7.8}$$

Here, the constrained language model for estimating $P(d \mid x, p)$ in Eq. (7.8) can be implemented as an adaptation of the target (smoothed) n-grams used in DEC-PREF (where p was already taken into account) based on the source sentence x.

The adapted weight of each n-gram (h_1^n) is the product of the original n-gram probability in DEC-PREF ($P(h_n \mid h_1^{n-1})$) and the largest probability of translating h_n from any source word in x; i.e., $\max_{1\le j\le |x|} P(x_j \mid h_n)$, where $|x|$ is the number of words in x. The lexical translation probabilities $P(x_j \mid h_n)$ are obtained from a stochastic dictionary estimated using a parallel corpus and the GIZA++ toolkit [7]. The acoustic models for estimating $P(v \mid d)$ in Eq. (7.8), are the same HMMs used in DEC and DEC-PREF.

7.3.4 Prefix Selection (IMT-SEL)

The most constrained scenario, called IMT-SEL, corresponds to a realization of Eq. (7.9). It is similar to IMT-PREF but here the human translator can only utter exact prefixes of the suggestion made by the IMT system (s'). These utterances are aimed at *selecting* acceptable prefixes of the system suggestions (hence the name, IMT-SEL). The possible amendments of the remaining parts of the suggestions can only be made by typing. We have

$$\hat{d} = \arg\max_{d} P(d \mid s') \cdot P(v \mid d). \tag{7.9}$$

In practice, Eq. (7.9) can be implemented as a search for $\hat{d}$ in the (small) set of possible prefixes of the target suffix $\hat{s}$; that is, $P(d \mid \hat{s})$ is estimated by a special finite-state language model in which only those d that are prefixes of $\hat{s}$ have non-null probability. The acoustic models for estimating $P(v \mid d)$ in Eq. (7.9) are the same HMMs as in all the previous cases.

7.4 Correcting Errors with Handwritten Text Recognition

On-line *Handwritten Text Recognition* (HTR) can be considered as an alternative (or complementary) modality to speech. In this case, the human writes down the correction of a target word in a graphic tablet or in a touch-screen. This correction can be another word or a gesture to indicate a word deletion or an insertion of a new word at a given point.

Although the scenario is quite similar to the one for speech, there are some differences. To begin with, the cursor is placed in a position using the pen by the human when she writes down the correction. This allows for a deterministic way of validating the prefix. Furthermore, as a result, a non-explicit mouse action is performed in a similar way to Sect. 7.2.1, which allows the system to take into account the valuable extra information encoded in the rejected suffix. In addition, the user is only permitted to introduce one word at a time, simplifying the recognition process. Of course, as in the speech interaction scenario, the touch-screen input is non-deterministic. Therefore, the user may need to correct the HTR decoding using the keyboard in case of error.

	Input	(x)	Si alguna función no se encuentra disponible en su red
0	System	$(\hat{s})$	If any feature not is available on your network
1	Handwriting	(t)	If any feature | is
	System	(d)	in
	User	(p)	If any feature | is
	System	$(\hat{s})$	not available at your network
2	Handwriting	(t)	If any feature is not available | in
	System	(d)	in
	User	(p)	If any feature is not available in↑
	System	$(\hat{s})$	your network
3	User	(p)	If any feature is not available in your network #
	Output	(h)	If any feature is not available in your network

Fig. 7.4 Example of IMT session for a task from Spanish to English for the Xerox corpus. The diagram shows the translation from the source sentence x to the target sentence h. At each iteration, s is the suffix proposed by the system. t are the pen strokes introduced by the user. If the decoding $\hat{d}$ of the pen strokes correct it is displayed in *boldface*. On the contrary, if $\hat{d}$ is incorrect it is shown in *red*. In that case, the correct word is introduced by the user using the keyboard, which results in a new validated prefix p. Finally, the # symbol marks the end of the string

Figure 7.4 is an example of this interaction modality. Initially, the system starts with an empty prefix. At the first iteration, the systems proposes a full hypothesis, which would be the equivalent to the output of a fully automated system. The user finds the first error, *not*, and amends it by handwriting *is* with on a touch-screen. The HTR system mistakenly recognizes *in*. Thus, the user falls back to the keyboard and enters *is*. Since the user validates sequentially from left to right, the system assumes that the prefix *if any feature is* is correct. Based on this validated prefix, the system produces a new suffix, in which the first word, *not*, has been automatically corrected. In the second iteration the user replaces *at* by the word *in*. Finally, the system suggests a new suffix that is correct and the user ends the process by accepting the sentence.

Let x be the source text and t a representation of the on-line handwritten word that corrects the first erroneous word s'_e of the previous suffix s'. The problem is to search for a transcription d of t that corrects the target word s'_e and a new suffix s that completes the target sentence from the consolidate prefix p (all the words in s' until the previous position of s'_e followed by d) as a translation of x. Following Eq. (1.26), the feedback is introduced by handwriting $f = t$ on a touch-screen. On the other hand, a left-to-right protocol ($h = p, s$; $h' = p, s'$) is assumed. We also assume independence of $P(s \mid p, s', d, x)$ on s' given the rest of the dependencies and we take into account that the position of s'_e is fixed in a deterministic way, therefore $P(d \mid p, s', x)$ in Eq. (1.26) can be written as $P(d \mid p, s'_e, x)$. Finally, the search problem can be formulated as

$$\hat{s} \approx \arg\max_{s} \max_{d} P(t \mid d) \cdot P(d \mid p, s'_e, x) \cdot P(s \mid p, d, x), \qquad (7.10)$$

where $P(t \mid d)$ is a regular morphological model for on-line handwritten text recognition (see more details in Sect. 3.5.2). Similarly to the speech modality, the last term, $P(s \mid p, d, x)$, is equivalent to the IMT model in Eq. (6.7) for which p and d has been concatenated into a new validated prefix. Finally, $P(d \mid p, s'_e, x)$ is a constrained language model. On the one hand, the language model must provide the probabilities for words following the prefix p which, at the same time, are among the possible translations of the words in x. On the other hand, s encodes non-explicit information of the user feedback, that is, the user is correcting a word s'_e in the predicted suffix s' which is known to be wrong. Thus, the constrained language model probability can be approximated as (assuming that $P(d \mid p, s'_e, x)$ does not depend on x given p)

$$P(d \mid p, s'_e, x) \approx \begin{cases} 0, & d = s'_e, \\ \frac{P(d|p)}{1-P(s'_e|p)}, & d \neq s'_e, \end{cases} \tag{7.11}$$

where $P(d \mid p)$ can be approximated by a n-gram conditioned to the prefix p.

Two problems must be tackled with Eq. (7.10). First, as the dynamic range of the estimated probabilities are quite different, it is necessary to balance the absolute values of these probabilities [9]. Second, the estimated probabilities are rough approximations to the true probabilities and need to be smoothed with more general, better estimated models. Log-linear models can be used to accomplish both things. They have been successfully applied for other natural language tasks [1, 8, 10]. Following this framework, the decision rule in Eq. (7.10) can be rewritten as

$$(\hat{s}, \hat{d}) = \arg\max_{s,d} \sum_{m=1}^{M} \lambda_m f_m(d, t, x, p, s'_e, s), \tag{7.12}$$

where we have a set of M feature functions $f_m(d, t, x, p, s'_e, s)$ and scale factors λ_m.

The following feature functions have been considered to form part of the log-lineal model. First, $f_{\text{hmm}} = \log P(t \mid d)$ is a morphological model for HTR that is modeled as a HMM. Second, $f_{\text{e}} = \log P(d \mid s'_e)$ is an error-conditioned model to assign zero probability to the word w that has been wrongly predicted by the IMT system and a uniform probability for the rest of the vocabulary. Third, $f_{\text{tr}} = \log P(s \mid d, p, x)$ is an IMT model. And finally, $f_{\text{1gr}} = \log P(d)$ as a 1-gram is added for smoothing.

7.5 Tasks, Experiments and Results

7.5.1 Results when Incorporating Weaker Feedback

The use of the pointer as input feedback (see Sect. 7.2) was evaluated through experiments on some of the corpora that were used for the baseline system.

First, results for including the non-explicit positioning PA into the IMT system are shown in Table 7.1. In such table, it can be seen that the non-explicit PAs allow us to obtain a relative improvement of about 11.3% for the XEROX corpus and 6.0% for the EU corpus without any additional action [15].

Table 7.1 Experimental results with the XEROX and the EU corpora when considering pointer actions. Results are given in WSR percentage

Corpus	Languages	WSR baseline	WSR considering positioning PA
XEROX	English–Spanish	41.7	37.8
EU	French–English	51.9	45.9

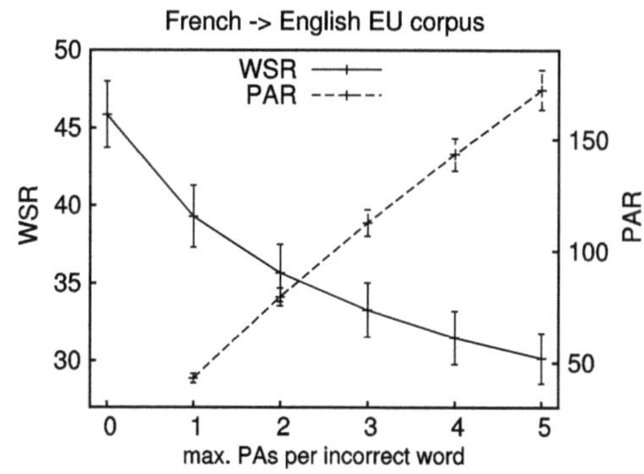

Fig. 7.5 WSR improvement when considering one to five maximum explicit PAs for translating the EU corpus. 95% level confidence intervals are shown

In addition, considering repeated PAs to find the right suffix yields further improvements [16], as can be seen in Fig. 7.5. Such improvements can achieve a further reduction of WSR by up to 30% relative. However, when increasing the maximum allowed amount of explicit PAs from 1 to 5, relative improvement in WSR drops significantly. For this reason, it is easy to imagine that a human user will rarely perform more than two or three PAs before actually typing in a new word. Despite this fact, it should be noted that by just asking the system to replace the suffix twice before actually typing in a word, the user might already be saving about 15% of word-strokes.

7.5.2 Results for Speech as Input Feedback

To measure the performance of the speech modality, the well known *Word Error Rate* (WER) has been used. It is explained in Sect. 6.4.3. *Sentence Error Rate* (SER) has been considered as well, which is computed as the percentage of incorrectly recognized sentences.

The experiments of speech enabled IMT have been carried out for the XEROX task explained at Sect. 6.4.2. For the speech experiments, a test corpus was acquired consisting of utterances of fragments of target-language (Spanish) sentences, extracted from the test part of the original parallel TT2 corpus. These utterances were used as a test-set to simulate real interactions of the IMT system with human

Table 7.2 Speech-decoding results (in %) for different scenarios

	DEC	DEC-PREF	IMT-PREF	IMT-SEL
WER	18.6	16.1	10.6	1.6
SER	50.2	44.4	30.0	3.6

translators.[1] For this acquisition, ten different users read aloud an average of 580 segments of sentences from the XEROX corpus, amounting to a total of 4 hours of speech signal. The speech data were acquired using high-quality microphones and 16 KHz sampling frequency. A 3-gram language model was trained using the Spanish XEROX corpus. Finally, the acoustic models were trained on a relatively large speech corpus, containing phonetically balanced spoken sentences in Spanish, which were acquired in this work [6]. This corpus was used here only to train the acoustic HMMs needed in all the speech-related experiments. See more details in Sect. 4.6 and [17].

Results for the different scenarios described in Sect. 7.3 are shown in Table 7.2. According to these results, speech recognition accuracy increases as the language model becomes more constrained. If only prefix-derived constraints are added to DEC, a modest improvement of 2.5 points of WER and 5.8 points of SER is obtained in DEC-PREF. By further including constraints derived from the source text, a more significant improvement is achieved in IMT-PREF: 5.5 points of WER and 14.4 points of SER (or 8.0 points of WER and 20.2 points of SER with respect to the least constrained baseline). The constraints added in the last scenario, IMT-SEL, are derived from the (simulated) suggestions of the IMT system. In this case, the improvement is very important: 9.0 points of WER and 26.4 points of SER with respect to the last scenario (or 17 points of WER and 46.6 points of SER with respect to the baseline).

These results clearly suggest that using knowledge about the source sentence is more important than using only user-validated prefixes. Moreover, if the translation difficulty of the test-set is taken into account (which according to Table 6.2 is quite large), the impact of using the translation information is remarkable. Therefore, better results are expected for IMT-PREF with less problematic texts and/or better (use of) translation models. Additionally, the decoding computational demands of the speech decoder are much less for the more constrained scenarios since the perplexity of their language models are lower.

The relative accuracy that can be achieved in the different scenarios has been assessed in terms of WER and SER. However, at least for the IMT-SEL setting, only the SER figure really matters, since it directly estimates the voice-driven cursor-positioning accuracy. The 3.6% SER achieved means that a manual (mouse or keyboard) correction of cursor position is required every 28 voice-driven successful

[1] Real experiments for IMT-PREF and IMT-SEL would involve having real human translators interacting with the system, which is prohibitive for this study; not only for the high costs involved, but also because of the associated lack of experimentation flexibility.

actions, on average. We think this figure can be easily improved by using better acoustic modeling for speech decoding.

7.5.3 Results for Handwritten Text as Input Feedback

The experiments of this modality evaluate the performance of the decoding algorithm in Eq. (7.12). Specifically, the interest is to evaluate the performance of the on-line HTR system, which has been assessed with the *Classification Error Rate* (CER). CER is the ratio between the number of misrecognized words and the total number of words.

The results presented in this section were performed on the XEROX English–Spanish corpus detailed in Sect. 6.4.2. From the experiments in Sect. 6.4.4, the words that were corrected by the user by typing the correct solution were gathered. With that list of words, a synthetic test corpus was generated from three held-out users from the UNIPEN dataset, which was introduced in Sect. 3.6.1. The words were generated by concatenating random characters from character instances of the same user. More details on how these words were produced can be found in Sect. 3.6.1. This set of generated samples established the test corpus, which was decoded using the on-line HTR subsystem is explained in detail in Sect. 3.5.2. With respect to the rest of the models used in Eq. (7.12), they where the same as obtained in Sect. 6.4.4.

Table 7.3 summarizes the results for different combinations of feature functions. The systems are, from left to right: a pure HMM system (f_{hmm}), a traditional on-line HTR system with a 1-gram ($f_{\mathrm{hmm}}, f_{\mathrm{1gr}}$), a log-linear (LL) model ($f_{\mathrm{hmm}}, f_{\mathrm{e}}, f_{\mathrm{tr}}, f_{\mathrm{1gr}}$), and a log-linear model with a menu for punctuation symbols (LL+menu). Values are average ER for the three users and relative improvements with respect to the baseline (HMM system) are presented as well. It is important to note that the log-linear model outperformed the traditional on-line HTR system. Besides, the addition of the menu for punctuation symbols provides remarkable improvements. The motivation of adding such menu will be explained in the next paragraph. With respect to IMT results, the user would have needed to correct the 31.9% of the words to achieve the reference translation (Sect. 6.4.4). The most important result that can be drawn is that just 1.6% of the total words of the translation are

Table 7.3 Summary of the CER results for various systems (combination of lambda parameters). R.I. are the relative improvements w.r.t. the baseline system (HMM). The systems are from left to right: a pure HMM system (f_{hmm}), a traditional on-line HTR system with a 1-gram ($f_{\mathrm{hmm}}, f_{\mathrm{1gr}}$), a log-linear (LL) model ($f_{\mathrm{hmm}}, f_{\mathrm{e}}, f_{\mathrm{tr}}, f_{\mathrm{1gr}}$), and a log-linear model with a menu for punctuation symbols (LL+menu)

System	HMM	HTR	LL	LL+menu
ER	18.7	11.0	10.6	5.0
R.I. (%)	–	41.2	43.3	73.3

needed to be written using a keyboard. Conversely, the rest of the errors (30.3%) of the total words) are amended with the touch-screen. The rest of the words remain untouched.

By looking carefully into the results of the on-line HTR system, six type of classes of errors were identified. A detailed analysis of the errors committed by the best system showed that most errors were provoked by short pen strokes (punctuation and up-to-three letter words). The case of *punctuation* is specially interesting since it covered 47% of the errors. Since the number of punctuation symbols is very limited, a special deterministic interface could be designed so that it is still quite touch-screen friendly. For example, when clicking on a punctuation symbol, a circular menu with the complete list of punctuation symbols could pop up. As this menu is completely error-free, the total number of errors produced by the touch-screen modality would be reduced by half. Besides, the cost for the user to introduce these symbols would be very reasonable and at no cost of ergonomics.

Finally, regarding the optimization of the log-linear model, it must be said that the lambda parameters were adjusted on a development corpus to optimize CER. It was observed that the optimum lambda values from the development set approximated quite well the test optimum values, which is a desirable feature. Additional experiments showed that if the lambda values were estimated separately for each user, the average CER would be identical (10.6% vs. 10.6%). Therefore, the estimation of these parameters can be deemed as rather robust to the variability of users.

7.6 Conclusions

One important research area when dealing with an IMT scenario is precisely how to provide the user with an appropriate interface so as to obtain the most benefit from the interaction paradigm. In this chapter, several alternatives have been presented. Some of them, such as the non-explicit positioning mouse actions, are almost transparent for the user, and present one example of how the users actions can be analyzed in order to make the user-machine interaction more efficient. Others, such as using handwritten text recognition or speech recognition for correcting errors, provide an almost orthogonal way of increasing the effectiveness of the synergy between the final human translator and the IMT system. In addition, the experiments have shown that coupling the IMT subsystem and the feedback subsystem can boost the performance of the feedback recognition compared to a decoupled independent feedback subsystem.

Although several possibilities have been explored in the present chapter, such interaction schemes are only examples of a much broader scenario. For instance, one could easily imagine a system which follows the user while it reads a given sentence by means of some sort of gaze tracking device. Such a system would open a whole new range of interaction schemes.

References

1. Berger, A. L., Pietra, S. A. D., & Pietra, V. J. D. (1996). A maximum entropy approach to natural language processing. *Computational Linguistics*, *22*, 39–71.
2. Brousseau, J., Drouin, C., Foster, G., Isabelle, P., Kuhn, R., Normandin, Y., & Plamondon, P. (1995). French speech recognition in an automatic dictation system for translators: the TransTalk project. In *Proceedings of the forth European conference on speech communication and technology (Eurospeech 95)* (pp. 193–196), Madrid, Spain.
3. Brown, P. F., Chen, S. F., Pietra, S. A. D., Pietra, V. J. D., Kehler, A. S., & Mercer, R. L. (1994). Automatic speech recognition in machine aided translation. *Computer Speech and Language*, *8*(3), 177–187.
4. Dymetman, M., Brousseau, J., Foster, G., Isabelle, P., Normandin, Y., & Plamondon, P. (1994). Towards an automatic dictation system for translators: the TransTalk project. In *Proceedings of the international conference on spoken language processing (ICSLP 94)* (pp. 691–694).
5. Khadivi, S., Zolnay, A., & Ney, H. (2005). Automatic text dictation in computer-assisted translation. In *Proceedings of the 9th European conference on speech communication and technology (Interspeech 2005)* (pp. 2265–2268), Portugal, Lisbon.
6. Moreno, A., Poch, D., Bonafonte, A., Lleida, E., Llisterri, J., Mariño, J. B., & Nadeu, C. (1993). Albayzin speech database: design of the phonetics corpus. In *Proceedings of the third European conference on speech communication and technology (Eurospeech 93)* (pp. 175–178), Berlin, Germany.
7. Och, F. J., & Ney, H. (2000). Improved statistical alignment models. In *Proceedings of the 38th annual meeting of the association for computational linguistics (ACL 2000)* (pp. 440–447), Hongkong, China.
8. Och, F. J., & Ney, H. (2002). Discriminative training and maximum entropy models for statistical machine translation. In *Proceedings of 40th annual meeting of the association for computational linguistics (ACL 02)* (pp. 295–302), Philadelphia, Pennsylvania, USA.
9. Ogawa, A., Takeda, K., & Itakura, F. (1998). Balancing acoustic and linguistic probabilities. In *Proceedings of IEEE international conference on acoustics, speech and signal processing (ICASSP 98)* (pp. 181–184), Seattle, WA, USA.
10. Papineni, K. A., Roukos, S., & Ward, T. (1998). Maximum likelihood and discriminative training of direct translation models. In *Proceedings of IEEE international conference on acoustics, speech and signal processing (ICASSP 98)* (pp. 189–192), Seattle, WA, USA.
11. Paulik, M., Stüker, S., & Fügen, C. (2006). Speech recognition in human mediated translation scenarios. In *Proceedings of 2006 IEEE Mediterranean electrotechnical conference (MELECON 06)* (pp. 1232–1235), Benalmádena, Málaga.
12. Reddy, A., & Rose, R. (2008). Towards domain independence in machine aided human translation. In *Proceedings of the 9th annual conference of the international speech communication association (Interspeech 08)* (pp. 2358–2361), Brisbane, Australia.
13. Reddy, A., & Rose, R. (2010). Integration of statistical models for dictation of document translations in a machine-aided human translation task. *IEEE Transactions on Audio, Speech, and Language Processing*, *18*(8), 2015–2027.
14. Reddy, A., Rose, R., & Désilets, A. (2007). Integration of asr and machine translation models in a document translation task. In *Proceedings of the 10th European conference on speech communication and technology (Interspeech 07)* (pp. 2457–2460), Antwerp, Belgium.
15. Sanchis-Trilles, G., González, M. T., Casacuberta, F., Vidal, E., & Civera, J. (2008). Introducing additional input information into IMT systems. In *Lecture notes in computer sciences: Vol. 5237. Proceedings of the 5th joint workshop on multimodal interaction and related machine learning algorithms* (pp. 284–295), Utrecht, The Netherlands.

16. Sanchis-Trilles, G., Ortiz-Martínez, D., Casacuberta, J. C. F., Vidal, E., & Hoang, H. (2008). Improving interactive machine translation via mouse actions. In *Proceedings of the conference on empirical methods for natural language processing (EMNLP 08)* (pp. 485–494), Waikiki, Honolulu, Hawaii.
17. Vidal, E., Casacuberta, F., Rodríguez, L., Civera, J., & Martínez, C. D. (2006). Computer-assisted translation using speech recognition. *IEEE Transactions on Speech and Audio Processing*, *14*(3), 941–951.

Chapter 8
Incremental and Adaptive Learning for Interactive Machine Translation

With Contribution Of: Daniel Ortiz-Martínez and Ismael García-Varea.

Contents

High-quality translation between any pair of languages can be achieved by human post-editing of the outputs of a MT system or, as mentioned in Chap. 6, by following the Interactive Machine Translation (IMT) approach. In the interactive pattern recognition framework, IMT can predict the translation of the next words in the output, and can suggest them to the human translator who, iteratively, can accept or correct the suggested translations. The consolidated translations obtained through the successive steps of the interaction process can be considered as "perfect translations" due to the fact that they have been validated by a human expert. Therefore, this consolidated translations can easily be converted into new, fresh, training data, useful for dynamically adapting the system to the changing environment. Taking that into account, on the one hand, the IMT paradigm offers an appropriate framework for incremental and adaptive learning in SMT. On the other hand, incremental and adaptive learning offers the possibility to substantially save human effort by simply avoiding the user to perform the same corrections again and again.

8.1 Introduction

IMT can be seen as an evolution of the SMT framework (see Sect. 6.2), where the same statistical models and search algorithms can be used with little modification.

A.H. Toselli et al., *Multimodal Interactive Pattern Recognition and Applications*, DOI 10.1007/978-0-85729-479-1_8,

Because of these similarities, a whole set of proposals for domain adaptation [2, 7, 9, 18, 21] that were initially introduced in the SMT framework can also be applied to IMT. However, human interaction offers another unique opportunity to improve the performance of the IMT systems by tuning the statistical models involved in the translation process. In particular, at each interaction, the text segments validated by the user together with the corresponding aligned source segments can generally be converted into new, fresh training data, useful for adapting the system to a changing environment. An early example of this can be found in the TransType framework, where a cache-based technique both for target language models and translation models is used [13]. Another example can be found in [4], where the output of a post-editing system is used for adaptation. More recently, in [16], a purely statistical IMT system with online learning capabilities is introduced, where the system can incrementally update the parameters of all of the different models that are involved in the translation process, and therefore automatically adapted to new users, new translation styles, or even to new target languages.

In the following sections, we describe different proposals that try to take advantage of user feedback to extend the statistical models of the IMT system. Specifically, in Sect. 8.2, an IMT system with online learning capabilities is described. In addition to this, other topics related with adaptation in IMT are presented in Sect. 8.3.

8.2 On-Line Learning

8.2.1 Concept of On-Line Learning

In the IMT framework, the target sentences validated by the user along with the corresponding source sentences constitute new training samples that can be used to extend the statistical models of the IMT system. Unfortunately, the vast majority of the existing work on IMT makes use of the well-known *batch learning* paradigm. In the batch learning paradigm, the training of the IMT system and the interactive translation process are carried out in separate stages. This paradigm is not able to take advantage of the new knowledge produced by the user of the IMT system. To solve this problem, the *on-line learning* paradigm to the IMT framework can be applied. In the on-line learning paradigm, the training and prediction stages are no longer separated.

The on-line learning paradigm has been previously applied to train discriminative models in SMT [1, 6, 11, 20]. The application of online learning techniques in IMT has not been extensively studied, one previous work is [5], where a very constrained version of on-line learning is presented. This constrained version of on-line learning is not able to extend the translation models due to technical problems with the efficiency of the learning process.

We present a purely statistical IMT system which is able to incrementally update the parameters of all the different models that are used in the system, including the translation model, breaking with the above mentioned constraints. Our proposal uses a conventional IMT system which is based on a log-linear model. Such a log-linear model is composed of a set of feature functions governing different aspects of the translation process. We will briefly describe the required techniques to incrementally update the statistical models used by the system. To do this, a set of sufficient statistics is incrementally updated for each feature function.

8.2.2 Basic IMT System

As was mentioned above, the basic IMT system that we propose uses a log-linear model to generate its translations. According to Eq. (6.3), we introduce a set of seven feature functions (from f_1 to f_7): a language model (f_1), an inverse sentence-length model (f_2), inverse and direct translation models (f_3 and f_4, respectively), a target phrase-length model (f_5), a source phrase-length model (f_6), and a distortion model (f_7).

The f_1 feature function is implemented by means of smoothed n-gram language models. In particular, we adopt an interpolated n-gram model with Kneser–Ney smoothing.

The f_2 feature function constitutes an inverse sentence-length model implemented by means of a set of Gaussian distributions whose parameters are estimated for each source sentence length.

The inverse translation model (feature function f_3) is implemented with an inverse phrase-based model. This phrase-based model is smoothed with an HMM-based alignment model [19] by means of linear interpolation. It is illustrative to consider the exact formulation of f_3 so as to later explain how it can be incrementally updated in the following section. Specifically, f_3 is defined as follows:

$$f_3(x, h, a) = \log\left(\prod_{k=1}^{K} P(\tilde{x}_k \mid \tilde{h}_{a_k})\right) \tag{8.1}$$

where x and h are the source and the target sentences, respectively, and the hidden alignment variable a determines a phrase alignment of length K between x and h. The probability of translation between phrase pairs, $P(\tilde{x}_k \mid \tilde{h}_{a_k})$, is defined as follows:

$$P(\tilde{x}_k \mid \tilde{h}_{a_k}) = \beta \cdot P_{\text{phr}}(\tilde{x}_k \mid \tilde{h}_{a_k}) + (1-\beta) \cdot P_{\text{hmm}}(\tilde{x}_k \mid \tilde{h}_{a_k}). \tag{8.2}$$

In Eq. (8.2), β is the linear interpolation parameter, $P_{\text{phr}}(\tilde{x}_k \mid \tilde{h}_{a_k})$ denotes the probability given by a statistical phrase-based dictionary used in regular phrase-based models (see [10] for more details) and $P_{\text{hmm}}(\tilde{x}_k \mid \tilde{h}_{a_k})$ is the probability given by an HMM-based alignment model defined at phrase level:

$$P_{\text{hmm}}(\tilde{x} \mid \tilde{h}) = \epsilon \sum_{b_1^{|\tilde{x}|}} \prod_{j=1}^{|\tilde{x}|} P(\tilde{x}_j \mid \tilde{h}_{b_j}) \cdot P(b_j \mid b_{j-1}, |\tilde{h}|) \tag{8.3}$$

where ϵ is a small, fixed number which accounts for the probability of the length of the source sentence (see [3] for more details), $b_1^{|\tilde{x}|}$ represents a word-level hidden alignment variable between $\tilde{x}$ and $\tilde{h}$, $P(\tilde{x}_j \mid \tilde{h}_{b_j})$ is the lexical probability and $P(b_j \mid b_{j-1}, |\tilde{h}|)$ is the alignment probability.

Analogously, feature function f_4 is implemented by means of a direct, smoothed phrase-based model.

Regarding the target phrase-length model (feature function f_5), it is implemented by means of a geometric distribution. The use of a geometric distribution penalises the length of the target phrases. A geometric distribution can also be used to model f_6, such distribution penalizes the difference between the source and target phrase lengths. Finally, we use again a geometric distribution to implement a distortion model for the phrase translations (feature function f_7). Such distribution penalises the reorderings.

The log-linear model, which includes the above described feature functions, is used to generate the suffix s given the user-validated prefix p. Specifically, the IMT system generates a partial phrase-based alignment between the user prefix p and a portion of the source sentence x, and returns the suffix s as the translation of the remaining portion of x (see [15]).

8.2.3 Online IMT System

After translating a source sentence x, a new sentence pair (x, h) is available to feed the IMT system. In this section we describe how the log-linear model described in the previous section is updated given the new sentence pair. To do this, a set of *sufficient statistics* that can be incrementally updated is maintained for each feature function $f_i(\cdot)$. A sufficient statistic for a statistical model is a statistic that captures all the information that is relevant to estimate this model. If the estimation of the statistical model does not require the use of the Expectation–Maximisation (EM) algorithm (e.g. n-gram language models), then it is generally easy to incrementally extend the model given a new training sample. By contrast, if the EM algorithm is required (e.g. word alignment models), the estimation procedure has to be modified, since the conventional EM algorithm is designed for its use in batch learning scenarios. To solve this problem, we apply the incremental version of the EM algorithm [12].

The parameters of the n-gram language model with Kneser–Ney smoothing that implements the f_1 feature function can be incrementally adjusted with an appropriate algorithm which is shown in [16]. Since the estimation does not involve the EM algorithm, the algorithm is relatively simple.

Regarding the f_2 feature function, its incremental estimation requires updating the parameters of a set of Gaussian distributions. This problem has been extensively studied in the literature, specifically, we apply the incremental update rules given in [8].

Feature functions f_3 and f_4 implement inverse and direct smoothed phrase-based models, respectively. Since phrase-based models are symmetric models, only an inverse phrase-based model is maintained (direct probabilities can be efficiently obtained using appropriate data structures, see [14]). It is interesting to see how this inverse phrase-based model can be incrementally updated, since, as will be explained below, such incremental update involves the application of the incremental version of the EM algorithm.

Given a new sentence pair (x, h), the standard phrase-based model estimation method uses a word alignment matrix between x and h to extract the set of phrase pairs that are *consistent* with the word alignment matrix (see [10] for more details). Once the consistent phrase pairs have been extracted, the phrase counts are updated following the equation:

$$P(\tilde{x} \mid \tilde{h}) = \frac{c(\tilde{x}, \tilde{h})}{\sum_{\tilde{x}'} c(\tilde{x}', \tilde{h})} \tag{8.4}$$

where $c(\tilde{x}, \tilde{h})$ represents the count of the phrase pair $(\tilde{x}, \tilde{h})$ in the set of consistent phrase pairs extracted from the training corpus.

The word alignment matrices required for the extraction of phrase pairs are generated by means of the HMM-based models used in the feature functions f_3 and f_4.

Inverse and direct HMM-based models are used here for two purposes: to smooth the phrase-based models via linear interpolation and to generate word alignment matrices. The weights of the interpolation can be estimated from a development corpus. Since the alignment in the HMM-based model is determined by a hidden variable, the EM algorithm is required to estimate the parameters of the model. However, the conventional EM algorithm is not appropriate for its use in our online learning scenario. To solve this problem, the incremental version of the EM algorithm that was mentioned above is applied. As was mentioned above, HMM-based alignment models are composed of lexical and alignment probabilities. Lexical probabilities are obtained following the equation:

$$P(u \mid v) = \frac{c(u \mid v)}{\sum_{u'} c(u' \mid v)} \tag{8.5}$$

where $c(u \mid v)$ is the *expected* number of times that the word v is aligned to the word u. The alignment probability is defined in a similar way:

$$P(b_j \mid b_{j-1}, l) = \frac{c(b_j \mid b_{j-1}, l)}{\sum_{b'_j} c(b'_j \mid b_{j-1}, l)} \tag{8.6}$$

and $c(b_j \mid b_{j-1}, l)$ denotes the expected number of times that the alignment b_j has been seen after the previous alignment b_{j-1} given a source sentence composed of l words.

Finally, the parameters of the geometric distributions associated to the feature functions f_5, f_6 and f_7 are left fixed. Because of this, there are no sufficient statistics to store for these feature functions.

8.3 Related Topics

8.3.1 Active Learning on IMT via Confidence Measures

As outlined in Sect. 1.3, the Interactive Pattern Recognition scenario allows to use the valuable user feedback signals produced in the interaction in an adaptive training process which progressively tunes the models to the specific task and/or to the way the user makes use of the systems in this task. Final outputs contain lot of information provided by the user to help the system refine or improve its hypothesis. For the IMT scenario this information consists in correct translations of the input sentences that can be used to improve the translation models as shown in Sect. 8.2.

Regarding the alternative IMT scenario presented in Sect. 6.2.1, confidence measures are used to reduce the effort required for the user, so final translations are composed of segments validated by the user and segments automatically translated by the system. This information can be used to perform a mixed active and semi-supervised learning to exploit both what the system thinks it knows about the unlabeled data and the new information provided by the user for the data the system is not confident enough of.

8.3.2 Bayesian Adaptation

In IMT, it is quite common to have a model trained on a given domain where lots of data are available, but the purpose is to translate another domain, where only few data are available. Such a problem has not been confronted as of yet in the context of IMT, although some work exists in the context of traditional SMT. This is the case of Bayesian adaptation [17], which is an instantiation of the Bayesian learning paradigm to the case of adaptation in SMT.

The weights of the log-linear combination in Eq. (6.3), can be adapted to new situations by the application of the MERT algorithm of Chap. 6, estimating a new set of weights on the adaptation data and substituting the old ones. However, if the adaptation set made available to the system is not big enough, MERT will most likely become unstable and fail in obtaining an appropriate weight vector. This situation is common in IMT.

The main idea behind Bayesian learning is that parameters are viewed as random variables which have some kind of a priori distribution. Given a training set T to build the initial models and an adaptation set A, the problem can be stated as

$$\begin{aligned}\hat{h} &= \arg\max_h P(h \mid x; T, A) \\ &= \arg\max_h \int P(\lambda \mid T, A) P(h \mid x; \lambda)\, d\lambda. \end{aligned} \tag{8.7}$$

In last equation, the integral over the complete parametric space forces the model to take into account all possible values of the model parameters (in this case, only the

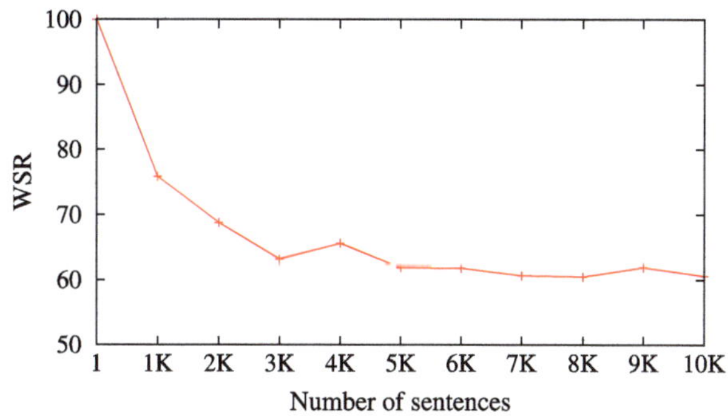

Fig. 8.1 WSR evolution when translating a portion of the XEROX English–Spanish training corpora by means of an online IMT system

λ in Eq. (6.3)), although the prior over the parameters implies that our model will prefer parameter values which are closer to our prior knowledge. Two assumptions are adopted: first, the output sentence h only depends on the model parameters (and not on the complete training and adaptation data), and second, that the model parameters do not depend on the actual input sentence x. Such simplifications lead to a decomposition of the integral into two parts: the first one, $P(\lambda \mid T, A)$ will assess how good the current model parameters are, and the second one, $P(h \mid x; \lambda)$, will account for the quality of the translation h given the current model parameters.

8.4 Results

We carried out experiments to test the IMT system with online learning techniques proposed in Sect. 8.2. The proposals that were presented in Sect. 8.3 have not yet been adequately tested in the IMT framework.

All the experiments were executed using the XEROX task described in Sect. 6.4. The XEROX task was used to perform IMT experiments in two different scenarios. In the first one, the first 10 000 sentences extracted from the English–Spanish training corpora were interactively translated by means of an IMT system without any pre-existent model stored in memory. Each time a new sentence pair was validated, it was used to incrementally train the system. The results obtained in this first experimentation scenario are shown in Fig. 8.1. In the figure, the evolution of the WSR measure as a function of the number of interactively translated sentences is represented. As can be seen, the results clearly demonstrate that the IMT system is able to learn from scratch. The results obtained for the translation from English to Spanish were similar for the rest of language pairs of the XEROX corpora, as is shown in [16].

Alternatively, we carried out experiments in a different learning scenario. Specifically, we compared the performance of a batch IMT system with that of an online IMT system when translating the XEROX test corpora. In this experiment, the statistical models used by both the batch and the online IMT systems were initialized by means of the XEROX training corpora. The obtained WSR results for the English–Spanish language pair are shown in Table 8.1.

Table 8.1 On-line learning results for the English–Spanish XEROX task

Task	System	WSR
XEROX (Eng–Spa)	batch	32.0
	on-line	26.6

As can be seen in the table, the proposed on-line learning techniques allow the IMT system to learn from previously estimated models (further results in this experimentation scenario can be found in [16]).

8.5 Conclusions

Human interaction offers a unique opportunity to improve the performance of the IMT systems by tuning the translation models. In particular, at each interaction of the IMT process, the text validated by the user along with the source sentence constitute new training data that can be used to extend the statistical models used by the system. The IMT techniques proposed in this chapter allow us to take advantage of such user feedback by means of different techniques, including online learning, active learning and Bayesian adaptation.

References

1. Arun, A., & Koehn, P. (2007). Online learning methods for discriminative training of phrase based statistical machine translation. In *Proceedings of the machine translation summit XII (MT Summit 07)* (pp. 15–20), Copenhagen, Denmark.
2. Bertoldi, N., & Federico, M. (2009). Domain adaptation for statistical machine translation with monolingual resources. In *Proceedings of the EACL 09 fourth workshop on statistical machine translation (WSMT 09)* (pp. 182–189), Athens, Greece.
3. Brown, P. F., Pietra, S. A. D., Pietra, V. J. D., & Mercer, R. L. (1993). The mathematics of statistical machine translation: Parameter estimation. *Computational Linguistics*, *19*(2), 263–310.
4. Callison-burch, C., Bannard, C., & Schroeder, J. (2004). Improving statistical translation through editing. In *Proceedings of the 9th EAMT workshop broadening horizons of machine translation and its applications*, Malta.
5. Cesa-Bianchi, N., Reverberi, G., & Szedmak, S. (2008). *Online learning algorithms for computer-assisted translation*. Deliverable D4.2, SMART: Statistical Multilingual Analysis for Retrieval and Translation.
6. Chiang, D., Marton, Y., & Resnik, P. (2008). Online large-margin training of syntactic and structural translation features. In *Proceedings of the conference on empirical methods in natural language processing (EMNLP 08)* (pp. 224–233), Honolulu, Hawaii.
7. Civera, J., et al. (2004). A syntactic pattern recognition approach to computer assisted translation. In A. Fred, T. Caelli, A. Campilho, R. P. Duin, & D. de Ridder (Eds.), *Lecture notes in computer science. Advances in statistical, structural and syntactical pattern recognition* (pp. 207–215). Berlin: Springer.
8. Knuth, D. E. (1981). *Seminumerical algorithms: Vol. 2. The art of computer programming* (2nd ed.). Reading: Addison-Wesley.

9. Koehn, P., & Schroeder, J. (2007). Experiments in domain adaptation for statistical machine translation. In *Proceedings of the ACL 2007 second workshop on statistical machine translation (WSMT 07)* (pp. 224–227), Prague, Czech Republic.
10. Koehn, P., Och, F. J., & Marcu, D. (2003). Statistical phrase-based translation. In *Proceedings of the human language technology and North American association for computational linguistics conference (HLT/NAACL 03)* (pp. 48–54), Edmonton, Canada.
11. Liang, P., Bouchard-Côté, A., Klein, D., & Taskar, B. (2006). An end-to-end discriminative approach to machine translation. In *Proceedings of the joint international conference on computational linguistics and association of computational linguistics (COLING/ACL 06)* (pp. 761–768), Sydney, Australia.
12. Neal, R. M., & Hinton, G. E. (1998). A view of the EM algorithm that justifies incremental, sparse, and other variants. In *Learning in graphical models* (pp. 355–368). Dordrecht: Kluwer Academic.
13. Nepveu, L., Lapalme, G., Langlais, P., & Foster, G. F. (2004). Adaptive language and translation models for interactive machine translation. In *Proceedings of the conference on empirical methods in natural language processing (EMNLP 04)* (pp. 190–197), Barcelona, Spain.
14. Ortiz-Martínez, D., García-Varea, I., & Casacuberta, F. (2008). The scaling problem in the pattern recognition approach to machine translation. *Pattern Recognition Letters*, *29*, 1145–1153.
15. Ortiz-Martínez, D., García-Varea, I., & Casacuberta, F. (2009). Interactive machine translation based on partial statistical phrase-based alignments. In *Proceedings of the international conference recent advances in natural language processing (RANLP 09)* (pp. 330–336), Borovets, Bulgaria.
16. Ortiz-Martínez, D., García-Varea, I., & Casacuberta, F. (2010). Online learning for interactive statistical machine translation. In *Proceedings of the 11th annual conference of the North American chapter of the association for computational linguistics (NAACL 10)* (pp. 546–554), Los Angeles, USA.
17. Sanchis, G., & Casacuberta, F. (2010). Bayesian adaptation for statistical machine translation. In *Proceedings of the 23rd international conference on computational linguistics (COLING 10)* (pp. 1077–1085), Beijing, China.
18. Sanchis-Trilles, G., & Cettolo, M. (2010). Online language model adaptation via n-gram mixtures for statistical machine translation. In *Proceedings of the conference of the European association for machine translation (EAMT 10)*, Saint-Raphaël, France.
19. Vogel, S., Ney, H., & Tillmann, C. (1996). HMM-based word alignment in statistical translation. In *Proceedings of the 16th international conference on computational linguistics (COLING 96)* (pp. 836–841), Copenhagen, Denmark.
20. Watanabe, T., Suzuki, J., Tsukada, H., & Isozaki, H. (2007). Online large-margin training for statistical machine translation. In *Proceedings of the joint conference on empirical methods in natural language processing (EMNLP 07) and computational natural language learning (CoNLL 07)* (pp. 764–773), Prague, Czech Republic.
21. Zhao, B., Eck, M., & Vogel, S. (2004). Language model adaptation for statistical machine translation with structured query models. In *Proceedings of the international conference on computational linguistics (COLING 04)* (pp. 411–417), Geneva, Switzerland.

Chapter 9
Interactive Parsing

With Contribution Of: José Miguel Benedí, Joan Andreu Sánchez and Ricardo Sánchez-Sáez.

Contents

This chapter introduces the *Interactive Parsing* (IP) framework for obtaining the correct syntactic parse tree of a given sentence. This formal framework allows us to make the construction of interactive systems for tree annotation. These interactive systems can help to human annotators in creating error-free parse trees with little effort, when compared with manual post-editing of the trees provided by an automatic parser.

In principle, the interaction protocol defined in the IP framework differs from the *left-to-right* interaction protocol used throughout this book. Specifically, the IP protocol will be of *desultory order*; that is, in IP the user can edit any part of the parse tree and in any order.

However, in order to efficiently calculate the next best tree in IP framework, in Sect. 9.4, a *left-to-right depth-first* tree review order will be introduced. In addition, this order also introduces computational advantages into the lookout of most probable tree for interactive bottom-up parsing algorithms.

The use of Confidence Measures in IP is also presented as an efficient technique to detect erroneous parse trees. Confidence Measures can be efficiently computed in the IP framework and can help in detecting erroneous constituents within the IP process more quickly, as they provide discriminant information over all the IP process.

A.H. Toselli et al., *Multimodal Interactive Pattern Recognition and Applications*,
DOI 10.1007/978-0-85729-479-1_9,

9.1 Introduction

Probabilistic Parsing is an important problem related to Natural Language Processing and Computational Linguistics, which has proven to be useful for Language Modeling [2, 8, 24], RNA Modeling [25], and Machine Translation [7, 35], among others [19]. In probabilistic parsing, a parse tree is obtained for an input sentence that represents syntactic relations between different parts of the sentence. This parse tree is obtained by using a probabilistic model and a parsing algorithm.

Probabilistic Context Free-Grammars (PCFG) are a powerful formalism that has been widely used for Probabilistic Parsing [1, 10, 23, 24, 30]. PCFG represent an appropriate trade-off between representation capability and time complexity of the algorithms that are able to use them. The good results obtained in parsing have made PCFG the most used formalism in order to tackle this problem. Therefore, we will focus on the use of PCFG as probabilistic models.

A possible classification of the parsing algorithms can be done based on the use of lexical information. In *lexicalized parsing*, lexical information is used in the parsing process in order to disambiguate between non-lexical rules [5]. The main drawback of the probabilistic lexicalized parsing is the high time complexity of the parsing algorithms. Alternatively, *unlexicalized parsing* can be used. In the last years, unlexicalized parsing has achieved very good parsing results with algorithms of lower time complexity [18, 23]. For unlexicalized parsing, algorithms can be grouped into two main approaches: those that are based on the Earley algorithm [12], and those that are based on the Cocke–Kasami–Younger (CKY) algorithm [15]. The Earley algorithm is a classical parsing algorithm that can deal with PCFG in general format. Alternatively, the CKY algorithm has a similar performance but it requires the PCFG in Chomsky Normal Form (CNF). Several reasons have made more popular the use of the CKY algorithm in the last years: first, the CKY algorithm makes easier the use of efficient techniques for obtaining a set of n-best parse trees [16]; second, in recent years, efficient A* algorithms have been proposed for unlexicalized parsing that are able to achieve very good performance [13, 18]; third, efficient maximum-entropy techniques have been devised for CKY-style parsing [6]; and fourth, efficient CKY-style parsing algorithms have been recently proposed for Machine Translation [9, 14, 34]. Throughout this section we will focus in probabilistic parsing with PCFG in CNF with the CKY-style algorithms, but similar ideas could be applied to the Earley algorithm with PCFG in general format, and other parsing formalisms.

In probabilistic parsing, given a sentence x and a PCFG G, the problem in which we are interested is to obtain the parse tree t that best represents the relation between the words of the sentence x according to model G. From a pattern recognition point of view, the probabilistic parsing can be formulated as

$$\hat{t} = \arg\max_{t \in \mathcal{T}} p_G(t \mid x), \tag{9.1}$$

where $p_G(t \mid x)$ is the probability of the parse tree t given the input string x using a PCFG G, and $\mathcal{T}$ is the set of all possible parse trees for x. In probabilistic parsing, a parse tree t that is associated to a string $x = x_1^n$ can be decomposed into subtrees t_{ij}^A, such that, A is the label of the root node and i, j are indexes delimiting the analyzed substring x_i^j. In this way, $t = t_{1n}^S$ where S is the axiom of the grammar. If the PCFG is in CNF, then the maximization in Eq. (9.1) can be carried out with a dynamic programming CKY-style algorithm. This CKY-style algorithm resembles the Viterbi algorithm for finite-state models, and therefore sometimes is also called a Viterbi algorithm. This algorithm fills in a $(n \times n)$ parse matrix $\mathcal{V}$ for a string of size n. Each element of $\mathcal{V}$ is a probabilistic non-terminal vector such that each component is defined as

$$\mathcal{V}_{i,j}[A] = \hat{p}\big(t_{ij}^A\big) = \hat{p}_G\big(A \stackrel{+}{\Rightarrow} x_i^j\big) \quad A \in N; 1 \leq i, j \leq n, \tag{9.2}$$

where N is the set of non-terminal symbols of the grammar, and $\hat{p}_G(A \stackrel{+}{\Rightarrow} x_i^j)$ is the probability of the most probable tree that generates the substring x_i^j from the non-terminal symbol A.

As we introduced in Chap. 1, within the syntactic and statistical pattern recognition world, we can tell apart two different usage scenarios for automatic systems. First, we have the cases in which the output of such systems is expected to be used in a vanilla fashion, that is, without validating or correcting the results produced by the system. Within this usage scheme, the most important factor of a given automatic system is the quality of the results. Although memory and computational requirements of such systems are usually taken into account, the ultimate aim of most research that relates to this scenario is to minimize the error rate of the results that are being produced [17].

The second usage scenario arises when there exists the need for perfect and completely error-free results. In such a case, the intervention of a human user validator/corrector is unavoidable. The corrector will review the results and validate them, or make the suitable corrections before the system output can be employed. In these kind of problems, the most important factor that has to be minimized is the human effort that has to be applied to transform the potentially incorrect output of the system into validated and error-free output. Measuring user effort has an intrinsic subjectivity that makes it hard to be quantized. Given that the user output, most research about problems associated to this scenario tried to minimize just the error rate of the system as well.

Only recently, more formal work in this direction has started to be carried out, in the form of Interactive Pattern Recognition (IPR) systems (see Chap. 1). These systems formally integrate the correcting user into the loop, making him part of an interactive system (see Fig. 1.4). In such systems the importance of the vanilla error rate per-se is diminished. Instead, the intention is to measure how well the user and the system work together. For this, formal user simulation protocols started to be used as a benchmark. This dichotomy in evaluating system performance or user effort applies to probabilistic parsing as well.

There are many problems within the parsing field where error-free results consisting in perfectly annotated trees are needed. Building correct trees is needed for tasks such as recognition of handwritten mathematical expressions [36] or creating new gold standard treebanks [11]. When using automatic parsers as a baseline for building perfect syntactic trees, the role of the human annotator is to post-edit the trees and correct the errors. This manner of operating results in the typical two-step process for error correcting, in which the system first generates the whole output and then the user verifies or amends it. This paradigm is rather inefficient and uncomfortable for the human annotator. For example, in the creation of the Penn Treebank annotated corpus, a basic two-stage setup was employed: a rudimentary parsing system provided a skeletal syntactic representation, which then was manually corrected by human annotators [20]. Additional works within this field have presented systems that act as a computerized aid to the user in obtaining the perfect annotation [4, 21]. Subjective measurements of the effort that is needed to obtain perfect annotations were reported in [4], but we feel that a more comparable metric is needed.

With the objective of reducing the user effort and making the laborious task of tree annotation easier, an IPR framework for probabilistic Interactive Parsing (IP) will be presented. In this IP framework, the user is located in the loop, embedding him as a part of the automatic parser, and allows him to interact in real time within the system. Thus, the IP system can use the readily available user feedback to make improved predictions about the parts that have not been validated by the corrector.

To reduce user effort in IPR systems in general, and in IP systems in particular, one approach that can be followed is adding information of the system that helps the user in finding the errors and so he can correct them in a hastier fashion. For the users of such systems it is important to know, not only that the output may be erroneous, but which parts of this more complex output blocks are more prone to be erroneous. Confidence Measures (CM) are a formalism that goes along this direction, allowing the system to assigning a *probability of correctness* for individual erroneous constituents of a more complex output block of a PR system.

In fields such as HTR, MT or ASR the output sentences have a global probability, or score, that reflects the likeness of the whole recognized or translated sentence of being correct. CM allow precision beyond the sentence level in predicting the errors: they allow one to label the individual generated words as either correct or incorrect. This enables systems to identify possible erroneous parts to the user, or to propose only those words that are likely to be correct. CM have been successfully applied in many completely automatic PR systems [26, 31–33]. Recently, CM have also been applied to IPR systems in the HTR [29] field.

In the following section we describe how the IPR framework can be stated for probabilistic IP. Then, we explore the use of CM to the IP framework, to asses how much is retained of their ability to detect erroneous constituents within the interactive process.

9.2 Interactive Parsing Framework

As presented in Sect. 9.1, it is necessary to consider the human user in the parsing process to achieve error-free parse trees. There are two possible approaches: by including the human user in a process of post-editing, or by incorporating the human user in the interactive recognition process itself. Following the guidance of this book, this latter approach is what we consider in this section. The IPR formal framework introduced in Chap. 1, and more particularly the case for explicitly taking interaction history into account (Sect. 1.3.2), can be directly applied to the IP problem.

According to IPR paradigm, in each interaction, the system should propose a new hypothesis (parse tree) compatible with the constraints imposed by the amendments made by the user in previous interactions. Initially, for a given input string, the system proposes a parse tree. Next, the user corrects a possible error of the proposed parse tree. Then, the system must provide a new parse tree compatible with the user correction. Obviously, this user correction restricts the set of solutions (parse trees) possible. This interactive process continues until a correct parse tree is achieved.

In principle, this interaction protocol differs from the *left-to-right* interaction protocol, raised throughout this book. Following the interaction protocol taxonomy described in Sect. 1.4.1, the IP protocol would be of *desultory order*. That is, in IP the user can edit any part of the parse tree and in any order. Then we will formally characterize the IP problem, and we will also analyze the implicit interaction protocols. In Sect. 9.4 we will return to analyze the interaction protocols for IP and we will propose some restrictions.

From a linguistic point of view, user annotation can be stated in terms of *constituents*. A constituent is a word sequence that functions as a single linguistic unit. More formally, from a parsing point of view, a constituent C_{ij}^A is defined by the nonterminal symbol (either a *syntactic label* or a *POS tag*) A and its span ij (the starting and ending indexes which delimit the part of the input sentence encompassed by the constituent). Notice that a parse subtree t_{ij}^A defines a constituent set $C(t_{ij}^A)$. This constituent set is composed of several constituents C_{su}^B, with $C_{su}^B \in C(t_{ij}^A)$ and $i \geq s \geq j$ and $i \geq u \geq j$ for all constituents in the set. However, note that a given constituent set C can be the result of different subtrees, if we consider cycles and unit rules.

In an IP approach, the user amends a particular constituent in every interaction for some parse tree t. More precisely, he points out a particular node of the tree and he amends the node label and/or its span. As in Sect. 1.3.2 (Eq. (1.13)), the interactive formal framework for probabilistic parsing can be defined as

$$\hat{t} = \arg\max_{t \in \mathcal{T}} p_G\big(t \mid x, C, C_{ij}^A\big), \tag{9.3}$$

where C_{ij}^A is the (feedback) constituent validated by the user in the last interaction; C is the set of constituents validated by the user (history); $p_G(t \mid x, C, C_{ij}^A)$ is the probability (using a model G) of a parse tree t given the input string x, the user feedback C_{ij}^A, and the history C; and finally $\mathcal{T}$ is the set of all possible parse trees for x.

At this point, we consider that the user feedback is deterministic (mouse and/or keyboard). That is, the decoding process of user feedback does not introduce new errors. In Sect. 1.3.5 we will see how to include a non-deterministic multimodal feedback using interaction information to help decoding non-deterministic feedback.

Note that the definition of C is general, so if we were to define a certain order in the user review process, then the set C would not only include the constituents directly amended by the user but also the components implicitly validated by each interaction with the IP system. As seen in previous chapters, this also happens in applications where the order of analysis is from left to right. In that case, when the user edits a word, this means that this implicitly validates the previous prefix.

In Eq. (9.3), the search algorithm should take into account the restrictions introduced by C and C_{ij}^A, that is, the search space defined by the possible parse trees. In both cases, the restrictions introduced by the user should limit the possible solutions represented in the parse matrix $\mathcal{V}$. Note that both C and C_{ij}^A produce, somehow, a partial labeled bracketing of the input sequence. In this way, and following [22], we define a *compatibility function* $c(Y, r, s)$ for all those subproblems defined on $\mathcal{V}$ (Eq. (9.2)) compatible with the constituents of C. In other words, given a subproblem $\mathcal{V}_{r,s}[Y]$, its compatibility with C can be defined using the following function:

$$\forall C_{pq}^X \in \left(C \cup \left\{C_{ij}^A\right\}\right)$$

$$c(Y, r, s) = \begin{cases} 1, & \text{if } (r, s) = (p, q) \wedge (Y = X), \\ 0, & \text{if } (r, s) = (p, q) \wedge (Y \neq X), \\ 1, & \text{if } (r, s) \neq (p, q) \text{ but are consistent}, \\ 0, & \text{otherwise}. \end{cases} \tag{9.4}$$

This function filters those derivations (or partial derivations) whose parsing is not compatible with the validated constituents. The span (r, s) is not consistent with the span (p, q) when $p \leq r \leq q < s$, or $r < p \leq s \leq q$.

The compatibility function between $\mathcal{V}_{r,s}[Y]$ and C_{pq}^X defined in Eq. (9.4) requires that when the spans are equal also the labels Y and X must be equal. However, if the grammar G has unary rules $(A \rightarrow B)$ then this restriction is excessive, and should be relaxed as $X \overset{*}{\Rightarrow} Y$ or $Y \overset{*}{\Rightarrow} X$.

9.3 Confidence Measures in IP

Annotating trees syntactically, even with the aid of automatic systems, generally requires human intervention with a high degree of specialization. This fact partially justifies the shortage in large manually annotated treebanks. Endeavors directed at easing the burden for the experts performing this task could be of great help. One approach that can be followed in reducing user effort within an IPR paradigm is adding information that helps the user to locate the individual errors in a sentence, so he can correct them in a hastier fashion. The use of the Confidence Measure (CM) formalism goes in this direction, allowing us to assign a probability of correctness for individual erroneous constituents of a more complex output block of a Pattern Recognition system.

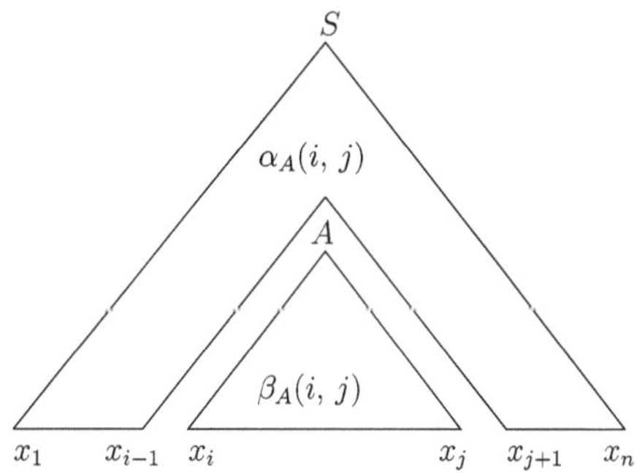

Fig. 9.1 The product of the inside and outside probabilities for each constituent comprises the upper part of Eq. (9.6)

It is interesting to see this issue from the perspective of interaction protocols introduced in Sect. 1.4.1. That section discussed two main types of interactive protocols: *passive*, when the user decides which parse tree (hypothesis) elements need supervision; and *active*, when the system decides which parse tree elements undergo user supervision. The IP paradigm framework seen so far is clearly based on a passive strategy. The introduction of CM associated to the parse tree elements provided by the system can be seen as a first step toward an active approach, where the system suggests/helps the user in the correction process.

However, until recent advances, the use of CM remained largely unexplored in probabilistic parsing despite having several applications of great interest within this field. Assessing the correctness of the different parts of a parsing tree can be useful in improving the efficiency and usability of an IP systems, not only by *coloring* parts with low confidence for the user to spot on, but also the automatic part of the interactive process by forcing the user to correct constituents with low confidence. Additionally, CM could also help improving the parsing process itself, either by being used as a component of an n-best reranker, or by being directly employed by a parsing system for recalculating parts with low confidence.

CM for parsing in the form of combination of characteristics calculated from n-best lists were explored in [3]. Computation of CM from n-best list makes sense mainly when the parsing algorithm prunes the search space by using some A* strategy [6]. However, when no pruning strategy is used in the parsing process, CM can be computed efficiently from the posterior probability of the tree constituent [27].

CM have been also explored in the IP framework. CM of each one of the parse subtrees (subproblems) can be calculated in terms of their posterior probability [27], which can be considered as a measure of the degree to which the subtree is believed to be correct for a given input sentence x. This is formulated as

$$p_G(t_{ij}^A \mid x) = \frac{p_G(t_{ij}^A, x)}{p_G(x)} = \frac{\sum_{t' \in \mathcal{T}} \delta(t_{ij}^A, t_{ij}'^A) p_G(t' \mid x)}{p_G(x)} \tag{9.5}$$

with $\delta()$ being the Kronecker delta function. Equation (9.5) is the posterior probability of the subtree t_{ij}^A given x. The numerator stands for the probability of all parse trees of x that contain the subtree t_{ij}^A (see Fig. (9.1)).

The posterior probability is computed with the well know *Inside* β and *Outside* α probabilities. The *Inside* probability is defined as $\beta_A(i,j) = p_G(A \stackrel{*}{\Rightarrow} x_i \ldots x_j)$, and it can be computed with the *Inside* algorithm. The *Outside* probability is defined as $\alpha_A(i,j) = p_G(S \stackrel{*}{\Rightarrow} x_1 \ldots x_{i-1} A x_{j+1} \ldots x_n)$ and it can be computed with the *Outside* algorithm [1]. In this way, Eq. (9.5) can be written as follows:

$$p_G\big(t_{ij}^A \mid x\big) = \frac{p_G(t_{ij}^A, x)}{p_G(x)} = \frac{\beta_A(i,j)\alpha_A(i,j)}{\beta_S(1,n)}. \tag{9.6}$$

It should be noted that the calculation of CM reviewed here is generalizable for any problem that employs PCFG, and not just IP tasks. In the experiments presented in Sect. 9.5, we show that the CM can be used within IP to detect erroneous constituents.

9.4 IP in Left-to-Right Depth-First Order

Parting from the general *desultory order* framework defined in Sect. 9.2 we can instantiate the *left-to-right* tree review order, similarly to what has been done in previous chapters through this book. For that, we take a cue from the prefix/suffix paradigm in order to introduce a predefined review order for the user checking the constituents in each parse trees: a left-to-right depth-first exploration order. In addition to seeming a reasonable and ergonomic review order for the structure of a tree (the reviewer would check constituents in a hierarchical order) this order also introduces computational advantages into the most probable tree lookout for interactive bottom-up parsing algorithms. Another key benefit of adopting this order is that it facilitates the automatic simulation of user interaction, allowing one to calculate metrics that estimate the amount of effort reduction.

This order can be formalized by defining a *prefix tree* $t_p(t, C_{ij}^A)$ that is defined for each correction performed by the user over a constituent C_{ij}^A. The *prefix tree* is comprised of all the ancestors of the corrected constituent and all constituents whose end span is lower than the start span of the corrected constituent. In terms of subtrees, the prefix tree can be represented with the following expression:

$$t_p\big(t, C_{ij}^A\big) = \big(t - t_{ij}^A\big) - \big\{t_{pq}^B \in t : p > j\big\} \tag{9.7}$$

with $t - t'$ meaning to remove the subtree t' from the tree t.

In terms of constituents, Eq. (9.7) is equivalent to

$$\begin{aligned} t_p\big(t, C_{ij}^A\big) = {} & \big\{C_{mn}^B \in C(t) : m \le i, n \ge j, d\big(C_{mn}^B\big) \le d\big(C_{ij}^A\big)\big\} \\ & \cup \big\{C_{pq}^D \in C(t) : q < i\big\} \end{aligned} \tag{9.8}$$

with $d(C_{ab}^Z)$ being the depth (distance from root) of constituent C_{ab}^Z. In Fig. 9.2d one can see that the slash-outlined part becomes the *prefix tree* and the dot-outlined subtree part becomes recalculated.

In this way, the history from Eq. (9.3) in Sect. 9.2 becomes the prefix $C = t_p(C_{ij}^A)$. Because of this, the compatibility function becomes further restricted:

$$\forall C_{pq}^X \in \left(C \cup \{C_{ij}^A\}\right)$$

$$c(Y,r,s) = \begin{cases} 1, & \text{if } (r,s) = (p,q) \wedge Y = X, \\ 0, & \text{if } (r,s) = (p,q) \wedge Y \neq X, \\ 1, & \text{if } (r,s) \neq (p,q) \wedge r \geq p \text{ and are consistent}, \\ 0, & \text{otherwise}. \end{cases} \tag{9.9}$$

Notice that the restriction $r \geq p$ comes from the converse of Eq. (9.7).

9.4.1 *Efficient Calculation of the Next Best Tree*

If we employ PCFGs as the underlying parse model for IP, then computing the next best tree as expressed in Eq. (9.3) becomes simpler when one uses a *left-to-right depth-first* tree review order.

The following calculation takes advantage of the fact that there are two types of subtrees that do not have to be recalculated: subtrees that are part of the prefix because they have already been implicitly validated, and subtrees that are not part of the prefix but do not descend from the parent of the corrected constituent. This follows from the fact that under the *left-to-right* review order we know that the parent of an amended constituent is already correct so, owing to the context-freeness of PCFG, a change in a constituent only affects its descendants and its right sibling subtrees at most.

In the following expressions we show how $\hat{t}$, which is the next best tree produced by the IP framework can be calculated in an efficient manner by reusing parts of $\hat{t}'$, the best tree obtained in the previous user iteration.

Let the corrected constituent be C_{ij}^A and its parent C_{st}^D then the next tree $\hat{t}$ can be calculated in the following manner:

$$\hat{t} = \arg\max_{t \in \mathcal{T}} p_G\left(t \mid x, C, C_{ij}^A\right) = \left(\hat{t}' - \hat{t}_{st}'^D\right) + \hat{t}_{st}^D \tag{9.10}$$

with

$$\hat{t}_{st}^D = \arg\max_{t_{st}^D \in \mathcal{T}_{st}} p_G\left(t_{st}^D \mid x_s^t, C_{ij}^A\right) \tag{9.11}$$

where t_{mn}^A is the subtree of t that has constituent C_{mn}^A as the root.

Equation (9.10) calculates the newly proposed tree $\hat{t}$ by subtracting the subtree rooted at the parent of the corrected constituent $(\hat{t}' - \hat{t}_{st}'^D)$ and appending a newly calculated subtree $\hat{t}_{st}'^D$, whose root is the parent of the corrected constituent and is calculated taking into account just the corrected constituent as shown in Eq. (9.11).

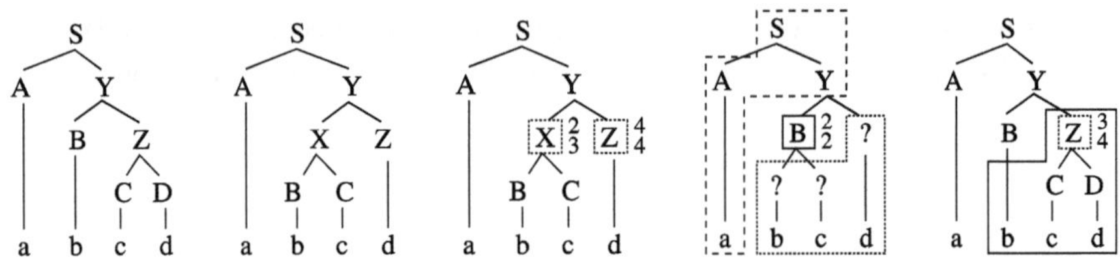

(**a**) Reference tree (**b**) Iteration 0: *Proposed output tree 1* (**c**) Iteration 0: *Erroneus constituents* (**d**) Iteration 1: *User corrected constituent* (**e**) Iteration 1: *Proposed output tree 2*

Fig. 9.2 Synthetic example of user interaction with the IP system. (**a**) The reference tree. (**b**) The system proposes an initial tree. (**c**) The user simulation subsystem looks at the tree and detects two incorrect constituents. (**d**) The first error is corrected by the user simulation subsystem. Note the implicitly validated prefix (*slashed outline*) and the recalculated part (*dotted outline*). (**e**) The system produces a new tree which equals the reference

This new maximization is more limited in extent and easier to perform because we only consider the last corrected constituent rather than the whole history of corrected constituents.

9.5 IP Experimentation

Based on the theoretical framework instantiated in Sect. 9.4, we devised an experimental setup to obtain an automatic assessment of user effort savings when using an IP system compared to a traditional system. The experimental setup is based on a user simulation subsystem that uses the gold reference trees to imitate system interaction by a human corrector and provides a comparable benchmark.

9.5.1 User Simulation Subsystem

Again, we devised an automatic evaluation protocol following the aforementioned left-to-right depth-first review order. The protocol is quite simple, and an example can be seen in Fig. 9.2a.

1. The IP system proposes a full parse tree $\hat{t}$ for the input sentence.
2. The user simulation subsystem finds the first incorrect constituent by exploring the tree in the order defined by the prefix tree definition (left to right, depth-first) and comparing it with the *reference tree*. When the first erroneous constituent is found, it is amended by being replaced by the correct one C_{ij}^{A}, operation which implicitly validates the prefix tree $t_p(C_{ij}^{A})$.
3. The IP system produces the most probable tree that is compatible with the validated prefix tree.

4. These steps are iterated until a final, perfect parse tree is produced by the IP system and validated against the *reference* by the user simulation subsystem.

9.5.2 Evaluation Metrics

With the user simulation in place, we need some metrics to measure the effort reduction. Parsing quality is generally assessed by the classical evaluation metrics, *Precision*, *Recall*, and *F-measure*:

- *Precision*: number of correct constituents divided by the number of constituents in the gold reference parse tree.
- *Recall*: number of correct constituents divided by the number of constituents in the proposed parse.
- *F-measure*:

$$2 \cdot \frac{\text{Precision} \cdot \text{Recall}}{\text{Precision} + \text{Recall}}.$$

However, for the assessment of an IP process, we need two comparable metrics: one that reports the amount of human correcting work needed to obtain the gold tree in a classical two-step process (i.e. the number of operations needed to post-edit the proposed tree in order to obtain the gold one); and a second one that measures the amount of effort needed to obtain the gold tree with the human interacting within the presented IP system.

We defined the following metric that measures the amount of effort needed in order to post-edit a proposed tree and obtain the gold reference parse tree, akin to the Word Error Rate used in Statistical Machine Translation and related fields:

- *Tree Constituent Error Rate (TCER)*: Minimum number of constituent substitution, deletion and insertion operations needed to convert the proposed parse tree into the corresponding gold reference tree, divided by the total number of constituents in the reference tree.

The TCER is in fact strongly related to the F-measure: the higher the F-measure is, the lower TCER will be.

Finally, the relevant evaluation metric that assesses the IP system performance represents the amount of effort that the operator would have to spend using the system in order to obtain the gold tree, and is directly comparable to the TCER:

- *Tree Constituent Action Rate (TCAC)*: Number of constituent corrections performed using the IP system to obtain the reference tree, divided by the total number of constituents in the reference tree.

9.5.3 Experimental Results

An IP system was implemented over the classical CKY-Viterbi algorithm. Experimentation was run over the Penn Treebank (English language) and the UAM Treebank (Spanish language). Within the Penn Treebank, sections 2 to 21 were used to obtain a vanilla Penn Treebank Grammar; test set was the section 23. We divided the UAM Treebank into two sets as well: the set used to obtain the grammars comprised was of the first 1 400 sentences of the corpus; and the test set consisted of the remaining 100 sentences.

Parsers based on CKY work with grammars in CNF, which is a subtype of CFG in which all the production rules must be in the form:

$$A \rightarrow BC \quad \text{or} \quad A \rightarrow a \quad \text{or} \quad S \rightarrow \epsilon. \tag{9.12}$$

Notice that for every CFG (or PCFG) there is an equivalent version of this grammar in CNF.

In order to obtain the CNF grammars from the vanilla PCFG for each of the languages we used the CNF transformation method from the toolkit NLTK.[1] In addition to obtaining a plain right-factored CNF transformation, the CNF method from the NLTK allows to augment the performance of the obtained unlexicalized binary grammars by introducing additional context information in the non-terminals names. This process is called grammar markovization and is controlled by the vertical (v) and horizontal (h) markovization parameters [18]. A plain right-factored CNF transformed grammar corresponds to a markovization with both v and h set to 0.

A basic schema was introduced for parsing sentences with out-of-vocabulary words: when an input word could not be derived by any of the preterminals in the vanilla treebank grammar, a very small probability for that word was uniformly added to all of the preterminals.

For our experiments we obtained several CNF grammars of different sizes through the use of different v and h values. Results for the metrics discussed on Sect. 9.5.2 for the different markovizations of the obtained grammars can be seen in Tables 9.1 and 9.2. We observe that the percentage of corrections needed using the IP system is much lower than the rate of corrections needed on just post-editing the proposed trees: from 42% to 47% effort reduction by the human supervisor. These results clearly show that an IP system can relieve manual annotators of a lot of burden in their task.

Additionally, we performed experimentation with CM used over an IP process, to assess their power to detect incorrect constituents. We assessed that CM retain all of their error detection capabilities during the IP process: they are able to discern between 18% and 25% of incorrect constituents at most stages of the IP process, with a bump up to 27% after about seven user interactions. The complete details can be found at [28].

---

[1] http://nltk.sourceforge.net/.

Table 9.1 Results for the test set of the Penn Treebank: F_1 and TCER for the baseline system; TCAC for the IP system; relative reduction between TCER and TCAC

PCFG	Baseline		IP	RelRed
	F_1	TCER	TCAC	
$h = 0, v = 1$	0.67	0.40	0.22	45%
$h = 0, v = 2$	0.68	0.39	0.21	46%
$h = 0, v = 3$	0.70	0.38	0.22	42%

Table 9.2 Results for the test set of the UAM Treebank: F_1 and TCER for the baseline system; TCAC for the IP system; relative reduction between TCER and TCAC

PCFG	Baseline		IP	RelRed
	F_1	TCER	TCAC	
$h = 0, v = 0$	0.57	0.48	0.26	46%
$h = 0, v = 1$	0.59	0.47	0.25	47%
$h = 0, v = 2$	0.62	0.44	0.24	46%
$h = 0, v = 3$	0.61	0.45	0.24	47%

Note that the presented experiments were done using parsing models that perform far from the latest F_1 results; their intention was to assess the utility of the IP schema. However, we expect that relative reductions with IP systems incorporating state-of-the-art parsers would be relevant as well.

9.6 Conclusions

In this chapter, we have introduced a novel Interactive Parsing framework which can be operated by a user to obtain error-free syntactic parse trees. This compares to the classical two-step schema of manually post-editing the erroneous constituents produced by the parsing system. In the general IP framework presented, the interaction protocol that we have initially defined is desultory type: the user can edit any part of the parse tree and in any order. However, to efficiently increase the computation of next best parse tree, a left-to-right depth-first tree review order has been introduced.

To make an automatic experimental assessment, we have simulated the user interaction with the system. Since we have the reference parser, this experimental feature has been possible. We have also defined and calculated some evaluation metrics. In general, the achieved results showed that in an IP system is produced a high amount of effort reduction for a manual annotator compared to a two-step system.

In addition, we have proved that using confidence measures to discriminate incorrect from correct constituents helps to some extent in the IP process. In this point, a purely statistical confidence measure (based on inside-outside estimated posterior probability of constituents) for probabilistic parsing has been introduced.

Finally, is important to note that, in addition to the automatic experimental evaluation reported in previous section, a complete IP prototype has been implemented (see Chap. 12) and made available to potential real users.

References

1. Baker, J. K. (1979). Trainable grammars for speech recognition. *The Journal of the Acoustical Society of America*, *65*, 31–35.
2. Benedí, J. M., & Sánchez, J. A. (2005). Estimation of stochastic context-free grammars and their use as language models. *Computer Speech & Language*, *19*(3), 249–274.
3. Benedí, J. M., Sánchez, J. A., & Sanchis, A. (2007). Confidence measures for stochastic parsing. In *Proceedings of the international conference recent advances in natural language processing* (pp. 58–63), Borovets, Bulgaria.
4. Carter, D. (1997). The TreeBanker. A tool for supervised training of parsed corpora. In *Proceedings of the workshop on computational environments for grammar development and linguistic engineering* (pp. 9–15), Madrid, Spain.
5. Charniak, E. (1997). Statistical parsing with a context-free grammar and word statistics. In *Proceedings of the national conference on artificial intelligence* (pp. 598–603), Providence, Rhode Island, USA.
6. Charniak, E. (2000). A maximum-entropy-inspired parser. In *Proceedings of the first conference on North American chapter of the association for computational linguistics* (pp. 132–139), Seattle, Washington, USA.
7. Charniak, E., Knight, K., & Yamada, K. (2003). Syntax-based language models for statistical machine translation. In *Machine translation summit, IX international association for machine translation*, New Orleans, Louisiana, USA.
8. Chelba, F., & Jelinek, C. (2000). Structured language modeling. *Computer Speech and Language*, *14*(4), 283–332.
9. Chiang, D. (2007). Hierarchical phrase-based translation. *Computational Linguistics*, *33*(2), 201–228.
10. Collins, M. (2003). Head-driven statistical models for natural language parsing. *Computational Linguistics*, *29*(4), 589–637.
11. de la Clergerie, E. V., Hamon, O., Mostefa, D., Ayache, C., Paroubek, P., & Vilnat, A. (2008). PASSAGE: from French parser evaluation to large sized treebank. In *Proceedings of the sixth international language resources and evaluation* (pp. 3570–3577), Marrakech, Morocco.
12. Earley, J. (1970). An efficient context-free parsing algorithm. *Communications of the ACM*, *8*(6), 451–455.
13. Gascó, G., & Sánchez, J. A. (2007). A* parsing with large vocabularies. In *Proceedings of the international conference recent advances in natural language processing* (pp. 215–219), Borovets, Bulgaria.
14. Gascó, G., Sánchez, J. A., & Benedí, J. M. (2010). Enlarged search space for sitg parsing. In *Proceedings of the North American chapter of the association for computational linguistics—human language technologies conference* (pp. 653–656), Los Angeles, California.
15. Hopcroft, J. E., & Ullman, J. D. (1979). *Introduction to automata theory, languages and computation*. Reading: Addison-Wesley.
16. Huang, L., & Chiang, D. (2005). Better k-best parsing. In *Proceedings of the ninth international workshop on parsing technology* (pp. 53–64), Vancouver, British Columbia. Menlo Park: Association for Computational Linguistics.
17. Jain, A. K., Duin, R. P., & Mao, J. (2000). Statistical pattern recognition: A review. *IEEE Transactions on Pattern Analysis and Machine Intelligence*, *22*, 4–37.
18. Klein, D., & Manning, C. D. (2003). Accurate unlexicalized parsing. In *Proceedings of the 41st annual meeting on association for computational linguistics* (Vol. 1, pp. 423–430), Association for Computational Linguistics Morristown, NJ, USA.
19. Lease, M., Charniak, E., Johnson, M., & McClosky, D. (2006). A look at parsing and its applications. In *Proceedings of the twenty-first national conference on artificial intelligence*, Boston, Massachusetts, USA.
20. Marcus, M. P., Santorini, B., & Marcinkiewicz, M. A. (1994). Building a large annotated corpus of English: The Penn Treebank. *Computational Linguistics*, *19*(2), 313–330.

21. Oepen, S., Flickinger, D., Toutanova, K., & Manning, C. D. (2004). LinGO redwoods. *Research on Language and Computation*, *2*(4), 575–596.
22. Pereira, F., & Schabes, Y. (1992). Inside-outside reestimation from partially bracketed corpora. In *Proceedings of the 30th annual meeting of the association for computational linguistics* (pp. 128–135). Newark: University of Delaware.
23. Petrov, S., & Klein, D. (2007). Improved inference for unlexicalized parsing. In *Conference of the North American chapter of the association for computational linguistics; proceedings of the main conference* (pp. 404–411), Rochester, New York.
24. Roark, B. (2001). Probabilistic top-down parsing and language modeling. *Computational Linguistics*, *27*(2), 249–276.
25. Salvador, I., & Benedí, J. M. (2002). RNA modeling by combining stochastic context-free grammars and n-gram models. *International Journal of Pattern Recognition and Artificial Intelligence*, *16*(3), 309–315.
26. San-Segundo, R., Pellom, B., Hacioglu, K., Ward, W., & Pardo, J. M. (2001). Confidence measures for spoken dialogue systems. In *IEEE international conference on acoustic speech and signal processing* (Vol. 1), Salt Lake City, Utah, USA.
27. Sánchez-Sáez, R., Sánchez, J. A., & Benedí, J. M. (2009). Statistical confidence measures for probabilistic parsing. In *Proceedings of the international conference on recent advances in natural language processing* (pp. 388–392), Borovets, Bulgaria.
28. Sánchez-Sáez, R., Leiva, L., Sánchez, J. A., & Benedí, J. M. (2010). Confidence measures for error discrimination in an interactive predictive parsing framework. In *23rd International conference on computational linguistics* (pp. 1220–1228), Beijing, China.
29. Serrano, N., Sanchis, A., & Juan, A. (2010). Balancing error and supervision effort in interactive-predictive handwriting recognition. In *Proceeding of the 14th international conference on intelligent user interfaces* (pp. 373–376), Hong Kong, China.
30. Stolcke, A. (1995). An efficient probabilistic context-free parsing algorithm that computes prefix probabilities. *Computational Linguistics*, *21*(2), 165–200.
31. Tarazón, L., Pérez, D., Serrano, N., Alabau, V., Terrades, O. R., Sanchis, A., & Juan, A. (2009). Confidence measures for error correction in interactive transcription of handwritten text. In *LNCS: Vol. 5716. Proceedings of the 15th international conference on image analysis and processing* (pp. 567–574), Salerno, Italy.
32. Ueffing, N., & Ney, H. (2007). Word-level confidence estimation for machine translation. *Computational Linguistics*, *33*(1), 9–40.
33. Wessel, F., Schluter, R., Macherey, K., & Ney, H. (2001). Confidence measures for large vocabulary continuous speech recognition. *IEEE Transactions on Speech and Audio Processing*, *9*(3), 288–298.
34. Wu, D. (1997). Stochastic inversion transduction grammars and bilingual parsing of parallel corpora. *Computational Linguistics*, *23*(3), 377–404.
35. Yamada, K., & Knight, K. (2002). A decoder for syntax-based statistical MT. In *Meeting of the association for computational linguistics*, Philadelphia, Pensilvania, USA.
36. Yamamoto, R., Sako, S., Nishimoto, T., & Sagayama, S. (2006). On-line recognition of handwritten mathematical expressions based on stroke-based stochastic context-free grammar. In *10th international workshop on frontiers in handwriting recognition* (pp. 249–254), La Baule, France.

Chapter 10
Interactive Text Generation

With Contribution Of: José Oncina and Luis Rodríguez.

Contents

Using a computer to produce text documents is essentially a manual task nowadays. The computer is basically seen as an electronic typewriter and all the effort required falls on the human user who has to, firstly, think of a grammatically and semantically correct piece of text and, then, type on the computer. Although human beings are usually quite efficient when performing this task, in some cases, this process can be very time consuming. Writing text in a non-native language, using devices having highly constrained input interfaces, or the case of impaired people using computers are only a few examples. Providing some kind of automation in these scenarios could be really useful.

Interactive Text Prediction deals with providing assistance in document typing tasks. IPR techniques are used to predict what the user is going to type, given the text typed previously. Prediction is studied both at the word level and at the character level but, in both cases, the aim is to predict multi-word text chunks, not just a single next word or word fragment. Empirical tests suggest that significant amounts of user typing (and to some extent also thinking) effort can be saved using the proposed approaches. In this chapter, alternative strategies to perform the search in this type of tasks are also presented and discussed in detail.

10.1 Introduction

Since the adoption of the written language by the ancient human societies, writing texts has become a very common task. The introduction of electronic computers has

A.H. Toselli et al., *Multimodal Interactive Pattern Recognition and Applications*,
DOI 10.1007/978-0-85729-479-1_10, © Springer-Verlag London Limited 2011

made this process significantly easier. Thanks to word processing software, computers allow us to generate text faster and more comfortably than ever. However, so far, the approach adopted is essentially the same as centuries ago. Computers are, essentially, much more sophisticated replacements of paper, pencil and eraser, but typing text is still a manual process and the incredible computational power that computers provide is barely used. Even in the most modern word processing developments, only basic tools such as orthographic and grammatical checkers and thesaurus are generally implemented to help the user in the generation of correct text.

The development of advanced assistance tools for generating text is thus of great interest for general-purpose word-processing applications and more so for applications needed in many other more specific environments where text-input is needed. In all the cases, the ability of automatically predicting what someone is going to type can save considerable amounts of human effort and could therefore be utterly helpful.

In some situations, the typing task can become too slow and uncomfortable. For instance, in devices such as mobile phones and PDA's, no satisfactory interfaces for text-input have been developed so far. In addition, even with adequate typing devices such as a conventional keyboard, people with certain disabilities can be unable to achieve a sufficient typing speed; and, unfortunately, for many of them text generation may be the only appropriate communication channel.

Different approaches to the text prediction problem can be found in the literature. Most of them only attempt to predict the next single word [4] or focus on measuring the accuracy of off-line text predictions [1]. Here, we consider a more general setting under the IPR paradigm where, not only single words, but multi-word fragments or full sentences are predicted.

10.1.1 Interactive Text Generation and Interactive Pattern Recognition

Providing assistance in text typing is a problem that could fit in the interactive transcription or translation frameworks presented Chaps. 2–4 or Chaps. 6–8. The basic process consists in predicting (or "completing") some portion of text based on the text previously typed. Using the terminology adopted in Chap. 2, the problem is to find a text *suffix* which is a suitable continuation for a given text *prefix*. However, there is a big difference in this case with respect to the problems considered in previous chapters of this book.

In the general IPR framework, the goal is to decode some input signal or data. In contrast, for text prediction, no input is available. That is, the only information source available to produce its outcome is the user feedback.[1] This makes the text prediction task more difficult since the system outputs can not constrained by input

[1] Actually, this formulation could be interpreted in a different way by considering the prefix as the input pattern leading to a *classical* Pattern Recognition problem.

patterns. Therefore, the set of possible system hypotheses is much larger and prediction accuracy is expected to be significantly lower than in the problems considered so far in this book.

Following the concepts introduced in Sect. 1.4.1, the text prediction problem clearly entails a type of passive interaction protocol "without input data", which can be formulated as in Eq. (1.37):

$$\hat{h} = \arg\max_{h \in \mathcal{H}} P(h \mid h', d). \tag{10.1}$$

In addition, as in Sect. 2.3, we can quite naturally assume a left-to-right processing protocol. This way the hypotheses, h, are text *suffixes* (called s from now on), and the history, h', along with the user feedback, d, correspond to the given text *prefix* (referred to as p in the sequel). Therefore, Eq. (10.1) becomes:

$$\hat{s} = \arg\max_{s} P(s \mid p). \tag{10.2}$$

Initially, no prefix is available, and the system makes an initial prediction. The user validates part of the prediction, selecting a correct prefix, and adds some text to this prefix (this corresponds to the feedback, d in Eq. (10.1)). Then, the system will complete this user-validated and corrected text and the process continues in this way until the whole text is satisfactory. Figure 10.1 shows an example of an ITG session.

Some practical aspects that arise in this task are worth discussing. On the one hand, the initial prediction (when no prefix is available) would be always identical, since the conditional probability in Eq. (10.2) only depends on an empty prior. Because of this, an initial prediction can be useless and it might be better to wait for the user to type something before starting the prediction process. Nonetheless, an initial prediction could be adequate in some applications involving the generation of documents starting with fixed or typical sequences of words.

Another practical problem arises because of the lack of input data. In all IPR tasks previously considered in this book, the input pattern is somehow used to estimate a best length for the prediction. On the contrary, in text generation, other strategies have to be developed for this estimation. Predicting just one word after the prefix seems to be the easiest strategy to do, but multi-word predictions can clearly be more beneficial. Predicting whole sentences, on the other hand, could be a considered a best choice, but a full-sentence language model would be needed and, so far, models of this kind have not proved sufficiently good for language modeling. Letting the user set the length of predictions is, maybe, a good alternative but letting the system itself deal with this problem could be worth it.

10.2 Interactive Text Generation at the Word Level

Now we address the development of an Interactive Text Generation (ITG) system. We consider this problem at the *word level* in this section and at the *character*

Step 1	
Prediction:	`Check the printer before sending jobs`
Prefix:	**Check the**
Amendment:	**Check the** *following*
Step 2	
Prediction:	**Check the following** `conditions before continuing`
Prefix:	**Check the following conditions**
Amendment:	**Check the following conditions** *to*
Step 3	
Prediction:	**Check the following conditions to** `ensure an optimum work`
Prefix:	**Check the following conditions to ensure an optimum**
Amendment:	**Check the following conditions to ensure an optimum** *performance*

RESULT: **Check the** *following* **conditions** *to* **ensure an optimum** *performance*

$$\text{WSR} = \frac{3}{9} = 0.33 \rightarrow 33\%$$

Fig. 10.1 Example of text generation session and the corresponding word stroke ratio (WSR) computation for producing the text "*Check the following conditions to ensure an optimum performance*". The system generates an initial prediction. Then, the user validates a correct prefix (*boldfaced*) and introduces a word amendment (shown in *italics*). The system, taking into account this information, generates a new prediction. The process is iterated until a correct, full sentence is achieved. In the final result, the user only had to type the two words shown in *italics*. The WSR is obtained by dividing the number of user word strokes between the overall number of words

level in the next section. We begin describing the models involved in ITG and then we consider search approaches to solve Eq. (10.2). With respect to the search approaches considered in previous chapters of this book, it is worth noting that, here, the lack of input data entails interesting simplifications, which lead to much simpler and more effective search techniques.

10.2.1 N-Gram Language Modeling

N-grams [2] are the most widely used language models in NLP applications. Our approach to text generation also lies on n-grams but taking into account some considerations that are discussed in the following paragraphs. As described in Sect. 2.4, the basic idea is to rely on the $n-1$ last words of the prefix to predict an appropriate continuation. Clearly, these models fail in benefiting from the whole wealth of information available and just a small part of it is actually considered. Nevertheless, n-gram language modeling (LM) generally entails important useful simplifications both in search and (mainly) in training, as discussed in Sect. 2.2.

10.2.2 Searching for a Suffix

The conditional probability maximization entailed by Eq. (10.2) can in principle be solved by Dynamic Programming as discussed in Sect. 2.5.1. Notice, however, that, because of the lack of input data, the decoding process here becomes easier than in text images or speech transcription solutions such as CATTI or CATS (Chaps. 2–4).

Here the problem only consists in constructing suffixes according to the given LM. At this point, we can anticipate a problem that will be discussed later. In most pattern recognition tasks, we have an input pattern to decode and the search algorithm can be stopped when the end of the pattern is reached. In ITG, no input exists and, therefore, no clue to stop predicting words is available. Moreover, due to the nature of the n-grams, the probability of a word sequence quickly drops with the number of words and longer predictions are penalized over shorter ones. Therefore, we will need a function, $F_{\text{length}}(.)$, which, given a prediction hypothesis, will return a score for this hypothesis according to its length. Taking into account all these considerations, the Algorithm 10.1 (called "*MaxPost*"), shown on p. 200, provides a (maximum posterior probability) solution to Eq. (10.2).

Surprisingly enough, the (*Viterbi* search) maximization of the posterior probability is not necessarily the best strategy for ITG. Recently, a better and simpler approach has been proposed [3], which will be discussed below.

10.2.3 Optimal Greedy Prediction of Suffixes

The *MaxPost* strategy actually aims at minimizing "whole line or sentence" errors; that is it assumes a 0–1 *loss function*, as outlined in Sects. 1.2.1 and 1.3.4, which leads to optimizing the number of whole sentences or lines correctly predicted.[2] In other words, the well-known *Sentence Error Rate* (SER) metric is the optimization goal for *MaxPost*.

In an interactive task like ITG, the real goal is to save user interaction effort and not necessarily maximizing the number of correctly predicted whole sentences or lines. As discussed in Sect. 1.3.4, adequate estimations of user interaction effort can be achieved by using different *loss* functions. Following this idea, an optimal strategy to predict suffixes in an interactive environment is proposed in [3]. This strategy turns out to entail a greedy-like search (called *Greedy* from now on) which constructs the final hypothesis just as a concatenation of locally optimal decisions. This strategy is described by Algorithm 10.2 on p. 201.

The superiority of the *Greedy* approach could be alternatively derived by applying the optimal decision rule properly. Without loss of generality, let us consider that exactly one word is predicted after the prefix. Only two possibilities arise: If

[2]Here we are considering that ITG works in a "sentence-by-sentence" or "line-by-line" basis. In NLP this approach is often followed since working with too long chunks of text is generally unpractical.

Algorithm 10.1: (*MaxPost* algorithm) Dynamic-programming Viterbi-like algorithm to search for the best continuation to a prefix. n-gram states are identified as substrings of length $n-1$. Therefore, if (for example) $n=3$, $q=w_{i-n+2}^{i}$ denotes a state identified as the 2-gram $w_{i-1}w_i$. It is assumed that, if $j<i$, w_i^j is the empty string (λ). The function $F_{\text{length}}(i,g)$ provides the length-conditioned score for an i-words sentence with likelihood g. Different implementations of this function are discussed in Sect. 10.2.4

```
input : user-validated prefix (p), vocabulary (V), maximum prediction length
        (maxLen), n-gram size (n), length score function (F_length)
output: whole sentence prediction
begin
    i = |p| + 1; q = p_{i-n+1}^{i-1};
    Q = {q}; // States
    G[q] = 0; // Likelihoods;
    W[q] = p; // Word sequences
    g_best = 0; w_best = λ
    while i < maxLen do
        Q' = Q; G' = G;
        W' = W; Q = ∅;
        forall q' ∈ Q' do
            forall v ∈ V do
                q = q'_2^{n-1} · v // concatenate v to w_{i-n+2}^{i-1}
                if q ∉ Q then
                    Q = Q ∪ {q};
                    G[q] = G'[q] P(v | q');
                    W[q] = W'[q'] · v;
                else if G[q] < G'[q] P(v | q') then
                    G[q] = G'[q] P(v | q');
                    W[q] = W'[q'] · v;
        g* = 0; w* = λ;
        forall q ∈ Q do
            if G[q] > g* then
                g* = G[q];
                w*=W[q]; //best result for length i
        if g_best < F_length(i, g*) then
            g_best = F_length(i, g*);
            w_best = w*; // best result so far
        i = i + 1;
    return w_best;
end
```

Algorithm 10.2: Greedy strategy to complete a user-validated prefix. Note that the greedy solutions shorter than *maxLen* are just the prefixes of the resulting w.

input : user-validated prefix (p), vocabulary (V), maximum prediction length ($maxLen$), n-gram size (n)
output: whole sentence prediction (w)

```
begin
  w = p; i = |p| + 1;
  while i < maxLen do
    v* = λ; g* = 0;
    forall v ∈ V do
      if g* < P(v | w_{i-n+1}^{i-1}) then
        g* = P(v | w_{i-n+1}^{i-1});
        v* = v;
    w = w · v*;
    i = i + 1;
  return w;
end
```

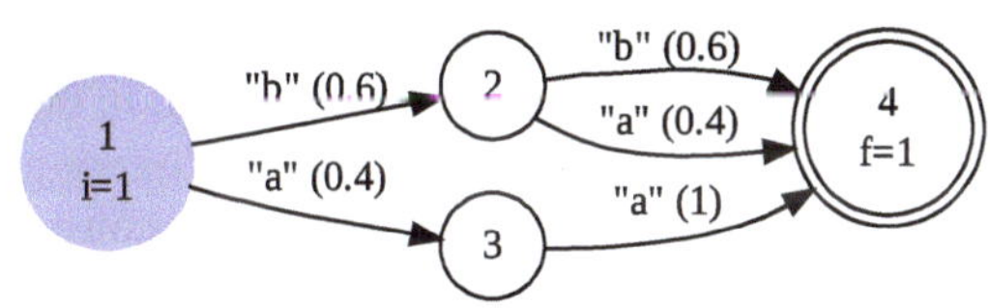

Fig. 10.2 Simple stochastic language model

the prediction was correct, the word is added to the prefix (thereby generating a new prefix) and the process is iterated; if the word was not correctly predicted, a word stroke is computed and the correct word is added, again, to form a new prefix. It is easy to see that this process is completely equivalent to the more general one with respect to the number of word strokes needed to produce a sentence. Therefore, the conclusions reached here can be applied, as well, to our multi-word prediction case.

From this new point of view, we can consider that we are addressing an iterative classification problem where, in each iteration, we have a prefix and we obtain a label class (the predicted word) for this prefix. By making the reasonable assumption that each classification step is independent from the previous ones, the optimal decision rule follows. This rule tells us that we have to maximize the posterior probability of the class (single word) given the pattern (prefix). This way, we should choose, in each iteration, the most probable word given the prefix, which turns out to be, indeed, a greedy prediction algorithm.

To illustrate and analyze the behavior of both strategies, *MaxPost* and *Greedy*, we show an example based on the simple LM shown in Fig. 10.2.

Let us suppose that the texts we want to generate are all the strings modeled by this LM; namely, *aa*, *ba* and *bb* (we assume here that each letter represents a single word). Now, we can compute the expected number of interactive steps (I) required to generate these texts when using *MaxPost*. The string aa is generated with probability 0.4 and does not need any interaction (notice that aa is the most probable text generated by the model). Next, the string ba, is generated with probability 0.24 and it needs one interaction step (with no prefix, *MaxPost* predicts the string aa and after setting b as a prefix, the string ba is finally achieved). Finally, the string bb is generated with probability 0.36 and two interaction steps. Therefore:

$$\textit{MaxPost}: \quad E(I) = 0 \cdot 0.4 + 1 \cdot 0.24 + 2 \cdot 0.36 = 0.96.$$

On the other hand, the *Greedy* approach starts predicting bb when no prefix is available, without needing any interaction step (the third addend in the equation below) and two and one interaction steps are needed for the strings aa and ba, respectively (first and second addends in the equation below). Therefore, the corresponding expected value for the *Greedy* approach is

$$\textit{Greedy}: \quad E(I) = 1 \cdot 0.4 + 1 \cdot 0.24 + 0 \cdot 0.36 = 0.64.$$

Thus, the *Greedy* approach is expected to require less overall interaction effort. But what can be expected about the prediction errors? We can notice that the (expected) number of prediction errors corresponds to the (expected) number of interactions. When the system fails to generate a perfect suffix a user interaction step is required. Therefore, we conclude that, in this case, the number of (single word) prediction errors is also minimized by *Greedy* and not by *MaxPost*.

This apparent *paradox* is solved by considering the proper loss function that *MaxPost* aims to optimize; namely, the number of full-suffix prediction error corrections, C. In the previous example, the expected value of this number, considering all the possible situations, can be easily computed: There are three different decision problems, given by the three different prefixes that the strings in the model can have: λ (the empty string), a and b. In the case of *MaxPost*, first consider the empty prefix, λ, which is produced with probability 1 and makes the algorithm predict the string aa; then, the correct suffix will be predicted with probability 0.4 (probability of aa) and, therefore, a wrong suffix will be suggested with probability 0.6 (probability of ba and bb). The second prefix, a, is generated with probability 0.4; in this case, the algorithm will predict the only possible suffix a and the probability of making a wrong prediction is 0. Finally, the prefix b is produced with probability 0.6 and b will be suggested as the best continuation; therefore, the probability of the correct prediction will be 0.6 (probability of b given b) and the probability of making a mistake will be 0.4 (probability of a given b). Thus, the expected value for *MaxPost* is

$$\textit{MaxPost}: \quad E(C) = 1 \cdot 0.6 + 0.4 \cdot 0 + 0.6 \cdot 0.4 = 0.84.$$

Similar considerations apply in the *Greedy* case, leading to

$$\textit{Greedy}: \quad E(C) = 1 \cdot 0.64 + 0.4 \cdot 0 + 0.6 \cdot 0.4 = 0.88.$$

10.2.4 Dealing with Sentence Length

As previously mentioned, the problem of determining when to stop generating words in ITG could be regarded, for simplicity, as one of the practical issues of the system. This way, simple solutions such as letting the user set a maximum prediction length can be adopted. Nevertheless, there is also an important problem related to the nature of the models used in predictions that can not be overlooked. When using a dynamic programming approach, a trellis containing all the explored hypotheses is constructed. Each stage of the trellis contains same-length hypotheses. Initially, the 1-word hypotheses are considered. Next, 2-words hypotheses are generated and evaluated and so on. On the other hand, an n-gram language model scores a sentence by computing the product of the probabilities of all the n-grams of the sentence. Since all these probabilities are numbers between 0 and 1, the fewer amount of n-grams in the hypothesis the higher the score is or, in other words, shorter predictions would have (in average) a better score than longer ones. In the most extreme case, our system would always produce a 1-word prediction. We propose two different alternatives to approach this problem.

The first one is based on normalizing each hypothesis probability by its length. This normalized *score*, $\mathcal{S}(s \mid p)$, can be better expressed by following the usual log-prob computation:

$$\mathcal{S}(s \mid p) = \frac{1}{l-k} \cdot \sum_{i=k+1}^{l} \log P\big(w_i \mid w_{i-n+1}^{i-1}\big), \qquad (10.3)$$

where $w = p \cdot s$, k is the length of p and l is the length of w.

According to this equation, the best hypotheses are those whose individual n-gram log-probabilities are higher on average. An important drawback of this approach is that, because of the normalization, the model is not a probabilistic model anymore and some of the desirable properties that characterizes this kind of models are lost.

As an alternative, we propose, a different approach which uses a separate model to account for the length (denoted as $P_l(\cdot)$). For instance, a Gaussian can be chosen to approximate the distribution over all the possible lengths. This Gaussian distribution can be easily maximum-likelihood trained on the training samples. Once an explicit length model is available, a linear interpolation is performed between the n-gram model and this new length model:

$$P(s \mid p) = \alpha \cdot P_l\big(|p| + |s|\big) + (1-\alpha) \cdot \prod_{i=k+1}^{l} P\big(w_i \mid w_{i-n+1}^{i-1}\big). \qquad (10.4)$$

In the case of the *Greedy* approach, this is not actually an issue. In *MaxPost*, multiple partial hypotheses are considered in parallel. In *Greedy*, however, a single prediction is constructed by just adding locally optimally computed words after the successive prefixes. That means that the length of the prediction does not significantly modify the content of the prediction itself That is, the best prediction of length m will always be a prefix of the best prediction of length $m+1$.

10.2.5 Word-Level Experiments

The evaluation method followed here is based on the use of the already defined *Word Stroke Ratio* (WSR) metric (cf. Sect. 2.6). An example of WSR computation is shown in Fig. 10.1.

Three different tasks are considered. The first two, EuTrans and Xerox, were already used in CAST (see Chap. 4). The third one, Albayzin, consists of a set of natural language queries to a geographic database. The main features of these corpora are shown in Table 10.1.

The experiments performed in this section aim at evaluating two different aspects of ITG. On the one hand, the prediction accuracy has to be measured. On the other, a comparison between the two techniques *MaxPost* and *Greedy* is needed to validate the optimality of the last one. In Table 10.2 the main results of the experiments are shown. In this table, the *Length Model* column refers to the linear interpolation shown in Eq. (10.4). The final two columns correspond, respectively, to the length normalization of Eq. (10.3) in the *MaxPost* approach and to predictions of a defined length in the case of the *Greedy* approach. The best result for each corpus is shown in boldface.

We can see that *Greedy* significantly outperforms *MaxPost* in all the corpora. It is noticeable, as well, that in simple tasks the system can accurately predict about

Table 10.1 Features of the corpora used

	EuTrans	Albayzin	Xerox
Test sentences	2 996	1 440	875
Running words	35 023	13 566	8 257
Running characters	188 707	81 246	53 337
Training vocabulary	688	1 271	10 913
Training sentences	10 000	9 893	53 740
Test-set perplexity (3-grams)	4.9	6.6	41

Table 10.2 WSR results on different corpora. A comparison between the two search algorithm proposed is shown for the three corpus considered. The columns under *Length model* show the result of interpolating the n-gram with a probabilistic length model under different values for the α parameter in Eq. (10.4). The column under *Length normalization* shows the result of applying a length normalization on this algorithm. The final column reports the results achieved by the greedy approach

Corpus	*MaxPost*						*Greedy*
	Length model (α)					Length norm.	
	0.1	0.3	0.5	0.7	0.9		
EuTrans	57.6	57.6	60.4	62.7	62.7	62.5	**50.9**
Albayzin	62.5	62.5	62.5	62.5	62.8	60.4	**53.6**
Xerox	79.6	79.6	79.7	80.0	80.0	77.3	**66.3**

half of the overall words in the reference sets. It is also worth mentioning that the *Xerox* test is the same as used in CAST, where a WSR of 18.6% was achieved. By comparing both results we can get a picture about the prediction accuracy lost because of the lack of input data.

10.3 Predicting at Character Level

The results shown in the previous section were obtained by considering each user interaction step as a whole-word correction. However, an alternative arises if we consider a character-based approach, where the user feedback consists of single keystrokes rather than whole words. This alternative would also entail estimating interaction effort in terms of *key strokes* (KSR), rather than *word strokes* (WSR), where the KSR is defined as the number of key strokes needed to achieve the reference tesx divided by running characters in this text.

In principle, it is clear when to estimate the text-generating user effort in terms of word or key strokes. For constrained interfaces, where the bottleneck is the very typing process, computing keystrokes seems to be reasonable, since a significant amount of time is spent in introducing the information instead of thinking about what it is going to be typed. Otherwise, if the bottleneck is not typing but finding (i.e., thinking) the right words to compose the intended text, it is the WSR what makes more sense.

In character-level interaction, as soon as the user types a single character, the system provides a continuation without waiting for a full word correction. The process is essentially the same as described for word-level ITG, but taking into account that, when searching for the suffix, we have to deal with incomplete words (that is, the final characters of the prefix can be a word-prefix and not necessarily a whole word). Under this premise, we firstly have to complete the final characters in the prefix, which will usually be an incomplete word. In Fig. 10.3 an example of interaction with a character-ITG system is shown, along with an example of KSR computation.

Formally, let c_{w_k} be the sequence of *characters* that comes after the last blank in the prefix. We have to search for a word $\hat{v}$ for which c_{w_k} is a prefix. In the case of an n-gram language model, this amounts to the following optimization equation:

$$\hat{v} = \operatorname*{arg\,max}_{v \in V : c_{w_k} \in \operatorname{pref}(v)} P\big(v \mid w_{k-n+1}^{k-1}\big) \tag{10.5}$$

where $\operatorname{pref}(v)$ denotes the set of all the prefixes of the word v.

10.3.1 Character-Level Experiments

Table 10.3 shows the results of character-level interaction on the corpora described in Sect. 10.2.5.

At this point, it can be interesting to recall the discussion about which measure (WSR or KSR) to adopt to better estimate the user interaction effort. In a normal

Step 1
Prediction: `Check the printer before sending jobs`
Prefix: **Check the**
Amendment: **Check the *f***
Step 2
Prediction: **Check the f** `inal configuration before continuing`
Prefix: **Check the f**
Amendment: **Check the f*o***
Step 3
Prediction: **Check the fo** `llowing conditions to ensure an optimum work`
Prefix: **Check the following conditions to ensure an optimum**
Amendment: **Check the following conditions to ensure an optimum *p***
Step 4
Prediction: **Check the following conditions to ensure an optimum p** `erformance`

RESULT: **Check the *fo*llowing conditions to ensure an optimum *p*erformance**

$$\text{KSR} = \frac{4}{65} = 0.06 \rightarrow 6\%$$

Fig. 10.3 Example of character-level text generation session and the corresponding KSR computation for producing the text "*Check the following conditions to ensure an optimum performance*". The system generates an initial prediction. Then, the user validates a correct prefix (**boldfaced**) and introduces an amendment (shown in *italics*). The system, taking into account this information, generates a new prediction. The process is iterated until a correct, full sentence is achieved. In the final result, the user only had to type the three characters shown in *italics*. A final acceptation keystroke is also assumed. The KSR measure is obtained by dividing the number of user strokes between the overall number of characters

Table 10.3 Character prediction results (KSR in %) corresponding to the *Greedy* approach. The previously reported WSR results for the same corpora are also included for informative purposes

Corpus	KSR	WSR
EUTRANS	14.1	50.9
ALBAYZIN	13.3	53.6
XEROX	19.5	66.3

situation where a user generates a whole text document in a desktop computer, it is not clear which estimation is more reliable. If the system is planned to help a user in how to write a document (that is, to suggest grammatical constructions, specific words, etc.), WSR seems quite adequate since words can be considered as the minimum meaningful units in human language and, therefore, the effort should be expressed in these terms. On the other hand, if ITG is to be used as an assistive technology in problematic environments, where the effort needed to merely do typing is significant, then KSR is clearly the metric to be adopted. The results obtained so far (on *simple* tasks) seem to suggest that, for the time being, ITG is only of moderate help to solve the first situation. On the contrary, the KSR results indicate that ITG turns out to be an interesting approach for constrained-typing situations.

10.4 Conclusions

In this chapter, a different type of application derived of the Interactive Pattern Recognition paradigm has been presented. The aim of this proposal is to provide assistance in the generation of text documents. The main difference with respect to other IPR applications is that no input pattern is available and the system only has the user feedback to produce the predictions. This makes the process more difficult in the sense that the possible set of adequate system outputs is less constrained than in the applications described in previous chapters.

One of the main contribution of this chapter is the adoption of a different, simpler, *greedy* search strategy which proves to be optimal to achieve the best possible continuation to a text prefix.

The experiments performed show that this kind of approach can save a significant amount of typing effort. This can be quite interesting when a user has to deal with situations where typing is a burdensome process.

References

1. Bickel, S., Haider, P., & Scheffer, T. (2005). Predicting sentences using n-gram language models. In *HLT'05: Proceedings of the conference on human language technology and empirical methods in natural language processing* (pp. 193–200), Morristown, NJ, USA. Menlo Park: Association for Computational Linguistics.
2. Jelinek, F. (1998). *Statistical methods for speech recognition*. Cambridge: MIT Press.
3. Oncina, J. (2009). Optimum algorithm to minimize human interactions in sequential computer assisted pattern recognition. *Pattern Recognition Letters*, *30*(6), 558–563.
4. Trost, H., Matiasek, J., & Baroni, M. (2005). The language component of the fasty text prediction system. *Applied Artificial Intelligence*, *19*(8), 743–781.

Chapter 11
Interactive Image Retrieval

With Contribution Of: Roberto Paredes and Franco Segarra.

Contents

This chapter presents search methods for image retrieval which are boosted using the user's supervision by means of the human–computer interaction methodology. Two contributions are presented which cover different aspects of this problem.

The first one deals with classical relevance feedback, content-based image retrieval, but with a formulation directly derived from the IPR paradigm adopted throughout this book. This formulation helps putting forward the improving role of "consistency" among the retrieved images. The second contribution considers the use of a complementary text-based "modality" to express the user relevance feedback information, which leads to improved retrieval results.

11.1 Introduction

This chapter presents two different approaches which aim at improving the results of the image retrieval problem by means of user interaction and multimodality. The first one is a relevance feedback approach which relies on the user feedback and image dissimilarities in order to provide better retrievals in an iterative way. It adopts a probabilistic model of the interactive process which leads to an algorithm to maximize the relevance of the images retrieved. The second approach is based on user relevance feedback as well, but we focus our attention on adding new modalities to the retrieval mechanism. In particular, we propose a multimodal retrieval system that uses both visual and textual features.

A.H. Toselli et al., *Multimodal Interactive Pattern Recognition and Applications*,
DOI 10.1007/978-0-85729-479-1_11, © Springer-Verlag London Limited 2011

11.2 Relevance Feedback for Image Retrieval

In this section we propose a probabilistic model to handle user interaction in information retrieval applications. User feedback in these applications usually consists of hints about the *relevance* of the information retrieved by the system. The model presented can be useful for general information retrieval systems but here we focus on image retrieval. Image retrieval has been investigated since the 1980s and, in the 1990s, content-based image retrieval (CBIR) became an active area of research. In CBIR, the objective is to find relevant images where the query is often described by an example image of the type of images that the user is looking for. In practice, CBIR is still far away from being a solved problem. One way to increase retrieval performance is to capitalize on user feedback, i.e., a user starts his query with an example image and is then presented with a set of hopefully relevant images; from these images the user selects those images which are relevant and those which are not (possibly leaving some images unmarked) and then the retrieval system refines its results, hopefully leading to better results after each interaction step.

Related Work Relevance feedback has been studied in the field of image retrieval and information retrieval nearly as long as the field of information retrieval exists [11]. An overview of the early related work on relevance feedback in image retrieval is given in [20]. Most approaches use the marked images as individual queries and combine the retrieved results. More recent approaches follow a query-instance-based approach [5] or use support vector machines to learn a two-class classifier [13]. In this work, we follow a probabilistic approach to model the relevance of candidate *image sets*. This leads to a significant boost in performance and also opens new ways to integrate consistency checks into the retrieval procedure. Another related field of research is browsing of image and video databases. The approach most closely related to the approach presented here is Bayesian browsing [18]. The formulation presented here follows the concepts for interactive pattern recognition first proposed in [19], which are developed in more detail in Chap. 1 of this book. A previous version of this work was presented in [10].

11.2.1 Probabilistic Interaction Model

The proposed probabilistic model and a greedy algorithm to solve the resulting interactive search problem are presented here. Notation, modeling and search are particularized for the image retrieval problem but they can be easily adapted to other information retrieval tasks.

Let U be the universal set of images and let $C \subset U$ be a fixed, finite *collection* of images. We assume the user "has in mind" some *relevant set* of images $R \subset U$. This set is unknown and the system's objective is to discover n images of it, among the images in C. The interactive retrieval process starts with a given query image, $q \in U$ proposed by the user. Then the system provides an initial set $X \subset C$ of n

images that are "similar" to q. These images are judged by the user who provides a *feedback* by selecting which images are relevant (and, implicitly, which are not relevant). Such feedback information is used by the system to obtain a new set of images X and the process is repeated until the user is satisfied, which means that he considers all images X to be relevant.

Following the framework stated in Chap. 1, at any step of this interactive process, the *history* can be represented as a set $H' \in C^m$, where $m \geq n$ is the number of images previously supervised by the user.[1] This set contains all the images that the user has considered to be relevant in previous interaction steps and other images provided by the system. In the current step, the (deterministic) feedback, $f \equiv d$, provided by the user, consists in marking as relevant some of the (previously unmarked) images from H'.

To optimize the user experience, we propose to maximize the probability that the images in X are relevant according to H' and d; that is:

$$\hat{X} = \arg\max_{X \in C^n} \Pr(X \mid q, H', d) \tag{11.1}$$

where we have ignored C since it is fixed for all the queries. Note that this equation is formally the same as the general equation (1.14) for interaction with explicit history representation and deterministic feedback.

In the task here considered, the initial query image can be considered just as one more image in the subset of relevant supervised images in H'. This way we can write

$$\hat{X} = \arg\max_{X \in C^n} \Pr(X \mid H', d). \tag{11.2}$$

That is, the interactive protocol in this task can be considered as an instance of Eq. (1.37), called "Interaction without input data" in Sect. 1.4.1.

Now, let $X' = (H', d)$ denote a "consolidated history", consisting of m images from which the subset $Q^+ \subset R$ (with $q \in Q^+$) is marked as relevant and the remaining ones, $Q^- \subset C - R$, are considered as non-relevant; that is, $X' = (Q^+ \cup Q^-) \in C^m$. According to Eq. (11.2), the images in the system hypothesis, $\hat{X}$, should be "similar" to the images in Q^+ (and may also be similar among each other) and "different" from images in Q^-. Using this notation, applying the Bayes' rule and dropping terms which do not depend on the optimization variable, X, Eq. (11.2) becomes

$$\hat{X} = \arg\max_{X \in C^n} \Pr(X' \mid X) \cdot \Pr(X). \tag{11.3}$$

For the first term of Eq. (11.3) we can use a model directly based on image distances:

$$\Pr(X' \mid X) \propto \prod_{x \in X} P(X' \mid x) \tag{11.4}$$

---

[1] Since H' can be the result of *several* interaction steps, the total number of supervised images, m, can be greater than the number of images retrieved in each interaction step, n.

where each term in the product[2] is a *smooth* version of the classical class-conditional probability estimate based on nearest neighbors [2] using a suitable image distance $d(\cdot,\cdot)$:

$$P(X' \mid x) = \frac{\sum_{q \in Q^+} d(q,x)^{-1}}{\sum_{q \in X'} d(q,x)^{-1}}. \tag{11.5}$$

Note that we use a product to combine probabilities in Eq. (11.4). This enables using the greedy search strategy proposed in Sect. 11.2.2 to find approximate solutions to Eq. (11.3).

For the second term of Eq. (11.3), we assume that the prior probability of a set X should be high if it is "*consistent*"; that is, if all its images are similar among them. Applying the chain rule, we obtain

$$\begin{aligned}\Pr(X) &= \Pr(x_1, x_2, \ldots, x_n)\\ &= \Pr(x_1)\Pr(x_2 \mid x_1), \ldots, \Pr(x_n \mid x_1 \cdots x_{n-1}).\end{aligned} \tag{11.6}$$

As before, each term of this product can be adequately modeled in terms of image distances:

$$\Pr(x_i \mid x_1 \cdots x_{i-1}) \propto \frac{P(x_1 \cdots x_i)}{P(x_1 \cdots x_{i-1})} \tag{11.7}$$

where

$$P(x_1 \cdots x_i) = \frac{1}{i(i-1)} \sum_{j=1}^{i} \sum_{k \neq j, k=1}^{i} d(x_j, x_k)^{-1}. \tag{11.8}$$

Intuitively, Eqs. (11.5) and (11.7), respectively, measure *relevancy* and *consistency* of images in X. Therefore, in practice, it is convenient to balance the importance of both factors by means of a parameter α, where $\alpha = 1$ denotes that no consistency information is used and $\alpha = 0$ denotes that only consistency information is considered. Taking this into account, Eq. (11.3) can be expanded as

$$\hat{X} \approx \operatorname*{arg\,max}_{X \in C^n} P(X' \mid x_1) P(x_1) \prod_{i=2}^{n} P(X' \mid x_i)^{\alpha} \left(\frac{P(x_1 \cdots x_i)}{P(x_1 \cdots x_{i-1})} \right)^{1-\alpha}. \tag{11.9}$$

In the following sections we describe an efficient procedure to find an approximately optimal set of images $\hat{X}$.

[2] We recall that only the notation Pr() stands for true probabilities; here we abuse the notation by letting $P()$ denote arbitrary functions used as models.

$\hat{X} = \textbf{GARF}(C, Q^+, Q^-)$ {
  for each $x \in C_{X'}$ $\{V = P(X' \mid x)\}$
  $\mathcal{B} = select(V, t);\ max = -\infty$
  for each $x \in \mathcal{B}$ {
    $x_{r+1} = x;\ S = \{x_{r+1}\}$
    for $i = r+2, \ldots, n$ {
      $x_i = \arg\max_{x \in \mathcal{B}-S} P(X' \mid x)^\alpha (\frac{P(x_{r+1},\ldots,x_{i-1},x)}{P(x_{r+1},\ldots,x_{i-1})})^{1-\alpha}$
      $S = S \cup \{x_i\}$
    }
    $sc = P(X' \mid x_{r+1}) \prod_{i=r+2}^{n} P(X' \mid x_i)^\alpha\ (\frac{P(x_{r+1}\ldots x_i)}{P(x_{r+1}\ldots x_{i-1})})^{1-\alpha}$
    if $(sc > max)$ {
      $max = sc;\ SBest = S$
    }
  }
  $\hat{X} = Q^+ \cup SBest$
  return $\hat{X}$
}

Fig. 11.1 GARF: Greedy approximative algorithm to determine the most relevant and consistent images. The value of t has to be tuned empirically

11.2.2 Greedy Approximation Relevance Feedback Algorithm

Let $C_{X'} = C - X'$ be the set of the images in the collection that have not been retrieved. In the following notation, m, r and $\bar{r}$ are the sizes of X', Q^+ and Q^-, respectively. We propose an algorithm to approximate the maximization presented in Eq. (11.9). This algorithm works as follows. First of all the r images in Q^+ are selected as the first r images in $\hat{X}$. The remaining $n-r$ images are to be selected from the set $C_{X'}$ since the images in Q^+ and Q^- have just been supervised by the user. This entails a slight modification of the maximization in Eq. (11.9):

$$\hat{X} \approx Q^+ \cup \arg\max_{X \in C_{X'}^{n-r}} P(X' \mid x_{r+1}) P(x_{r+1}) \prod_{i=r+2}^{n} P(X' \mid x_i)^\alpha \left(\frac{P(x_1 \cdots x_i)}{P(x_1 \cdots x_{i-1})}\right)^{1-\alpha}. \tag{11.10}$$

We assume that $\Pr(x)$ follows an uniform distribution, so the term $P(x_{r+1})$ is constant in the maximization process and can be dropped. To solve the maximization, the *t-best* images, $t \geq (n-r)$, with the highest values of $P(X' \mid x_i)$ are determined. We refer to this set as $\mathcal{B}$. Each image that belongs to $\mathcal{B}$ is tentatively hypothesized to be the first image, x_{r+1}. Subsequently, the following images can be determined by greedy maximization of the index Eq. (11.10), using the GARF algorithm shown in Fig. 11.1.

$\hat{X} = \textbf{GARFs}(C, Q^+, Q^-)\,\{$
  for each $x \in C_{X'}$ $\{V = P(X' \mid x)\}$
  $\mathcal{B} = select(V, n - r)$
  $\hat{X} = Q^+ \cup \mathcal{B}$
  return $\hat{X}$
$\}$

Fig. 11.2 GARFs: Simplified GARF algorithm not considering image consistency

11.2.3 A Simplified Version of GARF

If $\alpha = 1$, image consistency is not taken into account and thus the expression to maximize becomes

$$\hat{X} = Q^+ \cup \operatorname*{arg\,max}_{X \in C_{X'}^{n-r}} \prod_{i=r+1}^{n} P(X' \mid x_i), \tag{11.11}$$

which further simplifies the procedure. To maximize this expression, only those images with maximum values for $P(X' \mid x_i)$ have to be chosen, yielding the GARFs algorithm shown in Fig. 11.2.

Due to this simplification, GARFs is no longer an approximation, but an exact solution to Eq. (11.11) instead. We prefer to refer to this algorithm as GARFs because it can be considered as a simplified version of GARF. The computational complexity of GARFs is the same as the relevance feedback baseline methods presented in Sect. 11.2.6.

11.2.4 Experiments

The proposed algorithm is evaluated using a well known data set, Corel/Wang. For the sake of experimental clarity and reproducibility, in all the experiments, relevance feedback was simulated, i.e. no real users were involved. Nevertheless the methods proposed here can directly be used with any user interface that allows users to mark images as relevant and/or non-relevant in interactive retrieval processes such as that described in Chap. 12, or those presented in [8, 12].

WANG Database It consists of a subset of 1 000 images of the Corel stock photo database which have been manually selected and which form 10 classes of 100 images each. Example images are shown in Fig. 11.3a. The WANG database can be considered similar to common stock photo retrieval tasks with several images from each category and a potential user having an image from a particular category and looking for similar images which have cheaper royalties or which have not been used by other media. The 10 classes are used for user relevance simulation: given

Fig. 11.3 Example images from the WANG database

a query image, it is assumed that the user is searching for images from the same class. Therefore, to specify the ground truth, the remaining 99 images from the same class are considered relevant and the images from all other classes are considered irrelevant.

11.2.5 Image Feature Extraction

For our experiments, we choose to represent our images using color histograms and Tamura texture histograms. Although there are image descriptors that perform far better for special applications, it was recently shown that these features are a very reasonable baseline for general image databases [1]. Furthermore, the probabilistic model for relevance feedback investigated here can be applied on top of any image descriptor that allows for distance calculation between images. In the following, we describe how these features are compared and obtained.

To compare the histograms, we use the L_1 distance, which was shown to be identical to histogram intersection if the histograms share the same bins,

$$d(h, h') = \sum_{i=1}^{I} |h_i - h'_i|, \tag{11.12}$$

where h and h' are two histograms to be compared and h_i and h'_i are the ith bins.

Color Histograms Color histograms are among the most basic approaches and widely used in image retrieval [4, 14, 16]. To show performance improvements in image retrieval, systems using only color histograms are often used as a baseline. The color space is partitioned and for each partition the pixels with a color within its range are counted, resulting in a representation of the relative frequencies of the occurring colors. We use the RGB color space for the histograms, and split each dimension into eight bins leading to an $8^3 = 512$ dimensional histogram. We observed only minor differences with other color spaces, which was also observed in [15].

Tamura Features In [17] the authors propose six texture features corresponding to human visual perception: *coarseness*, *contrast*, *directionality*, *line-likeness*, *regularity*, and *roughness*. From experiments testing the significance of these features with respect to human perception, it was concluded that the first three features are very important. Thus, in our experiments we use coarseness, contrast, and directionality, calculate each of these values in a neighborhood for each pixel, quantize each of these values into eight discrete values and create a 512-dimensional joint histogram for each image. In the QBIC system [4] histograms of these features were used as well.

11.2.6 Baseline Methods

The proposed approach is compared with some baseline methods:

Simple Method The simple method is accomplished by performing the next search of $n-r$ images among the set of images in $C_{X'}$, keeping the relevant images, and performing the next search exactly equal as the initial one but over this reduced collection $C_{X'}$.

Relevance Score Relevance score (R) was proposed by [5], and has been inspired by the nearest neighbor classification method. Instead of only finding the best match for each query image among the database images, for each database image only the best matching query image is considered among the positive and negative query images. The ratio between the nearest relevant and the nearest non-relevant image is considered for ranking the images. In [5], R is computed as

$$R\big(x, Q^+, Q_-\big) = \left(1 + \frac{\min_{q_+ \in Q^+} d(x, q_+)}{\min_{q_- \in Q^-} d(x, q_-)}\right)^{-1} \tag{11.13}$$

and then images are ranked such that the images with smallest relevance score are presented first.

Rocchio Relevance Feedback Rocchio's method for relevance feedback [11] can be considered a de facto standard in textual information retrieval. In CBIR, it has been investigated in the context of the GIFT system [9]. In Rocchio relevance feedback, the individual query documents are combined into a single query according to

$$\hat{q} = q + w_+ \cdot \sum_{q_+ \in Q^+} q_+ - w_- \cdot \sum_{q_- \in Q^-} q_-, \tag{11.14}$$

where $\hat{q}$ is the new query, q is the query from the last feedback iteration and w_+ and w_- are weighting factors to determine the influence of relevance feedback; commonly the parameters are chosen $w_+ = |Q^+|^{-1}$, $w_- = |Q^-|^{-1}$.

Table 11.1 Precision (in %) for successive interaction steps, using different methods on the WANG database

Method	I_1	I_2	I_3	I_4	I_5
Simple	73.6	83.2	88.0	91.0	92.9
Rocchio	73.6	92.7	97.3	99.2	99.8
RS	73.6	92.2	97.8	99.5	99.9
GARFs	73.6	94.5	98.9	99.9	99.9

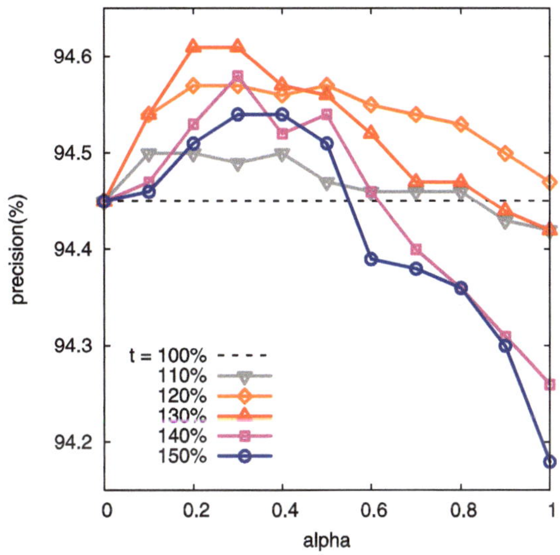

Fig. 11.4 Results using GARF on the WANG database for different values of α and t

Once $\hat{q}$ is determined it is used to query the database and find the most similar images.

In all the experiments, we set the number of images to be retrieved to $n = 20$ and the query image is always contained in set of retrieved images. Up to four feedback iteration steps were performed. The precision was measured for each iteration step obtaining five values for each method $I_1, \ldots, I_5$. The precision is the ratio of the relevant images among the n retrieved ones and is given in percent.

For the evaluation of the different relevance feedback methods on this database a Leaving-One-Out approach has been followed. Every image is used as query and the rest of the images are used as reference set C.

The results for the database are shown in Table 11.1. The simplified version of GARF obtains the best results. It is worth to mention that the user is interested to obtain high precision values for the first feedback iterations, and, in this case, GARFs is the best method.

Figure 11.4 shows the results of the GARF algorithm for the first feedback iteration (I_2) with varying α-parameter and the size of the set $\mathcal{B}$. The α parameter is varied from 0 (no consistency information considered, simplified GARF) to 1 (only consistency information considered). The size of the set $\mathcal{B}$, the t-parameter, is given relatively to the number of relevant images still needed, $n-r$. The results obtained for $t=100\%$ does not vary with respect to α because this value means that $\mathcal{B}$ has only $n-r$ images. The highest precision for the first feedback iteration is 94.62 and is obtained using GARF with $\alpha=0.3$ and $t=130\%$.

11.2.7 Discussion

In this subsection a novel probabilistic model for relevance feedback in image retrieval has been described. In contrast with other approaches, we incorporate consistency among the retrieved images in a probabilistic sound way. A simpler model which does not take into account such consistency is also proposed.

The results obtained by this simplified version are already clearly better than the results obtained by the state-of-the-art techniques tested. On the other hand the incorporation of the consistency model can increase the performance of the retrieval system even further. The improvements contributed by this consistency model have shown to be effective mainly when the classes of the images are *consistent* enough under an *appearance* point of view.

While these improvements are really marginal, they show that the novel approach to information retrieval proposed here provides a suitable framework to develop new techniques that better take advantage of all the information sources available.

11.3 Multimodal Relevance Feedback

Many research systems for web image retrieval use interactive relevance feedback techniques to integrate *keywords* and *visual features*. They require the users to specify the textual/visual combination and thus add heavy burden to the users. Therefore, an approach that can improve the retrieval accuracy of a search engine with less user involvement is valuable [6].

One of the most interesting issues in multimedia information retrieval is to use different modalities (e.g. text, image) in a cooperative way. The fusion between several methods usually leads to better results in precision. Some queries may be solved by just using visual information. If for example we think about "tigers", the visual part is really important and therefore the visual retrieval technique will perform much better. In other cases, visual information may not help at all but possibly available textual annotations may help solving the problem. In many other cases an adequate *fusion* between these two extremes can lead to a higher precision. Moreover, visual and textual information are usually "orthogonal". When the tagging is unsupervised, as in the present work, visual features make it easy to find similar looking images. On the other hand, with textual information we are able to find "*semantically*" similar images, but in order to find this similarity it is important to have clean and complete annotations for all the images.

Fig. 11.5 A Relevance Based Image Retrieval prototype using "fusion by refining", with several images selected as relevant

A recent tendency to fuse visual and textual features has been observed in different evaluation tracks such as TRECVID and ImageCLEF, with the belief that these sources of information more than competing are complementary, and that the actual problem may be reduced to finding a way of adequately fusing them. This kind of fusion is a sort of multimodal information retrieval, and it can be performed either as *early* or *late fusion*. Research on these two directions has already been developed, but current performance of these methods remains poor, showing the need of further research to find better fusion alternatives and to select better individual relevant models.

11.3.1 Fusion by Refining

The first approach is really obvious (see Fig. 11.5). The user introduces a text query in the web browser. Images have small captions or annotations, therefore the system searches for those images that textually correspond with the query. Then the system provides the user with visual examples and the user selects those images he considers relevant. This can be considered a simple case of multimodal interaction, since text information is used in the first iteration and then for the next iterations only visual information is needed. This is called "fusion by refining", since textual information is only used to provide a rough set of pictures, which are later refined using only visual techniques.

11.3.2 Early Fusion

It is a supervised learning process where images are trained manually and classified into different classes (Fig. 11.6). This type of fusion is commonly used in automatic annotation problems. It consists in linking image features with semantic concepts. After each image is selected into a class, a binary classifier is trained to detect the

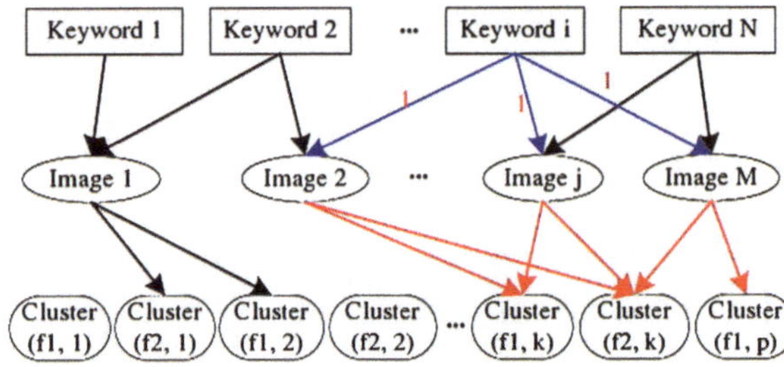

Fig. 11.6 Typical architecture in Annotation Based Image Retrieval systems with early fusion, where the keywords are combined with low level visual features

class. When a new image comes, the visual similarity to each class is computed. More or less, early fusion tries to discover the statistical dependencies between visual features and semantic concepts using unsupervised learning methods. Early fusion is difficult due to several reasons.

(1) The annotations of the images often contain keywords that are not strongly associated with particular visual features. They correspond to abstract concepts. Examples of such keywords are "friendship", "north" or "tournament".
(2) Even if there are some relationships between keywords and visual features, these relationships may be difficult to extract because there is a huge amount of possible visual features. In fact, visual features are continuous. Even if we use discretization techniques, the number is still too high to allow for associating features to some keywords. For example, for a set of images associated with the keyword "water", one would expect to extract strong relationships between the keyword and the texture or color. However, water in many images may only take a small portion or region of the image. There may be many other objects in the image making it really difficult to isolate the typical features of "water".

11.3.3 Late Fusion

Late fusion is the approach chosen here. This is motivated by the hypothesis that two images with a very strong visual similarity should share some common semantics [7]. Late fusion of independent retrieval methods is the simpler approach and it is widely used for combining visual and textual information for the search process. Usually each retrieval method is based on a single modality, or even, when several methods are considered per modality, all of them use the same information for indexing/querying (see Fig. 11.7). The latter reduces the diversity and complementariness of documents considered for the fusion and, as a consequence, the performance of the fusion approach tends to be poor [3]. In multimodal image retrieval, the sources of information are visual features extracted from the image and textual features in the form of associated captions. These sources of information have been mostly used individually and separately. In many tasks, with relatively clean figure captions, textual features have proved to be more effective than their visual counterparts. However, a problem generally found in both cases is the lack of generalization, which makes systems fail with varied sets of queries. A more specific

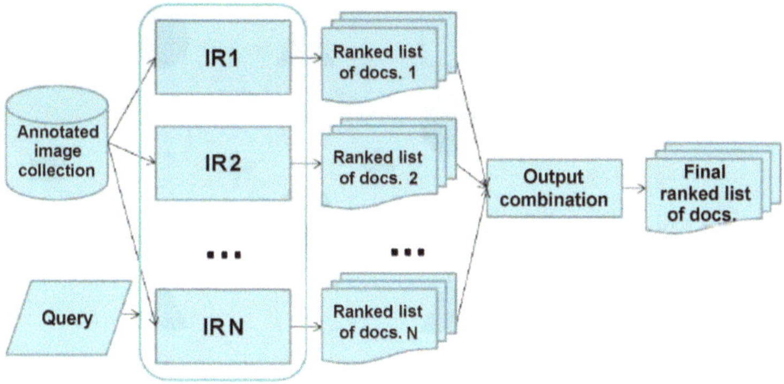

Fig. 11.7 Graphical General Diagram showing Late Fusion for heterogeneous methods. The output is combined for obtaining a single list of ranked documents

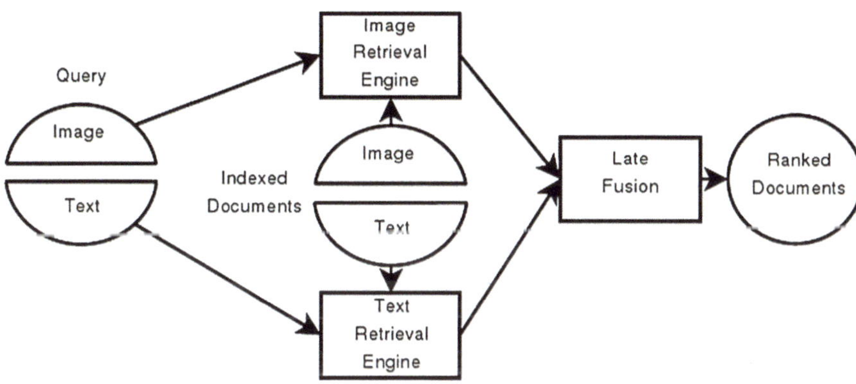

Fig. 11.8 Visual and textual late fussion

diagram showing this behavior for only visual and textual retrieval engines can be seen in Fig. 11.8.

For each query q, the N different retrieval methods work separately. This results in a set of N ranked list of documents or images. The information of the N ranked lists is used to obtain a single list of ranked documents, which is returned to the user in response the query q. The final list is obtained by assigning a score to each document appearing in at least one of the N lists. A high score indicates that the document is more likely to be relevant to query q. Documents are sorted in decreasing order of their score and the top k documents are considered for the final list of ranked documents.

In this work we consider a simple (yet very effective) score based on a weighted linear combination of the documents rank through the different lists. The proposed score takes into account redundancy of documents and the individual performance of each retrieval method. Diversity and complementariness are brought to play by the heterogeneousness of the considered independent retrieval methods (IRMs),

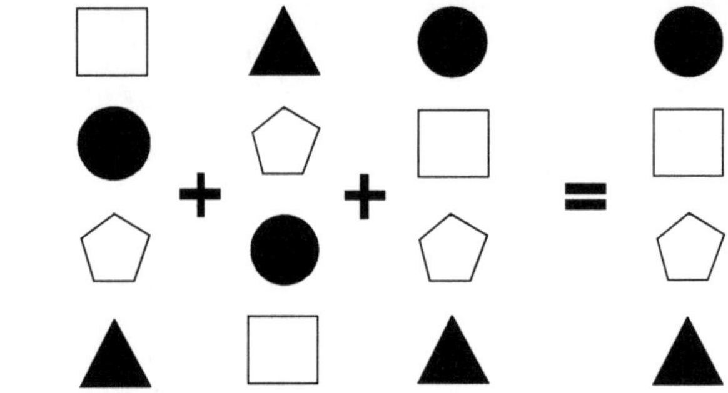

Fig. 11.9 Example of late fusion ranking algorithm

while redundancy is considered through the use of several IRMs per modality. Given a document (image plus text) x and N lists L_i, $1 \leq i \leq N$, a score $S(x)$ is computed as follows:

$$S(x) = \left|\{i : x \in L_i\}\right| \cdot \sum_{i=1}^{N} \frac{\alpha_i}{R(x, L_i)} \tag{11.15}$$

where $R(x, H)$ is the position of document x in the ranked list H and α_i, with $\sum_{k=1}^{N} \alpha_k = 1$, is the importance weighting for the ith IRM, which can be determined using prior knowledge. Documents appearing in several lists at the top positions will receive a higher score, while documents appearing in few lists or appearing at the bottom positions most of the times will be scored low.

If only two IRMs (visual an textual) are considered, a simpler linear combination can be used:

$$R(x) = \alpha R_v(x) + (1 - \alpha) R_t(x) \tag{11.16}$$

where $R(x)$ is the combined rank of x, α is the (now single) importance weight and $R_v(x) = R(x, L_v)$, $R_t(x) = R(x, L_t)$ are the visual and textual rankings, respectively.

Figure 11.9 illustrate these ideas. This is a simple and intuitive way of merging the output of IRMs which has proved to be quite useful in practice.

11.3.4 Proposed Approach: Dynamic Linear Fusion

At a given point, the visual and text retrieval engines have to cooperate in order to obtain a higher precision. But there is a main problem when using late fusion, the α value in the previous equation has to be *fixed* for each considered task. However, for a given task, no unique value of α may exist that is adequate for all the types of queries expected in this task. Mostly visual queries may need high values, while other queries, mostly textual, may need very low values. To deal with this dynamically variable weighting, we propose solving this maximization problem:

$$\begin{aligned}\hat{\alpha} &= \arg\max_{\alpha} \sum_{x \in Q^+} \sum_{y \in Q^-} R(y) - R(x) \\ &= \arg\max_{\alpha} \sum_{x \in Q^+} \sum_{y \in Q^-} \alpha\big(R_v(y) - R_v(x)\big) + (1-\alpha)\big(R_t(y) - R_t(x)\big)\end{aligned} \tag{11.17}$$

where $R()$, $R_v()$ and $R_t()$ are as in Eq. (11.16), and Q^+ and Q^- are the sets of relevant and non-relevant images, respectively, at the present step of the interaction process.

At each interaction step, the system proposes a set of images which the user marks as relevant or non-relevant. Without further disturbing the user, the weighting is updated on the base of the user's intention, determined by the images marked so far in the present query.

Intuitively speaking, the above equation searches for a best area under the ROC curve which would make the difference between the non-relevant images and the relevant images very high by globally ranking them as far as possible.

11.3.5 Experiments

To simulate the users' relevance feedback a set of 21 (text) queries was considered. For each of these queries, 200 images were crawled from the web using a public search engine and each image was manually taged as really relevant or not relevant

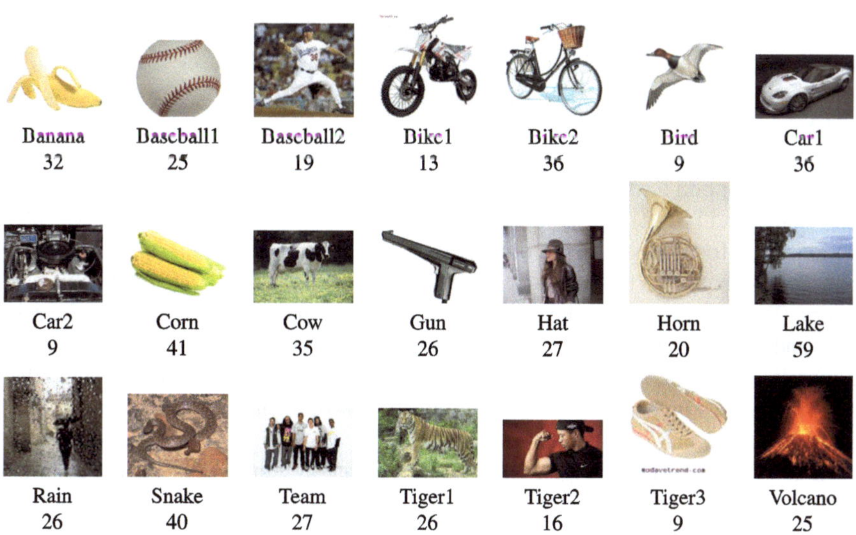

Fig. 11.10 Examples of relevant images (and total number of relevants) for each of the 21 inspected queries

Table 11.2 Queries and their descriptions as they appear in the test corpus

Query	Description
Banana	Real yellow bananas. Cartoon or drawn bananas are considered not relevant
Baseball1	Baseball balls
Baseball2	Baseball players in the baseball pitch
Bike1	Catalog motorbikes but not only with white background
Bike2	Catalog bicycles. People can appear but the bike appears completely
Bird	Birds flying
Car1	Real cars with no people or other cars around. Car appears completely
Car2	Car engines
Corn	Corn pictures with no human hands
Cow	Real cow on mountain, land or grass
Gun	Catalog guns with white background
Hat	People wearing hat and looking at the camera. Hats by themselves are not relevant
Horn	Trumpets
Lake	Panoramic landscape pictures with or without houses around the lakes
Rain	Pictures where one can appreciate rain falling
Snake	Not only snake heads but also some body must appear in the picture
Team	Group of people
Tiger1	Full body real tigers
Tiger2	Tiger Woods by himself. Either playing golf or not, but alone
Tiger3	Tiger sneakers or shoes
Volcano	With lava or fire around

for the corresponding query. A brief description of each query is given in Table 11.2 and image examples are shown in Fig. 11.10.

Given an image collection and the description of each image, we know which image is relevant or irrelevant to each query. This way the user feedback can be simulated automatically. In the experiments we simulate a user who wants N images to be seen at a time. In each iteration he would see N images and judge which are relevant or not according to the criteria specified for each query. Results reported below correspond to $N = 10$.

Figure 11.11 (left) shows evolution of the accuracy with the successive interaction steps for the best α in comparison with both pure text and visual retrieval, which was expected to perform worse than the average best percentage for each query. (We do not have all the relevant images of a concept; we only know the relevant and non-relevant images for an interaction step.) After one interaction step, the dynamic linear fusion approach proposed here performs better on the average than both modalities involved. Obviously it falls below best linear combination for each concept, which is just un upper bound.

It can be observed in Fig. 11.11 (right) that the system quickly gains accuracy with the progression of the user interaction steps. That is, the more information the system has about what the user considered relevant (and non-relevant) in previous steps, the better it can predict the best α for the current step. In the first step, there is a clearly ascendant slope toward the visual strategy, achieving high precision when

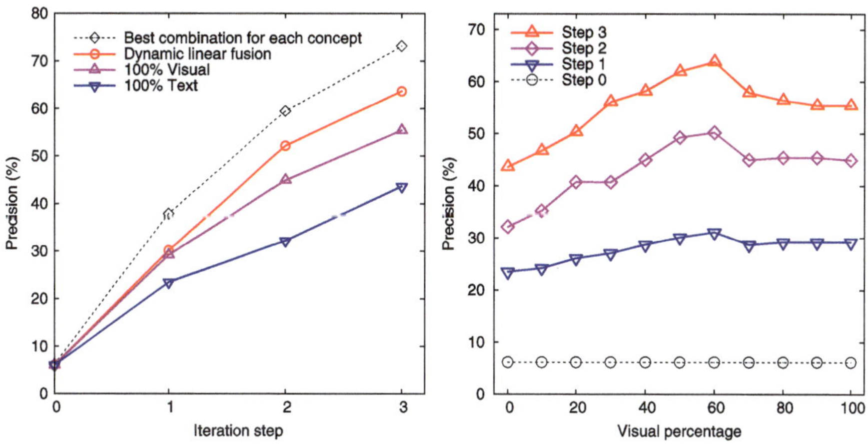

Fig. 11.11 RISE evaluation test results, for $N = 10$ images to be seen at a time. *Left*: Comparison of image retrieval techniques. *Right*: Precision as a function of α, for several feedback iteration steps

full visual search is used. However, in the following iterations the best precision is not obtained on the extremes, which shows the importance of having a dynamic user/query-adaptative α to achieve always the best precision.

An important fact about this α parameter is that it has no memory. The user can change her mind while looking at a query or concept. The user can start looking at "apples", choosing real, eatable apples. Then maybe she starts selecting as relevant the company "Apple". So, the user can change the value of α and the system will be tuned for her needs. This allows for much more flexibility in the relevance of results for the user.

11.3.6 Discussion

In this subsection we have considered several approaches for Relevance-based Image Retrieval. The first one, late fusion, mixes the visual ranking and the text ranking depending on a α value. This is a fixed value we need to know before using the method. Some experiments were done to prove that depending on the type of the query a different α is needed. If we took the best possible α for each query, we would have a much more precise system. This led us to propose the *dynamic linear fusion*. It learns from the user intentions the type of query the user is searching for and automatically computes an optimal α at each interaction step. The experimental results show that this dynamic value performs much better than each of the retrieval engines separately.

References

1. Deselaers, T., Keysers, D., & Ney, H. (2008). Features for image retrieval: an experimental comparison. *Information Retrieval*, *11*(2), 77–107.

2. Duda, R., & Hart, P. (1973). *Pattern recognition and scene analysis*. New York: Wiley.
3. Escalante, H. J., Hérnadez, C. A., Sucar, L. E., & Montes, M. (2008). Late fusion of heterogeneous methods for multimedia image retrieval. In *MIR'08: Proceeding of the 1st ACM international conference on multimedia information retrieval* (pp. 172–179), New York, NY, USA. New York: ACM.
4. Faloutsos, C., Barber, R., Flickner, M., Hafner, J., Niblack, W., Petkovic, D., & Equitz, W. (1994). Efficient and effective querying by image content. *Journal of Intelligent Information Systems*, *3*(3/4), 231–262.
5. Giacinto, G., & Rolli, F. (2004). Instance-based relevance feedback for image retrieval. In *Neural information processing systems (NIPS)*, Vancouver, Canada.
6. Jin, H., Tao, W., & Sun, A. (2008). Vast: Automatically combining keywords and visual features for web image retrieval. *International Conference on Advanced Communication Technology*, *3*, 2188–2193.
7. Lacoste, C., Chevallet, J. q. P., Lim, J. q. H., Le, D. T. H., Xiong, W., Racoceanu, D., Teodorescu, R., & Vuillemenot, N. (2006). Inter-media concept-based medical image indexing and retrieval with umls at ipal. In *CLEF* (pp. 694–701).
8. Moënne-Loccoz, N., Bruno, E., & Marchand-Maillet, S. (2005). Interactive retrieval of video sequences from local feature dynamics. In *Proceedings of the 3rd international workshop on adaptive multimedia retrieval, AMR'05*, Glasgow, UK.
9. Müller, H., Müller, W., Marchand-Maillet, S., & Squire, D. M. (2000). Strategies for positive and negative relevance feedback in image retrieval. In A. Sanfeliu, J. J. Villanueva, M. Vanrell, R. Alquezar, J. q. O. Eklundh & Y. Aloimonos (Eds.), *Computer vision and image analysis: Vol. 1. Proceedings of the international conference on pattern recognition (ICPR'2000)* (pp. 1043–1046), Barcelona, Spain.
10. Paredes, R., Deselaers, T., & Vidal, E. (2008). A probabilistic model for user relevance feedback on image retrieval. In *Proceedings of the 5th international workshop on machine learning for multimodal interaction, MLMI'08* (pp. 260–271). Berlin: Springer.
11. Rocchio, J. J. (1971). Relevance feedback in information retrieval. In G. Salton (Ed.), *The SMART retrieval system: experiments in automatic document processing* (pp. 313–323). New York: Prentice-Hall.
12. Rooij, O. d., Snoek, C. G. M., & Worring, M. (2007). Query on demand video browsing. In *ACM int. conf. on multimedia* (pp. 811–814), Augsburg, Germany.
13. Setia, L., Ick, J., & Burkhardt, H. (2005). Svm-based relevance feedback in image retrieval using invariant feature histograms. In *IAPR workshop on machine vision applications (MVA)*, Tsukuba Science City, Japan.
14. Smeulders, A. W. M., Worring, M., Santini, S., Gupta, A., & Jain, R. (2000). Content-based image retrieval at the end of the early years. *IEEE Transactions on Pattern Analysis and Machine Intelligence*, *22*(12), 1349–1380.
15. Smith, J. R., & Chang, S. q. F. (1996). Tools and techniques for color image retrieval. In *SPIE storage and retrieval for image and video databases* (Vol. 2670, pp. 426–437).
16. Swain, M. J., & Ballard, D. H. (1991). Color indexing. *International Journal of Computer Vision*, *7*(1), 11–32.
17. Tamura, H., Mori, S., & Yamawaki, T. (1978). Textural features corresponding to visual perception. *IEEE Transactions on Systems, Man, and Cybernetics*, *8*(6), 460–472.
18. Vasconcelos, N., & Lippman, A. (1998). Bayesian modeling of video editing and structure: Semantic features for video summarization and browsing. In *ICIP* (pp. 153–157), Chicago, IL, USA.
19. Vidal, E., Rodríguez, L., Casacuberta, F., & García-Varea, I. (2007). Interactive pattern recognition. In *LNCS: Vol. 4892. Proceedings of the 4th joint workshop on multimodal interaction and related machine learning algorithms* (pp. 60–71), Brno, Czech Republic.
20. Zhou, X. S., & Huang, T. S. (2003). Relevance feedback in image retrieval: A comprehensive review. *Multimedia Systems*, *8*, 536–544.

Chapter 12
Prototypes and Demonstrators

With Contribution Of: Luis A. Leiva, Vicent Alabau, Verónica Romero, Franco M. Segarra, Ricardo Sánchez-Sáez, Daniel Ortiz-Martínez, Luis Rodríguez, and Nicolás Serrano.

Contents

This chapter presents several full working prototypes and demonstrators of multimodal interactive pattern recognition applications. These systems serve as validating examples of the approaches that have been proposed and described throughout this book. Among other interesting things, they are designed to enable a true human–computer interaction on selected tasks.

To begin, we shall expound the different protocols that were tested, namely Passive Left-to-Right, Passive Desultory, and Active. The overview of each demonstrator is sufficiently detailed to give the reader an overview of the underlying technologies. The prototypes covered in this chapter are related to transcription of text images (IHT, GIDOC), machine translation (IMT), speech transcription (IST), text generation (ITG), and image retrieval (RISE). Additionally, most of these prototypes shall present evaluation measures about the amount of user effort reduction at the end of the process. Finally, some of such demonstrators come with web-based versions, whose addresses are included to allow the reader to test and practice with the different implemented applications.

A.H. Toselli et al., *Multimodal Interactive Pattern Recognition and Applications*,
DOI 10.1007/978-0-85729-479-1_12, © Springer-Verlag London Limited 2011

12.1 Introduction

Throughout this book, the multimodal interactive–predictive paradigm to pattern recognition (MIPR) has been theoretically studied. The proposed paradigm has been empirically validated on controlled laboratory experiments with computer-simulated users. Although this set-up provides a reasonable framework for research, it is relatively optimistic regarding user interaction when dealing with real applications.

In this chapter we present some implementations of prototypes for several MIPR tasks. They all entail a multimodal, interactive strategy, and they all fully integrate the user's knowledge into the Pattern Recognition (PR) process. These demo systems seek two goals: (1) allow potential users to have a quick view into the MIPR technologies, and (2) facilitate data acquisition to study real user interaction for evaluation purposes in a more realistic scenario. As we will expound in the next sections, the use of these prototypes may entail a drastic reduction of user effort without sacrificing usability—quite the opposite, since, as stated before, the Human–Computer Interaction (HCI) paradigm is considered the main actor in front of a PR scenario.

The organization of each section in this chapter is as follows. After a brief introduction, a description of the prototype's demonstration is presented. In each description, a user interaction protocol is both established and itemized. Then a section about the technologies involved in the creation of the prototype is introduced. Finally, a discussion about both the evaluation of the prototype (if available) and the main achieved results are delineated. In all user evaluations, there is a noticeable improvement over the traditional PR approaches. Thus, as commented in this chapter's preface, these demos serve as validating examples of the MIPR framework proposed and described throughout this book. User's feedback directly allows us to improve system accuracy, while multimodality increases system ergonomy and user acceptability. Multimodal interaction is approached in such a way that both the main and the feedback data streams help each other to optimize overall performance and usability. The prototypes presented below can be classified on the basis of the interaction protocols described in Sect. 1.4. Now we briefly introduce an outline of each prototype based on the above-mentioned schema.

12.1.1 Passive, Left-to-Right Protocol

The prototypes classified under this interaction protocol fulfill two requirements. On the one hand, this being a passive protocol, they are directed toward a full supervision, where a 'perfect' (high-quality) result is needed. On the other hand, in this interaction protocol a left-to-right order in the output constituents is assumed, which makes such protocol appropriate for human language processing tasks (notice that a right-to-left protocol is also perfectly applicable for those languages that require so, e.g., arabic or persian).

The passive, left-to-right protocol is defined by the next procedure: First, the system proposes a fully automatic output. Then, the user validates the longest prefix of the output which is error-free by entering some amendment keystrokes to correct the first error in the suffix. If the prototype supports multimodality, the interaction can be performed by different kinds of feedback channel, such as touchscreen pen strokes and/or other possible interaction modalities such as speech input. The system then suggests a suitable, new extended consolidated prefix based on the previous validated prefix, the multimodality decoding, and the keystroke amendments. These steps are repeated until the user is satisfied with the system's output.

The series of prototypes for natural language processing tasks that have been implemented following this protocol are introduced now.

Multimodal Interactive Handwritten Transcription (MM-IHT) Given a text image which corresponds to a line of a digitized handwritten document, the user transcribes the text in the image with the help of the system. Multimodality can be achieved by entering some pen strokes to amend the first error in the suffix.

Interactive Speech Transcription (IST) The user transcribes speech utterances from parliamentary proceedings, public speeches, video lectures, etc. Corrections are made by using the mouse and the keyboard.

Interactive Machine Translation (IMT) A document in a source language is loaded into the system. The application splits the document into sentences, which are then translated into a target language by using the keyboard, the mouse, and/or pen strokes.

Interactive Text Generation (ITG) The system works by predicting what the user is going to type based on the topic of the document, the context, and previously typed documents from the same user. Several input modalities can be used in order to adapt the system to different scenarios and/or user preferences.

Multimodal Interactive Parsing (MM-IP) The user generates interactively a syntactic analysis for an input sentence. One can perform modifications to the presented tree, using either the keyboard, the mouse, or other advanced input modalities.

As we shall see, most of these prototypes are built with the same communication toolkit [1], which offers an Application Programming Interface (API) that allows a TCP socket connection between client(s) and PR engine(s). Using sockets has several advantages over other communication channels. On the one hand it allows much faster message exchanging and lower latency responses. On the other hand, a multiuser environment can be easily implemented, so that several user across the globe can work concurrently on the same task. In addition, the web server and the PR engine do not need to be physically at the same place. Therefore, a dedicated PR engine can be run per task to deal with high CPU demanding corpora, or several web servers can be set up with the same task to serve an increasing amount of users.

Three basic functions summarize the above-mentioned API:

- `set_source`: selects the source phrase to be transcribed.
- `set_prefix`: sets the longest error-free prefix and amends the first error with keyboard strokes.

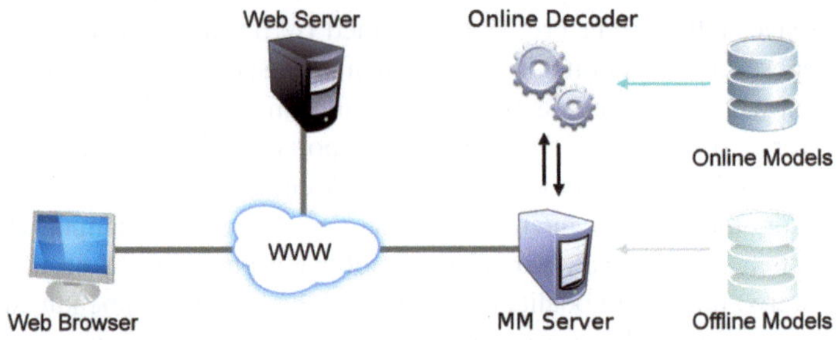

Fig. 12.1 Diagram of (common) system architecture for passive, left-to-right prototypes

- `set_prefix_online`: sets the longest error-free prefix and amends the first error with pen strokes.

Additionally, such prototypes share a common architecture, which is schematized in Fig. 12.1. The online form of such an architecture allows to carry out collaborative tasks with thousands of users across the globe, thus notably reducing the overall PR process. Since the users operate within a web browser window, the system also provides cross-platform compatibility and requires no disk space on the client machine.

12.1.2 Passive, Desultory Protocol

Like the previous protocol, here, the user is expected to supervise the whole system's output to achieve a high-quality result. However, in this case the user can perform the amendments in a desultory order. This is especially useful when the elements of the output do not have a particular order or hierarchy between them.

Many different scenarios can fall under this category. However, in this book we analyze the case of information retrieval where the user types a natural language description of an object she is looking for. The system outputs a set of objects matching this description so the user can select which ones fit her needs and which do not. The system, then, implicitly rejects the objects with negative feedback and tries to fill the set with new objects taking into account the user preferences from the previous iterations. The procedure stops when the user chooses not to reject any further object from the set. The goal is to obtain such a set in the minimum number of interactions.

Relevant Image Search Engine (RISE) The user looks for images that can be described by a sentence in natural language. She selects the images she likes and asks for more images, until she decides that the retrieved results are good enough.

12.1.3 Active Protocol

Contrarily to passive protocols, active protocols are not oriented toward a perfect solution but a trade-off between effort and output quality. In this scenario, the system typically selects actively a part of the solution for which it has a low confidence, and asks the user for the correct solution. The procedure stops when a certain compromise between user effort and recognition rate has been achieved. Note that in this protocol the order of the output constituent is not specially relevant, since the whole output does not need to be supervised by the user. Instead, it is the system that decides the parts to be corrected and the order in which they are presented to the user.

GIMP-based Interactive Document Transcription (GIDOC) This system provides a user-friendly, integrated support for interactive-predictive layout analysis, line detection and handwriting transcription. GIDOC is designed to work with large collections of *homogeneous* documents (i.e. similar structure and writing styles). The system pursues a similar goal to MM-IHT. However, in this case the documents are transcribed by partially supervising system hypotheses. Furthermore, statistical models are constantly being updated with an increasing number of available annotated documents.

12.1.4 Prototype Evaluation

It is worth mentioning that the cost of a formal field study of this kind of systems is exceedingly high, since it typically involves expensive work by a panel of experts (for instance, qualified paleographers, professional translators, or trained computational linguists). For that reason, we decided to start doing a preliminary exploration, recruiting regular computer users instead. By now, the IHT prototype is the only demonstrator that has been formally evaluated, since it was the most advanced overall. However, we plan to do so with all prototypes in a near future. We encourage the reader to try the freely available demos and draw their own conclusions.

12.2 MM-IHT: Multimodal Interactive Handwritten Transcription

Transcribing handwritten text is a laborious task which, in general, is currently carried out manually. As the accuracy of automatic handwritten text recognizers improves, post-editing the output of these recognizers is foreseen as a possible alternative. However, given the high error rates of current approaches, post-editing is usually both inefficient and uncomfortable for the users. As alternative, an interactive-predictive paradigm has gained an increasing popularity due to promising empirical results that estimated considerable reductions of user effort.

In this section we introduce a web-based demonstrator of the interactive multimodal approach presented in Chap. 3. This new multimodal interactive approach for handwritten transcription, also known as MM-CATTI, MM-IHT, or simply IHT for short, is shown to work quite well by an implemented web-based demonstrator. The reader can access the online demo at http://cat.iti.upv.es/iht/.

12.2.1 Prototype Description

In this prototype [22] the server–engine communication is made through binary sockets [1]. A web application loads initially an index of all available pages in the document to be transcribed (Fig. 12.3). The user then navigates to a page and begins to transcribe the handwritten text images line by line (Fig. 12.5). She can make corrections with any kind of pointing device (e.g. touchscreen or stylus), and also she can use the keyboard. If pen strokes are available, the IHT engine uses an on-line HTR feedback subsystem to decode them. Finally, taking into account the decoded word and the off-line models, the engine responds with a suitable continuation to the prefix validated by the user.

On the other hand, keystrokes data directly interact with the aforementioned IHT engine. All corrections are stored in plain text logs on the server, so the user can retake them in any moment. Other client–server communications, such as managing logs or loading the sockets interface, are made via AJAX (Asynchronous JavaScript And XML), thus providing a richer interactive experience.

User Interaction Protocol

In the MM-IHT web-based demonstrator, the user is tightly involved with the transcription process, where following a preset protocol, she validates and/or corrects the HTR output during the process. Such a protocol, which rules this interaction process, is formulated in the following steps:

- The IHT engine proposes a full transcription of the input handwritten text line image.
- The user validates the longest prefix of the transcription which is error-free and enters some on-line touchscreen pen-strokes and/or some amendment keystrokes to correct the first error in the suffix.
- If pen strokes were available, an on-line HTR feedback subsystem is used to decode this input.
- In this way, a new extended consolidated prefix is produced based on the previous validated prefix, the on-line decoded word and the keystroke amendments. Using this new prefix, the IHT engine suggests a suitable continuation of it.
- These previous steps are iterated until a final, perfect transcription is produced.

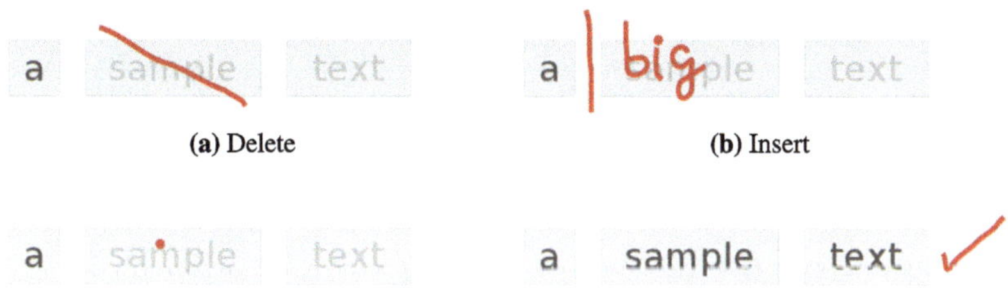

(a) Delete (b) Insert

(c) Reject (d) Accept

Fig. 12.2 An example of pen strokes-related operations in the MM-IHT prototype

The interaction between the user and the system is not only limited to write the full correct word, but other different operations can be carried out using both pen-strokes and/or keystrokes. The types of operations that can be carried out are the following.

Substitute The first erroneous word is substituted by the correct word. The validated prefix consists of all the words preceding the substituted word and the new correct word.

Delete The incorrect word is deleted. The validated prefix consists of all the words preceding the deleted word plus the word that follows the deleted word.

Reject All the words that precede the incorrect word constitute the validated prefix. The system proposes a new suffix where the first word is different to the incorrect word.

Insert A new word is inserted. The validated prefix are all the word precedent the inserted word, the inserted word and the word that follows the inserted word.

Accept The proposed transcription is fully validated.

In Fig. 12.2 one can see different interaction modes making use of pen-strokes. The user can write down the correct word directly, make a diagonal line to delete an erroneous word, make a vertical line followed by a word for inserting that word, or make a single click to ask for another suitable suffix continuation [20].

12.2.2 *Technology*

IHT Engine

The IHT engine combines all the information received from the client and compute a suitable solution. It follows the approach presented in Chap. 3, where both online and offline HTR systems are based on HMMs and n-gram language models.

The offline system is implemented using word-graphs. These word-graphs are a pruned version of the Viterbi search trellis obtained when transcribing the whole image sentence. In order to make the system able to interact with the user in a time-efficient way, they are computed beforehand.

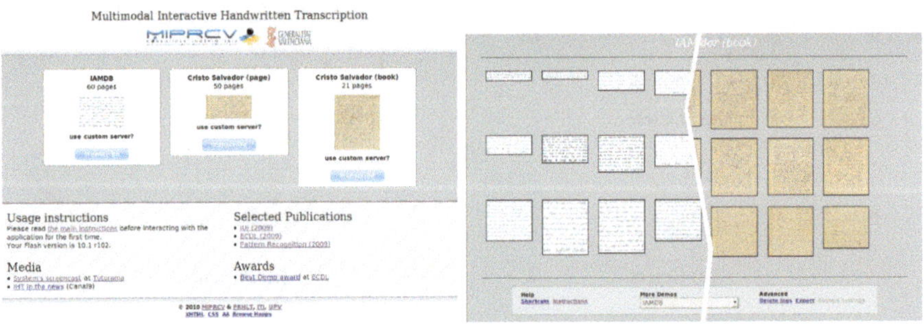

(a) IHT Index (b) Page selection

Fig. 12.3 Once a corpus is selected on the IHT index (**a**), a thumbnail for each page of the document is presented to the user (**b**)

Once the user selects the line to transcribe, the client application send to the IHT engine the `set_source` message. The IHT engine loads the word-graph corresponding to the selected line and proposes a full transcription as explained in Sect. 2.2 of Chap. 2.

When the user makes some correction, if pen strokes are available, the IHT engine uses an on-line HTR feedback subsystem to decode them. After preprocessing and extracting the features, as is explained in Sect. 3.5.2, the pen strokes are decoded following the last scenario presented in Chap. 3, taking into account information derived from the validated prefix and the previous suffix as shown in Eq. (3.13).

Once the pen strokes have been decoded, a new prefix can be generated taking into account the validated prefix, the new decoded word and the operation that the user has carried out (substitution, deletion, insertion, etc.). Then, this new prefix is parsed in the off-line word-graph, and a suitable continuation is provided following techniques described in Chap. 3. It could happen that the prefix was not in the word-graphs, so, the error correcting parsing explained in Sect. 3.2.2 is applied.

Web Interface

The Web Interface is responsible for showing the user interface and capturing the user actions on the different modalities of interaction, i.e, keyboard and pen strokes. On the main page (Fig. 12.3a) of the demonstrator the user must choose one of the available documents to transcribe by clicking on the "*transcribe*" button. Also, by clicking on "*use custom server?*" link, the user can specify a custom IHT engine while her session is active.

Once the user has selected the document to transcribe, an index of all pages in the corpus appears, allowing the user to navigate to any page. In Fig. 12.3b we can see different pages from the IAMDB modern English corpus and from the Spanish 19th century handwritten document "Cristo Salvador".

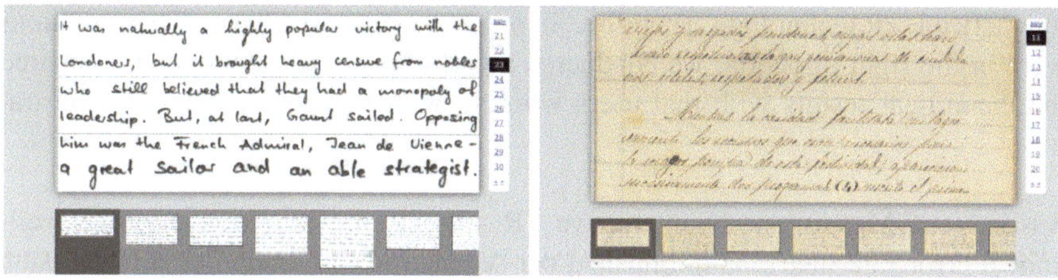

(a) IAM database **(b)** Cristo Salvador corpus

Fig. 12.4 Corpora examples for the IHT prototype

Fig. 12.5 Screenshot (detail) of two feedback modalities: keyboard input and e-pen

To begin with, once the user selects a thumbnail page from the index, the full page is loaded (Fig. 12.4). The center block is the page to transcribe itself. The tidy menu at the right side is a pagination item, to allow the user browsing all pages quickly. There is a page slider to allow a visual pagination of the selected corpus, and also a bottom menu intended to help the user with common tasks (such as closing session, changing the corpus, or displaying application shortcuts).

Then, the user can select a line from the current page by clicking on its image, and the system will propose an initial, full transcription. If no error is detected, the user chooses another text line image to transcribe. Otherwise, the user edits it interactively as explained before. All the corrections made by the user are stored in plain text logs on the web server. In this way, she can retake them at any moment.

12.2.3 Evaluation

The empirical tests on cursive handwritten tasks suggested that, using the IHT approach, considerable amounts of user effort could be saved with respect to both pure manual work and non-interactive, post-editing processing (see Sect. 3.1). While, of course, no definitive conclusions could be derived from these empirical tests, they clearly raised great expectations about the effectiveness and usability of this kind of interactive HTR technology. Therefore, in order to assess whether such expectations were in the right direction, we conducted a preliminary field study that compared the theoretical results with real users working with the implemented demonstrator.

Assessment Measures In interactive PR systems the importance of the well-known error rate metric is diminished per-se. Instead, the intention is to measure how well the user and the system work together. For this reason, to better judge the quality of the user transcriptions we used the two objective test-set-based measures introduced in Sect. 2.6: word error rate (WER) and word stroke ratio (WSR). Both metrics have proven to be useful for estimating the reduction in human effort that can be expected by using IHT with respect to using a conventional HTR system followed by human post-editing. On the other hand, in our subjective tests with real users we measured the time needed to fully transcribe each page with the different transcription possibilities (fully manual, post-editing, and IHT) as well as the residual WER (rWER)—defined as the WER which remains after the user has typed the transcriptions or corrected/accepted the transcriptions proposed by the system (this value is expected to be greater than zero due to human errors).

Corpus The corpus used on the experiments was the one identified as "Cristo Salvador" (CS), which has been previously presented in Sect. 3.6.1.

Participants Fourteen members from our Computer Science department volunteered to cooperate, aged 28 to 61 ($M = 37.3$, three females). Most of them were knowledgeable with handwriting transcription tasks, although none was a transcriber expert.

Apparatus The presented IHT demonstrator was modified to carry out the field study. We developed three kind of HTR engines to assist the document transcription: a trivial manual system, a post-editing system, and an interactive-predictive system. The user interface (UI) was common to all engines (see Fig. 12.4). Also, a logging mechanism was embedded in the web application. It allowed to register all user interactions in a fine-grained level of detail (e.g., keyboard and mouse events, client/server messages exchanging, etc.). The generated log files were reported in XML format for later postprocessing.

Procedure To carry out the experiments we used two pages (#45 and #46) from the test partition of the CS corpus. The WER and WSR of these pages are 24.5% and 23.0%, respectively. Participants accessed the web-based application via a special URLs that were sent to them by email. In order to familiarize with the UI, users informally tested each transcription engine with some test pages, different from the ones reserved for the user-test. Only three participants were aware of the existence of such a demonstrator prior to the study. Then, people transcribed the two user-test pages; each one with the three transcription engines. The two user-test pages for the field study were selected because they had very similar test-set-based performance

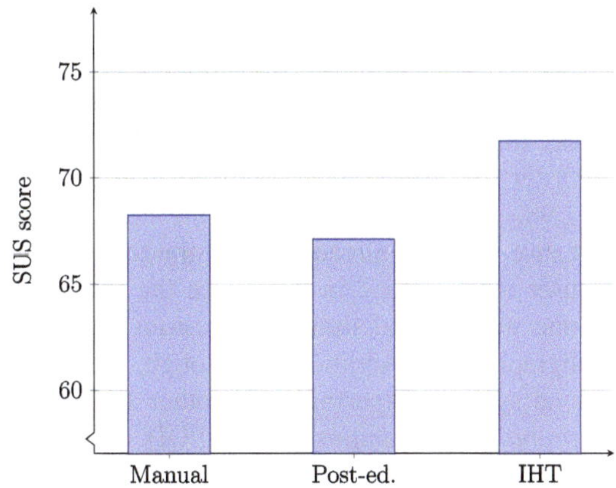

Fig. 12.6 User satisfaction, according to the SUS questionnaire

metrics (CS page #45: WER = 24.35%, WSR = 23.07%; CS page #46: WER = 24.69%, WSR = 23.04%; respectively). It is important to remark that nobody saw these pages before the study. For that reason, it is clear that the engine that were tested at first would lead to poorer results than the rest of engines—in the next trials users would need less effort in reading the image lines. Thus, to avoid possible biases due to human learnability, page #45 was transcribed in this order: manual, post-edition, and IHT. Then the order was inverted for page #46. Finally, participants filled out a SUS questionnaire for each engine, including a text field to enter free comments and ideas about their testing experience as well as give some insights about possible enhancements and/or related applicability.

Design A within-subjects repeated measures design was carried out. We tested two conditions: transcribing a page when it has not been seen before and when it has been seen at least once. Since both normality assumptions and homocedasticity in the data were met, we performed a four-way ANOVA experiment. The independent variables were time, rWER, and WSR, respectively.

Discussion of Results

In sum, we can assert that regarding effectiveness there are no significative differences, i.e., users can achieve their goals with any of the proposed systems. However, in terms of efficiency the IHT system seems to be the better choice. Regarding user satisfaction, Fig. 12.6 clearly shows that IHT is the most preferable of the three options. Now let us delve into a more detailed analysis in order to shed more light to the obtained results.

For the sake of saving time for the users, the post-editing engine was tested always as the second option. However, we must emphasize that the daily use of any system designed to assist handwriting transcription would involve not having seen previously any of the pages (users usually read a page once and at the same time they just transcribe it).

- *Analysis of Time*: Overall, post-editing attained the best time. This was expected, since for both user-test pages such system was tested after users had read each page once. However, the manual and IHT engines were tested under the same conditions, and we observed that IHT is approximately 1 minute faster. In any case, these differences are not statistically significant ($F_{2,76} = 1.98$, $p = 0.14$). In general, the last used system achieves the best time, because the user already knows the text. The remarkable result is that when the user reads a page in first place the chosen engine is not determinant, because one must spend time to accustom to the writing style, interpreting the calligraphy, etc. Additionally, though, we might count the number of times that one system outperforms the other for a given user, and thereby, measure the *probability of improvement* (POI) [4]. In this case the POI of the IHT engine with respect to the manual engine is 53%, and 42% regarding to post-edition.
- *Analysis of rWER*: Overall, IHT was the best choice regarding to residual WER in all situations, although the differences are not statistically significant ($F_{2,75} = 0.67$, $p = 0.51$). The interesting observation is that IHT is the most stable of the systems, even better than when using the manual engine on an already read page (the post-editing system was expected to perform similarly, since it was tested in both conditions in second place). We must recall that the more stable in rWER a system is, the fewer residual transcription errors are expected. In this case, considering the first time that the user reads a page, the POI of the IHT engine over the manual engine is 69%, and 68% with respect to post-edition.
- *Analysis of WSR*: Interestingly, the WSR when using the manual engine was below 100%, since there are inherent errors (some users were unable to correctly read all the lines). That means that some users wrote less words in their final transcriptions than they really should have to. Overall, ANOVA showed that IHT was the best performer in both conditions. Differences were statistically significant ($F_{2,76} = 1014.71$, $p < 0.0001$, $\eta^2 = 26.7$). This means that the number of words a user must write and/or correct under the IHT paradigm is always lower than with any of the other systems. Additionally, this fact increases the probability of achieving a high-quality final transcription, since users perform fewer interactions and are prone thus to less errors. In this case the POI of the IHT engine regarding the manual engine is 100%, and 65% with respect to post-edition. It is also interesting to note that, on average, the real WSR achieved by the participants is fairly close to the objective user-test based estimates for the same pages and even closer to the theoretical test-set estimates overall.
- *Analysis of User Subjectivity*: Regarding user responses to the SUS questionnaire, while no statistically significant differences were achieved ($F_{2,32} = 0.11$, $p = 0.9$), there is a clear tendency in favor of IHT (see Fig. 12.6). What is more, participants chose the manual engine over post-editing most of the time. This would explain why, considering difficult transcription tasks, users generally refuse to post-edit the output of a conventional HTR system, since it has too many recognition errors.

Most of the users' comments were alas related to the web UI rather than the transcription engines themselves. Some included "*when clicking on a text field, the whole word is selected*", "*it is hard to remember some [keyboard] shortcuts*", or "*a clear and visual user manual would allow not having to learn almost anything before using the system.*" Additionally, four users complained about the segmentation of lines, which "*made especially difficult reading those images where words had many ascenders/descenders.*" On the other hand, three users noticed that punctuation chars did not contribute to improve predictions in the IHT system. In fact, they were removed from the language models when training the IHT engine, since we used bi-grams and punctuation chars do not improve notably the predictions.

Limitations of the Study and Conclusion

There are a number of reasons why we were unfortunately not able to achieve statistically significant differences between the three tested engines in some cases. First, most of the participants had never faced neither any of the implemented engines nor the web UI before the study, so it is expected a logical learning curve prior to using such systems in a daily basis. Second, the web interface was just a prototype, and it is well known that a careful design of the UI is a primary factor to tap the possibilities of the IHT technology. Third, the pages were really deteriorated, making thus the reading difficult for the users. For that reason, there is a great difference between the first time that a user had to transcribe a page and the subsequent attempts. Fourth, the post-edition engine was not tested under the same circumstances as the other two engines, i.e., it was always used in second place. Thus an important bias was introduced in the comparison of the systems—although it was not the case for manual and IHT engines, which were both tested in the same conditions. Finally, due to the limited size of user sample, we had to include the outliers in the evaluation. However, despite the above mentioned limitations, there is a comprehensible tendency to choose the IHT paradigm over the other two systems. Additionally, as observed, the probability of improvement of an IHT engine over manual transcription or post-edition makes this paradigm worthwhile.

12.3 IST: Interactive Speech Transcription

The transformation audio speech signals into text is an important activity in many official institutions (e.g. the European Union parliament, U.N. sessions, Catalan and Basque parliaments in Spain, etc.) and private companies. However, speech recognition systems are not perfect. Special cases always appear which are not accounted for by automatic systems, leading to inaccurate and/or inadequate transcriptions. In practice, such systems generally need human postprocessing to correct the possible errors incurred by the system.

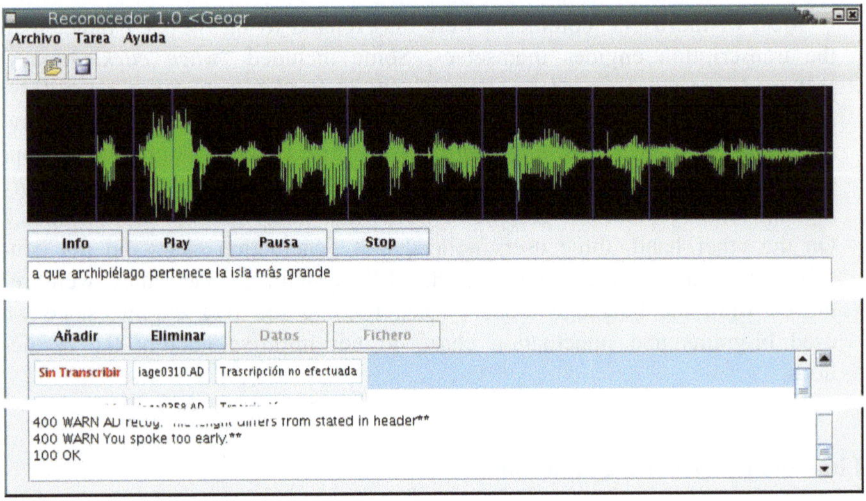

Fig. 12.7 MM-IST User Interface

In this section we introduce an Interactive Speech Transcription (IST) prototype [19] developped within the general Interactive Pattern Recognition approach presented in Chap. 4. This prototype provides an interactive framework for obtaining high-quality results while increasing the productivity with respect to the classical postprocessing techniques of speech transcription.

12.3.1 Prototype Description

A Java interface provides all the interaction mechanism to allow an efficient communication between the user and the prototype (see Fig. 12.7). Initially, the interface ask the user to create a new transcription project or to use a previously created one. A project is a set of audio files to transcribe. Along with these files a project stores the transcriptions already obtained. The main interface screen shows, on the one hand, the list of files in the current project so that the user can choose the file to be transcribed (see Fig. 12.8). On the other hand, the waveform of the current file is shown in a graphic panel and a text field is used to show the current system suggestion along with the different user interactions performed (see Fig. 12.9). The user can interact with this text field by using either the mouse or the keyboard to select the error-free prefix. In addition, the keyboard is used to amend the system suggestions.

User Interaction Protocol

It is similar to the protocol used in IHT discussed in the previous section.

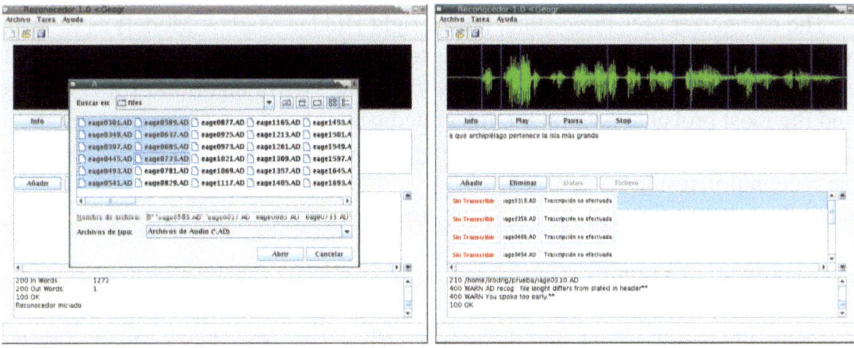

(a) (b)

Fig. 12.8 Loading a set of speech utterances to transcribe

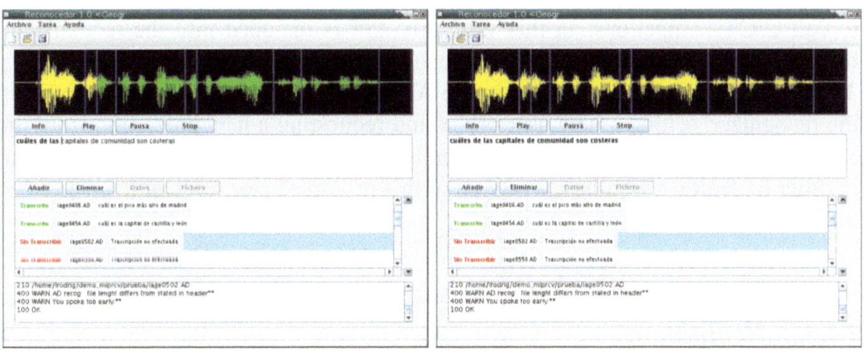

(a) (b)

Fig. 12.9 Using the IST prototype, discerning those utterance parts that are already transcribed (*yellow wave*) from those that are not (*green wave*)

12.3.2 Technology

Prediction Engine

The prediction engine is a general-purpose, speaker-independent, continuous speech recognizer (ATROS). This engine is a standalone application capable of recognizing speech in real time from a microphone input or from an audio file.

Given an input utterance, the recognizer initially preprocess the signal by performing a border detection algorithm and a pre-emphasis filter to increase the magnitude of the high frequencies present in the speech signal. Next, a feature extraction is performed to obtain a MFCC (Mel Frequency Cepstral Coefficients) vector for each frame in the input signal. Then, the energy along with the first and second derivatives are added to build the final feature vector for the frame. Once the feature extraction has been preformed, the recognition process is carried out.

The recognizer uses three-state, left-to-right Hidden Markov Models as acoustic models. Finite-state automata are used as lexical entries and, finally, language models are implemented as finite-state networks. The Viterbi algorithm [8] is used to find the most probable path on the integrated network (acoustic+lexical+language models). Finally, the word sequence associated with this optimal path is returned as the recognition result.

Communication Module

Since the prediction engine and the user interface have been developed in different languages, a communication module is needed to send the user feedback from the user interface to the engine and to collect the different predictions. This module is currently implemented by adding a communication API to the recognizer. This API is implemented by using the Java Native Interface (JNI) that allows a Java program to call C/C++ functions. In this way, this API is included into the recognizer's building process so that the interface can make the proper calls during runtime. Three main functions are defined in the API which are responsible for initializing the recognizer, setting a new user prefix and requesting a new prediction from the engine. It is worth mentioning that currently the CAT-API [1] is being implemented in order to deploy a web-based version of this prototype (see reference functions in Sect. 12.1.1).

12.3.3 Evaluation

To assess the IST approach discussed above, different experiments were carried out. The reader is redirected to Sects. 4.6 and 4.6.3. The empirical results showed a clear effectiveness of thc IST approach in the tested corpora.

12.4 IMT: Interactive Machine Translation

The WWW with its universal access to information and instant communication between users has created a physical and geographical freedom for translators that was inconceivable in the past [6]. Computer-Assisted Translation (CAT) is an alternative approach to Machine Translation, integrating human expertise into the automatic translation process. Interactive Machine Translation (IMT) [2] can be considered as a special type of the CAT paradigm. The IMT framework was later extended in [24], where the possibility of rejecting a given suffix was introduced. The above-mentioned IMT framework is shown to work quite well by a web-based architecture.

In this section we bring to practice the theory discussed in Chap. 6. In similar web-based natural language processing systems [21, 23], the user's feedback has shown to improve system accuracy, and increase both system ergonomics and

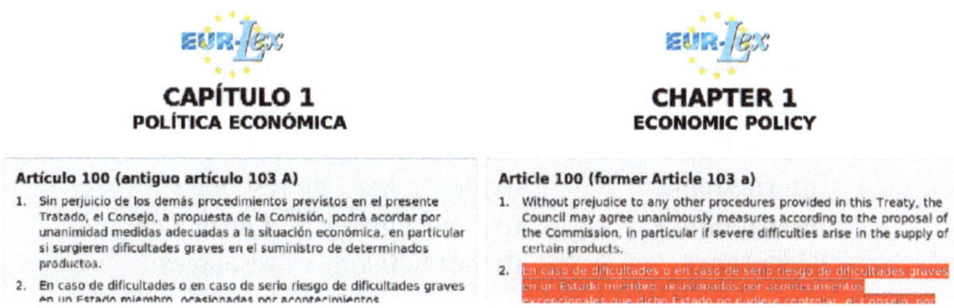

(a) Source document example, created from the EuroParl corpus.

(b) Translated example document, preserving original format and highlighting non-translated sentences.

Fig. 12.10 Translating documents with an IMT system

user's acceptability. Since the users operate within a web browser, this prototype also provides crossplatform compatibility and requires neither computational power nor disk space on the client machine. The reader can access the online demo at http://cat.iti.upv.es/imt/.

12.4.1 Prototype Description

This prototype is not intended to be a production-ready application. Rather, it provides an intuitive interface which aims at showing the functionality of an IMT system. Thus, two main aspects on which the architecture has been built are accessibility and flexibility. The former is necessary to reach a larger number of potential users. The latter allows researchers to test different techniques and interaction protocols reducing the implementation effort.

The proposed system [14] coordinates client-side scripting with server-side technologies, by using the CAT-API library [1]. At first, the web interface loads an index of all available corpora. Each corpus consists of a web document that is parsed from an automatically generated Translation Memory eXchange (TMX) file.[1] In this way, it is possible to recover the original format from source document and apply it back to the translated version of that document (see Fig. 12.10).

The user then navigates to a page and begins to translate the document by text segments. She can make corrections with the keyboard and also accomplish some mouse operations. User's feedback is then processed by the IMT engine. The IMT User Interface appears in Figs. 12.12 and 12.13.

User Interaction Protocol

The protocol that rules the interaction process has the following steps:

1. The system proposes a full translation of the selected text segment.

[1]TMX is an open XML standard for the exchange of translation documents.

source	Para ver la lista de recursos:
interaction-0	To view the resources list:
interaction-1	To view |a list of resources
interaction-2	To view a list[i]ng resources:
interaction-3	To view a listing [o]f resources:
acceptance	To view a listing of resources:

Fig. 12.11 IMT session to translate a Spanish sentence into English. On interaction-0, the system suggests a translation. On interaction-1, the user moves the mouse to validate (VP) the first eight characters "To view" and rejects (R) the next word; then the system suggests completing the sentence with "a list of resources". On interaction-2 the user moves again the mouse to accept the next six characters and presses the key *i* (KS). interaction-3 is similar to interaction-2. Finally, the user completely accepts (A) the present suggestion

2. The user validates the longest prefix of the translation which is error-free and/or corrects the first error in the suffix. Corrections are entered by amendment keystrokes or mouse-click operations.
3. In this way, a new extended consolidated prefix is produced based on the previous validated prefix and the interaction amendments. Using this new prefix, the system suggests a suitable continuation of it.
4. Steps 2 and 3 are iterated until the user-desired translation is produced.

System Interaction Modes

Our proposed system works both at full-word and character level, that is, the user can introduce modifications to the system by interacting with minimum and atomic text parts, respectively. The types of operations that can be carried out are grouped in four categories:

Validate prefix (VP) The text at the left of the mouse pointer is validated.
Key/Mouse stroke (KS/MS) The next character of the desired translation is inserted with the keyboard/mouse.
Reject (R) The text to the right of the pointer is wrong.
Accept (A) The text is finally correct.

Figure 12.11 shows an example of a typical IMT session involving the four interaction modes that have been described above (key stroke operations are represented by framed boxes and reject operations are represented by vertical bars).

12.4.2 Technology

In this section we describe the technology used to implement the IMT server and the web interface needed to communicate both client and server sides. On the one

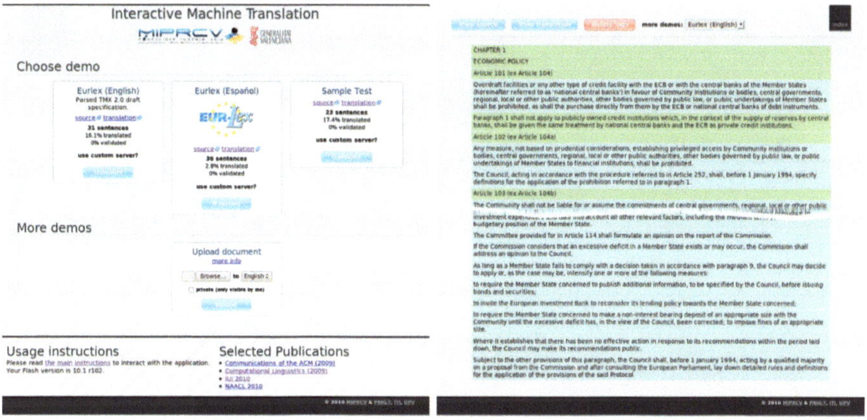

(a) IMT Index (b) Demo Layout

Fig. 12.12 IMT User Interface

hand, the client provides a user interface which uses the above-mentioned CAT-API library to communicate with the IMT engine through the Web. The hardware requirements in the client are very low, as the translation process is carried out remotely on the server. So virtually any computer (including netbooks, tablets or 3G mobile phones) should be enough to use this system. On the other hand, the server, which is unaware of the implementation details of the IMT client, uses and adapts the statistical models that are used to perform the translation.

Interactive CAT Server

The IMT server is based on the statistical phrase-based translation approach [9] to generate the suffixes completing the consolidated prefixes given by the user. State-of-the-art SMT systems use a log-linear combination of features to generate their translations. Among the features typically used in this log-linear combination, the most important of them are the statistical language model, which is implemented by means of n-gram language models, and the statistical translation model, which is implemented by means of phrase-based models. Standard SMT systems require little modification for its use in the IMT framework [2].

Web Interface

Client-Server communication is made via asynchronous HTTP requests, providing thus a richer interactive experience, and Server-Engine communication is made through binary sockets. All corrections are stored in plain text logs on the server, so the user can retake them at any moment, also allowing other users to help to translate the full documents.

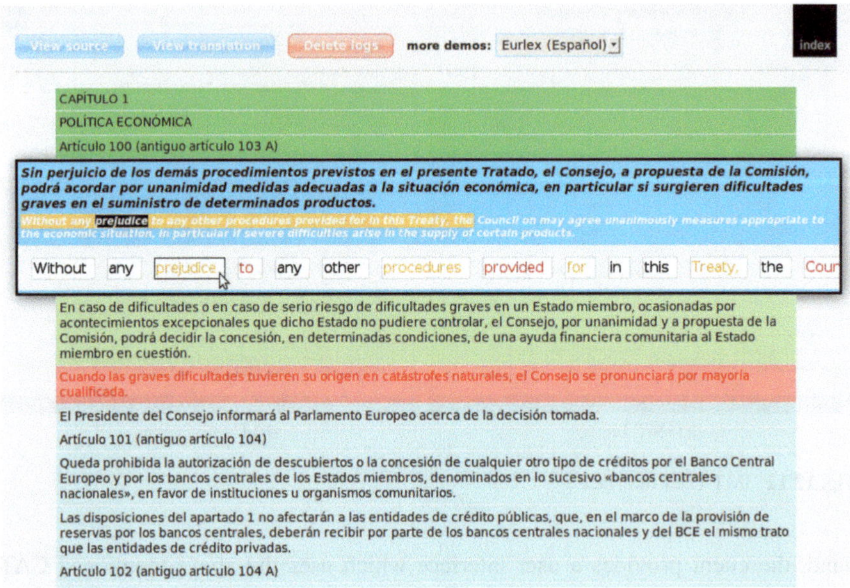

Fig. 12.13 IMT User Interface, using confidence measures to mark those words that presumably need to be verified or corrected by the user

12.4.3 Evaluation

Experimental results were carried out on different tasks (see Sect. 6.4). It is worth noting that the reported experiments simulate real users to measure the effort required to generate error-free translations. The results suggested that the proposed system can substantially reduce the typing effort needed to produce a high-quality translation of a given source text with respect to the effort needed to simply type the whole translation. Specifically, 80% and 70% typing effort reductions were obtained for the Xerox and the European Union corpora, respectively.

12.5 ITG: Interactive Text Generation

The time spent in typing (including, as well, thinking about what is going to be typed) is quite high in many real-world situations. In addition, in some situations, typing becomes a slow and uncomfortable task. For example, in some devices, such as mobile phones, no suitable input mechanisms are available. Moreover, some disabled people are not able to achieve a fast enough typing speed and, unfortunately, in some cases, this is the only way for them to communicate.

In this section we present a system that takes all these considerations into account for assisting users in text generation tasks. Previous approaches to this topic can be found in the literature. Most of them just attempt to predict the next single word

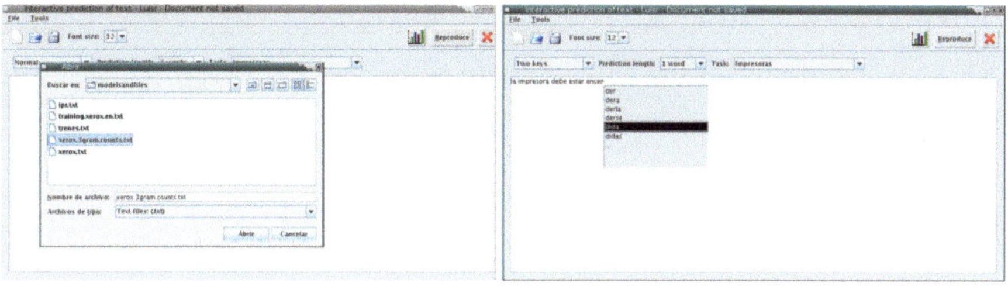

(a) (b)

Fig. 12.14 Loading a task-specialized corpus (**a**) and interacting with the ITG prototype (**b**)

and/or to complete the characters of each new word being typed by the user [30]. Other systems just focus on measuring the accuracy of off-line text predictions [3]. In the system presented in this section, however, a more general setting is considered where not only single words, but multi-word fragments or even full sentences, are predicted interactively.

12.5.1 Prototype Description

A prototype for interactive text prediction, based on the IPR framework, has been implemented. The main prototype features are summarized in the following list.

- A user profile is maintained to store preferences and interaction statistics.
- A language or a domain can be selected (that is, the language model to be used).
- Different interaction modes (see Sect. 12.5.1) and prediction options (word or character level, prediction length, etc.) are available.
- Predictions are integrated into the main text editor.
- The system maintains statistics about the usage.
- An additional tool can be used to record a user session, keeping track of all the user and system actions. This is aimed at using the prototype in play-back mode in order to analyze the behavior of both the user and the system.

During its normal operation mode, the system is also able to take advantage of the generated text to improve the statistical prediction models. The rationale behind this idea is to adapt the system to a specific user so that the system is able to learn the user's writing style (or a new task or domain, for instance). Moreover, the system could be still used if no previously trained models were available. This way, all the learning process will perform on-line. Initially, the system predictions will be useless but, as the user generates more and more text, these predictions will be improved as a consequence of this on-line training process. Eventually, we will have a prediction model specifically trained for the task being currently solved.

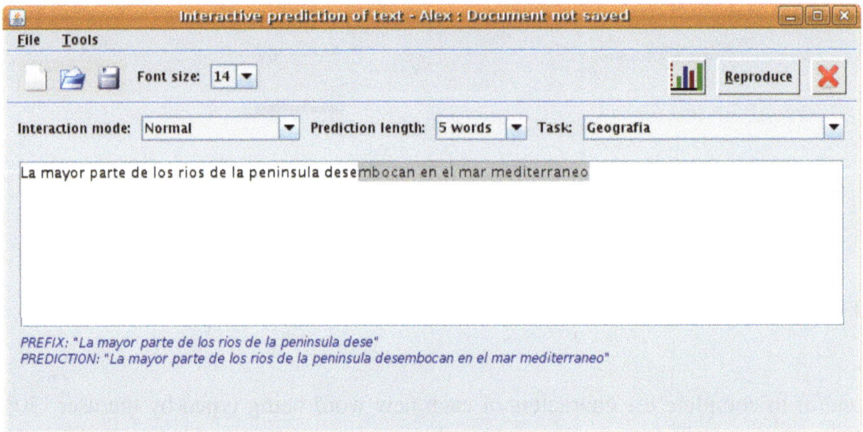

Fig. 12.15 Example of a sentence being edited using the keyboard-based interaction mode. The text in *white* background is the prefix consolidated so far, and the text in *grey* background is the current system suffix suggestion

System Architecture

The ITG prototype has been divided into two different subsystems: the User Interface (UI, see Fig. 12.14) and the prediction engine. The UI allows the user to interact with the system, as well as set the different configuration options. The main component in this UI is a text editor where the system displays the proposed suffixes while the user is typing. She can accept, modify or discard these suffix-suggestions just by using the keyboard or the mouse. This interface also displays statistics on the system usage and can replay a previously saved session. The prediction engine, on the other hand, searches for the most suitable suffix (or set of suffixes) according to the current prefix.

This division allows the prediction engine to be deployed in a separate computer, or even implement several engines on a distributed computing system (e.g., each computer can host a single language model). Taking this fact into account, the prediction engine can be placed in a server (or servers) allowing the use of thin clients (PDAs, mobile phones, etc.) to have access to this technology. The system is based on the MIPR CAT client–server architecture (see Fig. 12.1) using socket interfaces and the TCP protocol for communication among the different subsystems.

User Interaction Protocol

Given the text typed so far, the system produces a prediction that the user reads until a mistake is found. Next, such a mistake is corrected and the system provides a new continuation taking this correction into account (as can be seen in Fig. 12.15). In this scenario, we are interested in minimizing the number of user interactions (i.e. to save user effort). Under this criterion, a simple greedy strategy consisting in suggesting the most probable word given the text typed (prefix) so far turns out to be the optimal strategy for this scenario [13]. It is worth noticing that this can be easily extended to multi-word predictions by considering each predicted word as part of the current prefix, and repeating this process until reaching the desired amount of predicted words.

System Interaction Modes

Two different interaction modes have been implemented. One may note that, in addition to these modes, as it was previously discussed, the system can work at both word or character level.

The first option (Fig. 12.15) considers that a keyboard (or a similar input device) is being used. The user can achieve high typing performance and the predictions should not slow down the process. This mode predicts just one suffix, which is directly inserted after the text typed so far. This suffix is highlighted to indicate that it is not still validated. The user can validate part of the suffix, the whole suffix or ignore it completely. In any case, the system suggestions do not interrupt the user, who can keep typing all the time. It is not clear whether this modality is really useful for a normal typing session, although it can be really helpful for slow-typing users or to type text in a non-native language, for instance. In these cases, the system could be seen as a language generation assistant rather than a typing effort saver.

The second option (Fig. 12.16) allows the system to be used with just two keys. This option is planned for users who have some kind of physical impairment or with highly constrained input interfaces. In this case, a set of alternative suffixes (in the form of n-best list) is shown when pressing one of the two keys. At this point, the user can navigate (using the same key) within this list and choose any suggestion by pressing the other key. If no suitable continuations are found in the list, a new listing containing all the characters in the alphabet is displayed. In this way, the user can select an alternative continuation and, as soon as the user picks one of these characters, the system reacts by predicting a new suffix.

These two interaction modes have been implemented considering that the system has a standard keyboard. However, they can be easily adapted to any kind of hardware that allows a multi-state input (first option) or a two-state input (second option). For instance, the two-key option can be adapted with little effort to be used with a two-button mouse (or any kind of two-positions device).

12.5.2 Technology

The prototype is composed of three different subsystems:

- An automatic text predictor. Based on n-gram language models and implemented in C++.

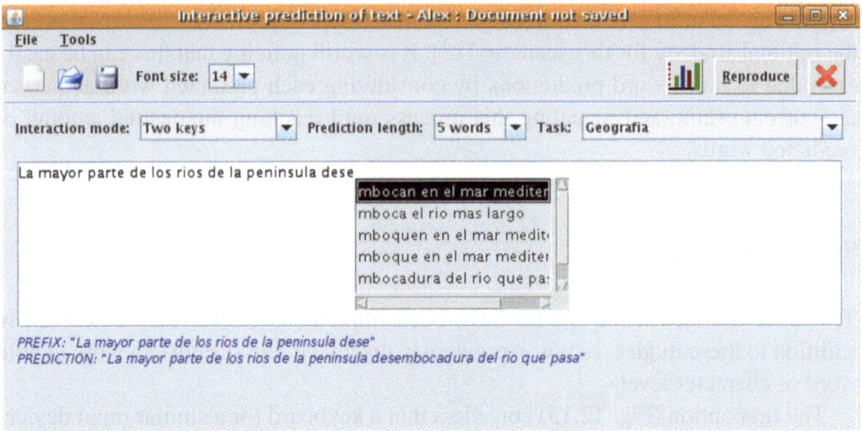

Fig. 12.16 Example of sentence being edited using the two-key-based interaction mode. Several suffixes are shown in a contextual menu at the current cursor position

- A Graphical User Interface. This interface provides all the interaction engine to allow an efficient communication between the user and the prototype. The interface has been implemented in Java.
- A communication module between the text predictor and the graphical interface, that sends the information derived from the user interaction to the predictor. This module is implemented by following a server-client approach and is based on the use of network sockets.

The technical details of the language modeling and searching strategy were detailed in Sects. 10.2.1 and 10.2.2, respectively.

12.5.3 Evaluation

In order to assess whether if the prototype could facilitate the user interaction with the computer, we performed some preliminary (and informal) experiments involving real users. Test users were split into groups according to their general experience with computer applications and to their skills about using standard input interfaces. Several sessions were performed by each user and finally a questionnaire was answered. Preliminary evaluations have shown that the prototype is highly usable in most of the cases. Nevertheless, those users with little experience with computers usually needed some kind of assistance.

Several experiments have been performed considering different tasks and calculating their corresponding metrics. The main evaluation was performed offline by using test sets and computing the Key and Word Stroke Ratio (KSR and WSR) metrics (see Sect. 2.6). In all tested scenarios the estimated effort saving was significant. For instance, in the simple EuTrans task, the system achieved a KSR of 14% and a WSR of 50%, and for printers' technical manuals (Xerox corpus) the KSR and WSR were 19% and 66%, respectively.

12.6 MM-IP: Multimodal Interactive Parsing

Parsing, also known as grammatical or syntactic analysis, is considered a fundamental problem in Computational Linguistics [10]. Parsing has been also applied to many other research fields aside from the Natural Language Processing (NLP) domain, since the concept of "sentence" can be easily extended to other objects, e.g., mathematical equations. Having perfectly annotated syntactic trees allows one to train and improve the statistical models of other NLP systems, such as machine translation, question answering, or discourse analysis, just to name a few. However, until now the grammatical construction of such trees has been done manually, implying thus a really laborious task.

In this section we introduce a multimodal prototype that operates over the WWW, which is based on the Interactive Parsing framework (IP from here onwards) presented in Sect. 9.2. It can be accessed online at http://cat.iti.upv.es/ipp/. In the prototype, user feedback is provided by means of traditional keyboard/mouse operations and, if available, pen strokes. Interaction through the user feedback allows to improve system accuracy, while multimodality increases both system ergonomy and user acceptability. Furthermore, owing to its web-based nature, this system allows for collaboration between several users across the globe.

12.6.1 Prototype Description

The prototype coordinates client-side scripting with server-side technologies, by using the CAT-API library [1]. The system architecture is based on the CAT network set-up (e.g. see Fig. 12.1). To begin, the user interface (see Fig. 12.17) loads an index of all available corpora. The user then navigates to the chosen corpus page and starts parsing the sentences one by one. She can make corrections both with the keyboard and the computer mouse. User's feedback is then processed by the IP server.

Multimodality is implemented in such a way that the interface accepts two types of human interaction, either by using the keyboard (a deterministic signal) and/or the mouse. The latter, in turn, provides two kinds of operations: *mouse actions* (i.e. clicks, draw movements) and *mouse feedback* (handwritten gestures)—a non-deterministic signal that needs to be decoded by an on-line HTR system, such as the subsystem depicted in Sect. 12.2.1. Both keyboard actions and mouse feedback are used mainly to modify the label of parsing tree's constituents. On the other hand, mouse actions are used to change the span of the above-mentioned tree's constituents (e.g. by clicking on a tree leaf the span is decremented; by drawing a line from a constituent to a word token the span is incremented).

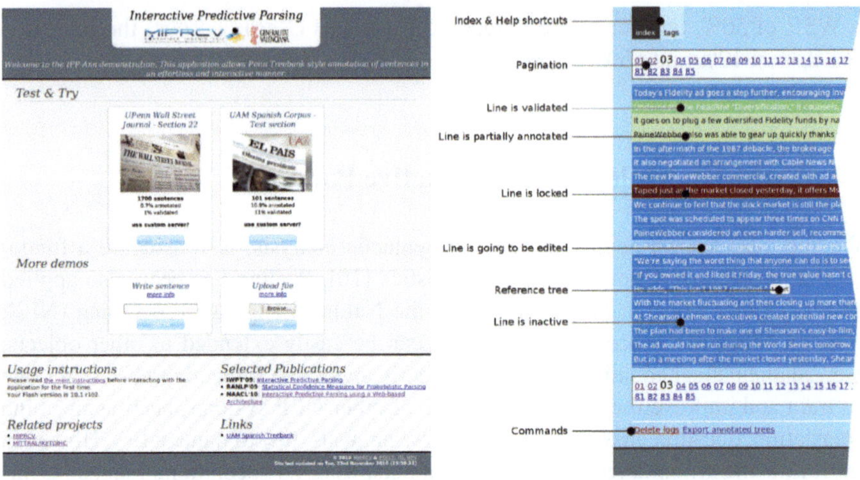

(a) Index page **(b)** Interface parts

Fig. 12.17 MM-IP layout description

Predictive interaction is approached in such a way that both the main and the feedback data streams help each other to optimize overall performance and usability. The first data stream relates to the validated subtree structure itself. The latter data stream takes into account the provided user information. As already mentioned, since the users operate within a web browser, the system also provides cross-platform compatibility and requires neither computational power nor disk space on the client machine. the client machine. See Fig. 12.18 for a layout of the GUI of this prototype.

Each validated user interaction is saved as a log file on the server side. In this way, the user can retake the tree from its latest state, also allowing other experts to help in parsing the full corpus.

User Interaction Protocol

Each parse tree t is composed by several constituents c_i. Each constituent is comprised of a label, either a *syntactic label* or a *Part-of-speech (POS) tag*, and a span (the starting and ending indexes which delimit the input sentence substring encompassed by the constituent).

The protocol that rules this process is formulated in the following steps.

1. The parsing server proposes a full parse tree t for the input sentence. The tree t is shown on the screen by the client interface.
2. The user finds the longest error-free prefix tree[2] and starts amending the first (incorrect) constituent c from the remaining suffix (either by entering on-line

[2]The tree visiting order is left-to-right depth-first.

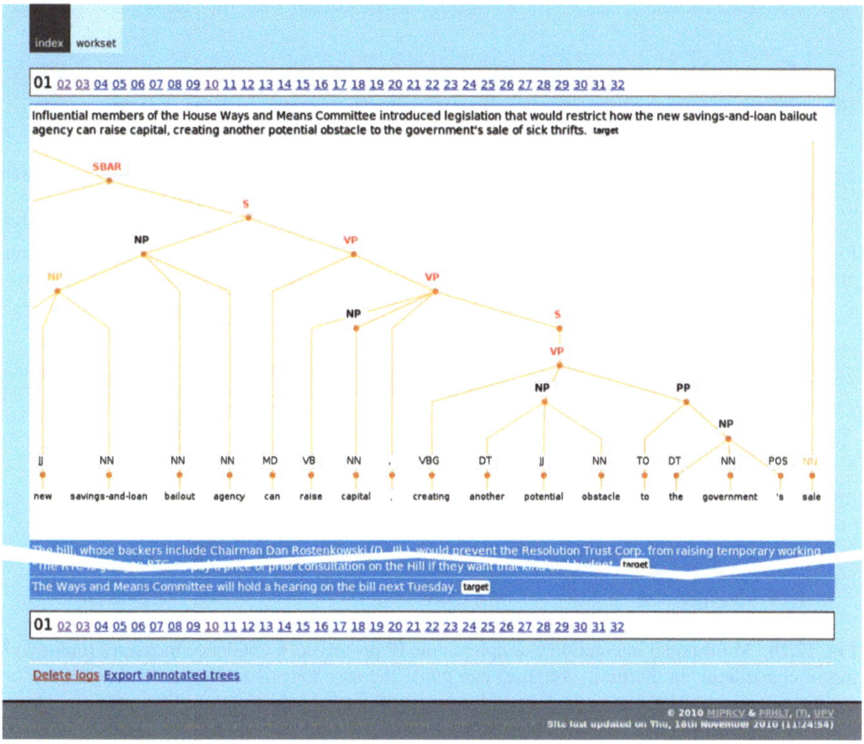

Fig. 12.18 MM-IP User Interface. Parse trees can be zoomed and/or panned for easing the human annotator's work

touchscreen pen-strokes or amendment keyboard strokes). This operation implicitly validates the prefix tree t_p.

3. The system decodes the user feedback, that is, the mouse/touchscreen pen-strokes or keyboard strokes. This user feedback can either affect the label or the span of the incorrect constituent c:
   (a) If the span of c is modified, the label is assumed to be incorrect. A partial constituent c^*, which includes *span* but no *label*, is decoded from the user feedback.
   (b) If the label of c is modified, the span is assumed to be correct. The corrected constituent c' is decoded from the user feedback.

   This step only deals with analyzing the user feedback, as the parsing server will not be contacted until the next step.
4. Either the partially corrected constituent c^* or the corrected constituent c' is then used by the client to create a new *extended consolidated prefix* that combines the validated prefix and the user feedback: either t_pc^* or t_pc'. The client sends the extended prefix tree to the parsing server and requests a suitable continuation for the parse tree, or tree suffix t_s:

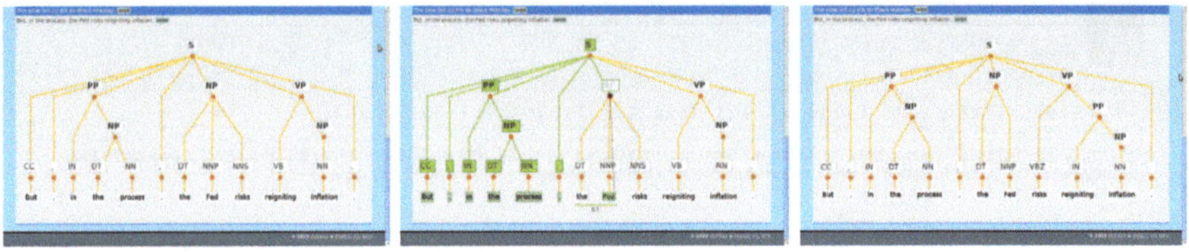

(a) System: Output tree 1 **(b)** User: Span modification **(c)** System: Output tree 2

Fig. 12.19 Mouse interaction example on the IP prototype. A constituent gets its span decremented using the mouse

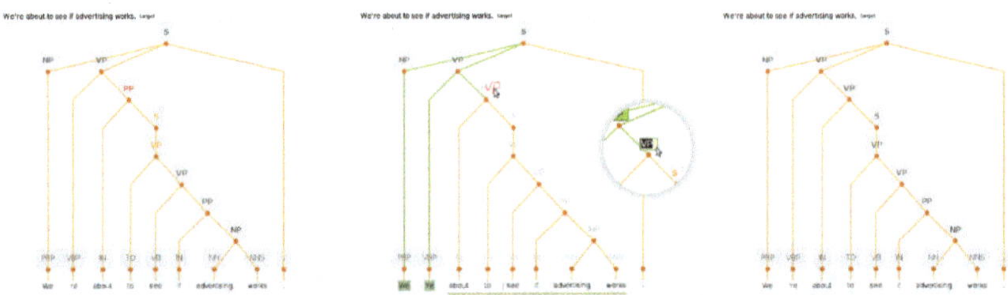

(a) System hypothesis **(b)** User feedback **(c)** System response

Fig. 12.20 Multimodal interaction example on the IP prototype. Confidence measures (color coding of constituents in the first subfigure) can guide the user toward a faster error detection. Correcting tree constituents can be performed by means of natural pen strokes or keystrokes (*enclosed circle* in (**b**)), leading to a new predicted tree

(a) If the extended prefix is partial ($t_p c^*$), the parsing server produces a suitable tree suffix t_s. The first element of t_s is the label completing c^*, followed by the remaining calculated constituents.
(b) If the extended prefix is complete ($t_p c'$), the parsing server produces a suitable tree suffix t_s which contains the remaining calculated constituents.

5. These previous steps are iterated until a final, perfect parse tree is produced.

Notice the similarities with the user simulation subsystem introduced in Sect. 9.5. Within this protocol, tree constituents can be deleted or inserted by adequately modifying the span of the left-neighboring constituent. In Figs. 12.19 and 12.20 one can see live interaction examples.

12.6.2 Technology

Parsing System

A customized CYK-Viterbi parser together with a grammar model is used as the parse server. We made available our system with two grammars, one for the English language constructed using roughly 40 000 sentences from the Penn Treebank, and one for the Spanish language constructed using 1 400 sentences from the UAM Treebank. Notice that the system performed well even with a grammar derived from a small number of sentences, like the one corresponding to the UAM corpus. Refer to Sect. 9.5 for more details on the implementation and grammar construction.

Web Interface

Client–Web server communication is based on asynchronous HTTP connections, providing thus a richer interactive experience—no page refreshes are required, only for changing the corpus to parse. The web server communicates with the IP engine through binary TCP sockets. Thus, response times are adequate. If mouse feedback is used to correct the label of constituents, an on-line HTR decodes the signal and passes the information back to the IP engine. Additionally, cross-domain requests are possible. So, the user can switch between different IP engines from the same user interface.

12.6.3 Evaluation

As mentioned on Sect. 9.5, it is expected that users employing this system would save around 40% of effort, compared to manually post-editing the output of the baseline system.

12.7 GIDOC: GIMP-Based Interactive Document Transcription

State-of-the-art technologies for automatic text transcription [17] can hardly deal with handwritten text or even with old-style printed text.

In this section we introduce a demonstrator of the approach presented in Chap. 5. GIDOC (Gimp-based Interactive transcription of text DOCuments) is a computer-assisted transcription prototype [26] for handwritten text images. It is a first attempt to provide integrated support for interactive-predictive page layout analysis, text line detection, and handwritten text transcription [18, 25]. GIDOC is built on top of the well-known GNU Image Manipulation Program (GIMP), and uses standard techniques and tools for handwritten text preprocessing and feature extraction, HMM-based image modeling, and language modeling.

12.7.1 Prototype Description

We decided not to build this prototype from scratch, but on top of GIMP, since GIMP gives us for free many desired prototype features. In particular, GIMP is Free

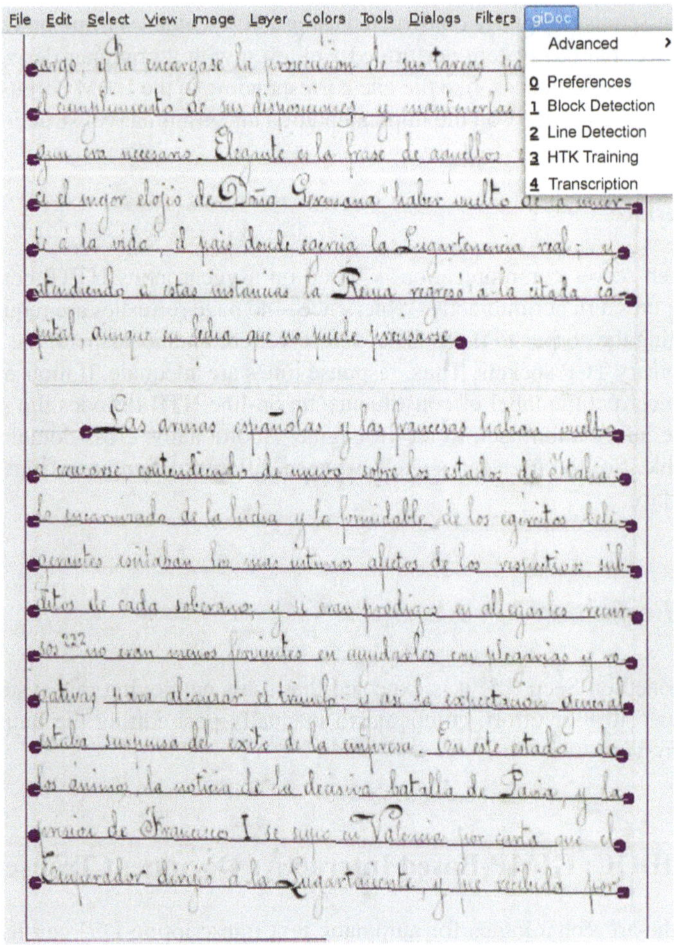

Fig. 12.21 Sample image window under the GIDOC menu

Software (GPL), multi-platform, multilingual, and provides: (1) a high-end user interface for image manipulation, (2) a large collection of image conversion drivers and low-level processing routines, (3) a scripting language to automate repetitive tasks, and, specially among others, (4) an API for the installation of user-defined plug-ins. Indeed, the GIDOC prototype is implemented as a set of GIMP plug-ins.

GIDOC is designed to work with (large) collections of homogeneous documents, that is, of similar structure and writing styles. They are annotated sequentially, by (partially) supervising hypotheses drawn from statistical models that are constantly updated with an increasing number of available annotated documents. And this is done at different annotation levels. To run GIDOC, one must first run GIMP and open a document image. GIMP will come up with its high-end user interface, which is often configured to only show the main toolbox (with docked dialogs) and an image window. GIDOC can be accessed from the menu-bar of the image window (see Fig. 12.21), by manipulating the six entries of its main menu:

- `Advanced`: a second-level menu where experimental features of GIDOC are grouped.
- `0:Preferences`: opens a dialog to configure global options, as well as more specific options for preprocessing, training and recognition.
- `1:Block Detection`: performs block detection on the current image.
- `2:Line Detection`: detects (straight) text baselines in the current block.
- `3:Training`: reads all text line images that have been already transcribed and trains from them statistical models for prediction of transcriptions.
- `4:Transcription`: opens the interactive-predictive transcription dialog of GIDOC.

As GIMP, GIDOC is licensed under the GNU General Public License, and it is freely available at http://prhlt.iti.es/w/gidoc. For a detailed review of the prototype's preferences one may see http://prhlt.iti.es/projects/handwritten/idoc/gidoc/manual/.

Block Detection

Detection of (textual) blocks logically precedes text line detection and handwritten text recognition. Technically, textual blocks are represented as closed paths with four handlers at the "corners", which can be graphically adjusted by the user. During its development, GIDOC has been mainly tested on a old book in which most pages only contain nearly calligraphic text written on ruled sheets of well-separated lines, as in the example shown in Fig. 12.21. As mentioned previously, GIDOC is designed to work with such homogeneous documents and, indeed, it takes advantage of their homogeneity. In particular, the Block Detection entry in the GIDOC menu uses a novel text block detection method in which conventional, memoryless techniques are improved with a "history" model of text block positions. An illustrative example is shown in Fig. 12.21, where a blue square encloses the text block.

Line Detection

Given a textual block, the Line Detection entry in the GIDOC menu detects all its text baselines, which are marked as straight paths. The result can be clearly observed in Fig. 12.21 and in the rightmost image of Fig. 12.22. As with the Block Detection, each baseline has handlers to graphically correct its position. Although each baseline has handlers to graphically correct its position, it is worth noting that the baseline detection method implemented works quite well, at least in pages like that of the example Fig. 12.21. It is a rather standard projection-based method [11]. First, horizontally-averaged pixel values or black/white transitions are projected vertically. Then, the resulting vertical histogram is smoothed and analyzed so as to

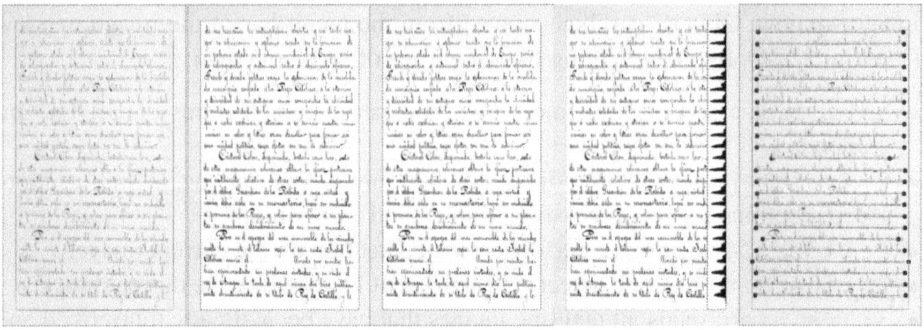

Fig. 12.22 Example of GIDOC Line Detection. *From left to right*: original image, contrast normalization, skew correction, vertical projection of black-to-white transitions, and baseline detection

locate baselines accurately. Two preprocessing options are included in `Preferences`; first, to decide on the histogram type (pixel values or black/white transitions), and second, to define the maximum number of baselines to be found. Concretely, this number is used to help the projection-based method in locating (nearly) blank lines.

The line detection method implemented in GIDOC is illustrated in Fig. 12.22. The original image is normalized in contrast, skew-corrected, and then a vertical projection of black-to-white transitions is computed, from which the vertical positions of baselines are derived.

Training

GIDOC is based on standard techniques and tools for handwritten text preprocessing and feature extraction, HMM-based image modeling, and language modeling [29]. Handwritten text preprocessing applies image denoising, deslanting and vertical size normalization to a given text (line) image. It can be configured through `GIDOC/Preprocessing` option. There is an option to use instead a customized procedure, and two options to define (bounds for) the locations of the upper and lower lines, with respect to the baseline.

HMM image modeling can be carried out with the well-known and freely available Hidden Markov Model ToolKit (HTK) [32], and the open source SRI Language Modeling toolkit (SRILM) [28]; or it can be trained using a free software built-in trainer. Training takes place using examples, therefore at least some pages have to be transcribed previously. As more transcriptions are available, better models are obtained. Hence, training must be called every few pages that have been transcribed. In this way the recognition system's performance is greatly improved. Specifically, two options are available in this process: train from the beginning all the models or re-estimate the current ones.

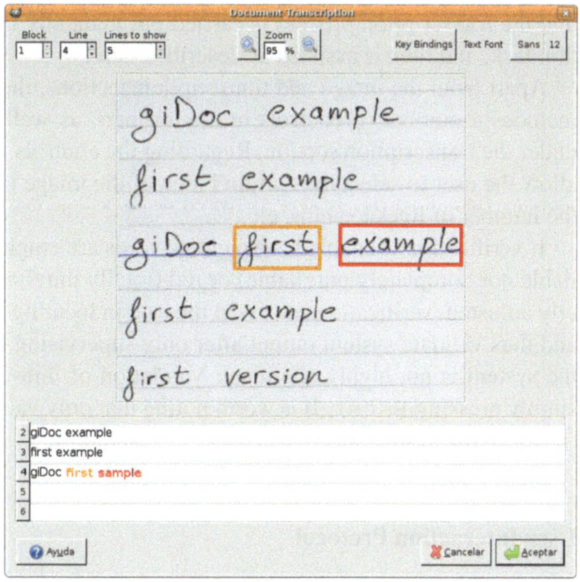

Fig. 12.23 GIDOC Interactive Transcription dialog

Transcription

The `GIDOC/Transcription` entry in the main menu opens an interactive transcription dialog (see Fig. 12.23). It consists of two main sections: the image section, at the middle part of the window, and the transcription section, at the bottom part. Text line images are displayed in the image section together with their transcriptions, if available, in separate editable text boxes within the transcription section. The current line to be transcribed (or simply supervised) is selected by placing the edit cursor in the appropriate editable box. Its corresponding baseline is emphasized and, whenever possible, GIDOC shifts line images and their transcriptions so as to display the current line in the central part of both the image and transcription sections. It is assumed that the user transcribes or supervises text lines, from top to bottom, by entering text and moving the edit cursor with the arrow keys or the mouse. However, it is possible for the user to choose any specific, desired order.

Each editable text box has a button attached to its left, which is labeled with its corresponding line number. By clicking on it, its associated line image is extracted, preprocessed, transformed into a sequence of feature vectors, and Viterbi-decoded using the HMMs and language models trained with `GIDOC/Training`. The Grammar Scale Factor (GSF) and Word Insertion Penalty (WIP) values to properly combine the HMM and language models are defined in the recognition section of `GIDOC/Preferences`. Also there is an option to adjust the *Beam* value and thus the computational cost to perform Viterbi decoding. In this way, there is not need to enter the complete transcription of the current line, but hopefully only minor corrections to the decoded output. Clearly, this is only possible if, first, text lines are correctly detected and, second, the HMM and language models are adequately trained, from a sufficiently large amount of training data. Therefore, it is assumed that the transcription process is carried out manually in early stages of a transcription task, and then is assisted as described here.

Apart from the image and transcription sections, the dialog shown in Fig. 12.23 includes a number of controls in the top part, as well as self-explanatory buttons under the transcription section. Regarding the controls in the top part, note that they allow the user to select the current block of the image to transcribe, the current line, the number of lines to show, etc.

If verification is enabled, suspicious words are emphasized in orange (neither reliable nor completely unreliable) or red (totally unreliable); see Fig. 12.23. If properly adjusted, verification can assist the user in locating possible transcription errors, and thus validate system output after only supervising those (few) words for which the system is not highly confident. Validation of lines after supervision is done by simply pressing `Enter`. It is worth noting that only validated lines are used to adapt (re-train) the system through `GIDOC/Training`.

User Interaction Protocol

The user follows a step-by-step process to fully transcribe a page, consisting on a given handwritten image. Firstly she opens an image and sets up the project preferences: `Preprocessing`, `Training`, and `Recognition` options. She then defines the text block in the image, by creating a rectangular selection containing the text block. The interactive transcription dialog appears and she transcribes manually a few lines, with the purpose of training the system. The system models are then generated and the user enters in an interactive transcription process, where he/she works on the detected lines one by one. It is worth noting that GIMP offers non-interactive functionality through the command line, so GIDOC can also work in this way. For example, it is possible to extract text lines from a (set of) handwritten image(s), preprocess them, and save the result in any directory.

12.7.2 Technology

As previously commented in Sect. 12.7.1, GIDOC is implemented as a set of GIMP plug-ins, and thus GIMP has to be installed in the first place. In addition, the training and prediction engines are based on the methods described in Chap. 5.

12.7.3 Evaluation

Early testing of the GIDOC prototype with real users revealed a time reduction in whole transcription tasks of 25% on average, in a moderately complex text documents. During its development, GIDOC has been used by a paleography expert to annotate blocks, text lines and transcriptions on a dataset called GERMANA [16]. The example shown in Fig. 12.21 corresponds to page 144 of such a dataset. The reader is redirected to Sect. 5.6 for a detailed evaluation of results based on this prototype.

12.8 RISE: Relevant Image Search Engine

The classical Content Based Image Retrieval (CBIR) approach helps to organize digital pictures by their visual content, and traditionally has involved a myriad of multidisciplinary fields such as computer vision, machine learning, HCI, database systems, statistics, and many more [7, 12, 31]. Two problems arise, though. On the one hand, it is not feasible to make the annotations of all images manually, and, on the other hand, it is not possible to translate some images (specially abstract concepts) into words—which is known as *the semantic gap* [27]. Relevance feedback (RF) is a query modification technique which attempts to capture the user's precise needs through iterative feedback and query refinement [7].

In this section we shall demonstrate the methodology described in Chap. 11, which is implemented in a Relevant Image Search Engine (RISE from here onwards) with late fusion. Fusion is used here to combine two *modalities* used to describe queries: *visual* or image-based and *semantic* or text-based. For some applications, visual similarity may in fact be more critical than semantic, and vice versa. The late fusion concept allows one to blend the amount of textual and visual information that will be used to retrieve similar images, overcoming thus with the inherent problem of the above-mentioned semantic gap. There is an online demonstration available at http://risenet.iti.upv.es/rise/.

12.8.1 Prototype Description

User Interaction Protocol

In sum, the user has in mind some relevant set of (unknown) images, and RISE's goal is to interactively discover n images of it, among the images in a fixed, finite collection of images C: The process is described as follows:

- Initially the user inputs a query q to the system.
- Then RISE provides an initial set $X_0 \in C$ of n images that are retrieved from a database according to a suitable criteria.
- These images are judged by the user, who provides a feedback by selecting which images are relevant (and, implicitly, which are not relevant).
- The system combines such feedback information with late fusion methods to obtain a new set of images X_1 depending of the nature of q, i.e., text-based or visual.
- The process is repeated until the user is satisfied, i.e., all retrieved images X_i are relevant to her.

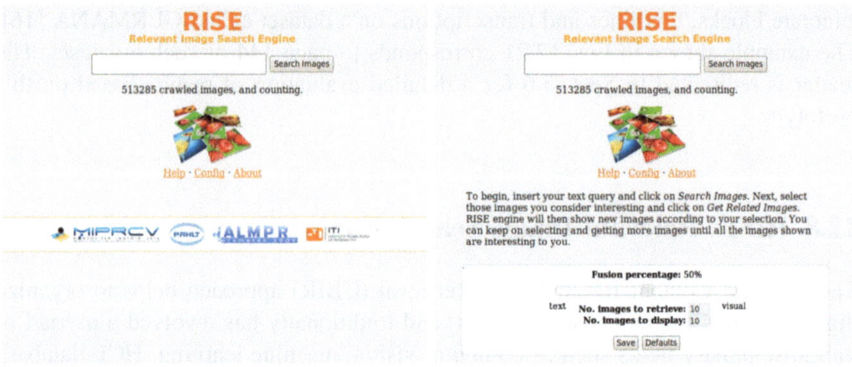

(a) (b)

Fig. 12.24 RISE index page

(a) (b)

Fig. 12.25 Interacting with the RISE prototype. The user typed the (ambiguous) query "tiger", and the system provides images related to the feline (**a**). However, the user was thinking of the sportsman Tiger Woods, so she validates those images she consider as relevant, and the system will use her feedback for improving their results in the next iterations (**b**)

Web Interface

On index page (Fig. 12.24a) the user can configure the fusion amount between text- and visual-based engines (see Fig. 12.24b). Once the user has submitted a query to the system, a set of images is shown, allowing the user navigate to interactively inspect some image properties such as dimensions, size, of referrer URL (Fig. 12.26).

12.8.2 Technology

We implemented a probabilistic model for user RF on CBIR, detailed in Sect. 11.2 (see also [15]), which is augmented with late fusion techniques. For this demonstrator we considered a simple (yet very effective) score based on a weighted linear combination of N-best lists, i.e., the best ranking of (relevant) images R_b is computed a as linear combination of visual R_v and text R_t rankings: $R_b(\%) =$

Fig. 12.26 RISE's User Interface. After introducing a text query, the user is presented with a set of images, having to select those she finds relevant (highlighted in *green*). Additional information is displayed when hovering on each image

$\alpha R_v + (100 - \alpha) R_t$, where α is automatically adjusted to account for the fusion percentage between visual and textual retrieval strategies. See details in Sect. 11.3.

Starting from Scratch

As starting point to build the image collection C, we used the Merriam-Webster's online dictionary to generate a list of queries to search for. After shuffling the 35 000 words in such an initial list we performed 1 500 searches for each dictionary entry among the main search engines (namely Google, Bing, and Yahoo) by using the GNU `wget` application (named *image crawler* from here onwards).

Gathering Images

The image crawler stores a thumbnail as well as the feature vectors in an optimized representation for searching, requiring thus minimal storage space; e.g, 1 000 000 retrieved images take up to just 10 GB overall, including all textual descriptors. The context in which an image appears is abstracted from the containing HTML document using the Latent Semantic Indexing (LSI) method. LSI works by statistically associating related words to the conceptual context of the given document. This structure is estimated by a truncated singular value decomposition (SVD) [5].

Automatic Image Tagging

The main code was implemented in Python, with the help of the Beautiful Soup HTML/XML parser library. The first part of the image tagging process consists in deleting all irrelevant elements (such as tables or scripts) from the retrieved web pages. The next step consists of assigning special importance to certain words with specific HTML tags, for example, one may assign different weights to the keywords appearing in the page title, headers, or in the attributes of the `img` tags. We also decided to use some of the related search engine's information. For instance, the closer to the first page of results is an image, the more important it is. A dictionary is thus created with the term frequency of each word that appears in the web document, alongside with the bag of weighted words. Then, and after applying some normalization routines (e.g., filtering stop words, lower-casing terms), image annotations are stored in the database (including their weights).

Retrieval Procedure

Initially we use text queries to narrow the initial set of images that will be presented to the user, i.e., she types in an input field what she is looking for. Then we employ the *query-by-similar-images* paradigm with late fusion in an interactive setting (see Sect. 12.8.1).

12.8.3 Evaluation

The evaluation and experiments are presented in Sect. 11.3.5. In general, we observed that depending on the query, a pure visual strategy may help achieving a complete set of relevant images while, in other cases, pure text retrieval performs better (take for instance the example commented in Fig. 12.25).

This is consistent with the performance results reported in Chap. 11, which compares the accuracy for the best α with both pure text and pure visual retrieval.

12.9 Conclusions

In this chapter we have introduced several demonstrators of multimodal interactive pattern recognition applications. These demos have served as validating examples of the MIPR framework proposed and described throughout this book. As observed, they involved many different real-world tasks, namely transcription of text images and speech, machine translation, text generation, parsing and image retrieval. Each of the seven introduced prototypes was based on one of the three types of user interaction protocols, and tapped the user feedback to enrich the system output. The most remarkable features are summarized as follows.

First, multimodal interaction has been approached in such a way that both the main and the feedback data streams collaborate to optimize the overall performance and usability. The interaction process is iterated until the user considers that the system output is wholly correct, so a perfect and high-quality output is guaranteed, since the user is tightly embodied on the system's inner processing. Second, an overview of each demonstrator has been sufficiently detailed to give the reader an overview of the underlying technologies. Most of the above-mentioned prototypes are being currently adapted to work as online demos, therefore being able to expand the potential audience. Third, all systems have been submitted to preliminary evaluation with real users. The resulting figures are definitely promising, validating thus the interactive–predictive paradigm off the lab. Finally, the reader is encouraged to test the available prototypes (e.g., the web-based versions), since the requirements on the client side are really low, and check the features that have been put into practice.

References

1. Alabau, V., Romero, V., Ortiz-Martínez, D., & Ocampo, J. (2009). A multimodal predictive-interactive application for computer assisted transcription and translation. In *Proceedings of international conference on multimodal interfaces (ICMI)* (pp. 227–228).
2. Barrachina, S., Bender, O., Casacuberta, F., Civera, J., Cubel, E., Khadivi, S., Lagarda, A. L., Ney, H., Tomás, J., Vidal, E., & Vilar, J. M. (2009). Statistical approaches to computer-assisted translation. *Computational Linguistics*, *35*(1), 3–28.
3. Bickel, S., Haider, P., & Scheffer, T. (2005). Predicting sentences using n-gram language models. In *Proceedings of human language technology and empirical methods in natural language processing (HLT/EMNLP)* (pp. 193–200).
4. Bisani, M., & Ney, H. (2004). Bootstrap estimates for confidence intervals in ASR performance evaluation. In *Proc. ICASSP* (pp. 409–412).
5. Cascia, M. L., Sethi, S., & Sclaroff, S. (1998). Combining textual and visual cues for content-based image retrieval on the world wide web. In *IEEE workshop on content-based access of image and video libraries* (pp. 24–28).
6. Craciunescu, O., Gerding-Salas, C., & Stringer-O'Keeffe, S. (2004). Machine translation and computer-assisted translation: a new way of translating? *Translation Journal*, *8*(3), 1–16.
7. Datta, R., Joshi, D., Li, J., & Wang, J. Z. (2008). Image retrieval: Ideas, influences, and trends of the new age. *ACM Computing Surveys*, *40*(2), 1–60.
8. Jelinek, F. (1998). *Statistical methods for speech recognition*. Cambridge: MIT Press.
9. Koehn, P., Och, F. J., & Marcu, D. (2003). Statistical phrase-based translation. In *Proceedings of the HLT/NAACL* (pp. 48–54).
10. Lease, M., Charniak, E., Johnson, M., & McClosky, D. (2006). A look at parsing and its applications. In *Proc. AAAI* (pp. 1642–1645).
11. Likforman-Sulem, L., Zahour, A., & Taconet, B. (2007). Text line segmentation of historical documents: a survey. *International Journal on Document Analysis and Recognition*, *9*, 123–138.
12. Moran, S. (2009). *Automatic image tagging*. Master's thesis, School of Informatics, University of Edinburgh.
13. Oncina, J. (2009). Optimum algorithm to minimize human interactions in sequential computer assisted pattern recognition. *Pattern Recognition Letters*, *30*(5), 558–563.
14. Ortiz-Martínez, D., Leiva, L. A., Alabau, V., & Casacuberta, F. (2010). Interactive machine translation using a web-based architecture. In *Proceedings of the international conference on intelligent user interfaces* (pp. 423–425).
15. Paredes, R., Deselaer, T., & Vidal, E. (2008). A probabilistic model for user relevance feedback on image retrieval. In *Proceedings of machine learning for multimodal interaction (MLMI)* (pp. 260–271).

16. Pérez, D., Tarazón, L., Serrano, N., Castro, F.-M., Ramos-Terrades, O., & Juan, A. (2009). The GERMANA database. In *Proceedings of the international conference on document analysis and recognition (ICDAR)* (pp. 301–305).
17. Plötz, T., & Fink, G. A. (2009). Markov models for offline handwriting recognition: a survey. *International Journal on Document Analysis and Recognition, 12*(4), 269–298.
18. Ramos-Terrades, O., Serrano, N., Gordó, A., Valveny, E., & Juan, A. (2010). Interactive-predictive detection of handwritten text blocks. In *Document recognition and retrieval XVII (Proc. of SPIE-IS&T electronic imaging)* (pp. 219–222).
19. Rodríguez, L., Casacuberta, F., & Vidal, E. (2007). Computer assisted transcription of speech. In *Proceedings of the Iberian conference on pattern recognition and image analysis* (pp. 241–248).
20. Romero, V., Toselli, A. H., Civera, J., & Vidal, E. (2008). Improvements in the computer assisted transciption system of handwritten text images. In *Proceedings of workshop on pattern recognition in information system (PRIS)* (pp. 103–112).
21. Romero, V., Leiva, L. A., Toselli, A. H., & Vidal, E. (2009). Interactive multimodal transcription of text images using a web-based demo system. In *Proceedings of the international conference on intelligent user interfaces* (pp. 477–478).
22. Romero, V., Leiva, L. A., Alabau, V., Toselli, A. H., & Vidal, E. (2009). A web-based demo to interactive multimodal transcription of historic text images. In *LNCS: Vol. 5714. Proceedings of the European conference on digital libraries (ECDL)* (pp. 459–460).
23. Sánchez-Sáez, R., Leiva, L. A., Sánchez, J. A., & Benedí, J. M. (2010). Interactive predictive parsing using a web-based architecture. In *Proceedings of NAACL* (pp. 37–40).
24. Sanchis-Trilles, G., Ortiz-Martínez, D., Civera, J., Casacuberta, F., Vidal, E., & Hoang, H. (2008). Improving interactive machine translation via mouse actions. In *EMNLP 2008: conference on empirical methods in natural language processing*.
25. Serrano, N., Pérez, D., Sanchis, A., & Juan, A. (2009). Adaptation from partially supervised handwritten text transcriptions. In *Proceedings of the 11th international conference on multimodal interfaces and the 6th workshop on machine learning for multimodal interaction (ICMI-MLMI)* (pp. 289–292).
26. Serrano, N., Tarazón, L., Perez, D., Ramos-Terrades, O., & Juan, A. (2010). The GIDOC prototype. In *Proceedings of the 10th international workshop on pattern recognition in information systems (PRIS 2010)* (pp. 82–89).
27. Smeulders, A. W. M., Worring, M., Santini, S., Gupta, A., & Jain, R. (2000). Content-based image retrieval at the end of the early years. *IEEE Transactions on Pattern Analysis and Machine Intelligence, 22*(12), 1349–1380.
28. Stolcke, A. (2002). SRILM—an extensible language modeling toolkit. In *Proceedings of the international conference on spoken language processing (ICSLP)* (pp. 901–904).
29. Toselli, A. H., Juan, A., Keysers, D., González, J., Salvador, I., Ney, H., Vidal, E., & Casacuberta, F. (2004). Integrated handwriting recognition and interpretation using finite-state models. *International Journal of Pattern Recognition and Artificial Intelligence, 18*(4), 519–539.
30. Trost, H., Matiasek, J., & Baroni, M. (2005). The language component of the fasty text prediction system. *Applied Artificial Intelligence, 19*(8), 743–781.
31. Wang, J. Z., Boujemaa, N., Bimbo, A. D., Geman, D., Hauptmann, A. G., & Tešić, J. (2006). Diversity in multimedia information retrieval research. In *Proceedings of the 8th ACM international workshop on multimedia information retrieval* (pp. 5–12).
32. Young, S., et al. (1995). *The HTK book.* Cambridge University, Engineering Department.

Glossary

3G	Third Generation (mobile networks)
AJAX	Asynchronous JavaScript And XML
API	Application Programming Interface
ASR	Automatic Speech Recognition
ATROS	Automatically Trainable Recognizer Of Speech
CAT	Computer Assisted Translation
CATS	Computer Assisted Transcription Speech Signals
CATTI	Computer Assisted Transcription of Text Images
CBIR	Content Based Image Retrieval
CE	Confidence Estimation
CKY	Cocke–Kasami–Younger algorithm
CM	Confidence Measure
CNF	Chomsky Normal Form
CS	Cristo Salvador Corpus (Old Handwritten Book)
CYK	Cooke–Yamakura–Kasami (algorithm)
DAG	Directed Acyclic Graph
DCT	Discrete Cosine Transform
DEC	Unconstrained speech DECoding
DT	Decision Theory
ECP	Error Correcting Parsing
EFR	Estimated eFfort Reduction
EM	Expectation Maximization
ER	Classification Error Rate
FER	Feedback Decoding Error Rate
FKI	Research Group on computer Vision and Artificial Intelligence
FS	Finite State
GIATI	Grammatical Inference Algorithms for Transducer Inference
GIDOC	Gimp-based interactive transcription of old text DOCuments
GIMP	GNU Image Manipulation Program
GPL	GNU General Public License
GSF	Grammar Scale Factor

A.H. Toselli et al., *Multimodal Interactive Pattern Recognition and Applications*,
DOI 10.1007/978-0-85729-479-1, © Springer-Verlag London Limited 2011

HCI	Human–Computer Interaction
HMM	Hidden Markov Model
HTK	Hidden Markov model ToolKit
HTML	Hypertext Markup Language
HTR	Handwritten Text Recognition
HTTP	HyperText Transfer Protocol
IAM	Institute of Computer Science and Applied Mathematics
IAMDB	IAM Handwriting Database (handwritten English text)
IHT	Interactive Handwriting Transcription
IMT	Interactive Machine Translation
IP	Interactive Parsing
IPP	Interactive Predictive Processing
IPR	Interactive Pattern Recognition
JNI	Java Native Interface
KSR	Key Stroke Ratio
LOB	Lancaster–Oslo/Bergen
MERT	Minimum Error Rate Training
MFCC	Mel Frequency Cepstral Coefficients
MI	Multimodal Interaction
MIPR	Multimodal Interactive Pattern Recognition
MM-CATTI	Multimodal Computer Assisted Transcription of Text Images
MM-IHT	Multimodal Interactive Handwriting Transcription
MM-IMT	Multimodal Interactive Machine Translation
MM-IP	Multimodal Interactive Parsing
MM-IST	Multimodal Interactive Speech Transcription
MM-ITG	Multimodal Interactive Text Generation
MT	Machine Translation
NLP	Natural Language Processing
ODEC-M3	Spontaneous Handwritten Paragraphs Corpus
OOV	Out Of Vocabulary
PA	Pointer Action
PA-CATTI	Computer Assisted Transcription of Text Images using Pointer Actions
PAR	Pointer-Action Rate
PDA	Personal Digital Assistant
POS	Part Of Speech
PR	Pattern Recognition
PRCFG	Probabilistic Context Free-Grammars
PWECP	Probabilistic Word Error Correcting Parsing
REA	Recursive Enumeration Algorithm
RF	Relevance feedback
SER	Sentence Error Rate
SFST	Stochastic Finite-State Transducers
SLM	Suffix Language Model
SMT	Statistical Machine Translation

SRI Stanford Research Institute
SRILM SRI Language Modeling
TCAC Tree Constituent Action Rate
TCER Tree Constituent Error Rate
TCP Transfer Control Protocol
TMX Translation Memory eXchange
TT2 TransType2
UI User Interface
WDAG Weighted Directed Acyclic Graph
WER Word Error Rate
WG Word Graph
WIP Word Insertion Penalty
WSJ Wall Street Journal
WSR Word Stroke Ratio

Index

A.H. Toselli et al., *Multimodal Interactive Pattern Recognition and Applications*,
DOI 10.1007/978-0-85729-479-1, © Springer-Verlag London Limited 2011

MIX
Papier aus verantwortungsvollen Quellen
Paper from responsible sources
FSC® C105338

If you have any concerns about our products,
you can contact us on
ProductSafety@springernature.com

In case Publisher is established outside the EU,
the EU authorized representative is:
Springer Nature Customer Service Center GmbH
Europaplatz 3, 69115 Heidelberg, Germany

Printed by Libri Plureos GmbH
in Hamburg, Germany